THE FRUGAL GOURMET
Cooks Three Ancient Cuisines

ALSO BY JEFF SMITH

The Frugal Gourmet (1984)
The Frugal Gourmet Cooks with Wine (1986)
The Frugal Gourmet Cooks American (1987)

THE
FRUGAL GOURMET

Cooks Three Ancient Cuisines

China, Greece, and Rome

JEFF SMITH

Craig Wollam, Culinary Consultant
Terrin Haley, Research Assistant
Illustrations by Chris Cart

WILLIAM MORROW
AND COMPANY, INC.
New York

TO MRS. MARY YOUNG
my adopted Chinese Auntie
who remains convinced that I was Chinese in a previous life . . .
I hope it is true!

AND TO
COLONEL JOHN YOUNG,
whose memory is on every page.

Permission to reprint has been kindly granted as follows:

Chinese Brine Pickles from Dragon Kiln.

Ha Gow Dough and Fun Gor Dough from *Favorite Dim Sum* by Lonnie Mock, Alpha Gamma Arts, Walnut Creek, CA, 1979.

Egg-Lemon Soup and Garlic Sauce both appeared originally in *The Frugal Gourmet*, copyright © 1984 by Jeff Smith.

Basic Brown Soup Stock, Basic Brown Sauce, and Pesto Sauce all appeared originally in *The Frugal Gourmet Cooks with Wine*, copyright © 1986 by Frugal Gourmet, Inc.

Baked Fish Archestratus, Shrimp Ananius, Roasted Quail Appetizers Homer, Barley Pudding with Lamb, and Pickled Asparagus, Greek Style all adapted from recipes in *The Complete Greek Cookbook* by Theresa Karas Yianilos, Avenel Books, New York, 1970.

Crispy Roast Pork from *Flavors of China*, Chinese Parents Service Organization, Trinity Printing, Seattle, 1975.

Pastitsio from *Greek Cooking in an American Kitchen*, St. Demetrios Cookbook Committee, 2100 Boyer Avenue East, Seattle, WA 98122.

Corn Crepes, Chinese Style, from *Sunset Magazine*, October 1985.

Onion Cakes from *Pei Mei's Chinese Cook Book, Volume I* by Pei Mei, T & S Industrial Co. Ltd., P.O. Box 53-319, Taipei, Taiwan.

Garbanzo Pizza from *Giuliano Bugialli's Classic Techniques in Italian Cooking*, copyright © 1982 by Giuliano Bugialli, reprinted by permission of Simon & Schuster, Inc.

Chinese Sesame Cookies adapted from *Chinese Cooking Our Way*, Chinese American Women's Club of Santa Clara County, Phoenix Press, Campbell, CA, 1971.

Library of Congress Cataloging-in-Publication Data
Smith, Jeff.
    The Frugal gourmet cooks three ancient cuisines : China, Greece, and Rome / Jeff Smith ; Craig Wollam, culinary consultant ; Terrin Haley, research assistant ; illustrations by Chris Cart.
    p. cm.
    Bibliography: p.
    Includes index.
    ISBN 0-688-07589-4
    1. Cookery, Chinese. 2. Cookery, Greek. 3. Cookery, Roman.
4. China—Social life and customs. 5. Greece—Social life and customs. 6. Italy—Social life and customs. I. Title. II. Title: Frugal gourmet cooks 3 ancient cuisines.
TX724.5.C5S597 1989
641.59—dc20   89-33238
                                                          CIP

Printed in the United States of America

First Edition

1 2 3 4 5 6 7 8 9 10

BOOK DESIGN BY RICHARD ORIOLO

ACKNOWLEDGMENTS

I must offer thanks to so many people who helped in the preparation of this book. All three ancient cuisines were equally giving. A cookbook, like the history of the cuisines of the world, is never a private matter. Never!

CHINA

Mrs. Mary Young, of San Francisco, the woman to whom this book is dedicated, has patiently taught me for years about the meaning of the world's oldest cuisine. I am so thankful.

Ken Hom, TV chef and author of several terrific books on Chinese cooking, took my assistant and me through Hong Kong. Ken is a kind and giving person, as are his Hong Kong friends, Willy Mark, Grace and Kendle Oei, and Justice and Mrs. Power. Thank you all.

The restaurant people of Hong Kong, particularly Frank Yuen and Pierre Tang of Maxim's, were most gracious to us, as were the people in the fine hotels of the city. Thanks to the Peninsula, the Regent Li Ching Heen Restaurant, and the Rainbow Room at Lee Gardens.

My thanks must go to Brenda Poon and the Hong Kong Tourist Association. This is a fine company that will make your stay in Hong Kong just a delight. The people in Hong Kong are even nice in the subway!

To my American Chinese friends I must also say thank you. Martin Yan and Bruce Cost (he is Chinese by decision) and to Sharon Jay, in Chicago.

SONG HAY! Hsieh, hsieh.

GREECE

The whole citizenry of Athens seemed to be helpful to us. The Greeks are so gracious that it is embarrassing, and yet you keep going back for more. Particularly helpful was the staff at the National Archeological Museum and my friends at the King Minos Hotel.

The many restaurants that welcomed us are listed among the recipes, but I must offer particular thanks to the characters at Taverna Sigalas, a great spot.

My Greek friends in Tacoma, Mrs. Koustela Stergachis and Mrs. Marie Arger, introduced themselves to me twenty-five years ago, and they have been teaching me ever since.

Finally, the people of Delphi were willing to share their Easter with us. Thanks to all of you, including the staff at the wonderful Hotel Amalia. *YASOU! Efharisto.*

ROME

I met Roberto and Micaela Bolzoni in Chicago and we became fast friends. He is with the American Embassy in Rome and I asked Micaela to act as our tour guide while in the Eternal City. Her sense of history, her grace and beauty, and the fact that she can talk anyone out of anything made our work delightful.

Carlo Middione, dear friend and the author of *The Food of Southern Italy,* told me about the markets and about some of his friends. Mrs. Jo Bettoja of Rome, and the Nasi family of Bologna, were just a blessing.

Ms. June di Schino, a beautiful woman who has become an authority on ancient Roman eating practices, was giving beyond belief, as was the Museo Nazionale Romano.

Finally, the restaurants and markets of Rome were most patient with us. Each of the restaurants is mentioned somewhere in the recipes. And to Prince Ugo of Rome, descendant of the caesars, thank you.
ALLA SALUTE! Grazie, grazie.

HOME

My crew from WTTW Television, Chicago, have always been patient and kind to me. The trips we made together to Rome, Athens, and Hong Kong stretched all of our bunch to the breaking point, I am sure. But I received nothing but support from Tim, my producer/director, Cynthia, my assistant producer, Bob, our sound man, and Roy, a cameraman who can get anything. And could this crowd eat!

Bill Adler, my book agent, has become a serious source of strength and insight. And my friends at William Morrow. Five years ago I would never have believed that I would become so attached to my editor, Maria Guarnaschelli, and the boss man, Al Marchioni. Chris Cart, my illustrator, has the most wonderful ability to understand what I am up to . . . and to put it into a drawing. He is charming and gifted, and I am thankful.

I will put my office crew in Seattle up against any crew in the country. Jim Paddleford, my business manager, Dawn Sparks, my secretary, and Terrin Haley, my research assistant, are committed to what I am trying to do and terribly skilled in their fields. Such a help!

Finally, thanks to Craig Wollam, my cooking assistant. His labors and insights have made an indelible impression on this book, and I thank him for his skill and commitment, and for his friendship.
HERE'S TO YOU! And thanks a million!

CONTENTS

INTRODUCTION: CREDIT MUST BE GIVEN!	**10**
GLOSSARY	**13**
Hints	14
Kitchen Equipment	15
Cooking Methods and Terms	23
Ingredients, Condiments, and Food Definitions	28
Herbs and Spices	39
Television Shows and Recipes	44
THE THREE ANCIENT CUISINES	**51**
CHINA AND ITS INVENTIONS	**52**
GREECE AND ITS INSIGHTS	**63**
ROME AND ITS TRAVELS	**70**
THE RECIPES	**79**
APPETIZERS	**80**
DIM SUM	**93**
Shrimp	95
Pork	99
Chicken	106
Beef	107
SOUPS	**111**
SALADS	**135**
SEAFOOD	**153**
Fish	154
Shellfish	168
Squid	186
Octopus	195
SAUCES AND CONDIMENTS	**199**
Sauces	200
Condiments	212

Sesame   216
Olives and Olive Oil   219

EGGS   **222**
POULTRY AND GAME   **228**
Chicken   229
Goose   248
Duck   251
Small Birds   264

MEATS   **273**
Lamb   274
Pork   286
Beef   305
Innards   320

DRIED FOODS   **334**
PASTA   **344**
RICE   **373**
DUMPLINGS   **387**
VEGETABLES   **397**
Artichokes   398
Asparagus   406
Beans   414
Chestnuts   425
Eggplant   434
Leeks   447
Mushrooms   456
Additional Vegetables   466

BREADS AND PIZZA   **469**
Breads   470
Pizza   484

DESSERTS   **489**

EPILOGUE: THE EARTH IS TOO SMALL FOR PRIVATE   **502**
    DINNER PARTIES
BIBLIOGRAPHY   **504**
INDEX   **507**

Introduction
Credit Must Be Given!

I cannot understand it! How can you call a dish "new" or "nouvelle" if you do not know the old dishes? The whole idea of calling something new before you have understood the history of a dish is totally inconsistent. Most people in our culture have not yet tasted the old cuisines so it is difficult to know what is new. The basic and wonderful flavors of the past belong to us as a culture, and these flavors have come from many sources. It is through the examination of the sources that one realizes what is new and what is simply repetition on a plate, along with a slice of kiwi fruit.

Do not misunderstand my concern here. I am very taken by the willingness of young chefs to try almost anything and any combination. I remain convinced, however, that a tasting of the creativity of the past would be very helpful in the quest for something new in the present. Chinese artists, for instance, are not expected to try to develop their own styles until they have mastered all the styles in painting that have preceded them. This takes many years, and the result is an artist with insight, with history. He knows what is new and what is not, and therefore he really does understand the meaning of innovation. Anything less is like a junior high student who rebels against all of the rules before he has even considered why the rules came into being. Therefore, duck with grapefruit and coffee-extract sauce is, for me, bizarre! Please learn to cook the duck first, cook it so that I know it is a duck. Learn to cook a duck Chinese style, or Greek style, or Roman style, and then try out some new recipes. Incidentally, Duck à l'Orange goes back to the first century in Rome. It was invented by an Italian! And credit must be given.

The necessity for giving credit to previous cuisines, thereby helping you understand your own cuisine, is the reason behind this book. The three ancient cuisines that most influenced the West were those of China, Greece, and Rome. The Chinese did it first. Everything from the first cooked meat to the first domesticated animals to the first metal cooking pot must be credited to the Chinese. And the Greeks! They taught us to make mayonnaise, baked pasta, basic white sauce (Béchamel), fancy breads, the frying pan as we know it today, the stewing pot brought to perfection, the Dutch oven, and the packed lunch. They even taught us to dip our bread in wine, though the Italians and French think it is their custom. Finally, the Romans took a whole style of cuisine from the Greeks, made some wonderful improvements upon it, and then, through their wild and warring travels, took this cuisine to the rest of Europe. When Catherine de Médicis moved to Paris in 1533 to marry Henri II she brought her Florentine cooks with her. The cooking of Paris was radically changed. Credit must be given.

Many other cuisines have influenced the West, the French being one of these. But French cooking, as we know it, is not ancient. It is excellent, but it is not ancient. The French really did not learn to cook until the beginning of the seventeenth century, and they are not embarrassed by that fact. They admit that the Greeks taught the Romans to cook and the Romans taught the French. Even the *Larousse Gastronomique* admits this! The French are wonderful cooks in our time, but the influences of the past must be shared with the young cooks, the sources must be acknowledged. Did you know that bouillabaisse is actually a Greek dish that came from Marseilles when the city was a Greek shipping port? Credit must be given.

This collection of recipes and comments is aimed at giving credit to the Chinese, Greeks, and Romans. The Chinese had great influence on the Western world, though we seem to have had little influence on them. The Chinese have always preferred their own ways and thus they have kept a rather closed house. But the Greek and Romans have had great influence on one another, and for me it has been fascinating trying to study some of these influences, and to taste the results.

Some of the bits of food history included in this volume will sound unimportant until you take time to consider the consequences of a particular event. The discovery of dried food, for instance, a process perfected by the Chinese, allowed trade routes to become established between the East and the West. And toast. This one sounds absurd, but Paxamos, a Greek of two thousand years ago, discovered that toasted bread will keep a long time in your pack, and thus the Greeks were able to carry an interesting diet with them while trading. Credit must be given.

Rome and China were linked in the pre-Christian era. The trade routes meant that silk and spices could flow into Rome, and with these items came stories of every culture encountered between Rome and the Orient. Feasting was changed, eating habits were modified, and diet was given wonderful variations.

Some of these recipes are included simply as nighttime reading material. I doubt that you will want to prepare them. Others have been included as a blatant attempt on my part to help you understand that Chinese, Greek, and Roman cooking are very different when prepared in their own lands. So I want you to travel to Hong Kong, to Athens, and to Rome. You will be much better prepared to judge whether or not a dish that you have found in America is really "new." After all, credit must be given.

Eat well!

—JEFF SMITH
Chinese New Year, 1989
The Year of the Snake

GLOSSARY

Hints

A Tortilla Press for Making Dim Sum Wrappers 97

A Bamboo Steamer for Properly Steamed Foods 97

If You Do Not Have Parchment Paper 101

Use Lettuce Circles for Steaming Small Dumplings 107

To Keep Meatballs from Sticking to Your Hands 108

To Remove Fat from Soup Stock 114

Add Iceberg Lettuce to Your Chinese Soups 121

Add Virginia Ham to Chinese Soups 123

To Sliver Green Onions 142

Use a Truffle Slicer for Shaving Hard White Cheeses 151

Roasting Sweet Bell Peppers 151

If Your Deep-Frying Oil Smells of Fish 160

For Finely Chopped Garlic 178

How to Clean Squid 188

On Cooking Squid 188

When Buying Olive Oil 221

When Cutting Poultry or Large Fish 271

To Make Hot Chinese Mustard 289

For Proper Chinese Chowing 293

Use the Serving Plate When Chowing 307

Avoid the High Cost of Flank Steak 308

When Browning Meats 317

Put Fresh Anise or Fennel in Innards 324

To Prepare Lettuce Cups 339

To Freeze Chow Mein Noodles 348

On Cooking Pasta Ahead of Time 368

On Cooking Pasta "Al Dente" 370

To Cook Rice Properly 375

Freeze Your Own Ravioli 393

Freeze a Batch of Gnocchi 396

Cleaning an Artichoke, Roman Style 400

On Cleaning Asparagus 407

Taste Before Salting 442

On Cleaning Leeks 448

Keep Your Deep-Frying Oil Fresh and Clean 468

For Making Breadsticks 482

Kitchen Equipment

KNIVES

Knives are the most important pieces of equipment in your kitchen. When purchasing such equipment you should be mindful of the following points:

1. Please do not buy knives that are cheaply made and designed to go into a dishwasher. (No good knife should *ever* be put into a dishwasher. They are made of stainless steel so that they are hard enough to take a dishwasher, but they cannot be sharpened.)

2. I prefer the standard old French chef's knife, not a designer gadget. The old model is hard to improve upon, and I have seen no improvement in function with the new "modern"-looking knives. Form follows function. A knife is for cutting. Buy one that does just that. My favorite knives are made in Germany by Der Messermeister company.

3. Buy good-quality knives of high carbon steel. They are now made to be nonstaining but are *not* stainless steel. Use a sharpening steel on them often to keep a good edge. If a sharpening steel makes you a bit nervous, use a Chantry knife sharpener. It is safe and works very well.

4. There is no such thing as a knife that never needs to be sharpened, any more than there is a plate that never needs to be washed. Good knives need sharpening and care, so never just throw them in a drawer.

Keep them in a rack, and in good repair. A dull knife is very dangerous since you have to work harder and thus are more apt to let the
knife slip and cut yourself.

5. I use the following knives constantly, but you may wish some other
   sizes. (I own about fifty knives. You don't need that many. Neither
   do I but I love good knives!)

   10-inch-blade chef's knife
   8-inch-blade chef's knife
   Boning knife
   Paring knife
   Long slicing knife (thin)
   Sharpening steel

Chinese cleaver: There are several thicknesses available. A thin one is
used for vegetables and a thicker one for cutting meat and hacking poultry.
Do not bother buying a stainless-steel cleaver. You cannot sharpen it.

POTS AND PANS

Good pots and pans make good cooking easy. Pans that are thin and
flimsy can offer only burning, sticking, and lumps. Buy good equipment
that is heavy. You will not be sorry.

Tips for Buying Good Equipment

1. Don't buy pots and pans with wooden or plastic handles. You can't
   put them in the oven or under a broiler.

2. Buy pans that fit your life-style, that are appropriate for the way you
   cook. They should be able to perform a variety of purposes in the
   kitchen. Avoid pans that can be used only for one dish or one particular style of cooking, such as upside-down crepe pans.

3. I do not buy sets of pans but rather a selection of several different
   materials that work in different ways. Most of my frying pans are
   aluminum with SilverStone lining. I have aluminum stockpots and
   saucepans. No, I do not worry about cooking in aluminum since I
   never cook acids such as eggs or tomatoes or lemon juice in that
   metal . . . and I always keep aluminum well cleaned, remembering
   never to store anything in aluminum pots or pans.

   I have copper saucepans for special sauces and some stainless-steel
   saucepans as well. These are heavy stainless with plain metal han-

dles, with an aluminum core sandwiched into the bottom. I also have a selection of porcelain-enameled cast-iron pans, Le Creuset being my favorite brand for that type of thing.

4. The pots and pans I use the most:

20-quart aluminum stockpot with lid
12-quart aluminum stockpot with lid
12-quart stainless-steel heavy stockpot with lid
4-quart aluminum *sauteuse,* with lid
10-inch aluminum frying pan, lined with SilverStone, with lid
Several cast-iron porcelain-coated casseroles, with lids
Copper saucepans in varying sizes, with lids
Chinese wok—I own six of them. See page 18 for descriptions.

MACHINES AND APPLIANCES

Please do not fill your kitchen with appliances that you will rarely use. I do not own an electric deep-fryer or an electric slow-cooking ceramic pot or an electric egg cooker or . . . you know what I am saying. Other pieces of equipment will work for these jobs, and have many other functions as well.

I do have:

Food mixer: Choose a heavy machine, one that will sit in one spot and make bread dough, grind meat, mix cake batters. I prefer a KitchenAid and have the large model with the five-quart bowl.

Food processor: While I use this machine less than my mixer, it is helpful. I have the medium-sized model.

Food blender: I have a heavy-duty model that will take a beating. Don't skimp on this machine.

Electric coffee grinder, small size: I use this for grinding herbs and spices, not for coffee. It is from Germany.

Espresso/cappuccino machine: A good one is expensive, but since my heart surgery I have been allowed only one cup of coffee per day. Caffeine is hard on the heart. A regular espresso has less caffeine in it than a regular cup of coffee, due to the way in which it is roasted and brewed. Since I am allowed only one cup I do a real deal on it! I own a Baby Gaggia, which is a professional-quality machine from Italy. It is expensive, but I have tried many and this is the best one.

Special Equipment

Pick and choose among these.
Most of them are just terribly helpful:

Flavor injector: This is a strange-looking
plastic device that resembles a
hypodermic needle and is used
for injecting flavors and juices into meats.

Garlic press: I cannot abide garlic in any form except fresh. Buy a Susi garlic press. Be careful in purchase as there are now many impersonators and they just do not work.

Lemon reamer, wooden: This is a great device, but since I began using it on television many companies have been producing copies that are just not the right size and shape for proper use. Buy a good one, even if you have seen a cheaper model.

Heat diffuser or tamer: This is an inexpensive gadget that you place on your gas or electric burner to even out or reduce the heat. It will save you from a lot of burned sauces.

Tomato Shark: This little gadget takes the stem out of a tomato in nothing flat. Be careful—there is a phony one on the market that doesn't work half as well.

Wooden spoons and spatulas: I never put metal spoons or gadgets into my frying pans or saucepans. Metal will scratch the surface, causing food to stick. Buy wooden gadgets and avoid that problem. I have grown very fond of tools made from olive wood as it is very hard and will last for years, even with regular use and washing. They cost more to start with but they will outlast the others by three times, at least.

Wok: I use my Chinese wok constantly. It is an ingenious device that is made of steel. Do not buy an aluminum or copper wok. The idea is to have a "hot spot" at the bottom of the wok, thus quickly cooking small amounts of food by moving them about in the pan. Aluminum and copper woks heat too evenly and the advantage of wok cooking is lost. Electric woks do not heat quickly enough, nor do they cool quickly enough. You can use your steel wok on an electric burner, though I prefer gas. If cooking with electricity, simply keep the burner always on high and control the temperature of the wok by moving it off and on the burner.

Bamboo steamers from China: These stackable steamers, usually three or four in a set, allow you to steam several dishes at once. The advantage that these have over metal steamers stems from the fact that bamboo  will not cause moisture to condense and drip on your food, as metal will. I use bamboo steamers for cooking Chinese foods and for warming up leftovers. I could not run a kitchen without them.

Sand pots: While these are not a necessity, they are fun to have. Great for use in the oven or on top of the stove. Find them in Chinatown.

Stove-top smoker: This is a wonderful device put out by Cameron and it is made entirely of stainless steel. The idea is to place it on the top 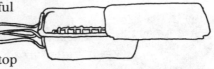 of your stove with a bit of alder or hickory sawdust in the bottom and you can smoke things in just a moment in your kitchen. These are an investment, but you will find yourself smoking all kinds of things. Instructions for use are found on page 27. Other sawdusts come with the device and can also be purchased in additional quantities. I remain partial to alder and hickory.

Stove-top grill: This is great for grilling peppers, bread, and other things right on top of the burner. It is called an *asador*, and it works very well.

Grill racks: Choose one or two sizes of these racks for grilling on the top of a griddle or on the barbecue. They are especially helpful in holding a fish together while you grill it Greek style.

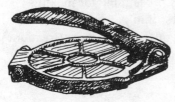

Tortilla press: This is very helpful in rolling out dough for Chinese dumplings. Buy a good one that is smoothly polished and you will have less trouble with sticking.

Dumpling maker, Chinese: This plastic gadget is cheap but clever. Helps you make Chinese filled dumplings in nothing flat.

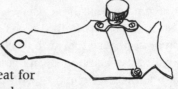

Truffle cutter for cheese: A very fancy gadget . . . but it does a great job on slicing thin bits of hard Italian cheeses. Great for pasta! I also use mine for shaving chocolate bars.

Cheese grater, hand-held: This little stainless-steel grater is wonderful for grating cheese on top of pasta. I use mine right at the table.

Ginger grater: This little porcelain piece works like a scrubboard to grate fresh ginger very quickly and very fine. From Japan.

Chopper/noodle cutter/breadstick maker: A German cutting device that I find just great for noodles and making thin Italian breadsticks.

Noodle bird-nest fryer: This two-basket device presses the fresh noodles together for deep frying. Also used for grated potatoes. The result is a fried "bird nest" basket.

Meat skewers: All kinds are available for making souvlaki and barbecued meat cubes. I prefer those made of stainless steel. These are easily found. The wide thick ones for ground meat will probably have to be made for you.

Apple parer/slicer: This is a great device for peeling and slicing apples. I use mine for making the best thin-cut potato fries that you can imagine. Great for shoestring potatoes, as well.

Apple parer/wedger: This little device cores and cuts an apple into wedges. Perfect for desserts, appetizers, or baking.

Pepper mill: The flavor of freshly ground black pepper is very different from that of the preground. Find a good mill and grind your own. I have several mills, but my favorite is a Turkish coffee grinder. These are expensive, but if you are a pepper lover you will love this device. Be careful that the one you buy comes with a guarantee that it can be adjusted for pepper.

Meat pounder: This device will flatten out slices of meat so that they are very thin. Great for Greek and Italian chicken, beef, and veal dishes.

Plastic sheeting: Sheeting is very helpful when you are pounding meat thin. It is inexpensive and available at most large lumberyards or hardware stores. Ask for clear vinyl sheeting 8 millimeters thick.

Fire extinguisher: A must for your kitchen. Buy one that will work on electrical fires as well as stove fires. Talk to the salesperson. You will sleep better at night.

Marble pastry board: These can be purchased in several sizes. I could not make pastry, bread, or pasta without one.

Stainless-steel steamer basket: This is a great help. I have two sizes, and they will adjust themselves to fit different pans. Great for steaming vegetables and not expensive.

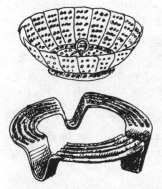

Steamer stand: This aluminum stand sits in the bottom of your kettle. A plate of food is placed on top and the pan becomes a steamer. You can also use this as a rack for a double boiler.

Fine strainer for skimming oil: If you do get into deep-frying, this very thin mesh strainer will help you keep the oil clean. From Japan.

Baking tiles: These will help you get a good crust on your bread. Whether or not you use a pan the tiles keep your oven temperature even. Salday makes these.

Pasta-rolling machine: This is the easiest way to make good pasta. I prefer rolled pasta to extruded, and this machine can also be used for making other thin doughs.

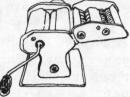

Ravioli cutters: These stamp forms are helpful if you decide to become a ravioli freak.

Wooden pasta fork: I love this old device. The metal or plastic mockeries of this gadget tear up the pasta.

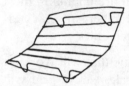

Roasting racks, nonstick: At last a roasting rack for a serious chicken lover. These work very well as the bird or roast does not stick to the rack.

Kitchen scale: Buy something that is fairly accurate. It will be helpful in baking perfect breads and in judging the size of roasts.

Mandoline: This is a wonderful device for cutting vegetables into thin slices or into julienne-style matchstick cuts. Be sure that you get a good one and be careful with it. You can cut yourself unless you use the guards properly. You can also cut french fries or vegetables with this.

Big dinner and serving plates: A dinner is much more exciting if served on large platters. Loneoak, in California, makes my favorite large white plates and serving platters. You can also find wonderful old serving platters in antique and junk shops.

Big wooden salad bowl: A good one will cost you some money, but if you like salad, you know that the greens will just not taste as good in metal or glass bowls as they will in wood.

Cooking Methods and Terms

AL DENTE

This is a wonderful Italian term that means to cook "to the teeth." It means nobody wants soggy pasta. Cook pasta to the teeth, or until it is barely tender, still a bit firm. It is much better that way . . . and the way Italians intended same to be eaten.

BLANCHING

Plunging a food product into boiling water for a very few minutes (the time varies and will be explained in each recipe). The food is then removed and generally placed in cold water to stop the cooking process. The purpose is to loosen the skin of a vegetable or fruit, to set the color of a vegetable, or to cook a food partially in preparation for later completion of the dish.

CHOW (stir-fry)

A basic cooking method in the Chinese kitchen. Generally a wok is used, but you can also do this in a frying pan. The food is tossed about in a hot pan with very little oil, in a process not unlike sautéing.

CORRECT THE SEASONING

When a dish is completed, a cook should always taste before serving. To correct the seasoning simply means to check for salt, pepper, or herbs to make sure that the dish has turned out as expected. A little correction at the last minute may be necessary.

DASH

Generally means "to taste." Start with less than $\frac{1}{16}$ teaspoon.

DEGLAZING A PAN

After meats or vegetables have been browned, wine or stock is added to the pan over high heat, and the rich coloring that remains in the pan is gently scraped with a wooden spoon and combined with the wine or stock.

DEVELOP

Developing a food product means that you have allowed it to sit for a time before serving so that the flavors might have a chance to blend or brighten.

DICE

This means to cut into small cubes; the size of the cube is generally stated in the recipe. For instance, a ¼-inch dice means a cube of that size. It is accomplished very quickly and easily with a good vegetable knife.

DREDGING IN FLOUR

Meats and fish, generally sliced thin, are rolled about in flour in preparation for frying or sautéing. The flour is usually seasoned.

DUSTING WITH FLOUR

Most often a fillet of fish or some type of shellfish (shrimps, scallops, etc.) is rolled in flour, and the excess flour is patted or shaken off. The idea is to have a very light coating on the food.

GRILLING

An ancient method whereby the food is cooked on a rack or skewer over hot coals or an open flame.

HACK

When cutting up chickens or thin-boned meats, one "hacks" with a cleaver, thus cutting the meat into large bite-size pieces and retaining the bone. The presence of the bone will help keep the meat moist during cooking. Do this hacking carefully.

LOOING

To gently cook a piece of meat (beef, pork, a whole chicken or fowl) in a broth composed of water, soy sauce, and spices. This is also known as "master sauce."

MARINATING

Meats or vegetables are soaked for a time in a flavoring liquid, such as soy sauce, wine, oil, or vinegar. The time of the marinating varies with the recipe.

MATCHSTICK OR JULIENNE CUT

Cut vegetable into thin slices, stack the slices, and then cut the slices into thin sticks, like matchsticks.

MINCE

A minced vegetable or herb is one that is chopped very fine. It is fine enough to be of a very coarse, granular nature. This pertains especially to garlic, onion, and herbs. The process is done by hand with a knife or a food processor.

PINCH OF HERBS OR SPICES

Usually means "to taste." Start with less than $\frac{1}{16}$ teaspoon, and then increase if you wish.

POACHING

Gently cooking fish, meat, or eggs in stock or water at just below a simmer. The liquid should just barely move during the poaching process. When fish or eggs are poached, a little vinegar or lemon juice is added to the liquid to help keep the food product firm.

PURÉE

When you wish to make a sauce or soup that is free of all lumps of any sort, purée the stock. This means that you put it in a food processor and mill it until it is free of all lumps, or run it through a strainer or sieve.

RECONSTITUTING

A procedure used for preparing dried foods, whereby the product is soaked in fresh water for a time. The food absorbs the water, so that its "life" is restored and it can be used properly in a given recipe. The process of drying food concentrates flavor and changes the texture, giving it a unique quality in the dish.

REDUCING

Boiling a sauce or liquid over high heat until it is reduced in volume, generally by half. The result is a very rich concentration of flavors.

ROUX

A blend of oil or butter and flour used to thicken sauces and gravies. The fat and flour are mixed together in equal amounts over heat. If a white roux is desired, the melting and blending are done over low heat for a few minutes. If a brown roux is desired, the flour is cooked in the fat until it is lightly browned.

RUBBED

When whole-leaf herbs, such as sage or bay leaves, are crushed in the hands so that their oils are released, the herbs are then referred to as having been rubbed.

SAND-POT COOKING

Using a ceramic lidded vessel originally designed to rest directly in an ash fire, thus cooking or stewing its contents. It can be used on the stove top, quite often with torn lettuce under the food inside. When the lettuce begins to cook, it creates a steaming action; then, as it begins to burn, it adds a unique flavor to the contents of the pot.

SAUTÉ

This term comes from a French word that means "to jump." In cooking, sauté means to place food in a very hot pan with a bit of butter or oil and to shake the pan during the cooking process so that the food jumps about. Thus one can cook very quickly over high heat without burning the food. It is not unlike Chinese chowing, or stir-frying.

SCALDED

Generally this term applies to milk in recipes and it simply means to heat the milk to just under simmering. The milk is scalded when it becomes very hot. It is not a boil at all.

SHOT

A liquid measurement that amounts to very little or to taste. A shot of wine is about an ounce, but a shot of Tabasco is less than $\frac{1}{16}$ teaspoon.

SMOKING AND TEA SMOKING

To cook or flavor food with smoldering wood. This can be done on the stove top with the Cameron smoker, providing there is a strong out-of-the-house exhaust system. Chinese black teas such as oolong or po nay can be added to the wood chips to enhance the flavor of the food you are smoking.

STEAMING

Cooking with steam as the heat source. See page 97 for a full discussion. This method is not to be confused with pressure cooking.

STIR-FRY

See Chow.

VELVETING

Deep-frying a food in oil at a temperature of about 280°F. This procedure is commonly used for shellfish. The shrimp, et cetera, is first marinated in a cornstarch and egg-white mixture. When deep-fried, a pale light coating is formed. This process also has a very tenderizing effect.

Ingredients, Condiments, and Food Definitions

CHINESE INGREDIENTS

ABALONE

Shellfish that can be found in Chinese markets in cans. Very expensive! It is also eaten fresh on the west coast of the United States.

BEAN CURD

Cheeselike product made from soybean milk. Buy fresh in cakes at Oriental markets or in produce sections of most supermarkets. It can also be purchased in cans, but the flavor is far inferior. Fresh bean curd looks very much like a five-inch rectangular block of soft but firmly shaped white cheese.

BEAN SPROUTS

You will find these fresh in most produce sections. The canned variety is so tasteless that you should omit them if you cannot find fresh ones.

BOK CHOY

A vegetable resembling Swiss chard in shape, but much lighter in color and flavor. A member of the mustard family, it can be found fresh in most supermarket produce sections and Oriental markets.

CELERY, CHINESE

Looks like common celery but has much thinner stalks and a brighter flavor. Find fresh in Oriental markets.

CELLOPHANE NOODLES

Noodles from China made from the mung bean, the same bean from which bean sprouts grow. Find in Oriental markets and some supermarkets. Also called glass noodles, *sai fun,* or bean threads.

CHESTNUTS, CHINESE DRIED

Find in Oriental markets already peeled and dried. Chinese chestnuts are slightly smaller than the Western variety.

DUCK, DRIED

Find in Chinese markets. These ducks have been cut down the breastbone, flattened out, and dried. Soak in water before using.

DOW SEE

See Fermented Black Beans

EGGPLANT, CHINESE

There are many types. The most common is purple in color, thin and long in shape compared to the varieties in the West. Also called Japanese eggplant. Can be found in Oriental markets and some supermarkets.

FERMENTED BLACK BEANS

Fermented black beans are a classic condiment in Chinese cuisine. Buy in Oriental markets, and keep in tightly sealed glass jars. No need to refrigerate.

FOO YEE

Fermented bean curd. Find in any Chinese market.

FUNGUS, BLACK

Chinese dried fungus, also known as "cloud ears" or "tree ears." Find in any Oriental market.

FUNGUS, WHITE

Related to black fungus, but white in color and very delicate. Found in Chinese markets.

GARLIC AND RED CHILI PASTE

Very hot Chinese sauce made of red peppers and garlic. Find in Oriental markets, or substitute garlic and Tabasco. It is worth the effort to find this delicious sauce.

GARLIC CHIVES

Light green in color, long thin stalks with a small bud on the tip. Find fresh in some Chinese markets.

GLASS NOODLES

See Cellophane Noodles

HOG MAWS

The actual stomach lining of the pig. Sometimes called pork tripe. Find in Oriental markets.

HOISIN

A soybean and pepper sauce common to Chinese recipes. Find in some supermarkets and in any Oriental market.

HOT BEAN SAUCE

Found canned or in jars in Oriental markets. It is *mein see* with hot pepper oil. That blend would be a good substitute.

HOT PEPPER OIL

May be purchased in Oriental markets.

JELLYFISH, DRIED

Also known as salted jellyfish. Packaged in folded sheets or already sliced. Find in Oriental markets.

LILY BUDS, DRIED

Dried lily flowers that have not blossomed. Look like little golden strands when dried. Buy in small packages in Oriental markets.

LOP CHONG

Chinese sweet pork sausage. Find in any Chinese market.

LOTUS ROOT

Found fresh in many Chinese markets, or in cans. Starchy, and when sliced displays a beautiful hollow pattern.

MEIN SEE

The remains of the process of making soy sauce. Very rich soybean condiment used in many Chinese dishes. Can be found in Oriental markets under this name or soybean jam or condiment. Refrigerate after opening.

MUSHROOMS, CHINESE

Find in Oriental markets. Soak in water before cooking. Trim the stems and save for chicken soup.

NAPA CABBAGE

Sometimes called Chinese celery cabbage, it can be found in many supermarket produce sections and Oriental markets.

OLIVES, SALTY AND SWEET (LAM SEE)

Dried olives, pitted, found in Chinese markets. Substitute dried Italian olives.

OYSTERS, DRIED

Removed from the shell and dried. Reconstitute in water for use. Found in small packages in Chinese markets.

OYSTER SAUCE

Classic cooking sauce from China. While actually made from oysters, it has no strong fishy taste. Found in Oriental markets. Refrigerate after opening.

PICKLED SHALLOTS (KUE TAO)

Shallots pickled in vinegar, sugar, and salt. Can be purchased in Oriental markets in bottles or cans.

POTATO STARCH

Starch made from dried potatoes ground into flour.

RED CHILI PASTE WITH GARLIC

See Garlic and Red Chili Paste. Same product.

RED DATES

Dark red in color, found in Chinese markets in the dried form. Use in double-boiled soups (page 123) and other dishes.

RED VINEGAR, CHINESE

Rice vinegar with spices and color added. Can be found in any Chinese market.

RICE WINE

Called *shao hsing* in Chinese markets. Basic to Chinese cooking. A good dry sherry is fine for a substitute.

RICE WINE VINEGAR

Delicious vinegar used in Chinese cooking. Find it in Oriental markets.

SAI FUN

See Cellophane Noodles

SCALLOPS, DRIED

Air-dried, resemble the common sea scallop. Reconstitute in water to use. Also called *conpoy*. Find in Chinese markets. Expensive.

SEAWEED SHEETS, DRIED

Also known as *nori.* Used in Chinese Seaweed Soup (page 118). Find in Oriental markets.

SESAME OIL

Used as a flavoring in Oriental cooking, not a cooking oil. Find this at an Oriental market. Used for flavoring a dish at the last minute. The health-food store version is not made from toasted sesame seeds, so the flavor will be very bland.

SESAME PASTE

Ground sesame seeds, oil, and salt. Purchase in any Oriental market. Used in sauces and dressings. Make your own (page 217).

SESAME SEEDS

Buy in bulk in Oriental markets. Roast them by stirring them in a hot frying pan until lightly browned, or on a baking sheet in a hot oven.

SESAME SEEDS, BLACK

Purchase in small packages in Oriental markets.

SHRIMP, DRIED

Tiny bay shrimp that have been dried. Any Chinese market will carry them.

SHU-MEI WRAPPERS OR GYOZA SKINS

A round flat noodle used to make dumplings and dim sum. Quite often used for Pork Shu-Mei (page 99). Find in any Chinese market.

SOUTHERN HAM

See Virginia Ham

SOYBEAN CONDIMENT

See Mein See

SOY SAUCE

Light, Chinese: To be used when you don't want to color a dish with caramel coloring, which is what dark soy contains. Do not confuse this with "Lite" soy sauce, which is lower in salt and flavor. Find in Oriental markets. I prefer Wing Nien brand. It is the very best quality and made by the company founded by my adopted Chinese uncle, Colonel John Young. This book is dedicated to his wife and to his memory.

Dark, Chinese: Used in dishes in which you wish to color the meat and sweeten the flavor with caramel sugar. Most common soy sauce. Buy good quality. I prefer Wing Nien brand. See explanation above.

SQUID, DRIED

Has a flat appearance when dried. Much larger than the familiar "calamari." Reconstitute in water to use. Find in Chinese markets; sometimes it can be found already soaking in water.

STICKY SWEET RICE

Very starchy rice, used in the making of Pearl Meatballs (page 300) and other dishes. Found in any Oriental market.

SWEET BEAN SAUCE

Find canned in any Chinese market. Use *mein see* with a bit of sugar for a substitute.

SWEET RED BEAN PASTE

Thick starchy paste used in Eight-Treasure Rice Pudding (page 490). Find in Oriental markets.

SWEET PICKLED RED GINGER (SUERN GEUNG)

Ginger packed in sugar syrup with red food color. Can be purchased in Oriental markets in bottles or cans. Very sweet.

SWEET PICKLED WHITE CUCUMBER (CHA GWA)

Chinese white cucumber packed in sugar syrup and salt. Can be purchased in Oriental markets in bottles or cans. Very sweet.

TARO ROOT

A starchy vegetable from China. Its shape and size are similar to that of a russet potato. Found fresh in most Oriental or Chinese markets.

TEA, OOLONG AND JASMINE

Oolong, a dark tea from China. Jasmine, a lighter tea with a flower-blossom flavor. Both are great for "smoked" dishes as well as for drinking. Can be found in any Oriental market.

TURNIP BALL, DRIED

A preserved vegetable from China used in the making of a good Chinese Chicken Soup (page 113) and other dishes. Found in Oriental markets.

VIRGINIA HAM

Also known as Southern ham or by the brand name Smithfield. A salty dry cured ham resembling the Chinese Yunnan ham. Used in very small amounts for flavoring dishes. Find these hanging in Chinese markets and meat shops or fancy delicatessens.

WATER-CHESTNUT FLOUR

A starch ground from dried water chestnuts. Find in any Chinese market.

GREEK INGREDIENTS

BÉCHAMEL SAUCE

Basic white sauce made of milk or stock and thickened with a roux of flour and butter; also known as cream sauce (page 205).

BRINE-CURED OLIVES

Sometimes called Greek olives or Calamata olives. Imported. Find in Italian markets, delicatessens, and supermarkets. California black olives are a very poor substitute.

BULGUR WHEAT

Coarse-ground processed wheat. Buy in bulk in health-food shops and good delicatessens.

CALAMATA OLIVES

See Brine-Cured Olives

FETA CHEESE

Soft white Greek cheese made from goat's milk. Buy in delicatessens. Domestic varieties made from cow's milk are available but not as good as imported feta from Greece.

GRAPE LEAVES

The leaves of the grapevine. Find in supermarkets and delicatessens packed in jars in brine.

KEFALOTYRI CHEESE

Hard cheese from Greece, made from sheep's milk. Purchase in good delicatessens. Good grating cheese.

KASSERI CHEESE

Hard cheese from Greece, good for grating. Find in delicatessens and cheese shops.

MIZITHRA CHEESE

Hard cheese from Greece, made from sheep's milk. Purchase in good delicatessens. Good grating cheese.

ORZO PASTA

Pasta shaped like rice. Great for pilaf. Find in Middle Eastern or Italian shops or in a good delicatessen.

PHYLLO DOUGH (FILLO)

Thin sheets of dough for Middle Eastern baking. Can be found in most delicatessens. Also called fillo dough.

PITA BREAD

Middle Eastern flat bread. Also known as pocket bread. Purchase in any supermarket, deli, or Middle Eastern shop.

SALT COD, DRIED

Codfish that has been cured with salt. Also known as *baccalà*. Must be soaked in water a long time before use. Buy in good delicatessens and seafood shops. This is common in both Greek and Roman cooking.

TARAMAS

Fish eggs from the carp. Purchase in small jars in Greek shops and good delicatessens.

ITALIAN INGREDIENTS

ANCHOVIES

Used for salads and pasta dishes in Italian cooking. Buy in cans from Portugal or Spain. Very salty.

ARBORIO RICE

Special rice from Italy used in making Risotto (page 383).

BACCALÀ

See Salted Cod, Dried, page 36.

CAPERS

Pickled buds used in salads and dressings. Found in any good supermarket.

CHESTNUTS, ITALIAN DRIED

These have been peeled and dried. Buy in Italian markets and delicatessens. Expensive.

FONTINA CHEESE

Rich semisoft cheese from Italy. Purchase in Italian markets or good delicatessens.

MORTADELLA

Famous sausage made in Bologna, Italy. Domestic brands can be found in Italian markets and delicatessens.

MUSHROOMS, DRIED EUROPEAN

Cepe, boletus, or porcini. These are delicious, but if they come from Europe they will be terribly expensive. Find an Italian market that brings them in from South America, and you will pay about $15 to $20 a pound. The real Italian dried mushrooms will cost you a fortune! You may also find some that are domestic. In any case, keep them in a tightly sealed jar at the back of your refrigerator, where they will keep for a year.

PANCETTA

Italian-style bacon with a flavor all its own. Find in Italian markets and good delicatessens. Regular bacon can be substituted, but it is not as good.

PARMESAN CHEESE

Hard cheese from Italy, made from cow's milk. Generally used for grating on salads and pasta dishes. Find in Italian markets, delicatessens, or supermarkets. Not as expensive as Pecorino Romano (see page 38).

PECORINO ROMANO CHEESE

Hard cheese from Italy made from sheep's milk. Rich flavor; common in Italian cooking. Buy in good delicatessens and Italian markets. Parmesan cheese is the best substitute.

PESTO

A sauce of northern Italian origin, made from fresh basil, olive oil, garlic, cheese, and pine nuts. Great on pasta or in soups and on vegetable dishes. Best to make your own. For recipe see page 211. You can purchase this frozen or in glass jars at Italian markets.

PINE NUTS

Expensive little treasures that actually come from the large pinecone of Italy. Find in Italian markets, or substitute slivered almonds.

POLENTA

Coarse cornmeal used in Italy. You can find this in any Italian market.

PORCINI

See Mushrooms, Dried European

PROSCIUTTO

A very firm and salty ham from Italy. The imported version is illegal in America but you can find fine domestic versions in Italian markets. Primo brand from Canada is quite good. Buy very little at a time, as it is very rich. Have the butcher slice it thin. You may substitute sliced Virginia ham or, in some recipes, a fully cured uncooked ham will do.

RADICCHIO

Resembles our purple cabbage, but smaller in size and has a bitter taste. Find in most supermarkets. Expensive.

RICOTTA CHEESE

White curd-type cheese. Find in delicatessens or in the dairy section of any supermarket.

SEMOLINA

A very coarse-ground flour made from hard durum wheat. Buy in an Italian grocery. Ideal for making fresh pasta, and the flavor is superior to farina, which may be used as a substitute.

Herbs and Spices

CHINESE HERBS AND SPICES

CORIANDER

The dry, whole seed is common in Mediterranean cooking. The fresh plant, which looks like parsley, is common in Chinese, Indian, and Mexican cuisines. You may see the fresh form in your supermarket listed as cilantro or Chinese parsley.

FIVE-SPICE POWDER

A Chinese blend of spices. Find in any Oriental market, or blend equal amounts of powdered cinnamon, ginger, anise, fennel, and clove. Some blends contain a bit of black pepper.

GARLIC

The bulb, of course. Use only fresh. I like mine from the garlic capital of the world, Gilroy, California. My friends at Christopher Ranch weave garlic braids that hang in the kitchen for up to a year. Just pull off a bulb as needed. This is a common and important ingredient in all three ancient cuisines. And buy a good garlic press (page 18).

GINGER, FRESH

Very common in Chinese dishes. Buy by the "hand," or whole stem, at the supermarket. Keep in the refrigerator, uncovered and unwrapped. Grate when needed. Also used in ancient Rome.

MALT SUGAR

Necessary ingredient in making a true Peking Roast Duck. Can be purchased dry or in liquid form. Easy to find in Chinese markets.

MSG

A powder made from seaweed or soybeans. Used as a natural flavor enhancer. Some people seem to be allergic to it and talk of Chinese Restaurant Syndrome, in which they have a headache or light chest pains when eating food containing too much monosodium glutamate (MSG). Few are bothered by this natural chemical and I use it now and then. IT SHOULD BE USED SPARINGLY, JUST AS YOU USE SALT.

MUSTARD, DRY

Absolute necessity if you love salad dressings. And when mixed with water, makes Chinese hot mustard dip. I buy Colman's, from Britain.

PEPPERCORNS, BLACK

Buy whole, and always grind fresh.

RED PEPPER FLAKES, HOT, CRUSHED

Also labeled "crushed red pepper flakes." Buy in bulk, and use sparingly. The seeds make this a very hot product. Common in both Chinese and Roman cuisines.

STAR ANISE

Anise seeds in whole form in the shape of five-pointed stars. Wonderful flavor. Buy whole in any Chinese or Oriental market.

SZECHUAN PEPPERCORNS

A wild peppercorn from China, sometimes called *fagara*. Not hot but very flavorful. No substitute. Find in any Chinese market.

WHITE PEPPER, GROUND

White peppercorns in the powder form. Important ingredient in good Chinese cooking.

Greek Herbs and Spices

ALLSPICE

Not a blend of spices at all, but a single one. Very common in the Greek kitchen. Buy it ground because it is hard to grind yourself.

CARAWAY SEED

This ancient dried seed used by the Greeks and the Romans is excellent for baking fresh breads.

CINNAMON

Very common in Greek cooking. Hard to grind your own, so buy it in the powder form. Also used by the Romans.

CLOVES, WHOLE AND GROUND

I use both the ground and the whole. Common in Greece and Rome.

DILLWEED

Both fresh and dried are used in Greece and Rome. The fresh is a great addition to a tossed salad.

GARLIC   (Page 39)

MAHLEB

Small seed that is ground fresh for wonderful Greek breads. Hard to find. Try Greek shops as it is worth the search. No substitute.

MINT

The dried form is common in both ancient Greek and Roman dishes; it also makes great tea. Fresh mint can be grown in the backyard; when cooking with it, use twice the amount in recipes calling for dried mint. Fresh mint is also good in salads.

OREGANO

Basic to the kitchen. For salads, meats, sauces. You can grow your own, but the best comes from Greece. Buy whole, dried.

PARSLEY, DRIED AND FRESH

I rarely use dried because fresh is better. However, dried holds up better in salad dressings. Buy whole. Fresh parsley can be purchased in the supermarket or you can grow your own. I like the Italian variety, which has a flat leaf and a bright flavor. Basic to Greek and Roman cooking.

PEPPERCORNS, BLACK   (Page 40)

ROMAN HERBS AND SPICES

BASIL

Common in Italian cooking. Buy it fresh or dried, whole at the supermarket. You can also grow your own.

BAY LEAVES

Basic to the kitchen for good soups, stews, et cetera. Buy whole, dried, or if your area is not too cold, grow a bay laurel tree. I have one in Tacoma.

CARAWAY SEED   (Page 40)

CINNAMON   (Page 41)

CLOVES, WHOLE AND GROUND   (Page 41)

CORIANDER, LEAF AND SEEDS   (Page 39)

CUMIN

An ancient Roman spice. Can be purchased by the can in powder form, or buy the whole seed and grind it. The flavor is much brighter with the whole seed.

FENNEL SEED

Resembles anise or licorice in flavor. Produces that special flavor in Italian sausage. Buy it whole or grind it as you need it. Common in Ancient Rome.

GARLIC   (Page 39)

JUNIPER BERRIES

These are to be found dried in good spice shops. They will remind you of the flavor of English gin. Used in ancient Rome. There is no substitute.

LOVAGE

Ancient Roman herb that resembles celery, with thin stalks and a leafy top. Common celery leaves can be substituted, but the flavor is not as bright. Similar to Chinese celery (page 29).

MARJORAM

Common kitchen herb, light in flavor. Used in Roman cooking. Buy whole, dried.

MINT, FRESH AND DRIED   (Page 41)

PARSLEY, DRIED AND FRESH   (Page 42)

PEPPERCORNS, BLACK   (Page 40)

RED PEPPER FLAKES, HOT, CRUSHED   (Page 40)

ROSEMARY

Basic to the cooking of Italy. Grow your own or buy it whole dried.

THYME

An ancient Roman herb used extensively in soups, stews, and sauces and for seasoning meats. Buy it whole, dried, or grow your own.

Television Shows and Recipes

SHOW NUMBER AND TITLE

501   APPETIZERS
Walnuts Fried with Sugar
(page 85)
Chinese Brine Pickles *(page 83)*
Barbecued Pork Strips *(page 288)*
Bean Sprout and Szechwan Pepper Salad *(page 139)*
Glass Noodles with Peanut Sauce
(page 356)
Looed Beef *(page 312)*
Shredded Chicken Sesame
(page 84)
Smelt Antipasti *(page 90)*
Peperonata *(page 91)*
Tzatziki *(page 86)*
Taramasalata *(page 87)*

502   DIM SUM
Ha Gow *(page 96)*
Shrimp Toast *(page 97)*
Shrimp Boats *(page 97)*
Shrimp-Stuffed Mushrooms
(page 98)
Pork Shu-Mei *(page 99)*
Pork and Taro Meatballs
(page 100)

Beef Meatballs *(page 107)*
Stuffed Bean Curd *(page 103)*
Hot and Spicy Squid *(page 109)*
Spicy Pork Tripe *(page 104)*
Spareribs with Black Beans and
Pepper Sauce *(page 105)*
Fried Wontons *(page 106)*

503   CONDIMENTS
Salad Mykonos *(page 149)*
Spinach with Olive Oil, Garlic,
and Lemon Juice *(page 467)*
Lettuce with Foo Yee
(page 467)
Oenogarum *(page 215)*
Steamed Fish with Soybean
Condiment and Bean Curd
(page 158)
Shrimp and Oyster Sauce
(page 173)

504   SOUPS
Chinese Chicken Soup Stock
(page 113)
Bean Curd Soup *(page 114)*
Peas and Egg Soup *(page 115)*

Seaweed Soup *(page 118)*
Double-Boiled Soups *(page 123)*
Tripe Soup with Egg-Lemon
Sauce *(page 325)*
Roman "Rag" Soup *(page 133)*

505   SAUCES
Greek Tomato Sauce *(page 204)*
Okra in Greek Tomato Sauce (re-
fer to Artichokes in Greek To-
mato Sauce, *page 405)*
Egg-Lemon Sauce *(page 205)*
Italian Tomato Sauce *(page 208)*
Basic Brown Sauce *(page 207)*
Sauce Bolognese *(page 209)*
Green Sauce for Boiled Meats
(page 209)
Chinese Dip Sauces *(page 201)*

506   MUSHROOMS
Dried Abalone with Mushrooms
(page 336)
Pork and Egg with Tree Fungus
in Pancakes *(page 460)*
Mushrooms Stuffed with Feta
Cheese *(page 462)*
Pasta with Mushrooms Natalie
(page 464)
White Fungus Soup *(page 461)*
Double-Boiled Soups *(page 123)*
Mushroom Omelet Apicius
(page 465)
Pizza with Two Mushrooms
(page 488)

507   EGGS
Baby Corn and Quail Eggs
(page 225)
Tea Eggs *(page 223)*
Salted Eggs *(page 224)*
Steamed Pork with Salted Eggs
(page 226)
Asparagus with Cheese and Eggs,
Italian Style *(page 413)*
Egg, Artichoke, and Tuna Pizza
(page 487)

508   HONG KONG
Pork Shu-Mei *(page 99)*
Ha Gow *(page 95)*
Fried Dumplings (see Rolled
Dumplings, *page 390)*
Chinese Roast Duck *(page 252)*
Wonton Dumplings *(page 391)*
Chow Mein, Cantonese Style
(page 347)
Looed Goose *(page 249)*
Chinese Fish Salad *(page 142)*

509   LEEKS
Chinese Lamb and Leeks
(page 448)
Chicken with Leek Belts
(page 450)
Boiled Leeks with Cabbage
Apicius *(page 453)*
Beans and Leeks Apicius
(page 452)
Artichokes and Leeks *(page 452)*
Fava Beans with Leeks *(page 453)*
Leeks and Juniper Berries
(page 454)
Leek Cakes *(page 451)*

510   LAMB
Roast Lamb, Italian Style
(page 285)
Roast Lamb, Greek Style
(page 281)
Lamb and Tomato Sauce, Greek
Style *(page 278)*
Lamb with Orzo Pasta, Greek
Style *(page 280)*
Greek Lamb and Pasta Salad
(page 146)
Lamb Hot Pot, Mongolian Style
(page 276)
Chinese Dip Sauces *(page 201)*
Chinese Lamb and Leeks
(page 448)

511   PORK
Crispy Roast Pork *(page 490)*
Barbecued Pork Strips *(page 288)*

Barbecued Spareribs *(page 289)*
Slow-Simmered Pork Roast
(page 292)
Bird's Nest Meatballs *(page 299)*
Pearl Meatballs *(page 300)*
Pork with Celery, Greek Style
(page 302)
Roast Pork, Roman Style
(page 303)

512   BREAD
Ancient Roman Bread *(page 480)*
Old Greek Bread *(page 475)*
Focaccia Romana *(page 482)*
Chinese Steamed Bread
(page 472)
Chinese Fried Bread Strips
(page 472)
Peking Pancakes *(page 474)*
Corn Crepes, Chinese Style
(page 473)
Onion Cakes *(page 475)*
Greek Sesame Bread *(page 477)*
Sesame Circles *(page 478)*
Greek Easter Bread *(page 478)*

513   ATHENS
Stuffed Grape Leaves with Egg-
Lemon Sauce *(page 380)*
Barley Pudding with Lamb
(page 283)

514   CHESTNUTS
Roasted Chestnuts *(page 430)*
Chestnuts Soaked in Wine
(page 431)
Chestnuts Soaked in Ouzo
(page 431)
Chestnut Focaccia *(page 482)*
Chestnut Pasta *(page 432)*
Chestnut Polenta *(page 432)*
Chestnuts and Lentils Apicius
(page 433)
Sweet Chestnut Purée *(page 500)*
Italian Chestnut Jam Cake
(page 501)

Chinese Beef and Chestnut Stew
(page 427)
Chinese Chicken with Chestnuts
(page 428)
Peking Dust *(page 495)*
Water Chestnuts and Green
Beans *(page 429)*
Shrimp Chowed with Water-
Chestnut Flour and Gin
(page 429)

515   FISH
Fish with Celery in Hot Plate
(page 156)
Steamed Fish with Soybean Con-
diment and Bean Curd *(page 153)*
Braised Fish Oi Mann *(page 159)*
Steamed Fish with Black Beans
(page 160)
Small Fish Deep-Fried in Olive
Oil *(page 162)*
Baked Fish Archestratus
(page 164)
Greek Fish Chowder *(page 163)*
Assorted Fried Seafood *(page 165)*

516   DUCKS
Peking Duck *(page 254)*
Duck Like a Mandolin *(page 255)*
Stewed Duck with Mushrooms
(page 256)
Chinese Roast Duck *(page 252)*
Steamed Dried Duck and Pork
(page 257)
Tea-Smoked Duck *(page 258)*
Looed Duck Feet *(page 260)*
Greek Duck with Olives
(page 261)

517   ROME
Pasta Carbonara, Roman Style
(page 366)
Deep-Fried Vegetables Piperno
(page 467)
Celery and Mushroom Salad
Savini *(page 149)*
Italian Flag Salad *(page 150)*

518 DESSERTS
Eight-Treasure Rice Pudding
(page 490)
Fried Custard *(page 492)*
Cherries in Almond *(page 493)*
Sweet Almond Cream Soup
(page 495)
Peking Dust *(page 495)*
Halvah Cake *(page 496)*
Strawberry Yogurt with Honey
(page 497)
Ricotta Pie, Roman Style
(page 498)
Italian Chestnut Jam Cake
(page 501)
Wine and Cookies *(page 500)*

519 EGGPLANT
Eggplant with Soybean Condi-
ment and Hoisin *(page 437)*
Eggplant Shoes *(page 442)*
Eggplant Stuffed Greek Style
(page 439)
Eggplant, Roman Style *(page 445)*
Eggplant Slices Baked *(page 443)*
Eggplant Salad *(page 444)*
Eggplant and Pork Mandar-Inn
Restaurant *(page 438)*

520 RELIGIOUS DISHES
Grilled Liver, Greek Style
(page 325)
Greek Easter Bread *(page 478)*
Fish Stew for Christmas Eve
(page 166)
Chinese New Year Noodles
(page 355)
Quick Chinese Roast Chicken
(page 242)

521 DUMPLINGS
Chinese Boiled Dumplings
(page 388)
Pot Stickers *(page 390)*
Rolled Dumplings *(page 390)*
Wonton Dumplings *(page 391)*

Chicken and Spinach Ravioli
(page 392)
Gnocchi with Cheese *(page 395)*
Gnocchi Fried *(page 396)*
Gnocchi with Sauce Bolognese
(page 396)

522 SQUID AND OCTOPUS
Cleaning Squid *(page 188)*
Squid Balls *(page 187)*
Two Squid, Chowed *(page 189)*
Seafood Salad Da Franco
(page 191)
Baby Octopus Salad *(page 198)*
Octopus Spaghetti Zorba
(page 196)
Stuffed Squid, Greek Style
(page 194)
Octopus in Wine and Tomato
Sauce *(page 197)*
Squid and Spinach *(page 193)*

523 SESAME
Sesame Almond Chicken Wings
(page 241)
Fish Fillets with Sesame
(page 161)
Shredded Chicken Sesame
(page 84)
Tahini, Homemade *(page 217)*
Tahini Bean Dip *(page 88)*
Chinese Sesame Cookies
(page 494)

524 PASTA
Chow Mein, Cantonese Style
(page 347)
Chow Fun Noodles *(page 349)*
Cold Chow Fun and Pork Roll
(page 351)
Meat-Stuffed Chow Fun Rolls
(page 353)
Noodles in Oyster Sauce
(page 354)

525 OLIVES AND OLIVE OIL
Deep-Fried Squid, Italian Style
(page 192)

Olive and Pepper Salad
(page 152)
Olive Bread *(page 483)*
Green Olive Soup *(page 134)*
Fish with Olives and Bean Curd
(page 161)
Steamed Pork with Chinese
Olives *(page 301)*
Rice Congee *(page 378)*
Chinese Fried Bread Strips
(page 472)

526   ASPARAGUS
Blanching Asparagus Apicius
(page 411)
Asparagus Custard Apicius
(page 412)
Asparagus with Beef and Black
Beans *(page 408)*
Cold Asparagus, Chinese Style
(page 407)
Pickled Asparagus, Greek Style
(page 410)
Cold Asparagus, Greek Style
(page 409)
Asparagus with Oil and Tomato,
Greek Style *(page 409)*

527   BEANS
Smoked Bean Curd *(page 416)*
Bean Curd with Pork *(page 416)*
Long Beans with Beef *(page 417)*
Fresh Fava Beans, Roman Style
(page 422)
Beans, Artichokes, and Peas
(page 423)
Lima Beans with Greek Tomato
Sauce *(page 418)*
Black-Eyed Pea Salad Sigalas
(page 419)
White Beans, Greek Style
(page 420)
Pasta and Bean Soup *(page 421)*

528   CHICKEN AND GOOSE
Chinese Poached Chicken
(page 230)

Beggar's Chicken *(page 233)*
Chicken with Two Onions in
Sand Pot *(page 234)*
Chicken Baked with Honey and
Soy Sauce *(page 232)*
Looed Goose *(page 249)*
Goose Chiu Chow Style
(page 250)
Fricassee of Chicken, Roman
Style *(page 244)*
Chicken with Sweet Bell Peppers
(page 246)
Devil's Chicken *(page 245)*
Roasted Chicken, Greek Style
(page 243)
Chicken Roll, Greek Style
(page 244)

529   RICE
Fried Rice *(page 375)*
Rice Congee *(page 378)*
Sticky Sweet Rice with Meats
(page 377)
Chinese Sausage on Steamed
Rice *(page 379)*
Risotto with Mushrooms
(page 383)
Risotto with Mushrooms and
Herbs *(page 384)*
Risotto with Champagne
(page 384)
Stuffed Grape Leaves with Egg-
Lemon Sauce *(page 380)*
Stuffed Tomatoes Hydra
(page 381)
Squid Pilaf *(page 192)*

530   ARTICHOKES
Cleaning Artichokes *(page 400)*
Artichokes Sautéed in Wine
(page 401)
Artichokes, Jewish Style
(page 400)
Artichokes Chilled, Roman Style
(page 401)
Artichokes Stuffed, Roman Style
(page 403)

Artichokes in Greek Tomato
Sauce *(page 405)*

531   BEEF
Poached Meatballs in Egg and
Lemon Sauce *(page 313)*
Fried Meatballs *(page 314)*
Meatballs in Tomato Sauce
(page 314)
Beef Slices with Rosemary
(page 316)
Pepper Onion Beef *(page 308)*
Smoked Meatballs *(page 310)*
Looed Beef *(page 312)*
Looed Beef in Sand Pot
(page 312)

532   UNUSUAL FOODS
Jellyfish Salad *(page 137)*
Duck and Jellyfish Salad
(page 138)
Spareribs with Lotus Root
(page 301)
Bird's Nest Soup *(page 125)*
Looed Duck Feet *(page 260)*
Looed Chicken Feet (Refer to
Looed Duck Feet, *page 260)*

533   TAKE-OUT FOODS
Barbecued Spareribs *(page 289)*
Barbecued Pork Strips *(page 288)*
Chinese Roast Duck *(page 252)*
Quick Chinese Roast Chicken
(page 242)
The Antipasti Bar *(page 90)*
Headcheese Appetizer *(page 92)*
Focaccia Romana *(page 482)*
Souvlaki *(page 282)*
Pita Bread with Olive Oil, Grilled
(page 479)
Cheese Pies *(page 88)*
Spinach Pies *(page 89)*
Strawberry Yogurt with Honey
(page 497)

534   DRIED FOODS
Jellyfish Salad *(page 137)*
Dried Abalone with Mushrooms
(page 336)
Dried Scallop and Chive Soup
(page 337)
Dried Oysters and Pork in Let-
tuce *(page 338)*
Chinese Sausage, Dried Duck,
and Roast Pork Sand Pot
(page 340)
Steamed Pork with Mushroom
and Dried Squid *(page 339)*
Steamed Dried Duck and Pork
(page 257)
Salted Cod in Cream Sauce
(page 342)
Salted Cod, Greek Style
(page 341)
Garlic Sauce *(page 206)*

535   GRILLING
Ground Meat on Skewers
(page 284)
Grilled Lamb Cubes, Greek Style
(page 285)
Firebrick Grill *(page 285)*
Fish Grilled Greek Style
(page 164)
Pita Bread with Olive Oil, Grilled
(page 479)
Mongolian Lamb *(page 277)*
Grilled Sweet Red Peppers
(HINTS page 151)

536   INNARDS
Looed Beef Tongue *(page 321)*
Looed Pork Tripe *(page 322)*
Pork Tripe in Hot Sauce
(page 323)
Stewed Oxtail, Chinese Style
(page 324)
Tripe, Roman Style *(page 329)*
Oxtails, Roman Style *(page 330)*
Fried Innards, Roman Style, Ed-
mondo *(page 331)*
Tongue in Sweet and Sour

Sauce, Roman Style *(page 333)*
Lamb Innard Soup for Easter
(page 327)

537　PASTA II
Pasta with Sweet Red Peppers
and Anchovies *(page 364)*
Pasta Ears with Cauliflower
(page 365)
Pasta Ties with Cabbage
(page 369)
Pappardelle with Pesto *(page 370)*
Pastitsio *(page 358)*
Pastitsio Baked with Phyllo
(page 360)

538　PIZZA
Peking Pancakes *(page 474)*
Garbanzo Pizza, Old Roman Style
(page 485)
Chestnut Focaccia *(page 482)*

Pizza Dough *(page 487)*
Pizza with Assorted Toppings
(page 487)
Rustic Pizza *(page 488)*

539　SHELLFISH
Velvet Prawns *(page 170)*
Velveted Scallops in Celery
(page 176)
Steamed Shrimp with Special
Sauce *(page 172)*
Crab in Black Bean Sauce
(page 178)
Shrimp Ananius *(page 181)*
Shrimp in Greek Tomato Sauce
with Feta *(page 182)*
Baby Snails in Greek Tomato
Sauce *(page 183)*
Seafood Salad, Roman Style
(page 185)

THE THREE
ANCIENT CUISINES

China and
Its Inventions

T here is no culture in the world that is more obsessed with food than the Chinese, and it seems to have always been that way. When the Chinese are not involved in the actual preparation of a meal, they are talking about the next meal. The sense of anticipation that centers around the family table is like nothing that I have ever seen in other cultures. Further, in their quest for the proper celebration of food, the Chinese have invented or discovered nearly every kind of cooking piece and cooking process, and they were probably the first in history to use them. Yet many books on food history begin with Sumeria, pass through Greece and Rome, and head for Paris, with China receiving a minor mention. That is an absurd way to do history.

THE CHINESE MIND-SET

"A man cannot be too serious about his eating,
for food is the force that binds
society together."

—CONFUCIUS

The Chinese preoccupation with food is not due to the fact that they have known starvation. Many cultures have passed through starving times but have never reached the culinary heights attained by the Chinese. Nor is their fascination with food due to their willingness to try anything and everything, though they have. Rather, the Chinese see themselves as a part of nature and its processes, and the celebration of food is a very matter-of-fact event. It is not a *part* of living, it *is* living. The sharing of a meal is what seems to hold the culture together, and even their common greeting to one another, *"Chi fan le mei you?,"* actually translates as "Have you eaten yet?" It is close to our "How are you?," but of course it centers around food.

In order to better understand the integral role that food plays in the culture, we need to admit that a culture cooks in a particular way because of the way it thinks. That is true in the West, but I have come to believe that the Chinese also think in a particular way because of the way they cook. The meal passes on to the members of the family a certain insight into history, family ties, holidays, celebrations—in short, into one's place in the scheme of things.

The concept of the Tao is important here. It refers to the belief that there is a natural order and flow to things, a place for all and each in the cosmos, and everything is somehow tied to this proper order or Way. When one is in tune with the Way, things go as they are intended to go. It is very different from the Western belief that we must be at odds with creation, be in charge, remake or reshape everything.

The Way of the Tao means that those who understand it try to get into the flow of things rather than make things into something else. For instance, in Western art we generally use oil paints when preparing a portrait. The oil remains wet for weeks and we can keep pushing it about until we get what we want, which is usually a bust, the person from the waist up, on his own, alone in the frame. The Chinese artist uses ink on rice paper, and he has one chance to catch what he sees or feels, only one chance. The Chinese portrait of a man will more often show a mountainside, with trees and rivers, great cloud formations, and mystical beauty. And there, down in one corner, stands the man. He is in the midst of the flow of the Way, of the cosmos, of the order of things. And he seems to be content to stand there.

Chuang-tze, a classic writer on the Way of the Tao, tells of the life of a chef. A chef who does not understand must always be sharpening his cleaver since he is always hacking away at reality. A Taoist chef rarely sharpens his cleaver since he knows where to place the blade effortlessly and thus separate the joints and meat from the bone. It appears as work without effort, but it amounts to work based on insight.

In terms of cooking this means that you do not force foods into becoming something that they are not. The covering over of one food with the sharp or overwhelming flavor of another is therefore considered very bad taste among the Chinese. For them a sauce must support, not cover over, a flavor. It also means that in order to bring each food product in a particular dish to its own point of fulfillment, you must cook several ingredients separately, and then join them together in the wok at the last moment. In this way you have contrast in both flavor and texture, all in the same dish. In our culture we are fond of a certain blending and equalizing, consistency and smoothness, a sort of democratic method of cooking. Thus, we are fond of stews, not contrasts.

The doctrine of contrasts in China, Yin/Yang, means that things are defined by other things. Woman is not the opposite of man, since she is woman only when a man is present. And man is only man when a woman is present. Otherwise he is just a person. Each defines the other; they do not battle one another.

These philosophical concepts give rise to all sorts of eating and cooking habits. Americans like to value privacy so we use separate plates for each person and we sit at square tables, thus showing our independence. The Chinese, understanding themselves in a much more communal way, eat from a common bowl in the center of the table, a table that is always enormous and round so that each person may always see the others, face to face. That is probably the only way that such a culture, one in which everyone has always lived so close to everyone else, could possibly work.

One further observation, this one about chopsticks. The idea that chopsticks are primitive is about as astute as the wisecrack about being hungry an hour after eating Chinese food. American-Chinese food, which is filled with celery and bean sprouts and little else, might leave you with hunger, but not real Chinese cooking. Nor are the chopsticks primitive. Willie Mark, a serious gourmet in Hong Kong, claims that the Chinese knew of the knife and fork before they settled on the use of chopsticks. That was news to me, but it is obvious that the Chinese do not use knives and forks at the table because they think butchering food at the table is somewhat barbaric. Better for the chef to chop everything in the kitchen so that it can be eaten by the guest without effort, and with delight. No, the chopping is not done so that one may eat faster. The Chinese spend more time at table than any other people I know, and it is not a matter of efficiency here. It is a matter of philosophy and courtesy and taste.

Finally, the above philosophical concepts allow the Chinese to enjoy their food unabashedly. They do not seem to be burdened with the guilt that is associated with food in our Puritan culture. Enjoy! That's the message. And enjoy food to your good health; the Chinese use food to prevent illness and to heal illness. They are the oldest nutritionists and herb doctors in the world. So, to the table!

THE FIRST COOKS
AND FIRST RESTAURANTS

The first person to cook meat, according to the anthropologists, was Peking Man. That was about 250,000 B.C. Meat sitting on a rock near a fire was probably discovered to be more flavorful than raw meat, and then it happened. Peking Man put some meat on the end of a stick, the first cooking device, and roasted it over the fire. Since it was probably a good-sized piece of meat, he shared it with his associates. There! First Chinese restaurant!

Actually, the first restaurant did appear in China. Prior to the T'ang dynasty (618 B.C.) the Chinese enjoyed the old custom of stopping off for rest and food at a Buddhist or Taoist monastery during a pilgrimage to the holy temples. Later, the Emperor came forth with an edict that these institutions should be kept in good condition for receiving secular guests, since an important goal of both religions was the welfare of all living beings. Thus was born the restaurant.

It is true that Rome had street shops, but these really must be considered take-out houses. The Romans picked the idea up from the Greeks, the inventors of take-out food, it seems to me. But the Romans provided no place to sit and you were expected to take the food to your residence, if you had one. The Chinese, on the other hand, had complete eating houses where you might even stay overnight. These predated anything else that could possibly be called a restaurant.

The Chinese also had take-out houses. The lack of fuel in the Old World meant that few homes could have kitchens, and those that did generally had the fire in the middle of the room. It was out of the question to have two fires going at once, one for cooking and one for heating the house. There was no central heating aside from the cooking fire, so the whole family gathered about that flame. The frugality of the Chinese meant that they would go often to take-out shops that had meat already cooked. Baked goods could be purchased across the street. And, finally, as the last stop, one could visit the special shop for boiling water for your teapot. We find this system strange, but please consider that we are terribly inefficient and burn incredible amounts of fuel all for the sake of privacy. The Chinese just do not think that way.

By the Sung dynasty (A.D. 960–1279) great restaurants were common in China. Marco Polo, who came a bit later, was amazed at the restaurants, hotels, taverns, and teahouses. All of these ventures were operated with paper money, something that Mr. Polo had never seen. The Chinese invented that, too!

The restaurants of China served meals that are hard to believe. It was not at all uncommon for the wealthy classes to go to an evening meal that consisted of forty courses. Many of the first dishes would simply be brought into the dining room in order to show the skill of the chef, and no one was expected to eat these decorative delights. They were returned to the kitchen, where the staff consumed the food. And since the rule was to serve the best dishes at the last, one had to know how many courses were being served so that one might know when to begin eating in earnest. While the number of courses is no longer so great, I have eaten in Hong Kong with older gentlemen who sit through a feast of many courses with little interest. Finally, near the end of the meal they begin eating everything in sight . . . the best dishes, of course. And I, I am too full to eat anything since I lack the discipline and insight and training to eat in a formal Chinese restaurant. I simply cannot wait, and the old men knew it!

It is still possible to find banquets of twenty-eight courses in Hong Kong, but they are three-day meals. I have eaten in Beijing and I have eaten in Chinese restaurants all over the Western world. The best Chinese food in our time is not to be found on the mainland since the government is so desperate for money that the quality food is shipped out to Hong Kong, and that is exactly where you will find the most profound and exciting Chinese food available . . . anywhere.

Be prepared to taste many schools of Chinese cooking in Hong Kong. The nation of China has many different ethnic and cultural groups within its borders, so I suppose we should not even use the term "Chinese food." It makes no more sense than the term "American food." What region are you talking about? Boston is certainly different from Dallas, which is different from Seattle. The schools of cuisine in China are many and run from lighter dishes in the south to western dishes that are so hot you are shocked.

THE OLDEST
CHINESE COOKBOOK

We don't know if it is the first Chinese cookbook, but it is certainly the oldest one we have. We have all kinds of claims as to the oldest cookbook, some going back to clay tablets from southern Babylonia around 1700 B.C. Other claims are based on references to earlier volumes that we no longer have. Such is the case with the oldest Chinese cookbook.

My friend Bruce Cost, the fine author of *Ginger East to West* and *Bruce Cost's Asian Ingredients,* has found a jewel. He has a manuscript that goes back to A.D. 535 in China. A government official from the Shandong Province, one Jai Sixie, offered a book that contained recipes from earlier books that we do not have, but the recipes go back to the sixth century B.C. Bruce is beside himself and busily translating the text. It will be called *How to Steam a Bear.*

Many recipes in the book are just as we see them today. Chinese eggplant braised in soy, ginger, and scallions with Szechwan peppercorns. I had the dish the other night in Chinatown. Bruce also claims that this book proves that the Chinese invented prepared mustard, not the French; *sashimi* and *sushi,* not the Japanese; and yeast breads, things that we did not know the Chinese appreciated prior to the time of Christ. All of the current methods of Chinese cooking are explained in this ancient text, and the roasting sections are just wonderful. They were into grilling—we call it barbecuing—long before we expected it. They even invented the meatloaf!

I have already ordered my copy of the book.

THE CHINESE KITCHEN

In the old days the kitchen of a wealthy family was out in back of the house. The smoke from the fire and the noise of the kitchen could not be contained in the house. If you were very wealthy the kitchen was attended by a large staff. But as far as I can understand the method, the basic plan and equipment were always pretty much the same.

The wok, or large round frying pan, was placed over a small burner of charcoal or over a large ceramic stove that could take several woks at once. The pan itself, the wok, originally developed as a result of Chinese inventiveness and a sense of frugality. There is probably some connection between the helmet used by the invading Mongols during the Bronze Age and the pan itself. Food could be cooked in the helmet over the fire. It was also a very frugal use of fuel since the heat is concentrated in a small area in the bottom of the pan, or helmet. In my opinion a good carbon-steel wok, well seasoned, is a must for cooking Chinese food. It is one of the oldest devices we have for the kitchen and I can see no way of improving it.

The kitchen also had a series of clay pots, called sand pots because of the crude method used in casting them, and the bamboo steamers, of course. Ovens for roasting were found only in the houses of the wealthy. The old cleaver and usual cutting boards were also present.

The quality of the porcelain soup bowls and dishes would depend on the wealth of the family.

The methods of cooking have changed little:

Stir-frying or Chowing Food is tossed about in the wok over high heat. Little oil is needed and the heat is kept high, thus sealing in the flavors of the ingredients.

Steaming or Jing Food is placed in bowls in bamboo steaming racks, or on the racks themselves. The result is very tender and moist food.

Deep-frying or Jow Food is quickly deep-fried in peanut oil. This seals the food and offers a wonderful crusty coating.

Pan-frying or Jin Just as in our system.

Red Cooking or Loo Soey The meats are simmered slowly in soy sauce, ginger, spices, and wine until tender and close to heaven.

Roasting or Shew Meats and birds are oven-roasted.

In addition, foods are smoked, barbecued, and grilled, much as we do in our culture.

THE FOOD PRODUCTS

You will not need to find terribly special ingredients for the recipes in this book. Oh, the Chinese do enjoy some food products that appear strange to us, and I have tasted most of them. I enjoy sea slug or sea cucumber, bird's nest soup, shark fin, and eggs preserved in lime. The only dish I have ever been offered by a Chinese chef that I did not like was sour bamboo. I still cannot get into that one.

The ingredients for all the Chinese recipes are explained in the recipe itself or in the glossary.

A FINAL OBSERVATION

Westerners seem to think that Chinese table manners are a bit different. Please understand that, as I said above, the Chinese enjoy food un-abashedly and without hesitation. Therefore they do not pretend that they are *not* eating when they are. That is our game in the West. The Chinese meal celebration may feature everything from burping at the table to reaching clear across the table in order to reach some special tidbit. So, they admit that they are eating . . . and everyone will be eating with their mouths open. However, you will never see a Chinese blow his nose at the table. That is a gross deed, according to the Chinese, that only Westerners would do.

Relax and enjoy this most profound and most ancient cuisine of the world.

WHEN IN HONG KONG

Hong Kong is one of the great cities of the world, and it certainly does not act like the rest of China. The mainland Chinese have always kept to themselves, preferring their own culture and habits to those of the outsiders who attempted to break into the Chinese life-style. This pro-vincial attitude was common even during the days of the silk routes that ran from Rome to central China prior to the Christian era. The Romans wanted to talk and gossip but the Chinese kept to themselves. Not so with Hong Kong. Not at all!

Hong Kong's history is bound up with the pirates and smugglers who founded the city two hundred years ago. The Opium Wars, the trade with Great Britain, the relationships established with every other major country in the world, make Hong Kong Island a very different and more open culture than the one you will find on the mainland of China. I think it is the best food city in the world and I urge you to go there. The city population is five and a half million, and another four and a half million visit each year. It is about time you got in on it. Traveling in Hong Kong is just a delight!

The following restaurants and markets will interest you.

Hong Kong Markets

I owe the discovery of these markets to my dear friend, Ken Hom, Chinese cooking instructor and cookbook author. He knows Hong Kong!

The food markets are most unusual and exciting. Go to the Central Market in Hong Kong, in the Central District. Live ducks are being freshly killed, fish are being cleaned, and it is a little much if you have a weak stomach.

Graham Street in the Central District has some of the most beautiful produce you have ever seen. Noodles, eggs, bean curd, everything. Be prepared to hike uphill for three or four blocks.

Dried-food markets on Des Voeux Road in downtown Hong Kong. Dried snakes, fish, mushrooms, almost everything you can imagine.

Yaumati District in Kowloon. Open street stalls, butchers, produce, poultry, and color. Tons of color. Don't miss the pots and pans shops on Canton Road and upper Shanghai Street.

You will enjoy the Tin Hau Temple in the same neighborhood.

Hong Kong Restaurants

The Maxim's Restaurants are all very good. For fine dim sum go to Maxim's Palace in Causeway Bay. The Sichuan Garden in Central Hong Kong is excellent, as is the Peking Garden and the Chiu Chow Garden. You will be happy in any of these places. Your hotel staff can give you instructions as to location.

Spring Deer Restaurant in Kowloon. Wonderful Peking duck and not very expensive.

Great Shanghai in Kowloon. This place is big, friendly, and very authentic. Want to try looed duck tongues? Moderate in price.

King Heung Restaurant in Causeway Bay. Some of the best food I had in Hong Kong. Peking style, moderate in price.

Wu Kong Shanghai in Kowloon near the Peninsula Hotel. Great food and moderate in price. Have their vegetarian goose. Tell Mr. Kong that I sent you.

City Chiu Chow Restaurant, Ocean Center, Kowloon. It is a madhouse but the food is great. Moderate in price.

Carriana Chiu Chow in Causeway Bay. Elegant, delicious, and expensive.

Capitol Dim Sum Restaurant on Nathan Street, Kowloon. Good dim sum and inexpensive.

I am sorry to report that the King Bun Dim Sum House, the one that you saw on my television show, has closed. Problems with a lease. What a pain!

Sun Tung Lok, Kowloon, specializes in dried seafoods. Very delicious, very elegant, and verrrrry expensive.

Li Ching Heen, at the Regent Hotel in Kowloon. Real class, rather nouvelle Chinese, and expensive. Great for a special party.

Rainbow Room at the Lee Gardens Hotel, Hong Kong Island. Fine food, pricy and classy. Great Peking duck and roast suckling pig.

Oi Mann Seafood Restaurant in the Lau Fau Shan fishing village outside of Kowloon. A day trip you will never forget. Moderate in price and all of the fish is alive when you arrive. Ask at hotel for directions. You must go. Tell Mr. Mann I sent you.

Greece and
Its Insights

HISTORY

It is impossible to discuss the food of Greece without discussing history, art, and philosophy . . . then food. In the early days, during the time of Sophocles (400 B.C.), it was common for poets and philosophers to sit about talking, or writing, about food. It was, and it remains, an integral part of the culture. Food and cooking were listed among the arts, and entertaining with food was another way of understanding and celebrating Greek life and culture.

Plato, Homer, Aristotle, Demosthenes, Aristophanes, Aesop, all discussed food as they discussed history and the rest of the arts. Since the cooks of the day were also priests (they alone knew how to prepare and butcher meats for the sacrificial rites that gave rise to the Greek banquet), it is easy to see why cooking was the prerogative of men. Dining in Greece has always been both a religious and artistic celebration. Even the term *gastronomy* is an ancient Greek word meaning the art and science of good eating. And did they eat! Homer records banquets involving enough meat and wine to take care of people for weeks, and it was done to honor both the gods and a hero of some sort.

Greek culinary art became highly sophisticated during the period of Alexander the Great (fourth century B.C.) when the Greeks spread their culture as far east as the heart of Asia and along the shores of the entire Mediterranean basin. As a result of their travels they came in contact with just about all the foods that we are familiar with in our time. Foods came in from all over the Mediterranean world, as well as from Persia and India.

FOOD
AND EATING HABITS

We have some interesting recipes and menus from that time through the goodness of one Archestratus, who traveled and wrote, and certainly ate, during the fourth century B.C. While his original series of articles—a cookbook, really—has been lost, we do have many references to them through such scholars as Athenaeus, a Greek writer of the third century A.D., who quoted Archestratus's works extensively. For instance, we know from these writings that the early Greeks preferred their meat boiled first; then it was roasted, if desired. They seemed to think that only peasants consumed rare meat as we do now. Further, they were fond of cooking with wine, gratinéeing with cheese, making meat broths and gravy stews, and stuffing birds. They also stuffed meats, fish, and fig and grape leaves. So many sauces contained cheese that I expect we must also credit the Greeks with the invention of cheese sauce. Archestratus also was firm on the number of persons who should eat at a table, the number being no more than five. How could you talk if you had more than five people at the table? So we should salute this writer not only for his wisdom but for his timing. He offered one of the first real cookbooks in the Western world, certainly the largest collection of recipes to survive those early times.

One of the principles of the table that was celebrated in the early days of Greece was that of moderation. All went well until the Greeks came in contact with the Persians, serious cooks and eaters, all. The ideals of the Spartans, whose name we still use today, who were very careful and moderate at table, were dumped when the peoples of Athens and Sparta began to understand the lushness of a Persian banquet. Thus began the change from the old habits to a newer form of celebration among the powerful and wealthy Greeks.

A Greek breakfast in the early days consisted of bread soaked in wine, a practice that the French still enjoy. Wonderful breads were available, better than any others to be found in the Mediterranean world. And the wines! Wines were cultivated in Greece, of course, but they were also imported from the rest of what we now call Western Europe.

The Greeks seem to have invented the practice of four meals a day, a practice we still continue, if you count the evening snack. They also developed the sack lunch. When one attended the theater in the old days it was outdoors, of course. Since there was no electric lighting, the plays would begin at the first sign of dawn. Greek theater fans would come armed with their breakfast of bread to be dipped in wine, and of course some olives, and cheese, and oil for the bread. We are talking about a serious meal here, not just a breakfast snack. When the players first noticed the sunlight they would cry, "Hail, rising orb!," and the Grecians would nod approvingly, all the time spitting out olive pits and happily munching on wonderful breads. Thus, the first packed lunch. It became a custom to ask guests in to share dinner and urge them to bring their own wine and food. "Bring your pitcher and supper chest!"

In the time of Homer meat was a major part of the diet. But with the growth of agriculture, the raising of animals for food became grossly expensive, and the whole culture turned to eating breads and grains. They realized that feeding the animals valuable grain was simply not feasible in terms of space and resources. The animals would eat up everything! That has happened throughout much of the world, though we Americans have gone back to meat, refusing to admit that it is not an ecologically sound practice. Meat must be for flavoring, as it is in the Greek diet today, and it should not be used as the basis of the whole diet.

One never saw butter in the ancient Greek diet. You still don't see much of it. The blessed olive offered oil that would provide flavor and lubrication in cooking, so butter was looked down upon. The Greek navy developed as a result of the desire of the Greeks for their beloved oil. Shipping lanes had to remain open, and thus the navy.

The movement of the olive-oil shippers throughout the Mediterranean gave the Greeks the chance to further influence the eating habits of the Western world. Each of the established ports was to feel the influence of the Grecian kitchen. Marseilles, in southern France, was to learn about the original fish stew, *kakkavi*, which the French simply renamed *bouillabaisse*. White sauce, bread for breakfast, which was later to become pizza, toast, and baked pasta. All of these Greek inventions began to influence Western cuisines.

Cooks were highly respected in Greece, and they were not brought in as slaves, as later in Rome. The cook was highly paid and he could be hired in the marketplace. For a special dinner he would bring his staff as well as the pots and pans. A good cook could become quite wealthy since he was allowed a kind of copyright on a new dish, a copyright that was not to be broken for one full year. Famous cooks thus were very much in demand. Everyone wanted to taste the chef's latest dish. They could also pick up some extra cash in the marketplace by selling the leftovers from a feast! It was all perfectly understood and acceptable.

When the Byzantine Empire fell to the Turks in 1453 the respected chefs fled to the monasteries. After all, they had always been associated with food and butchering as a religious rite. While in the monastery they wore clothes like those of the monk, complete with the tall black hat with a puff in the top. Eventually they changed the color of their uniforms to mark them from the priests, and we have the birth of the chef's cap. Even that is Greek!

From the Persians the Greeks picked up the practice of lying on a couch while eating. Food was generally eaten with the fingers since silverware was not popular nor was it used until the seventeenth century. Bread accompanied every course, both for the sake of eating and for the sake of wiping one's mouth, the used piece of bread then being thrown to the dogs. A small and necessary finger bowl was served with the meals as well.

One of the great Greek contributions to the art of dining was the symposium. Following the evening meal the climax of the night centered around the finishing of the wine and the discussion to follow. When the guests were sufficiently intoxicated, and the conversations and hymns completed, the party was finished.

THE KITCHEN

The Greek kitchen of the old days absolutely fascinates me. They had most of the pots and pans that we use now, but they were instrumental in developing the frying pan. The pot fork was a Greek invention as well, and remember that forks were never used at the table. They were simply used to remove boiled meat from the great pots. I am also convinced that the Greeks invented the concept of the Dutch oven, theirs being an enclosed clay baking dish on three feet. A fire was placed underneath the device and more coals heaped on the flat top. Food was

put into the oven through a small door in the side. I saw one of these in the wonderful National Museum in Athens, and it was dated 1500 B.C.! I also found a grill, probably the original barbecue, and it was made at the same time. You can see page 285 for instructions for your own.

Further, we know that the kitchens had to be large since the records list so many kitchen helpers and cooks. Be mindful, now, of the fact that only the wealthy had such kitchens, but these centers did influence the eating habits of the Western world at that time.

SOME CONCLUSIONS

You must go to Greece. I have traveled there three times so far, and I would leave tonight if it were not for the deadline on this book. American tourists tell me that the food is boring, but that is because they eat in the hotels, agencies of the government destined to serve mediocre food at government-controlled prices. Greece has been in the forefront of creative cooking since Athena called forth the olive tree in Athens. Don't put up with poor food! Go to the restaurants and the tavernas. Taste the wines and talk to the people. Tour the islands and the ancient cities such as Corinth and Athens. I expect that you will better understand why Theresa Yianilos, author of the wonderful *The Complete Greek Cookbook*, offers this profound remark:

''The Greeks' fierce pride in their heritage has kept the basic culture intact. Whether a slave under Roman rule, a captive under Turkish domination, or a newly arrived immigrant, the Greek is always aware that he is the direct descendant of men like Plato, Homer, Aristotle, Demosthenes, Aristophanes. The Greek who begins life in a new land on the bottom step of society as a dishwasher needs only to remember how Aesop left a legacy of poetry while cooking as a slave."

Such confidence. She is Greek!

CHRONOLOGICAL TABLE

A brief chronological table will help you understand the various influences that the Greeks encountered. Yianilos was helpful in preparing this list of events.

900 to 158 B.C. Greece became a powerful military force in the Mediterranean, with bases or colonies on the coast of Asia Minor, Cyprus, Egypt, Gaza, Italy, France, Spain, Sardinia, Persia, and India. The Greeks brought to the colonists their foods, such as olives and olive oil, cheese, figs, wheat, barley, wine, and honey, as well, of course, as Greek cuisine. In return they were influenced by all with whom they came in contact. Foods from foreign lands poured into Greece through the agency of the Greek navy, a navy necessary to the protection of the olive-oil trade routes that Greece had established all over the Mediterranean.

600 B.C. Already the Greeks knew how to bake dozens of different kinds of raised breads. The Egyptians, who were fine bakers, having learned to make leavened bread from the Jews, offered the bread secrets to the Greeks. They in turn began baking breads that contained seeds and spices and herbs and flowers, even wine. This was the beginning of what you and I know as bread.

150 B.C. Rome became the major power in the Mediterranean and it conquered Greece. The Romans loved Greek culture and took on Greek teachers for their children and Greek cooks for their kitchens . . . all as slaves.

A.D. 330 Greeks and Christian Romans overpowered the Roman state and moved the seat of culture from Rome to Byzantium, which they renamed Constantinople. The Byzantine world had the blessings of Greek art, language, and literature, plus Roman laws and government.

500. The barbarian Huns invaded Corinth. The Huns disgusted the Greeks—they used knives to cut their food at the table, a gross practice, and they preferred a fat called "butter," which the Greeks considered a body salve, not a substitute for fine Greek olive oil.

800. Crete became Muslim and the *Kritiki* had to abstain from their favorite meat: pork.

The Bulgars (Bulgarians) crossed over the border and taught the Greek mountaineers the secret of making yogurt.

1000. Romanian nomads invaded and taught the Greeks how to make a hot spiced preserved beef called *pastourma*, "pastrami."

1200. The Venetians settled in coastal regions of Greece.

Crusaders brought in new ways of making wines, and the lemon seed, which they had discovered in Palestine.

1300–1400. Serbs, Italians, and Franks came to Greece bringing pasta.

1453. Constantinople fell to the Ottoman Turks. They changed the name of the Byzantine Christian city to Istanbul and ordered the Turkish language to be spoken. Greek dishes thus took on Turkish names. Greek cooks began to add great amounts of garlic to meat and vegetable dishes to please the Turkish palate.

1821. The Turks began to lose control over Greece, but Turkish cooking left a distinct impression on the Greek cuisine.

New influences moved in. The British brought potatoes, tea, beef, margarine, and ginger beer. The French returned the recipes that they had borrowed hundreds of years before, most of them greatly improved.

1945. Americans entered Greece after World War II and brought new methods of agriculture . . . and such questionable gifts as ham and eggs, bacon, hamburgers, hot dogs, french-fried potatoes, sodas, and milk shakes. And corn on the cob, a dish that you now see roasted on charcoal braziers in the city squares of Athens.

MODERN GREECE

The Athens Market

Athens is a most wonderful city for touring. The cabs are cheap and generally honest and the markets are fascinating. After you have seen the National Archeological Museum and the Parthenon, you must visit the open food markets on Athinas Street. It is located between Monastiraki Square and Omonia Square. Believe me, you cannot miss it. Go in the morning so that the great hallway of butchers is open. Don't miss the fish stalls, the sausage peddlers, or the produce stalls, either.

The second market area that will astound you is the Flea Market just off Monastiraki Square. You can buy stuff in these backstreets that will tickle them back home.

The Restaurants

When you visit Athens you might want to try some of the following restaurants. I have eaten well at each of these. Just remember The Frugal Gourmet's Rule for Eating in Greece: *Don't eat in the hotels.*

Taverna Sigalas. Right behind the old church in Monastiraki Square. Good food at very reasonable prices. You can eat out in the square if you wish. Be sure and see the kitchen.

Keunan Souvlaki is located around the corner from Taverna Sigalas near the entrance to the Flea Market. Wonderful grilled lamb sandwich in pita bread.

Pelopenese Grill offers wonderful grilled pork, chicken, and lamb. All cooked over charcoal the old way. Dinner is cheap. Just behind Omonia Square.

Fast Food Tunnel. Channing and Jason's favorite place in Athens. Real Greek food in take-out places. Omonia Square.

Taverna Ideal. Near Omonia Square. Good for lunch or dinner. Moderate prices and good food. The hotel desk man will know the place.

Taverna Delphi. Near Syntagma Square, NIKIS 13. Very good food and you are welcome to look at the kitchen.

Vasilenas. ETOLIKOU 72, Piraeus. This place is a joy! Eighteen courses and the price is fixed. Eat till you pop, moderate price. Worth the trip to Piraeus. Watch the cabbie on this one as he might try and take you for too much money. Piraeus is a tourist trap. This place, however, is legit.

Taverna Anna. This is a wonderful, more formal restaurant in North Filotheh, a suburb of Athens. It is worth the cab ride. Opens for dinner at about 9:00 in the evening. Beautiful buffet.

There are several restaurants along the waterfront in Piraeus. It is a notorious tourist trap, but if you insist on going you can trust the food at Kokkini Varka. Be sure you see the prices before you sit down.

Rome and
Its Travels

Rome is filled with history and wonderful food. It is the birthplace of many sophisticated forms of art, architecture, and government, forms that we now take for granted, and it is the center of some of the most historically profound uses of food in the world. But while the ancient Romans proudly recorded their accomplishments in every field that you could imagine, including architecture, philosophy, war and conquering techniques, political and governmental systems, and art history, there is very little written about their food and daily diet. What we do have, however, is fascinating. June di Schino, a wonderful South African woman who adopted Rome—or Rome adopted her—has offered the most helpful and insightful material for Roman food history.

THE HISTORY

The Eternal City was founded around 700 B.C. with the union of several villages and tribes. Romulus, who, legend has it, was raised along with his brother by a she-wolf, became the first king, thus the name of the city. Kings ruled the area until 509 B.C. when the Roman Republic was founded, and the government was run by elected officials until 44 B.C. During this time the Roman armies conquered most of Europe and a good part of the Mediterranean, and their food and diet were very much influenced by the nations that they conquered, especially Greece. It became very "in" to enjoy Hellenistic or Greek art and values, and certainly Greek food. Greek cooks were brought into Roman households and with the cook came the food. Many of these cooks were slaves, others were hired by the house. The vast majority of the cooks of the day were nevertheless Greek. I must also note that the majority of the Greeks had no slaves. In Rome even the most humble householder went around with a train of eight slaves in attendance. Slaves were considered a necessity in Rome, not a luxury, close to the mind-set of our South during the nineteenth century. The more nations the Romans conquered, the more slaves poured into Rome, and the cheaper the price per person became.

In 44 B.C. the warring Romans called for a new governmental form and Roman democracy fell before the head of the heroic soldiers, a man who then declared himself emperor. His name was Julius Caesar. You will remember that he kept siding with the peasants rather than the wealthy class and he was finally assassinated by members of the Senate.

Interestingly enough, the site of the theater in which Caesar was murdered is now a restaurant. Perfect for my business! This murder marked the end of the Roman Republic and the beginning of the Roman Empire. The emperors who followed became incredibly powerful and the Empire very wealthy. For the next two hundred years Rome lived high, high indeed. The time of the Pax Romana eventually lapsed into a time of gross excesses at the table, excesses that lasted until, and probably contributed to, the Fall of Rome in the fifth century A.D.

THE DIET

The very early Romans lived primarily on grains. They ground many different types of seeds and grains and cooked them into an ancient form of polenta, *puls*. In other words, they lived on mush. When wheat flour was introduced during the third century B.C. a much more palatable type of bread was produced.

Vegetables have always been important to Romans. They still are! Onions, garlic, cabbage, and turnips were common, and wild mushrooms were very much appreciated, especially by the wealthy classes. Asparagus, wild in those times, and artichokes, remain two vegetables popular with Romans since the very early days.

Fish among the early Romans was rare, as was beef. Up until the fourth century B.C. cattle were considered primarily as work animals, and they were rarely eaten. Pork seems to have been fairly common, but it generally was reserved for some sort of religious holiday. Goats, sheep, pigs, and poultry were the most common domesticated animals, and these seem to have been eaten more often than fish, even though Rome is only thirty miles from the sea. They just were not fond of fish.

The early Romans were fond of olives, having learned about them from the Greeks. Olive oil became a regular part of the diet, as did Greek wines. As the Romans became more interested in growing grapes and olives, the lands reserved for grains began to diminish. The eventual popularity of cattle for meat also changed the whole agricultural structure, and the Romans finally suffered great grain shortages. Many scholars contend that this was a contributing factor in the Fall of Rome.

While bread was reserved for the wealthy classes in the early days, the peasants living on *puls*, the introduction of flour and Greek bakers brought bread to everyone during the early days of the Republic.

With the importing of the Greek chefs things began to look up for Roman diners. The wealthy classes could afford kitchens and chefs, but the peasants generally bought cooked meat from shops, street shops of great filth. Cheeses were both made locally and imported, and cooked pork was readily available in the street markets. Lamb became more popular, but it has always remained expensive.

The goose was very popular in Rome, a popularity that has been maintained. The Romans developed a method of feeding a goose with figs in order to fatten the livers for rich pâtés. Chickens were kept for eggs, and the birds seldom eaten. Eggs were very popular and we can probably thank the Romans for the invention of the omelet.

Fish gained popularity in later days and the Romans are to be credited with the first fish farms in the Western world. The Romans also prized oysters and raised them in private ponds and lakes or had them imported.

The average Roman ate quite well during the days between the late Republic and the early Empire.

MEALS AND TABLEWARE

The first meal of the day for the average Roman was simply bread dipped in wine, a custom picked up from the Greeks. One might also include an egg, some cheese, or perhaps a garlic sauce with olives and figs. Doesn't that sound like an eye-opener? A snack was consumed before noon and the biggest meal of the day was offered in the late afternoon.

The wealthy Romans did not recline on couches at dinner until they had met the Greeks, and the Greeks picked up the habit from the Persians. The practice became very popular for two reasons. First, the position allowed the eater to consume more food, and second, it was a comfortable position for falling asleep. This is hardly the way in which we now judge the comfort of our guests!

Since the Roman spent his dinnertime on one elbow, reclining on the couch, it was impossible to use a knife and fork. The meal was eaten with the fingers and the only piece of tableware that was used was the spoon. Among the middle class each person brought his own spoon to the dinner party. The host was not expected to provide them. Among the very wealthy, during the days of the decline of the Empire, the host would often give away gold spoons as a sign of his wealth and importance. The guests were obligated to take the gold spoon with them following the meal. Can you imagine the hosts talking after the meal and making that terribly important and insulting discovery? "Oh, no. They didn't take all of the tableware!"

If you were not invited to one of these meals you could always eat in the many taverns that provided wine, food, and . . . whatever. "Whatever" was generally a bit more expensive. And, further, you would not have a spoon in a tavern, only a knife. No, you did not recline but ate sitting upright on a stool or bench.

The eating position of free citizens was very important in the ancient world. The practice of reclining at meals was also common in the Holy Land, which means that our typical picture of the Last Supper of Jesus is historically wrong. The group would not have been at table but in a room of couches, probably heavy stone couches. You might want to read an essay on this very topic called *Now I Lay Me Down to Eat*, by Bernard Rudofsky (see Bibliography).

The equipment to be found in a Roman kitchen was creative and not far from what we use now. Please remember that only the wealthy had such kitchens, but they were filled with pots and pans, frying pans and portable ovens, many of these items coming from Greece. The Romans took the crude Greek pot fork, a device for removing boiled meats from a pot, and embellished it until it became a thing of great beauty. The Romans had a wonderful ability to take an idea from another culture and improve upon both the functionality of the item and its aesthetic value. They still do this!

The Roman kitchen had just about everything we see in the kitchen nowadays with the exception of gas and electricity. The kitchen was run instead on slave power. Slaves were so cheap at the time that one could afford an enormous kitchen staff, and the chief cook, or chef, was very often able to make a fortune from presents and wages and thus buy his freedom.

As interest in food grew with the growth of the Republic, so did the need for a special room for cooking. The Greeks had special rooms for dining and cooking in their homes and the Romans decided that these were necessary for their life-style as well. Prior to this time, during the time of the first kings, every activity in the house took place in one room, a room with an open hearth where the food was cooked. Smoke from the fire escaped through a hole in the ceiling, but only after blackening the walls. Thus the main room of the house was called the atrium, for *ater*, meaning "coal black."

THE ROMAN COOKBOOK

We really do not know who this fellow was, this Apicius. We do know that there were at least three different fellows with same name and all seemed capable of adding something to a cookbook. What we have from the first century A.D. in Rome is probably a compilation of recipes attributed to this Apicius character, later authors adding a few recipes here and there with the recipes gaining a bit of authority since they were attributed to the famous Roman cook. In any case, the collection of recipes comes to us intact and they are fascinating.

The man himself, if we stick to the most famous of the three, must have been a character. He loved to cook and eat, and it was the custom in those days for the men to be the cooks. Women were not expected to appear in the kitchen during formal parties. Often they were not even invited to the banquets, unless they were expected to perform special functions such as dancing, or whatever. (For an explanation of "whatever," please see above.) In any case, Apicius loved his dinner parties and spent a great deal of money setting them up. Remember, now, that this was during the first century A.D. He once heard about some shrimp that were larger than anything that could be found near Rome, these shrimp being in Africa. He immediately called for a ship and set off to sail for his dinner. Days later, when he approached the shores of Africa, he was shown samples of the fabled crawfish or shrimp. "Why," he yelled, "they are no bigger than those of my Rome!," whereupon he pulled up anchor and returned to Rome, having neither set foot on the soil nor tasted the shrimp. Years later he realized that he was down to just a million dollars or so and he had just spent ten million on feasts. He was so terrified of starving to death that he had a final feast and then drank poison. Now, this is the kind of cookbook author who should have met my editor, Maria Guarnaschelli. She could have straightened him out!

The cookbook remains a fascinating document. Several translations are available today (see Bibliography) and we gain an interesting bit of insight into the flavors favored at that time.

Seasonings were used with a heavy hand, seasonings that included salt and pepper, saffron, ginger, laser (an aromatic resin), myrtle berries, cloves, cardamom, poppyseed, laurel, anise, celery, fennel, cumin, parsley, and the ever-present *garum*, a solution of salt and fermented fish which is probably close to what we now call *nuc moom* from the Vietnamese kitchen. The above list certainly would not have been found in the Greek kitchen; they still do not use much in the way of herbs and spices. But the Romans, that was something else. The *garum* sauce probably came from the Middle East through Greece, and then the Romans took it with them on the road. It went with them into India where tamarind and ginger were added and then the Romans brought it into England. The sauce that we now know as Worcestershire is the result of such a journey.

Given the recipes, we can make some general observations about the food of the time. The Romans had a tendency to mix sweet with salty, much like our pickled peaches. Their chief meat, pork, was usually salted and often cured, such as our hams. Red meats were boiled first, and then roasted. They disliked rare meats. They were also fond of casseroles, something taught them by the Greeks, and pies filled with all sorts of things. Many different types of birds were eaten, including figpeckers, chicken, goose, duck, partridge, pheasant, peacock, swan, crane, and flamingo, though the latter birds were seen only on the tables of the extremely wealthy.

We must give credit to the Romans for developing a wonderful menu of sausages and forcemeats, though it appears that they learned about the dishes originally from the Greeks. The Romans ate with fingers and perhaps a spoon, since they were always lying on one side. The finger foods that sausages and forcemeats could provide were perfect for such a meal.

THE EXCESSES

We must remember that most of the Roman peasants and middle class lived not on the fancy foods mentioned above but on gruels, *puls*, and bread. Innards were almost given away by the butchers and these became popular with the lower classes. The menu for the aristocracy was something else.

The first century A.D. saw the appearance of the formal banquet and the use of many slaves in serving. During a time of relative peace and prosperity I suspect that the Roman wealthy classes became bored and thus turned the banquet into the most lavish and gross exercise of excess that we have ever seen at table. The first emperors, Julius, Augustus, and Tiberius, seemed to have rather modest dining habits, but after Tiberius the emperors and their friends just went crazy at banquets. Claudius ate and drank until he fell asleep in front of his guests and Domitian once called the entire Senate together to determine how best to cook an enormous turbot. Heliogabalus had menus embroidered onto the tablecloths. Caligula and Cleopatra used to drink expensive pearls crushed and dissolved in vinegar, and they served their guests loaves and meats of gold. And then, there was Heliogabalus.

Heliogabalus was not a small, informal party man. He loved eels and kept tubs of them at his residence. Food for the eels was provided by the flesh of Christians from the gross displays at the Colosseum. He would eat the brains of six hundred ostriches at a single dinner, and the themes of the banquets were just unbelievable. Artificial ceilings were built into the dining rooms, and when they were opened, gifts would rain on the guests. One such affair featured tons of flowers petals that fell when the ceiling was pulled back . . . and four guests suffocated to death. Such nice evenings! The greater the waste, the more absurd the extravagance, the more succesful the dinner was deemed. And if the evening got to be too much for you it was expected that you would make a dash to the "vomitorium." It was all part of the evening's entertainment, and it marked the beginning of the decline and fall of the Empire.

THE FALL

The Empire of Rome began around 700 B.C. and lasted until about A.D. 450. During that time the Romans experienced every form of good cooking that we now know, and they knew of almost every food product that we now know. They took these cooking practices and food products to the rest of the world through their travels and conquering efforts, and the world was changed.

The early kings of Rome tended their own gardens, and the final Emperors of Rome simply consumed themselves to death. The motto of Rome, Senatus Populusque Romanus, S.P.Q.R., referred to the Senate and People of Rome only during the Republic. By the end, the citizens were driven to eating anything they could get their hands on since the government ceased to provide for the citizenry.

At this point we must ask the question, Who conquered whom? The Romans swept into Greece and took back to Rome food products, eating methods, cooking methods, chefs, teachers for their children, art forms—in short, a whole new mind-set. The Greeks believe that indeed *they* conquered Rome, not the reverse. I can understand how they feel.

ROME AT PRESENT

Rome is one of the most wonderful cities for touring. The food is superb and the city is quite ready for your visit. Just remember to bring your walking shoes and assume that many taxi drivers are dishonest. With that, plan a trip to Rome.

The Markets

You must go to the Campo de' Fiori. This is a great city square jammed with food and flower stalls. Be prepared to spend a few hours.

The market at Piazza Vittorio Emanuele is the biggest in Rome. If you can't buy it there, you don't need it. Wonderful open food displays. Plan to spend several hours.

Neighborhood markets are fun, too. There is a good one each morning on Via Metauro, near Villa Borghese.

Da Franco is a seafood house. All courses are seafood, and the price is fixed. Very informal joint that is strictly for the Romans. Just great and inexpensive for what you get. Via dei Falisci and Via degli Equi.

Edmondo, an old Roman-style house that specializes in innards. Not expensive, filled with locals, and tons of color. Circonvallazione Clodia 90. Tell Edmondo that I sent you. Wonderful place!

Da Pancrazio is on the site of the assassination of Julius Caesar. Really! Campo de' Fiori. Very nice, a little formal, good food, somewhat expensive. Great for your visit to Rome.

La Carbonara, Campo de' Fiori market square. A fine eating house with one of the best antipasti tables I have ever seen. Moderate in price by Roman standards. Have the Pasta La Carbonara.

Romolo, with a wonderful Roman garden in the back. Good food, a little more than moderate. Via di Porta Settimiana 8.

Piperno is a very famous restaurant in the Jewish Ghetto. Ask directions and bring lots of money. The food is just terrific. If during artichoke season you must have artichoke, Jewish style.

Da Giggetto al Portico d'Ottavia. The name is also the address. Good food in the middle of the fascinating Jewish Ghetto. Moderate in price.

Vecchia Roma, near the Jewish Ghetto, Piazza Campitelli 18. One of the best restaurants you will find in Rome. Good staff, nice garden for eating, very fresh food. Expensive but worth it.

Cesarina serves Bolognese food. Wonderful grilled meats and *bollito*, boiled-meat dinners. Via Piemonte 109, medium expensive.

Er Moccoletto is near the American Embassy. Wonderful food and a charming atmosphere. Great antipasti table. Fairly expensive but worth the price. Via Lucania 35.

THE RECIPES

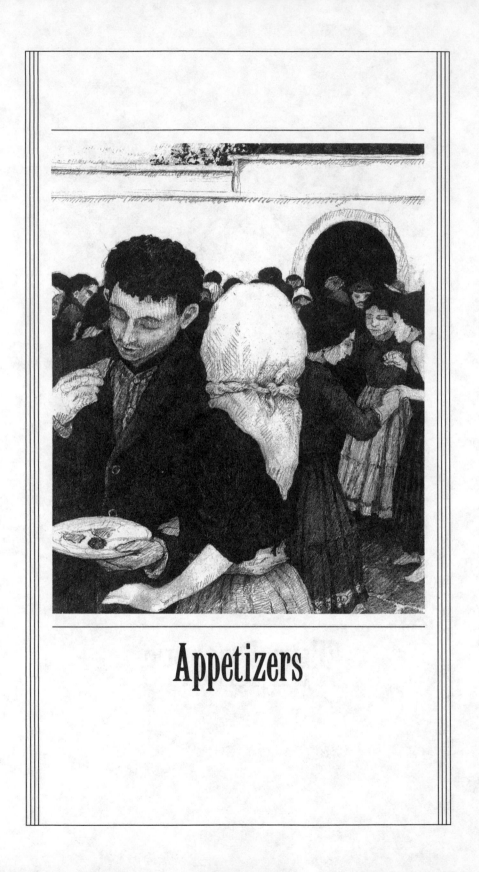

Appetizers

I t is hard for Americans to understand the meaning of an appetizer because we see the meal as a single unit. In all three of our ancient cultures, the meal was always viewed as a series of courses. The idea was to come together and eat with friends, family—and perhaps a few politicians that you had to include. The meal *was* the evening, not an event prior to it.

For two thousand years the Chinese have been famous for banquets of many courses. In early times the feasting was expected to continue for two or three days, the first day being just a sort of enticement and celebration of that which was to come. Great dishes would be prepared and brought into the dining room only to be smelled, gazed upon, admired, and finally passed to the servants. Why fill up on the early dishes when one knows that the best dishes are served last? The Chinese still enjoy this sense of anticipation, and these appetizer dishes from China are very typical of modern banquets, though some of the dishes go back hundreds of years.

The Greeks held lavish banquets and the guests could certainly tell what was coming just from gazing upon the first courses. The Romans, of course, who later brought the concept of the formal banquet to its high point and its downfall, had as many as fifteen early courses before the main table was offered. I use the word "downfall" since the Romans really did eat to excess on the strangest things, things that could only be eaten by a people who had come to a point of boredom with food . . . and art . . . and life. However, in our time, one of the greatest treats you can enjoy in Rome is the first dishes, the *antipasti,* literally, the plates "before the meal."

When you read these recipes, some of which are very old, think of the table, the people you wish to entertain, and the fact that it is still possible to enjoy a meal for the evening, and I mean the entire evening. That is how it was done in each of our three ancient cuisines.

CHINESE COLD PLATE

The first course in a formal Chinese meal is always to be seen as an anticipation of what is to come. Thus, an elaborate opening dish, made up of a wonderful assortment of delicacies, is a great compliment to the guests, and a signal to "get serious." The only problem is that you must discipline yourself so that you do not fill up on these first creations. They are meant to prepare the palate for at least ten other dishes that will follow.

You may think up your own cold-plate variations, and some ideas might come from the chapter on Dim Sum. Barbecued Pork would be good as an opening course. However, most of the opening dishes would traditionally be served cold or lukewarm. Place each variation on its own plate in the center of the table. Each of your guests can help themselves, eating from their own small private plates. Fresh plates are then offered and the meal is on its way! You can make a very elaborate display of this opening course.

I would suggest the following:

Cold Looed Beef *(page 312)*
Walnuts Fried with Sugar *(page 85)*
Shredded Chicken Sesame *(page 84)*
Glass Noodles with Peanut Sauce *(page 356)*
Bean Sprouts and Szechwan Pepper Salad *(page 139)*
Chinese Brine Pickles *(page 83)*

CHINESE BRINE PICKLES

(Dragon Kiln)

MAKES 4 CUPS
OF PICKLES

These pickles are so easy to make that it is almost embarrassing. While the recipe is common, this one comes from the Dragon Kiln people, who import wonderful and inexpensive cooking pieces from China. This recipe comes with their Chinese pickling jar.

2 *tablespoons salt*

1 *tablespoon Szechwan peppercorns (page 40)*

2 *to 4 small dried red chile peppers*

½ *cup boiling water*

3½ *cups cold water*

4 *to 5 slices fresh ginger, each the size of a 25-cent piece*

1 *tablespoon vodka or dry sherry*

4 *cups* total *of any combination of the following, cut into bite-size pieces:*
   Broccoli stems,
   Napa or Chinese celery cabbage,
   Carrots,
   Cauliflower,
   Daikon,
   Green string beans,
   Red sweet bell peppers

In a mixing bowl combine the salt, peppercorns, chile peppers, and boiling water, and stir until the salt dissolves. Stir in the cold water, fresh ginger, and vodka or sherry. Put the vegetables of your choice into a Chinese pickling jar or 2-quart glass jar. If using a Chinese pickling jar, seal with water according to the instructions. If using a regular glass jar, simply cover with plastic wrap. Do not wrap tightly as gas must escape. Allow the pickles to sit, unrefrigerated, for 24 hours and serve.

The pickles will keep for several days if sealed and in the refrigerator.

SHREDDED CHICKEN SESAME

SERVES 6–8
AS AN APPETIZER

This dish can be served as a salad course with a garnish of lettuce or served on crackers as an appetizer. Be careful or your guests will fill up on this dish before the main courses are served!

1 chicken, 2¾ pounds, lightly boiled, skin removed and discarded, boned and shredded. Use the bones and skin for a later soup stock (See Chinese Poached Chicken, page 230)

THE SESAME GARLIC DRESSING

1 teaspoon sugar

½ teaspoon MSG (optional)

2 tablespoons light soy sauce

2½ tablespoons sesame paste (page 217) (tahini works fine)

1 tablespoon sesame oil

1 tablespoon cider vinegar or Chinese red vinegar

1 tablespoon chopped green onion

½ teaspoon grated fresh ginger

2 cloves garlic, crushed

¼ tablespoon Chinese hot pepper oil, or to taste

Place the shredded chicken in a bowl. Mix the remaining ingredients together to form a salad dressing. Toss with the chicken and arrange on a platter. Garnish with more chopped green onion, if desired.

WALNUTS FRIED
WITH SUGAR

SERVES 8
AS AN APPETIZER

A delightful appetizer from China. Ken Hom, a fine Chinese cooking teacher, who appears on television, and a dear friend, taught me this one. It is great with cocktails or may be served as a part of the first appetizer course. Remember, in the ancient world nuts of any kind were very expensive, so the host would show off by serving something like this.

1 *pound walnut meats, halved*

THE SYRUP

2 *cups water*

1 *cup sugar*

2 *star anise, whole*

1 *cinnamon stick*

3 *tablespoons honey*

4 *cups peanut oil for deep frying*

Preheat the oven to its lowest temperature and then switch it off.

Bring a 2-quart saucepan filled ¾ full of water to a boil. Add the walnuts and blanch for 2 minutes. Remove the nuts from the pan and drain, discarding all water.

Mix the syrup ingredients together in the same saucepan. Bring to a simmer and add the nuts. Lightly boil, uncovered, for 10 minutes, or until the syrup begins to thicken. Remove the nuts with a slotted spoon and place on a baking pan and dry in the warmed oven for at least 2 hours.

Heat the oil in a deep fryer or wok to about 360°. Fry the nuts in small batches for about 2 minutes or until the nuts turn dark brown. Do not allow them to burn. Remove to a tray and allow to cool.

GREECE

TZATZIKI

SERVES 10–12
AS A FIRST COURSE

You will find this dish in every taverna, or eating house, in Greece. Our whole family loved the dish and we have learned to make it here at home. It goes back a long way into Greek history, along with the habit of eating all sorts of food hand-dipped into wonderfully thick mixtures such as this one. Channing, my oldest son, tasted this variation in my test kitchen. He turned to my assistant and told him that I did not really know how to make a good tzatziki. "Put in more garlic!" he howled. This version is his, and it *is* better than mine.

This Greek appetizer is just delicious served as a dip with small wedges of pita bread.

4 cups fresh yogurt, unflavored

1 medium cucumber, peeled and coarsely grated

4 cloves garlic, crushed

2 tablespoons olive oil

½ teaspoon dried dillweed

Salt and freshly ground black pepper to taste

Additional olive oil for garnish

Place a piece of cheesecloth in a colander and pour in the yogurt. I always make my own so that it will be good and tart. Allow the yogurt to drain for several hours. Use the whey in a soup or in baking.

Place the grated cucumber in another colander and allow to drain for 2 hours.

Mix together all ingredients except the additional olive oil and chill. Place in serving dishes and drizzle additional olive oil on top. Serve as a spread for bread or as a dip for vegetables. This is generally served as a first course.

NOTE: Store this dish covered in the refrigerator and it will keep well for 2 or 3 days. Add to salad dressings for an unusual and delicious flavor. Or smear it on a slice of dark rye bread for a late-night snack.

TARAMASALATA

SERVES 6–8
AS A FIRST COURSE

You will find this dish everywhere in Greece. It is a delicious spread for bread or a wonderful dip for a first course. The basis for this mixture is a cod roe that is whipped with other ingredients until it is lighter than mayonnaise.

By the way, did you know that the Greeks invented mayonnaise?

4 *ounces taramas*
  (Find this in any Greek or
  Middle Eastern deli. It
  comes in 8- or 10-ounce
  jars and keeps well under
  refrigeration. Do not buy
  taramasalata that has
  already been mixed. You
  want to make your own!)

5 *slices fresh white bread,*
  crust removed
  Juice of 2 lemons
1 *cup olive oil*
½ *yellow onion, peeled and*
  coarsely chopped
1 *cup mashed potatoes*

Place all ingredients in a food processor and blend until all is smooth.
  Serve as a dip with bread and vegetables.

TAHINI BEAN DIP

MAKES 4 CUPS

This paste is common throughout Greece and the whole of the Middle East. I love the stuff, having been introduced to it by my Lebanese Uncle Vic when I was a child. This Greek version is a bit different from the Middle Eastern version in that it includes vinegar and cayenne pepper.

2 cans (15½-ounce size) garbanzo beans

¼ cup olive oil

1 tablespoon white wine vinegar

¼ cup peeled and coarsely chopped yellow onion

2 cloves garlic, chopped coarsely

Pinch of cayenne pepper

½ cup tahini

Salt to taste

Open both cans of garbanzos and drain the juice from *one*. Pour the contents of both cans into a food processor and add all other ingredients. Process until very smooth. Serve as a dip for crackers, olives, pita bread, cucumber slices.

CHEESE PIES

MAKES 8–10 PIES

This is not only a wonderful appetizer but it does very well as a luncheon dish. In Athens you can purchase these in the street and munch as you walk about the city during lunchtime.

FILLING

1 pound feta cheese, crumbled

3 eggs, beaten

1 tablespoon olive oil

1 tablespoon chopped parsley

½ pound butter, melted but not hot

1-pound package of prepared phyllo dough

Mix the ingredients for the filling.

Now, calm down! These are really easy to make. Put a couple of sheets of waxed paper on your counter. Open the phyllo package and unwrap the dough. Now you must work quickly as the dough will dry out in very little time. Place a sheet of dough on the counter and quickly brush it with some of the melted butter. Place another sheet on top of the first and brush it with a little more butter. Place 2 tablespoons of filling at the narrow end of the dough and begin to roll it up in the dough. Use

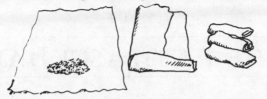

wide rolls rather than narrow ones. After two rolls, fold one side to the center. Roll one more time and fold the other side to the center, thus giving you a neat package. Continue rolling and place the package, seam side down, on an oiled baking sheet. Brush the top with more butter and continue with the next one.

Bake at 400° for 25 to 30 minutes, or until the pies are a light golden brown. Serve warm.

SPINACH PIES

MAKES 8–10 PIES

This is a very famous dish in Greece. Spinach and dill, along with the cheese, make a superb filling for the phyllo bundle.

FILLING
2 *packages frozen chopped spinach, defrosted and squeezed dry*
4 *eggs*
½ *pound feta cheese, crumbled*

1 *bunch green onions, chopped*
¼ *cup chopped parsley*
¼ *cup chopped fresh dill* or 1 *tablespoon dried dill*
½ *pound butter*
1-*pound package prepared phyllo dough*

Prepare the filling and roll and bake the pies just as in the recipe above.

ITALY

THE ANTIPASTI BAR

In the old days of Rome several courses were brought to your couch. While we don't generally have time to lie about on a couch, we do have time to calm down and open the Italian meal with an assortment of little things *antipasti*, "before the main part of the meal." In Rome you can wander into wonderful shops and just fill up a plate with tasty morsels. It is almost enough to satisfy you for the evening.

The Antipasti Bar would contain any of the following, and you can use these for your own antipasti course at home.

Cold veal, sliced thin with lemon and olive-oil dressing
Cold pasta salad

Artichokes, cooked and chilled   Prosciutto, thin-sliced

White bean salad   Headcheese Appetizer *(page 92)*

Garbanzo salad   Smelt Antipasti *(page 90)*

Olives of all kinds   Peperonata *(page 91)*

Salami, thin-sliced   Mortadella *(page 92)*

SMELT ANTIPASTI
(Vecchia Roma)

SERVES 8
AS AN APPETIZER

I found a dish very close to this one in the Vecchia Roma restaurant near the Jewish Ghetto in Rome. Its history probably goes back to ancient Roman times since it uses raisins and pine nuts, two favorite food products during the first century.

This dish can be served with crackers or as an antipasto course.

1 cup flour, seasoned with salt and pepper

1 pound fresh smelts

1 cup olive oil

2 cloves garlic, crushed

1 teaspoon crushed whole dry rosemary

1 teaspoon crushed whole dry sage

$\frac{1}{4}$ teaspoon dried hot red-pepper flakes

$\frac{1}{4}$ cup red-wine vinegar

$\frac{1}{2}$ medium yellow onion, sliced thin

$\frac{1}{4}$ cup white seedless raisins

$\frac{1}{4}$ cup pine nuts, toasted for a few minutes in a 350° oven

Chopped parlsey for garnish

Dredge the smelts in the seasoned flour. Pan-fry in $\frac{1}{4}$ cup of the olive oil. Do not overcook; $1\frac{1}{2}$ minutes per side should be ample. Remove to a cooling rack or paper towels.

In a pan sauté the garlic, rosemary, sage, and red-pepper flakes in $\frac{1}{2}$ cup olive oil for just a few moments. Add the wine vinegar and reduce for a couple of minutes. Set aside.

In another pan sauté the onion slices in the remaining $\frac{1}{4}$ cup oil until they are limp. Do not brown the onion.

When the smelts are cool, remove the heads and cut lengthwise to debone. Arrange on a platter with the skin side down. Add the sautéed onion, raisins, and pine nuts to the vinegar and herb reduction. Pour all of this over the smelts.

Garnish with parsley.

PEPERONATA

SERVES 8
AS AN APPETIZER

This makes a very attractive appetizer when served with crackers or tiny slices of French bread. Allow each person to place a bit of the mixture on the fresh bread. If the bread is covered ahead of time, the dish will be soggy.

6 *flat anchovy fillets*

2 *cloves garlic, crushed*

5 *tablespoons olive oil*

4 *red sweet bell peppers,
each cut into 8 long strips*

4 *ripe tomatoes, medium,
coarsely chopped*

1 *medium yellow onion,
peeled and sliced thin*

2 *tablespoons red wine
vinegar*

6 *green olives, pitted and
sliced*

2 *tablespoons capers, small
or chopped*

*Salt and fresh ground
black pepper to taste*

Sauté the anchovies and garlic in the oil until the anchovies turn to a paste. Add the pepper strips and sauté, covered, for about 15 minutes.

Add the remaining ingredients and simmer until the tomatoes become tender.

MORTADELLA

Mortadella is the ancestor of what we call bologna, but it is far superior to the salty but flavorless product we know. It comes from the city of Bologna, and there they eat mortadella as a first course regularly. It is sliced thin and offered with wonderful bread, or I have even had it cut into good-sized cubes that you can simply eat with your fingers. Find a good brand of this sausage in an Italian delicatessen. I am fond of Primo brand from Canada.

HEADCHEESE APPETIZER

Place slices of Italian headcheese on a large platter and splash with a dressing of olive oil, lemon juice, and a tad of good red-wine vinegar. Salt and pepper will also be needed. This is a wonderful first course, but you must buy good headcheese to start with.

Dim Sum

The celebration of dim sum is one of the most civilized events I know. It is not a breakfast meal, nor is it lunch, though it can function as either of these. It is more of a brunch that is enjoyed among friends who take one another to enormous dim sum houses that will seat up to one thousand persons. The staff in the restaurant wheels carts about, chanting out the names of the items on their carts as they pass by. The patrons simply point to what they want on the cart and the dishes are placed on the table. When the meal is finished the dishes are counted and you are charged accordingly. Tea is a must with the meal, of course, and it is assumed that you will take a great deal of time to eat and talk and drink tea . . . and choose the various dim sum. The restaurant may offer four hundred different kinds, which means you would have to go back several times in order just to see the varieties pass your table, let alone eat them all.

The name of this style of food, "dim sum," literally means "little jewels that tug at the heart." The Chinese, however, do not see this as snack food. It is far from that. The selection includes meat-filled dumplings, steamed or deep-fried, shrimp in tiny noodle bags, round meatballs of pork or beef. Little plates of spareribs and spicy squid will be found on the carts, and beautiful one-bite pastries made of rice flour and stuffed with a hundred different fillings. The "tug at the heart" is supposed to come from the beauty of the delicacies, but the tug that comes at my heart stems from the pain of not being able to taste everything in the place!

The history of some of these dishes goes back two thousand years and many have wonderful symbolic meanings. For instance, during the New Year Festival dumplings that look like little money bags are served in order to wish wealth for the New Year upon the guest. One emperor in the early days was so fond of dumplings that the staff made them and froze them in crocks in the ground so that they could be ready to serve him whenever he hungered for his favorite food. Did the Chinese invent frozen foods? I think there is some good evidence for this.

You can make these tasty jewels at home with only a little practice. The shouts and cheers that you will receive when you serve this food will make the time involved very much worth it. Or you can just read about these dishes and then go to a major Chinatown in this country and enjoy. I think my recipes are very good, so you might just offer your own dim sum parties and be the happier for it.

I love these dishes . . . and I have to confess that once when I finished lunch with my cousin David in San Francisco, we counted seventeen plates on the table. Eating it all took some doing, but I have never forgotten that meal.

You might also consider:

Barbecued Spareribs *(page 289)*

Chicken Wings in Five Spices *(page 236)*

Chinese Boiled Dumplings with Hot Sauce *(page 388)*

Pot Stickers *(page 390)*

Looed Chicken Feet *(page 260)*

Looed Duck Feet *(page 260)*

Fried Wontons *(page 108)*

Hot and Spicy Squid *(page 109)*

Steamed Meat-Stuffed Buns *(page 109)*

SHRIMP

HA GOW

MAKES 24 HA GOW

This is my favorite dim sum. I have eaten them in Hong Kong, San Francisco, Seattle, New York, Vancouver, B.C., and I can never get enough. My love for shrimp is brought to fulfillment in this wonderful delicacy, the name of which refers to the shape and is translated as "cat's paw." Any cat would go crazy over these things.

NOTE: The Ha Gow Filling can be used for several other dim sum, recipes for which follow.

HA GOW FILLING

½ pound raw shrimp, peeled and chopped very coarsely

¼ pound precooked salad shrimp, chopped coarsely

2 ounces pork fat, chopped fine

¼ cup coarsely chopped bamboo shoots

¼ teaspoon ground white pepper

¼ teaspoon grated fresh ginger

½ teaspoon salt

½ teaspoon sesame oil

1 tablespoon finely chopped green onion, white part only

1 egg white

1 tablespoon dry sherry

1 tablespoon cornstarch

Place all in a bowl and mix well, by hand. I mean, use your hand! Keep stirring and whipping with your fingers until the ingredients form a smooth and rather firm stuffing. This will take about 2 minutes.

HA GOW DOUGH

From *Favorite Dim Sum*. I have made changes only in the amount of water.

2 tablespoons potato starch*

1 cup wheat starch†

¼ teaspoon salt

½ cup plus 3 tablespoons boiling water

1 teaspoon lard

Additional wheat starch for dusting

Measure both starches and salt into a small mixing bowl. Quickly pour the boiling water into the starches while stirring with chopsticks until you get a partially cooked dough. Do not overwork the dough. Quickly add the lard in little pinches and then knead until smooth. A marble board is great for this. When the dough is smooth, after about 2 minutes' kneading, cover it with the mixing bowl and allow it to rest for 15 minutes before shaping.

To shape the dumplings, pull just a tad more than 1 teaspoon of dough from the ball. Keep the remainder of the dough covered with the bowl. Roll the small amount into a ball and place onto the floured marble board. Roll out into a circle about 3 inches in diameter. Place 1 teaspoon of the shrimp filling in the center of the circle of dough and fold over into a half-moon. Use a tiny bit of water for sealing the edges. Be sure

*Available in most fine groceries and delicatessens
†Can be purchased in any Chinese market

to gently press out all the air. If you wish, you can form little pleats in the dough for added decoration.

Steam on an oiled bamboo steaming rack (see below) for 12 minutes.

HINT: A TORTILLA PRESS FOR MAKING DIM SUM WRAPPERS. Try using a lightly oiled tortilla press to press the ball of dough out to an initial stage. Then dust with flour and quickly finish the rolling by hand. This works great!

HINT: A BAMBOO STEAMER FOR PROPERLY STEAMED FOOD. These can be found in most gourmet shops or Oriental markets. The steamer racks are placed in a wok with water in the bottom. Several dishes can be steamed at once since steam does not carry flavors. So clever! The advantage of bamboo over metal is that bamboo will not cause water to condense on your food. A metal lid will.

SHRIMP TOAST

Trim the crust from slices of white bread and cut each slice into 2 rectangles. Add ½ cup chopped water chestnuts to 1 cup of Ha Gow Filling and smear a bit on each slice of bread. Press in raw sesame seeds. Deep-fry in oil at 360° until golden brown. Delicious!

SHRIMP BOATS

Cut a green sweet bell pepper in half and remove the seeds and stem part. Cut each half into 4 little boats or shells. Fill each with some of the Ha Gow Filling and gently fry each boat, shrimp side down, in a very little oil in a covered frying pan. Cook just until the shrimp begins to brown, about 3 minutes. The pepper should still be a bit crisp.

SHRIMP BALL WITH PINE NUTS

Make small 1½-inch balls of Ha Gow Filling. Roll in raw pine nuts. Deep-fry in peanut oil at 360° until golden. These are very beautiful snacks.

SHRIMP-STUFFED MUSHROOMS

MAKES 12 DIM SUM

Soak 12 Chinese dried mushrooms in water for 3 hours. Trim away the stems and, using paper towels, pat the mushrooms dry. Place the mushrooms top side down and place a bit of Ha Gow Filling paste on each. Place them on a plate in a steamer and steam for 15 minutes.

EGGPLANT STUFFED WITH SHRIMP

*SERVES 6 AS PART
OF A DIM SUM MEAL*

In the Hong Kong dim sum houses, a cart with propane burner is circulated about the restaurant. As she moves along, the server fries these great delicacies so that they are very hot when she comes to your table. This is another great dim sum dish.

½ *pound Chinese or Japanese eggplant (the long gorgeous kind available in Chinese markets)*

2 *tablespoons peanut oil*

1 *clove garlic, crushed or chopped fine*

2 *tablespoons chopped green onions*

1 *teaspoon sesame oil*

1 *teaspoon sweet bean sauce (page 34)*

½ *teaspoon hot bean sauce (page 30)*

1 *cup Ha Gow Filling (see page 96)*

Do not peel the eggplant but cut the vegetable into small rounds, on an angle, about 1 inch thick.

Heat 1 tablespoon of the oil in a wok and add the garlic. Chow for just a moment and then add the green onions and the eggplant slices. Add the remaining ingredients, except for the Ha Gow Filling, and chow until the eggplant is tender but not soggy, about 5 minutes. Remove the pieces of eggplant to a tray to cool.

When cool, put a bit of the Ha Gow Filling on each. When completed, pan-fry them with the remaining 1 tablespoon oil in a SilverStone-lined frying pan. Cook them, uncovered, just until the shrimp filling is cooked, about 4 minutes.

PORK

PORK SHU-MEI

When I was a very young boy I used to save my allowance and travel down to Chinatown, in Seattle, to have pork shu-mei for brunch. These are easy to make and are probably the most popular dim sum that I know. They resemble little money bags and are offered at Chinese New Year since they help anticipate wealth.

THE FILLING

1 *pound lean ground pork, finely chopped*

2 *tablespoons light soy sauce*

2 *tablespoons dry sherry*

1 *teaspooon freshly grated ginger*

½ *teaspoon ground white pepper*

1 *tablespoon sesame oil*

½ *teaspoon MSG (optional)*

Pinch of sugar

1 *tablespoon chopped green onion*

1 *egg white*

1 *tablespoon cornstarch*

1 *teaspoon salt*

4 *tablespoons medium chopped bamboo shoots or water chestnuts (optional)*

2 *cloves garlic, crushed*

THE WRAPPER

1 *package shu-mei skins or Gyoza skins, available at the supermarket*

Mix all of the ingredients for the filling together, and mix them well. Place about ¾ tablespoon of filling in the center of each noodle wrapper and bring up the corners so that you have a little money bag. Leave the top open so that you can see some of the meat. For fun you might put 1 frozen green pea on the top of each for added color.

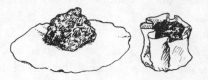

Steam in an oiled bamboo steamer for 15 minutes, on high heat.

NOTE: You can also add a bit of shrimp to this dish. It adds a great deal of flavor. Try about ½ cup of chopped fresh shrimp.

DEEP-FRIED SHU-MEI

Prepare the recipe as above and deep-fry the dumplings in peanut oil at 360° until golden brown and the inside is cooked to your taste.

QUAIL EGG SHU-MEI

Prepare Pork Shu-Mei and place 1 cooked quail egg on the top of each dumpling. Push it down a bit into the meat and steam as instructed.

Cooked quail eggs, all peeled and ready to go, can be purchased in the can at any Chinese grocery.

PORK AND TARO MEATBALLS

Prepare a batch of Pork Shu-Mei Filling (page 99). Roll 1½-inch balls of the mixture in finely grated taro root. Deep-fry these at 360° for a very attractive and delicious treat.

Taro root can be found in any Oriental market.

STEAMED POT STICKERS

Prepare a batch of Pot Stickers (page 390) and steam them on tiny pieces of parchment paper so that they do not stick to the bamboo steamer. Steam for about 20 minutes and serve.

HINT: IF YOU DO NOT HAVE PARCHMENT PAPER, use sheets of plain white typing paper and rub them with oil. That is what parchment paper is!

FUN GOR

MAKES 24 DIM SUM

The dough, or wrapper, on this one has a light and transparent look since you use cake flour and boiling water. When steamed the dough has a rather "pearly" look and it is delicious.

THE DOUGH
(From *Favorite Dim Sum*)

1 *cup Swans Down cake flour*

¼ *teaspoon salt*

½ *cup boiling water*

½ *teaspoon lard*

Additional flour for dusting

THE FILLING

¾ *pound pork, coarsely ground*

1 *tablespoon light soy sauce*

1 *tablespoon dry sherry*

¼ *teaspoon freshly grated ginger*

1 *clove garlic, crushed*

6 *water chestnuts, coarsely chopped*

2 *tablespoons grated carrot*

2 *tablespoons coarsely chopped Napa cabbage*

2 *tablespoons chopped fresh cilantro*

¼ *cup dry roasted peanuts, coarsely chopped*

2 *tablespoons coarsely chopped Western-style cabbage*

1 *egg white*

1 *tablespoon cornstarch*

Pinch of sugar

½ *teaspoon salt*

¼ *teaspoon ground white pepper*

Mix well all of the ingredients for the filling.

Prepare the wrappers in the same way that you prepare Ha Gow wrappers (page 96). Try to use Swans Down cake flour for best results.

Shape the dumplings and fill them just as you do the Ha Gow. When you have filled and sealed the dumpling, set it down, seam straight up, and put a few finger pleats in the seam. Place in an oiled bamboo steaming rack (page 97) and steam for 15 minutes over high heat. They should sit right up in the rack.

STUFFED BEAN CURD SKIN, PAN-FRIED

You may have trouble finding fresh bean curd skin unless you live in a large city with a bustling Chinatown. Seattle, New York, Chicago, San Francisco, Los Angeles, Boston, and Washington, D.C., will have this product in the Chinese markets.

Prepare a batch of Shu-Mei Filling (page 99), adding some chopped garlic chives or regular chives. Chopped cabbage is good in this dish as well.

Soak the sheets of bean curd skin in tepid water for just a few moments until they soften a bit.

Place a portion of soaked bean curd skin, about 6 inches by 8 inches, on the counter and put 2 tablespoons of filling on one end of the skin. Roll it up like a spring roll or burrito, folding the sides in so that you have a neat package. Pat the rolls dry on a kitchen towel. Dip each in an egg wash made of whole eggs, 1 tablespoon of water for each, and a dash of sesame oil. Dust each with cornstarch and pan-fry on medium heat in a bit of peanut oil until they are golden brown. Flatten them out a bit and pan-fry slowly on both sides.

Try deep-frying these in order to warm them up just before serving.

STUFFED BEAN CURD

MAKES 20 DIM SUM

These are especially appropriate for a larger dim sum celebration because they can be made ahead and then simply steamed to finish the cooking. I love these little pillows of goodness.

1 *batch Pork Shu-Mei Filling (page 99)*

1 *cake bean curd, firm style*

Oil for deep frying

OYSTER GRAVY

¾ *cup water*

2 *tablespoons oyster sauce*

1 *teaspoon sesame oil*

Pinch of sugar

1 *tablespoon cornstarch mixed with 1 tablespoon cold water*

Cut the bean curd into 2 pieces, the long way. Then cut into ¾-inch slices and cut each slice into 2 triangles. Place in a colander and allow to drain for 1 hour. Pat dry with paper towels and deep-fry at 320°, in two batches, until they are a light golden brown and they float. Drain on paper towels.

Cut a deep slash in the long side of each triangle. Do not go through to the edges. Fill the pocket with the meat filling. Go ahead and leave a bit overflowing from the pocket. Place in a glass pie plate or dish and steam for 30 minutes.

In the meantime, prepare the oyster gravy by bringing the water to a boil and stirring in the rest of the ingredients. Stir carefully over medium heat until thick.

Drain the water from the steaming dish and top the bean-curd pockets with the oyster gravy.

SPICY PORK TRIPE

SERVES 6–8 AS
A DIM SUM COURSE

Some things come by on the dim sum cart and only the Chinese will order them. What a shame it is that most other Americans will not try the very best dishes. This is a favorite of mine, but you must cook it for a long time.

1½ pounds pork tripe (hog maws)

2 green onions cut into 3-inch pieces

1 dried turnip ball (page 34), chopped and rinsed well

2 tablespoons peanut oil

1 tablespoon finely chopped garlic

1 teaspoon freshly grated ginger

1 tablespoon fermented black beans (dow see), rinsed

2 green onions, chopped

2 tablespoons light soy sauce

2 tablespoons Chinese rice wine or dry sherry

½ tablespoon garlic and red chili paste (page 30)

½ tablespoon sesame oil

2 tablespoons cornstarch mixed with 3 tablespoons water (optional)

Cut the tripe into strips about 4 inches long and ½ inch wide. Blanch in boiling water for 5 minutes and discard the water.

Cover the tripe with fresh water and add the green onions cut in 3-inch pieces and the dried turnip. Cover and simmer until the tripe is tender, about 1 hour. Longer if you prefer, of course.

Drain the tripe well, discarding the water. Heat a wok and add the peanut oil, garlic, and ginger. Chow for a moment and add the tripe. Toss in the oil and then add the remaining ingredients, except the cornstarch solution. Cook to your taste and then thicken the sauce, if you wish, with the cornstarch and water, stirring as you add.

To reheat for a dim sum party, simply steam in small bowls.

SPARERIBS WITH BLACK BEANS AND PEPPER SAUCE

SERVES 6 AS
A DIM SUM COURSE

This is another dish that causes traffic jams among the dim sum carts in Hong Kong. Everyone wants an order and the chaos is infectious. Easy to prepare, they will just make a dim sum party.

1 *pound pork spareribs, cut into 1-inch pieces (Have the butcher cut them for you on his band saw)*

MARINADE

3 *tablespoons light soy sauce*

2 *tablespoons Chinese rice wine or dry sherry*

1 *teaspoon ginger, freshly grated*

2 *tablespoons peanut oil*

3 *cloves garlic, chopped fine*

½ *teaspoon salt*

1 *tablespoon fermented black beans* (dow see), *rinsed*

Pinch of sugar

1 *teaspoon garlic and red chili paste (page 30)*

Blanch the ribs in boiling water for 1 minute. Drain well. Soak in the marinade for 20 minutes. Heat a wok and chow the ribs until lightly browned. Remove from wok and drain the oil. Add the fresh peanut oil, garlic, and salt. Chow until the garlic browns just a bit and then add the remaining ingredients. Return the ribs to the wok and toss in the sauce. Place in a steaming dish and steam for 45 minutes to an hour, or until the ribs are very tender.

VARIATION: You can also avoid browning the ribs. Just add 1 table-spoon cornstarch to the marinade and continue with the dish. When steamed the cornstarch will form a wonderful gravy on the ribs.

GARLIC RIBS WITH GREEN PEPPER AND BLACK BEANS

Use the same recipe as above but omit the garlic and red chili paste and add ½ green sweet bell pepper, cored and diced into ½-inch pieces. Add the pepper just before steaming the dish.

CHICKEN

CHICKEN SHU-MEI

Use the same recipe as for the Pork Shu-Mei (page 99) but substitute ground chicken for the pork. The chicken product can be found frozen in your supermarket and the result will please everyone at your table. It will also contain less fat.

CHICKEN AND CHINESE CHIVE SHU-MEI

You can use regular chives for this but the Chinese chive has a much brighter garlic flavor. As a matter of fact, it is sometimes found in the Chinese markets listed as "garlic chives." It is worth the search . . . but then you know me and garlic!

1 *pound ground chicken (page 106)*	*Pinch of sugar*
½ *cup finely chopped Chinese garlic chives*	1½ *teaspoons sesame oil*
1 *clove garlic, crushed*	1 *tablespoon cornstarch*
1 *tablespoon dry sherry or Chinese rice wine*	1 *teaspoon salt*
1 *tablespoon light soy sauce*	½ *teaspoon ground white pepper*
½ *teaspoon freshly grated ginger*	*Additional whole chives for "belts"*
½ *teaspoon MSG (optional)*	24 *Shu-Mei wrappers (page 99)*

Mix all ingredients together, except the chives for the "belts." Whip by hand, using your hand, until the mixture holds together very well. Form into shu-mei just as in the pork recipe (page 99). Blanch the whole chives in very hot tap water just for a moment. Tie one chive around the neck of each chicken-chive dumpling so that it looks like it is wearing a little green belt. Steam in an oiled bamboo steamer for 15 minutes (page 97).

HINT: USE LETTUCE CIRCLES FOR STEAMING SMALL DUMPLINGS. Simply cut iceberg lettuce into small circles using a small cookie cutter. Place a little circle of lettuce under each dumpling or shu-mei. No stick and lots of flavor.

BEEF

BEEF MEATBALLS

MAKES ABOUT 20 DIM SUM

This is a quicky. Buy good hamburger and do something very special in almost no time at all. I love these meatballs and they can be used in Hoko Pot soup (page 116) or chowed with vegetables . . . should you ever have any left over. I really doubt that you will have this problem.

1 *pound lean ground beef*

1 *tablespoon dark soy sauce*

1 *tablespoon Chinese rice wine or dry sherry*

¼ *teaspoon ginger, freshly grated*

1 *teaspoon sugar*

2 *green onions, chopped*

1 *egg, beaten*

1 *tablespoon cornstarch*

1 *teaspoon sesame oil*

2 *cloves garlic, crushed*

1 *teaspoon soybean condiment* (mein see)

2 *teaspoons finely grated orange peel*

¼ *teaspoon MSG (optional)*

1 *bunch spinach or mustard greens, fresh, for garnish*

Mix all ingredients together, with the exception of the garnish. You need to whip this dish to make it smooth, so I suggest an electric mixer . . . but it must be a good one. Otherwise, do it by hand and beat the blazes out of this stuff.

Roll into small meatballs about 1¼ inches in diameter. Press some of the greens into a steaming bowl and top with the meatballs. Steam the meatballs in several dishes, steaming each, or all together, for that matter, for about 15 minutes. It is best to use your bamboo steaming racks for these dishes (page 97).

> **HINT: TO KEEP MEATBALLS FROM STICKING TO YOUR HANDS** simply moisten your hands in between each molding of a meatball. Works great!

ADDITIONAL DIM SUM

FRIED WONTONS

I don't really care for these but they seem to be common fare on American/Chinese restaurant menus. So here is the recipe.

Deep-fry some prepared Wonton Dumplings (page 391) in fat at 360° until golden brown. Drain.

Prepare a dip of plum sauce (purchased in the can) thinned with a bit of hot water or Chinese Chicken Soup Stock (page 113).

Dip the hot wontons into the sauce. That's it. I apologize for my lack of enthusiasm but I will admit that these are much better than those you find in restaurants.

HOT AND SPICY SQUID

SERVES 4–6 AS
A DIM SUM COURSE

When the dim sum cart passes me and I see Hot and Spicy Squid I am a wreck. No matter how much I have already eaten I always order a plate of this wonderful seafood.

1 pound squid, cleaned and cut into ⅓-inch circles (page 188)

2 tablespoons peanut oil

1 tablespoon finely chopped garlic

1 teaspoon freshly grated ginger

2 green onions, chopped

2 tablespoons light soy sauce

2 tablespoons Chinese rice wine or dry sherry

Shot of hot pepper sauce such as Tabasco or 1 teaspoon garlic and red chili paste (page 30) (This is more legit!)

1 teaspoon sesame oil

2 tablespoons cornstarch mixed with 3 tablespoons water

Prepare the squid and set aside. Heat a wok and chow the oil, garlic, and ginger for about 1 minute over high heat. Add the green onions and the soy, along with the squid. Chow just until hot and add the remaining ingredients, adding the cornstarch mixture last and stirring until the mixture is thick.

Remove from heat and serve immediately, or cool and place in small dishes. Reheat for serving by steaming for about 4 minutes.

STEAMED MEAT-STUFFED BUNS
(Ham Bow)

MAKES 24 HAM BOW

This is certainly one of the most popular dim sum dishes in Chinese restaurants, whether they be in Hong Kong, Beijing, or San Francisco. The buns take a bit of time to prepare but they are delicious and fun to eat.

BREAD DOUGH

2 packages fast-rising yeast

½ cup lukewarm water

1 tablespoon sugar

1 cup milk, heated to lukewarm

4¼ cups regular flour

FILLING

½ pound Chinese Barbecued Strips (page 288), chopped into medium-small dice

2 green onions, chopped

¼ cup fairly finely chopped Chinese celery cabbage (Napa)

1 tablespoon hoisin sauce

½ tablespoon oyster sauce

½ teaspoon sesame oil

Pinch of salt

1 tablespoon light soy sauce

1 teaspoon sugar

1 tablespoon cornstarch dissolved in 1 tablespoon water or cold chicken stock

THE DOUGH

Sprinkle the yeast over the lukewarm water and then add the sugar. Allow to stand and then stir in the yeast. Add the warm milk. Be careful that this is only lukewarm or tepid, about 90°. Stir in the flour and knead until smooth. I do all of this with my KitchenAid mixer. Place the dough on a plastic countertop and cover with a large metal bowl. Allow to rise until double in bulk, around an hour. When properly risen, punch the dough down and allow to rise another 30 minutes.

THE FILLING

While the dough is rising, prepare the filling. Combine all ingredients in a wok, except for the dissolved cornstarch, and chow just until the mixture is hot. Thicken with the cornstarch and allow the filling to cool.

THE CONSTRUCTION

Punch the dough down and knead for 1 minute. Roll the dough into a snake about 1 foot long and divide the dough into 24 pieces. Roll each into a ball and then roll out into a 4-inch circle. I do this on a marble board so that I do not have to use too much additional flour.

Fill each bun as you roll it. Place a little more than a teaspoon of filling in the center of the dough circle. With your fingers, gather the sides of the dough up around the filling in loose folds, meeting at the top. Pinch the dough together so that it will hold. Place the filled bun upside down on a 2-inch square of waxed paper and place in a bamboo steamer. When all the buns are finished, cover the steamer with the lid and allow the dough to rise until not quite double in size. In about 30 minutes the dough should spring back slowly when pushed gently with your finger. Steam them for 15 minutes. Serve with a bit of Chinese mustard (page 40).

Soups

W ho invented soup? This most glorious of dishes, a dish that seems to transcend all cultures and all geographical barriers, has been with us since ancient peoples discovered that they could heat things in water held in the stomach lining of an animal. What an amazing technological step forward that was!

And the grass basket, if tightly woven, could be made waterproof. Foods were boiled in these baskets by adding hot rocks from the fire. Then the great advance called "The Clay Pot," and the soup was on! Copper, bronze, and iron cooking pots soon offered a whole new means of cooking by boiling in a liquid, and everyone knew that the liquid left in the pot was the best part. It would warm the heart, relax the body, and calm the spirit.

The peasants of our three ancient cuisines must be credited with wonderful discoveries once they had a pot in which to cook. Boiling foods was the simplest way of cooking and it eventually became one of the most sophisticated methods of food preparation. The peasants have always taught the upper classes how to eat. Soup was invented out of sheer hunger and frugal necessity . . . and now it is a dish in its own right.

In ancient China soup was often served as the last course, not the first as in our culture. And it did not need to be complex. A few chicken bones and a dried mushroom or two and you have a soup that is thousands of years old. Or perhaps you use the water in which the rest of the dinner has been cooked, a practice that the frugal Chinese still observe. With a light and simple stock, great dishes are prepared, such as the famous sharkfin or even bird's nest soups . . . these being two of the most expensive soups that I know of anywhere in the world. The recipes follow, of course.

The Greeks must be credited with the invention of "Fish in the Pot," which they call simply "The Pot," *kakavia*. They taught the French to make such a soup when Marseilles was a Greek shipping town, though the French name for "pot" gave the dish the title of *bouillabaisse*. And the Greeks taught the Romans to make the same soup. Greek soups are heavy and rich, just like the Greek mind. The Greek recipes in this section go back so far that some cannot be traced. I love the tripe soup!

The Romans took on the Greek cooks and learned a great deal from them. In Rome in our time you can find soups that are so old that one soup actually has the name "As Old as Adam." The range in Roman soups, and in Italian soups in general, is much wider than in either of our two earlier cultures. The Romans took the task of making soup very seriously and you can have anything from a simple bread soup to a vegetable soup, a minestrone, that will bring you to tears.

These were all peasant soups in the beginning. The people of the region of Liguria claim that they invented minestrone. During the time of the Crusades the soldiers from Genoa attempted to provide their leader with soup for a meal. They asked all the peasants in town to contribute herbs and vegetables, and the soldiers provided the stock. The soup became known as minestrone and do you know the name of their leader? It was Godfrey of Bouillon.

Enjoy the soups!

You might also like to consider:

Tripe Soup with Egg-Lemon
  Sauce *(page 325)*

Pasta and Bean Soup *(page 421)*

White Fungus Soup *(page 461)*

Clear Mushroom Soup *(page 461)*

CHINA

CHINESE CHICKEN SOUP STOCK

MAKES 4½ QUARTS

This is basic to the Chinese kitchen. It is easy to prepare and wonderfully versatile. One batch of this and you have a thousand possibilities for filling the soup bowl with wonderful things.

You will notice the practice of properly blanching the chicken pieces first. This is the way that a clear and light Chinese soup stock is made.

5 *pounds chicken backs and*
  necks

2 *slices fresh ginger, each*
  the size of a 25-cent piece

2 *Chinese dried turnip balls*
  (preserved turnip or
  preserved radish) (page
  34), coarsely chopped and
  rinsed with fresh water

Place the bones in a 12-quart stockpot and cover with water. On high heat bring the bones barely to a simmer. We do not want to cook the soup yet so do not let it do more than just simmer. Foam and scum will form on the top of the pot. You do not want this to boil. Drain the bones, discarding the water, and rinse well with cold water. Add 1 quart of fresh water for each pound of bones, along with the ginger and rinsed dried turnip. Bring to a simmer and cook 1 hour, uncovered.

Strain the soup stock and discard the solids. Remove the fat by using a plastic tube (see below) or simply chill the stock overnight and remove the fat when it has congealed.

> **HINT: TO REMOVE FAT FROM SOUP STOCK** use a plastic tube and siphon the strained stock from beneath the layer of fat. The tube can be purchased at a hardware store and should be ½-inch diameter. Wash and use regularly with your soup stocks.

BEAN CURD SOUP

SERVES 4

This should probably be called "peasant style" since it is so very common in China, but I love the stuff and make it often.

- 1 quart Chinese Chicken Soup Stock (page 113)
- ½ pound pork, trimmed and cut julienne
- 1 cake bean curd, firm Chinese style (page 28), cut into ½-inch cubes and drained
- 1 cup bok choy (page 28) or mustard greens, chopped

Salt and ground white pepper to taste

1 fresh egg

GARNISH
Green onion, chopped
Sesame oil

Bring the stock to a simmer and add the pork. Cook for 6 minutes and add the bean curd and the bok choy or mustard greens. Bring to a boil and add salt and white pepper. Pour into a serving bowl and crack the raw egg into the bowl. It will cook on the way to the table. Garnish with the sesame oil and chopped green onions. Stir the egg into the soup at the table and serve.

PEAS AND EGG SOUP

SERVES 4

This is the common "egg flower" soup that you find in Chinese/American restaurants. It is a good dish if you use good soup stock.

1 *quart Chinese Chicken Soup Stock (page 113)*

1 *10-ounce package frozen peas*

¼ *cup sliced water chestnuts*

3 *eggs, beaten*

1 *teaspoon Chinese red vinegar*

Salt and white pepper to taste

GARNISH

Green onions, chopped

Sesame oil

Bring the stock to a simmer and add the peas and water chestnuts. When all is hot, add the beaten eggs very slowly in a stream. Count to ten and stir the pot slowly. You should have lovely thin streams of egg. Add the remaining seasonings and garnishes and serve.

ABALONE SOUP

SERVES 8–10

This is a great favorite of mine. When I thirteen years old I used to save my allowance and travel to the old Tai Tung restaurant in Seattle. They would prepare this dish for me and I have never forgotten it. Now canned abalone is terribly expensive, something like $15 a can . . . but the soup is just wonderful. Prepare this for some kind of a state occasion such as your birthday or your lover's birthday . . . or maybe it should be served on a slow Monday.

6 cups Chinese Chicken Soup Stock (page 113)

1 16-ounce can abalone (available in Chinese markets), sliced thin, the liquid reserved

¼ pound pork, cut in a medium dice

4 Chinese dried mushrooms, soaked for 6 hours, drained and sliced julienne

¼ cup sliced water chesnuts

1 cup thinly sliced bok choy or Chinese celery cabbage (Napa)

Salt and white pepper to taste

GARNISH

Green onion, chopped

Sesame oil

1 egg

Bring the stock to a heavy simmer and add the juice from the canned abalone. Add the pork and mushrooms. Simmer for 10 minutes and add the water chestnuts, abalone, vegetable, and salt and pepper. Bring to a simmer again, being careful not to let this boil. You do not want to toughen the abalone. Place in a serving bowl and add the garnishes. The raw egg is cracked into the bowl just before serving. It will cook on the way to the table. Stir in the egg when you present this absolutely smashing soup.

HOKO POT

The fun of cooking soup at the table is increased if you own a Hoko Pot. This device is much like an angel-food-cake pan on a stand. The pan is filled with soup stock and glowing hot charcoal pieces are dumped into the center tube. The soup is cooked in this way and everyone simply helps him/herself to the pot.

This is probably a very old method of cooking going back three thousand years to the Shang Dynasty in China. Metal helmets were an invention of the time and soldiers would cook soup in them by simply placing them in the fire. The wok also is no doubt connected with this history.

The ingredients depend on what you have on hand.

Fill the Hoko Pot with hot Chinese Chicken Soup Stock. Heat the stock in a pan on the stove and pour it into the table device. Or you can use an electric hot plate and a soup pot, right on the table. Add one thin slice of fresh ginger for each quart of stock.

Have the charcoal already burning, just before dinner. *Remember that this can be done only in a well-ventilated room.* Place the Hoko Pot on a deep tray and set it on a mat in the middle of the table. Add several cups of water to the tray so that the table is not damaged by the heat. The water should run inside the bottom chamber of the Hoko Pot. After you have poured the stock into the pot, cover the container with the lid. Using metal tongs and a heavy protective metal tray, drop several burning charcoal briquets into the chimney of the cooker. Do this with the windows open so that you do not get sick from the charcoal fumes.

Now you are ready for the feast!

Place any or all of the ingredients below in the pot. Remember that anything goes, but you must first put in the things that take the longest to cook. Put in a few things, have a glass of wine with your guests, and then put in a few others. Eventually all will be finished at the right time and your guests may serve themselves from the pot. You may go on cooking more, if you wish, and the remaining soup is served as the last course.

Control the heat of the pot by placing a Chinese teacup filled with water over the top of the vent or chimney. The fire will calm down immediately.

POSSIBLE INGREDIENTS

Cook in this order.

Pork, lean and cut julienne style

Chinese mushrooms, soaked first for 3 hours and cut julienne

Beefsteak, cut julienne

Chicken, boneless, cut julienne

Bean curd, cut into ½-inch cubes

Beef Meatballs left over (page 310)

Deep-Fried Pork Balls left over (page 299)

Cooked ham, cut julienne

Green onions, cut Chinese style (page 142)

Sugar-pea pods

Shrimp, large and peeled

Chinese greens of any kind, sliced

Anything else that you can think of . . .

Garnish the soup with a bit of sesame oil and perhaps some white pepper as it cooks.

Remember to wait a bit for the pot to heat up between additions. The wait is worth it!

NOTE: You might also wish to serve one or even several dip sauces. Several possibilities are offered on pages 201–202.

SEAWEED SOUP

SERVES 6

This is a wonderful soup and certainly a very old one. Both the Chinese and the Japanese enjoy seaweed in their soups, though the Chinese are much more likely to make a meal of this saltwater vegetable instead of using it just for flavoring.

6 cups Chinese Chicken Soup Stock (page 113)

1 slice fresh ginger, the size of a 25-cent piece, cut julienne

2 tablespoons peanut oil

1 teaspoon salt

¼ pound lean pork, diced medium

3 dried Chinese mushrooms, soaked for 3 hours, drained, and cut julienne

6 water chestnuts, peeled and sliced

¾ ounce dried seaweed sheets (commonly called nori in Oriental markets)

¼ cup cooked ham, cut into thin slivers

Salt and white pepper to taste

GARNISH

Green onion, chopped

Sesame oil to taste

1 teaspoon white vinegar

1 raw egg

Bring the stock to a simmer. In the meantime, chow the ginger with the oil and salt in a hot wok. Cook just until the ginger begins to brown and add this mixture to the soup stock. Add the pork and mushrooms and simmer for 15 minutes. Add remaining ingredients, except the garnishes and egg, and simmer for 6 minutes. Place in the serving bowl and add the garnishes. Stir the raw egg into the soup at the table.

FISH AND LETTUCE SOUP

SERVES 4–5

Fish and iceberg lettuce sound too simple to be attractive. Here is one of the secrets of fine Chinese cuisine, simplicity. You can throw this soup together in nothing flat, and you will relish the delicate flavors.

½ *pound very fresh white fish, boneless fillet sliced thin (cod or snapper will do well)*

MARINADE

1 *tablespoon light soy sauce*
¼ *teaspoon MSG (optional)*
1 *tablespoon peanut oil*
Pinch of ground white pepper

3 *cups iceberg lettuce, sliced taco style*

1 *slice fresh ginger, the size of a 25-cent piece, cut julienne*
1 *tablespoon peanut oil*
¼ *teaspoon salt*
4 *cups Chinese Chicken Soup Stock (page 113)*
1 *tablespoon Chinese rice wine or dry sherry*

GARNISH

Sesame oil, few drops
White pepper, ground, to taste

Slice the boneless fish and soak in the marinade.

Prepare the lettuce and set aside. Chow the ginger, oil, and salt just until the ginger begins to brown a bit. Add this to the soup stock and bring to a heavy simmer. When you are *actually ready to serve*, drain the marinade from the fish and add the fish to the pot, all at once, along with the lettuce and the rice wine or sherry. Bring back to a simmer and remove from the stove. You do not want to overcook this soup. Add the sesame oil and pepper for garnish and serve immediately.

HOT AND SOUR SOUP

SERVES 8–10

This is a classic coming from the northern regions. You will be surprised at how simple this is to prepare . . . and better than what you find in most of the American/Chinese neighborhood restaurants. I make this for my sons on occasion, and it is always a great hit.

6 cups Chinese Chicken Soup Stock (page 113)

2 tablespoons light soy sauce

¼ pound lean pork, cut into ¼-inch dice

6 dried Chinese mushrooms, soaked for 3 hours, drained, and cut julienne

¾ teaspoon ground white pepper or more to taste

¼ cup white vinegar, more or less to taste

5 tablespoons cornstarch mixed with 5 tablespoons water

Salt, if necessary

½ cup bamboo shoots, cut thin julienne

¼ cup dried black fungus (cloud ears, page 29), soaked for 1 hour, drained, and shredded

1 cake bean curd, cut into ¼-inch cubes

4 eggs, beaten

GARNISH

Cooked ham, cut into slivers

Green onions, chopped

Sesame oil to taste, a few drops

Grated carrot

Fresh-ground black pepper to taste

Bring the stock to a simmer and add the soy, pork, and mushrooms. Simmer for 10 minutes, add the pepper and vinegar, and thicken with the cornstarch mixed with water. Taste for seasonings and add the bamboo, fungus, and bean curd. Bring to a simmer again and pour in the eggs in a very thin stream over the surface of the soup. Count to ten and stir a few times very slowly. Egg threads will have formed. Add the garnishes to the pot and serve. You may wish to add additional vinegar.

You may wish to add more fresh-ground black pepper as well.

VARIATION: If you really want this to be ''hot,'' try adding some garlic and red chili paste (page 30). That will make them sit up at the table!

SCALLOP, ASPARAGUS, AND MUSHROOM SOUP

SERVES 6–8

This one blends a bit from the East and a bit from the West. It is very light and unusually good.

6 cups Chinese Chicken Soup Stock (page 113)

4 dried Chinese mushrooms, soaked for 3 hours, drained, and cut julienne

½ pound fresh or frozen asparagus, cut into ½-inch pieces

2 tablespoons peanut oil

2 cloves garlic, chopped fine

¼ teaspoon salt

2 tablespoons light soy sauce

½ pound bay scallops or small scallops

2 eggs, beaten

White pepper, ground, to taste

GARNISH

Green onions, chopped

Chinese parsley, chopped

Sesame oil, a few drops

Bring the stock to a simmer and add the mushrooms. Cut the asparagus and set aside. Heat a wok and chow the peanut oil, garlic, and salt until the garlic barely begins to brown. Add the asparagus and chow just until it is hot and not quite tender. Add this mixture to the soup along with the soy and scallops. Bring to a simmer and add the beaten eggs in a thin stream over the top of the soup. Count to ten and stir slowly a couple of times. Add the white pepper and garnish, and serve.

Do not overcook this soup. The asparagus should taste fresh and still be quite green in color.

> **HINT: ADD ICEBERG LETTUCE TO YOUR CHINESE SOUPS.** The flavor of cooked lettuce, and the texture that it imparts, will surprise you. Try it in any kind of Chinese soup.

VELVET CHICKEN AND SWEET CORN SOUP

SERVES 4–6

This is a very popular soup at formal banquets in China. Corn, which came from America, became a mainstay in the diet of many of the peoples from the north, and Chinese ingenuity certainly has given us some new ways to appreciate our native grain. This one should become a family favorite.

½ pound chicken breasts,
boneless, cut into ¼-inch-
thick strips

MARINADE

2 egg whites, beaten

2 tablespoons cornstarch

⅛ teaspoon salt

3 cups peanut oil for deep
frying

THE SOUP

1 17-ounce can creamed
corn

3 cups Chinese Chicken Soup
Stock (page 113)

1 tablespoon light soy sauce

Salt and ground white
pepper to taste

Sesame oil, a few drops,
for garnish

Cut the chicken and pat dry on paper towels. Mix with the egg-white marinade and refrigerate for ½ hour. Heat the oil in a saucepan or wok to between 280° and 300°, no hotter. Deep-fry the chicken strips in the oil just until they are barely tender. They will not brown.

Heat the creamed corn along with the soup stock and light soy. When hot add the chicken and season to taste with the salt and pepper. Add the sesame garnish and serve.

DOUBLE-BOILED SOUPS

This style of cooking soup sounds confusing until you remind the Westerner what a double boiler looks like. Our prepared Chinese Chicken Soup Stock (page 113) is cooked and then placed in a porcelain double-boil soup container. You can find these pots under the Dragon Kiln Brand from China and they are sold in Chinatowns or some gourmet equipment shops.

 Special ingredients are added to the pot, along with the soup, and the pot is covered and placed in a pan of boiling water, thus making a double boiler. The soup is cooked for the second time very slowly so that the flavors are rich and warming.

Try your skill at some of the following double-boiled soups. You do not need recipes since the ingredients are actually up to you.

Chicken with Mushrooms
    Small pieces of chicken and dried mushrooms
Ginseng Chicken
    A piece of dried ginseng root and chicken
Chicken Feet, Red Dates, Peanuts, and Dried Mushroom
    This one is supposed to be very good for curing all sorts of diseases. Yes, I said chicken feet, not legs.

SHARK FIN SOUP

SERVES 6–8,
AS IT IS VERY RICH

When you see this on a fine Chinese menu you will also see a very high price. Shark sounds cheap to you but it is prepared in a very costly way. If you wish to buy a whole fin, skin and bone intact, be prepared to work with it for about 5 days before it is ready to serve. That is a bit much! Purchase prepared shark fin at any good Chinese grocery. Simply tell the clerk what you want to make and he will show you shark fin that is ready for the soup pot.

¼ pound refined shark fin, prepared shredded type, soaked in water overnight

2 green onions, cut into several pieces

2 pieces fresh ginger, each the size of a 25-cent piece

6 cups Chinese Chicken Soup Stock (page 113)

¼ pound lean pork, cut julienne

¼ cup bamboo shoots, cut thin julienne

5 Chinese dried mushrooms, soaked for 3 hours, cut julienne

2 tablespoons Chinese rice wine or dry sherry

Salt to taste

¼ teaspoon MSG (optional)

2 egg whites, beaten until fluffy and double in bulk

GARNISH

Ham slivers

Sesame oil, a few drops

Soak the shark fin overnight. Drain and place in fresh water to cover, along with the green onion and the ginger. Bring to a boil and turn off the heat. Cover and allow to cool. Drain and remove the onion and ginger. Place in a 4-quart soup pot and add the soup stock and simmer, covered, until tender, about 20 minutes.

Add the pork, bamboo shoots, and mushrooms. Simmer for 10 minutes and then add the wine and taste for salt. Add the optional MSG and pour the fluffy egg whites over the top of the soup. Very gently stir in the egg whites. Add the garnishes and serve.

BIRD'S NEST SOUP

SERVES 4–5

This is one of the most famous soups in China. A small bird lives on an island just off the coast of the land of the Emperors. The island has little natural vegetation so the sparrow gathers twigs and grass at the tideline on the beach. With these pieces a nest is made. Mother Nature has endowed the bird with the ability to regurgitate a gelatinous liquid with which to glue the nest together. The nests are gathered, after the birds have left, and meticulously cleaned. What remains is simply gelatin with a very light flavor of fish. It is really very wonderful.

You can buy nests for soup all cleaned and ready for the pot. Any good Chinese market will have them for you. When you see the price on the bird's nests you will understand that this soup is served only on special occasions . . . very special occasions. The cost for enough nest to make *two* batches of this soup will be somewhere between $30 and $40. Calm down and at least *read* the recipe; it is a very interesting dish.

1¾ *ounces cleaned bird's nest*

2 *cups water*

2 *slices fresh ginger, each the size of a 25-cent piece*

4 *cups Chinese Chicken Soup Stock (page 113)*

2 *tablespoons cornstarch mixed with 2 tablespoons water*

Salt to taste

2 *eggs, beaten*

Ham, cut julienne, very fine, for garnish

Soak the bird's nest overnight in fresh water. Using a fine mesh strainer drain and rinse the nest. Place in a saucepan and add 2 cups of water and the ginger slices. Simmer for 5 minutes and drain in the strainer, discarding the ginger. Pick out any impurities and add to the soup stock and simmer for ½ hour.

Stir in the cornstarch mixed with water and cook to thicken. Add salt to taste and pour the beaten eggs in a thin stream over the top of the soup. Count to ten and gently stir the eggs into the soup.

The shredded-ham garnish will go nicely on the top of this very delicately flavored soup.

GREECE

FISH STOCK

Y ou really don't need a recipe for such a thing. It is so easy to make that you will read this once and never refer to it again, but I hope you make it often. It is great to have a fine fish stock in your refrigerator so that you can create soups, sauces, and fish stews without any pain at all. This will freeze well in 1-quart plastic containers.

Pick up fresh fish bones, skin, heads, and tails. Just tell your fishmonger what you are preparing and he will take good care of you. Be sure that everything is very fresh.

Rinse the bones in fresh water and then place in a soup pot. Add 1 quart of water for each pound of bones and a few chopped carrots, yellow onions, celery ribs, and a bit of salt and pepper. Do not oversalt as you may wish to reduce the stock. Bring to a boil and then turn to a simmer. Cover and cook for 1 hour. Strain the stock and discard the solid material. Chill.

AVGOLEMONO SOUP

SERVES 10–12

T his soup is a classic. The lemon has been common in Greece for a thousand years and when they go to the market to buy lemons they do not buy them one or two at a time. They buy them in big bags the way we buy potatoes! I cannot even think of Greek cooking without the cleansing flavor of lemon. The flavor of lemon and egg, *Avgolemono,* is found in sauces, baked dishes, and soups.

This must be considered one of the classic soups of the world.

2 cups milk

2 tablespoons cornstarch

6 egg yolks, beaten

2 quarts Basic Chicken Stock (page 129)

½ cup long-grain rice

½ stick (⅛ pound) butter

Chopped parsley to taste

1 cup fresh lemon juice

Grated lemon peel to taste (optional)

Salt and pepper to taste

Stir the milk and cornstarch together and then beat in the egg yolks. Set aside. Bring the stock to boil in a 4-quart soup pot and add the rice. Cook, covered, until the rice is puffy and tender, about 25 minutes. Remove the soup from the heat and add the milk and egg mixture, stirring carefully. Continue to cook for a moment until all thickens. Remove from the heat again and add the butter, chopped parsley, and lemon juice. You may wish to add some grated lemon peel as well. Add salt and pepper to serve.

FISH SOUP AVGOLEMONO

SERVES 10

The Greeks invented the fish stew. This version, and there are many versions of this dish, is heavy and rich with the flavor of egg and lemon. During the summer months when eggs were scarce in the old days, a version was served minus the eggs. I prefer this one.

2 quarts Fish Stock (page 126)

1 medium yellow onion, peeled and coarsely chopped

1½ cups coarsely chopped ripe tomatoes

1 cup coarsely chopped celery tops

1 cup olive oil

½ pound cod fillets, boneless, cut into 1½-square pieces

½ pound mussels, trimmed of their beards, soaked in cold water for 1 hour, and drained

½ pound medium prawns, shelled

8 egg yolks

Juice of 2 lemons

Chopped parsley for garnish

Prepare the fish stock.

In a heavy 6-quart stockpot sauté the onions, tomatoes, and celery tops in the olive oil until the onions are transparent, about 15 minutes. Add the fish stock to the pot and bring to a simmer. Add the cod and simmer for 3 minutes. Add the mussels and simmer for 3 minutes more. Just as the mussels begin to open add the shrimp and continue cooking for about 2 more minutes, or until the shrimp have changed color and are a bit opaque. Strain the seafood from the pot. Mix the egg yolks and lemon juice together, beating until a froth is formed. Stir into the hot stock and cook gently, stirring all the time, until the soup is thickened. Return the seafood to the pot and bring up to serving temperature. Season with salt and pepper. Garnish with parsley and serve.

BASIC LAMB STOCK

MAKES ABOUT
3 QUARTS

This stock is another basic in the Greek household, and it has been for a long time. The Greeks have been eating lamb for thousands of years and they rarely waste any part of the animal. The recipe is simple and it is necessary to several other recipes in the Greek portions of this book. You cannot buy a commercial lamb stock in any form. Don't let anyone tell you that you can!

3 *pounds lamb bones, cut into 1-inch pieces (You may use up to ½ of this weight in pork neck bones)*

1 *yellow onion, peeled and quartered*

3 *ribs of celery, coarsely chopped*

2 *carrots, unpeeled, chopped*

1 *handful parsley, stems and all*

8 *black peppercorns, whole*

Place the bones in a large stockpot and rinse with very hot tap water. Drain and just cover with fresh *cold* water. Add vegetables and peppercorns and bring to a simmer. Skim the froth that forms on the top of the soup. Simmer, covered, for 3 to 4 hours. You may need to add additional water.

Note that the stock will taste a bit flat to you since we have not added salt. Salt will be added when you use the stock in a soup, sauce, or stew.

ITALY

BASIC CHICKEN STOCK

There is no way that you can run a proper kitchen without having fresh stocks on hand. If you buy commercially prepared products you are generally getting little more than salt, and in a very expensive form. I know it sounds like lots of work but to tell the truth stocks are very easy to make, and they are not expensive. Cook one day a week and fill the refrigerator and freezer with the blessed liquids that free you to be creative and comforting when cooking. Chicken stock is one of those necessary and comforting fluids.

3 *pounds chicken backs and necks*

4 *ribs celery, coarsely chopped*

6 *carrots, unpeeled, sliced thick*

2 *yellow onions, peeled and quartered*

8 *peppercorns*

Place the chicken backs and necks in a soup pot and rinse with very hot tap water. Drain and add 3 quarts of fresh *cold* water to the pot, along with the other ingredients. Bring to a simmer and cook for 2 hours. Be sure to skim the froth that forms when the pot first comes to a simmer.

The stock will taste a bit flat to you since it has no salt. Salt will be added when you use the stock in the preparation of soups, sauces, or stews.

ZUPPA IMPERIALE
(Bologna)

SERVES 8

Some dishes are just simply fun to cook. This is such a dish. It was given me by my friend Mrs. Nasi in Bologna, Italy. The pasta shops there sell this "cubed noodle" ready to go . . . but I think you can do better on your own. It is very simple and provides a most hearty meal.

THE CUBED NOODLE

4 *eggs*

4 *tablespoons semolina flour (page 38)*

6 *tablespoons freshly grated Parmesan cheese*

3 *tablespoons butter, melted*

Additional oil and butter for frying:

1 *tablespoon butter*

2 *tablespoons olive oil*

Mix all ingredients for the cubed noodle together. Heat a large frying pan and add the additional butter and olive oil. Fry the mixture very lightly on both sides. It should not be discolored. Allow to cool and cut into tiny cubes.

THE SOUP

6 *cups Basic Chicken Stock (page 129)*

The Cubed Noodle

Parmesan cheese, freshly grated

Salt and freshly ground black pepper to taste

Parsley for garnish, chopped

When ready to serve, heat the stock to a simmer. Add the cubed noodles, a bit of cheese to taste, salt and pepper, and garnish with the parsley. Serve very hot and enjoy a very old-world food product.

ITALIAN FISH SOUP

SERVES 8

This wonderful soup from Italy looks like a bouillabaisse from France . . . but it is not. The Greeks taught the Romans to make this dish . . . though it did not contain tomatoes, of course. Tomatoes were brought to Europe from the Americas during the fifteenth century.

This version is quick and easy since I use Italian Tomato Sauce that I have prepared ahead.

½ cup olive oil

3 leeks, cleaned and sliced, white part only

2 cloves of garlic, diced fine

1 yellow onion, peeled and chopped

1 cup chopped celery

1 cup fresh mushrooms, sliced

6 cups Fish Stock (page 126), clam nectar, or water

1 cup Italian Tomato Sauce (page 208)

1 cup dry white wine

Cayenne pepper to taste

Salt to taste

1 pound white fish, boneless fillet, cut into small pieces (seabass, cod)

2 pounds, combined, of any or all of the following:
Clams, soaked in fresh water 1 hour and drained;
Crab;
Shrimp in the shell;
Mussels, cleaned and prepared as in Fish Soup Avgolemono (page 127);
Squid, cleaned and cut into ½-inch circles (page 188);
Baby octopus, cleaned (page 198)

Chopped parsley, for garnish

Heat a large heavy soup pot and add the olive oil. Sauté the leeks, garlic, onion, celery, and mushrooms until the onions are clear. Add the stock or nectar, Italian Tomato Sauce, and white wine. Bring to a heavy simmer and taste. Add the cayenne pepper and salt to taste.

Prepare the seafood and add to the pot, remembering to add first those things that take the longest to cook. Clams and mussels would go in first. When they are almost cooked add the remaining seafood and simmer until all is tender.

Garnish with the parsley and serve.

Basic Brown Soup Stock

MAKES 5 QUARTS OF STOCK

The Old World has always had basic soup stocks on hand. The frugal cook was not about to throw out anything since he could not afford our luxury of waste. The bones of any and every creature were used for stock, and the stock eventually became the basis of another meal, in the form of either a soup, a sauce, or a gravy. You will need to make a batch of this now and then. It freezes well and it has a much better flavor than the only other possible substitute, canned beef stock. Please do not even think of using a bouillon cube. It is nothing but salt!

5 *pounds bare beef rendering bones, sawed into 2-inch pieces*

1 *bunch carrots, unpeeled and chopped*

3 *yellow onions, unpeeled and chopped*

1 *bunch of celery, chopped*

Tell your butcher that you need bare rendering bones. They should not have any meat on them at all, so they should be cheap. Have him saw them up into 2-inch pieces.

Roast the bones in an uncovered pan at 400° for 2 hours. Be careful with this, because your oven may be a bit too hot. Watch the bones, which you want to be toasty brown, not black.

Place the roasted bones in a soup pot and add 1 quart water for each pound of bones. For 5 pounds of bones, add 1 bunch carrots, 1 bunch of celery, chopped, and 3 yellow onions, chopped with peel and all. (The peel will give lovely color to the stock.)

Bring to a simmer, uncovered, and cook for 12 hours. You may need to add water to keep soup up to the same level. Do not salt the stock.

Strain the stock, and store in the refrigerator. Allow the fat to stay on the top of the stock when you refrigerate it; the fat will seal the stock and allow you to keep it for several days.

ROMAN "RAG" SOUP
(Stracciatella)

SERVES 8
AS A FIRST COURSE

I love the often amusing names that we put upon food products. The "rags" in this soup come about when you pour an egg batter into the hot broth. As you gently stir, the little pieces of torn egg appear. The Chinese would call this "egg flower," but I will bet that your kids will get a bigger kick out of "rags" in their soup.

This is a very popular soup in Rome and has been so for hundreds of years.

THE SOUP

4 cups Basic Chicken Stock (page 129)

4 cups Basic Brown Soup Stock (page 132) or canned

Salt and freshly ground black pepper

THE "RAGS"

3 eggs, beaten

4 tablespoons semolina or regular flour

4 tablespoons freshly grated Parmesan cheese

1 teaspoon finely grated lemon peel

Pinch of salt

GARNISH

Italian parsley, chopped

Parmesan cheese, freshly grated

Mix the stocks for the soup in a large soup pot. Bring to a simmer and season to taste with the salt and pepper.

Beat the eggs, flour, and cheese together. Add the lemon peel and salt and ¼ cup of the mixed soup stock.

Move the simmering pot from the heat and pour the rag batter into the soup in a thin stream, pouring carefully all over the surface of the soup. Return to the heat and stir with a wooden spoon as the tatters and rags cook. Simmer for about 2 minutes. Serve very hot with the parsley and cheese garnish.

GREEN OLIVE SOUP

SERVES 6–8
AS A FIRST COURSE

I cannot claim this dish as either Roman or Greek. I tasted it in a restaurant in this country and fell in love with it. All I can say is that a Greek or Roman would love this dish. It is a serious celebration of the olive!

2 cups green olives, pitted

3 tablespoons olive oil

½ medium yellow onion, peeled and sliced

2 cloves garlic, crushed

1 quart Basic Chicken Stock (page 129)

1 cup whipping cream

6 tablespoons flour cooked with 3 tablespoons olive oil to make a roux (page 26)

Black pepper, freshly ground, to taste (No salt will be necessary due to the olives)

4 shots Tabasco

⅓ cup dry sherry

GARNISH

Sliced pimento-stuffed green olives

Garlic-bread croutons

Soak the olives in cold water for 1 hour. Drain and coarsely chop the olives. Heat a frying pan and add the oil, onion, and garlic, along with ⅔ of the olives. Sauté until the onions are transparent. Puree this mixture in a food processor along with 1 cup of the stock. Place this mixture in a 4-quart saucepan and add the remaining stock. Simmer for 20 minutes and add the cream. Whisk in the roux and simmer, stirring constantly, until thickened. Add pepper to taste and the remaining chopped olives, Tabasco, and dry sherry. Heat to serving temperature and serve with the sliced olive and crouton garnish.

Salads

What we call a salad in our time is a long way from the first leaves and roots that were eaten by our ancestors. What has developed in our three cultures is just amazing.

The Chinese have traditionally used almost anything and everything as a food product. This openness was due partly to creativity and partly to necessity. Starvation is no fun . . . and finding wonderful new things to eat is! Please do not be put off by the salads from China. If you have never tried dried-jellyfish salad you are in for a fabulous treat, and the raw-fish salad is one of my favorite dishes in the whole world.

The Greek salads that follow all reflect the fact that the Greeks traveled a great deal and were willing to try all sorts of things. It is interesting that the Greeks have never been terribly concerned about admitting that they had received a dish from another culture . . . contrary to some Western European cultures who claim to have invented everything but the light bulb. You will love the Greek Village Salad with Cabbage, and the Salad Mykonos is just the most simple and delicious green dish that you can imagine.

Our American love for mixed salads probably came from the Romans. Since the time of the Emperor Domitian, who ruled Rome during the first century A.D., the people of the Eternal City have enjoyed a salad at the beginning of their meal. I have not bothered to offer you a simple green Roman salad, but I can tell you that the wonderful markets in Rome carry tiny lettuce leaves of all kinds, each picked leaf by leaf. None of this chopping and hacking at lettuce; the leaves are delicate and lovely just as they are. You can see from the Italian recipes I have selected that a salad can also function as an antipasto.

You might also consider:

Peperonata *(page 91)*

Chinese Duck Salad *(page 259)*

JELLYFISH SALAD

This is a bit unusual, I will admit. One wonders how destitute you have to be in order to catch jellyfish, salt them, and then dry them in the sun. Later, the dried fish is sliced thin, refreshed in water, and made into many dishes, this salad being the most famous. I can only say that I am glad for that first person who tried such a thing because this is one of the *great* dishes in Chinese cuisine—I promise. The texture is a bit firm and tender at the same time, and the Chinese love that sort of confusion in the mouth and tastebuds.

It will take some doing to find the dried jellyfish, but if you are near a big Chinatown you should have no problem.

I love this stuff, and so do my sons. Jason named this "rubber-band salad" and, when he was little, he used to get a kick out of serving this to his very young friends. "It's rubber-band salad," he would say. Only after the kids had eaten several helpings would he tell them what it was. That night I would get calls from parents asking me to explain what their child was talking about.

It may be an unusual salad for Westerners, but it is not unusual in China.

1 *pound dried jellyfish (to be found in Chinatown)*

DRESSING
¼ *teaspoon salt*
½ *teaspoon MSG (optional)*
2 *tablespoons sesame oil*
2 *tablespoons light soy sauce*

½ *teaspoon sugar*
1 *teaspoon garlic and red chili paste (page 30) or hot mustard or horseradish*
1 *tablespoon rice wine vinegar*

1 *cup fresh bean sprouts*

Cut the jellyfish into ⅛-inch-thin strips. Rinse with water and place in a stainless-steel or glass bowl. Cover with water and refrigerate. Change the water every 30 minutes for a total soaking time of 2½ hours. Drain.

Heat 2 quarts of water to boiling and remove the pan from the heat. Allow to cool for 5 minutes and then plunge the drained jellyfish into the water. Wait 5 seconds and drain and rinse in ice-cold water. I put ice cubes in the bowl at this point. This is the critical step. Do this whole step in a hurry or your jellyfish will not be tender and tasty. Drain well.

Mix the dressing and toss with the jellyfish and bean sprouts.

VARIATION: You may wish to add Chinese mustard (page 40) or even hot horseradish to this dish. I will follow you anywhere for jellyfish salad with hot horseradish!

DUCK AND JELLYFISH SALAD

I had this dish for the first time in San Francisco. I was so taken by it that I have worked out a method of duplication. This is very serious eating, which means it is also very serious cooking.

Prepare a batch of Jellyfish Salad (page 137). Also prepare a batch of Duck Salad (page 259) using regular roast duck, not smoked duck. (Leftover Peking Duck is just great with this dish . . . but then, who has leftover Peking Duck?) Also, omit the bean sprouts in the Duck Salad.

Toss the two salads together and then serve over a head of thinly sliced iceberg lettuce, sliced "taco style." This is just outstanding!

BEAN SPROUT AND SZECHWAN PEPPER SALAD

SERVES 4 AS PART
OF A CHINESE MEAL

The wonderful pinelike flavor of the Szechwan peppercorns gives this salad its depth. Actually it is a warm salad and very easy to prepare.

3 tablespoons peanut oil

1 teaspoon whole Szechwan peppercorns

1 pound fresh bean sprouts

1 green sweet bell pepper, cored and cut julienne

1 teaspoon salt

½ teaspoon sugar

½ teaspoon MSG (optional)

2 teaspoons white vinegar

Heat a wok and add the oil. When the oil barely begins to smoke add the peppercorns and chow for just a moment. Remove the pan from the heat and allow the oil to cool a few minutes. Remove the peppercorns, leaving the oil in the wok. Heat the wok and oil again and lightly chow the sprouts and green pepper, and remaining ingredients. Toss and serve. Or you may chill this and serve it later.

CHICKEN WITH BLACK BEAN SALAD

This is so easy that I will just describe it for you. Use leftover Chicken Chowed with Black Beans (page 235). Debone it and chop it up. Toss with shredded lettuce, cucumbers cut julienne, and Sesame Oil Salad Dressing (below). I like to add a shot of hot sauce such as Tabasco.

SESAME OIL SALAD DRESSING

MAKES APPROXIMATELY
¾ CUP

Your enjoyment of this light and tasty dressing need not be restricted to Chinese salads. It is good on just about any kind of vegetable salad, and will certainly give your dinner party an unusual twist.

2 *tablespoons light soy sauce*   ¼ *cup rice wine vinegar*
3 *tablespoons sesame oil*   ½ *teaspoon sugar*
3 *tablespoons light salad oil*   *Black pepper, freshly*
                                     ground, to taste

Blend all ingredients together and toss with fresh salad greens. You will not need to add salt to this dressing, though you might wish to put a bit of salt on the salad, depending on the ingredients.

MING'S CHICKEN SALAD

SERVES 6 AS A
MAIN LUNCHEON COURSE OR
8–10 AS A CHINESE DINNER COURSE

Chicken salad is not an uncommon dish in fancy Chinese restaurants in San Francisco. Ming's Restaurant, in Palo Alto, serves a dish very close to this one. It is perfect for a summer meal or a meeting at which you wish to feed a good-size group of people but do not want to do any cooking.

This dish is prepared in several stages and then thrown together at the last minute.

CHICKEN SESAME DEEP-FRIED

8 chicken thighs (about 1 pound)

MARINADE

2 tablespoons light soy sauce

½ teaspoon freshly grated ginger

2 tablespoons Chinese rice wine or dry sherry

¼ teaspoon ground white pepper

1 egg white, beaten

½ cup flour

½ cup cornstarch

½ cup sesame seeds

6 cups peanut oil for frying

THE NOODLES

2 ounces cellophane (sai fun) noodles (page 29)

THE DRESSING

3 tablespoons light soy sauce

½ tablespoon dry mustard (I prefer Colman's English)

3 tablespoons sesame oil

Juice of ½ lemon

¼ cup rice wine vinegar

½ teaspoon five-spice powder

1 teaspoon salt

½ teaspoon freshly ground black pepper

4 tablespoons peanut oil

½ teaspoon sugar

THE SALAD

12 green onions, slivered (see **HINT** below)

1 bunch Chinese parsley, chopped

½ cup thinly sliced water chestnuts

2 quarts shredded iceberg lettuce

Prepare the marinade and marinate the chicken thighs for 20 minutes. Drain and mix with the egg white. Mix the flour, cornstarch, and sesame seeds together and dredge the thighs in this coating mix.

Using a pair of kitchen shears cut the dry noodles into 2-inch lengths. Deep-fry at 360° for just a moment. Be sure to have tray covered with paper towels ready for draining the noodles. They will cook in just a second or two and will puff up greatly. Fry them in 3 different batches and drain them well. Set aside.

Deep-fry the chicken thighs at 360° until golden brown and crunchy, about 14 minutes.

Prepare the dressing and chop the vegetables. Debone the chicken thighs and julienne the meat. Toss all together except the noodles. They should go in last, just before serving. They are the source of the crunchiness that makes this salad so fresh and appealing.

VARIATION: Try substituting a couple of handfuls of crushed potato chips for the crunchiness of the deep-fried chicken. Use Chinese Poached Chicken (page 230) instead of frying the chicken. I know it sounds strange but it is a delicious variation.

> **HINT: TO SLIVER GREEN ONIONS** simply cut the onions in half the long way. Lay the halves flat side down on the cutting board and cut lengthwise into long thin strands. Cut these strands, on an angle, into 1-inch-long pieces.

CHINESE FISH SALAD

SERVES 6–8 AS
PART OF A CHINESE MEAL

The first time I ever tasted this dish I was shocked. I had no idea that the Chinese had been enjoying raw fish prepared in this way and I began to wonder if they were behind Japanese sashimi and Mexican ceviche. No matter. This salad is so totally unusual and delicious that your guests will cheer you on. It does take a bit of time to chop and slice everything, but you will surely become converted and see it as a simple and outstanding dish.

Be sure the fish is very fresh. The salad dressing and lemon juice firm up the fish a bit so that it really does not taste raw at all. It is almost "cooked" by the lemon juice.

This dish was a gift to me from my beloved friend Mrs. Mary Young. I served it one night at a formal party at my first restaurant, and I told no one what it was. They ate it, loved it, and begged for more. Only at the second serving did I tell them what it was. "Raw fish salad," said I. One woman, whose plate had been absolutely licked clean, yelled, "I didn't like it!" Such a loss. Don't let the thought of raw fish soaked in lemon put you off. What do you think pickled herring is?

1½ pounds fresh fish fillet, such as cod or sea bass, completely skinless and boneless

Juice of 1 lemon

½ cup dry-roasted unsalted shelled peanuts, chopped medium coarse

2 tablespoons sesame seeds, roasted

1 bunch Chinese parsley, chopped coarsely

6 green onions, cut julienne

*3 tablespoons Chinese sweet pickled scallions (kue tao), cut julienne

*2 tablespoons Chinese sweet pickled red ginger (suern geung), cut julienne

*3 tablespoons Chinese sweet pickled white cucumber (cha gwa), cut julienne

DRESSING

½ teaspoon dry mustard (Colman's English)

½ teaspoon ground cinnamon

1 teaspoon sugar

½ teaspoon salt

3 tablespoons light soy sauce

½ tablespoon sesame oil

2 tablespoons hot peanut oil (I heat mine in the microwave in a glass measuring cup)

1 cup crushed potato chips

Cut the fish into very thin slices. Be sure that you have removed or cut away all bone. Marinate the fish in the lemon juice while you prepare the rest of the ingredients.

Mix the dressing. Be sure that the oil is quite hot. It helps blend and brighten the flavors in the dressing.

Toss all ingredients, except for the crushed potato chips, in a salad bowl with the dressing. Add the chips just as you are serving and toss again.

*Can be purchased in any Chinese market.

GREEK SALAD DRESSING

The flavor of this simple dressing is common throughout Greece. The quality of the wonderful Greek olive oil, that from Sparta being my favorite, and the common use of fresh lemons, makes this dressing a natural. I will give you a recipe but all you really need is an explanation. Try it on any salad, and on fish, on meat, on shellfish, on . . . who knows.

¾ cup good Greek olive oil   Salt and pepper to taste
¼ cup fresh lemon juice

That is it! Just mix the oil and lemon 3 to 1 and season. It is great on any kind of salad. You might like to add a bit of oregano now and then. The very best oregano in the world comes from my beloved Greece.

GREEK VILLAGE SALAD WITH CABBAGE

I dislike coleslaw. No, let me be honest. I hate coleslaw! I know that this sounds un-American but I have never learned to like chopped raw cabbage—until I had this dish at Taverna Sigalas in Athens. It is simply the old Greek salad that you find in any really good Greek restaurant, but it is made with cabbage instead of lettuce. It is terrific!
Use any amount of the following, according to your taste.

White or yellow onions, peeled and sliced very thin
Green sweet bell peppers, cored and sliced thin
Feta cheese, cut up into tiny pieces
Greek olives

Greek Salad Dressing (above)

Oregano, whole and crushed by hand, to taste

Cabbage, cut as for coleslaw

Cherry tomatoes, or regular tomatoes (very ripe, *please*), cut or sliced to salad size

Cucumber, peeled and sliced thin

Salt and freshly ground black pepper to taste

Place the onions, peppers, feta cheese, and olives in a bowl and add enough Greek Salad Dressing, along with some oregano to taste, for your entire salad. Let this marinate for 1 hour.

Toss all remaining ingredients together with the marinated vegetables and dressing. Taste for salt and pepper and serve.

VARIATION: Of course you can use green lettuce instead of the cabbage. That would be the more traditional way and it is always a refreshing change from plain green salads.

SARDINE AND MACARONI SALAD

SERVES 6
AS A FIRST COURSE

I tasted this in a Greek village. It is common village food, I suppose, since canned sardines are always on hand and it is a wonderful change from normal summer pasta salads.

1 *pound dry pasta, cooked just until barely tender, rinsed, drained, and chilled. Shells are great for this dish.*

2 *3¾-ounce cans of sardines, drained on paper towels*

DRESSING

1 *cup mayonnaise*

1 *cup olive oil*

2 *tablespoons chopped capers*

1 *teaspoon oregano*

Salt and freshly ground black pepper to taste

Lettuce leaves for garnish

Prepare the pasta and chill. Mix the dressing and toss with the pasta and drained sardines. Serve in lettuce-leaf cups.

GREEK LAMB AND PASTA SALAD

SERVES 6–8
AS A LUNCHEON COURSE OR
8–10 AS A DINNER SALAD

This is not a dish that I found in Greece . . . but it certainly tastes Greek. Craig, my cooking assistant, and I developed this dish one night when unexpected visitors called and announced their coming. The dish is a great way to use up good roast lamb, provided that the meat has not been overcooked. Overdone lamb should be fed to the cat! (Unless you have a Greek cat. In that case he wouldn't eat overcooked lamb.)

1 pound dry penne pasta, cooked just until firm, rinsed, and chilled

1 pound medium-rare lamb, cut julienne

2 medium yellow onions, peeled and sliced thin

3 tablespoons olive oil for frying the onions

½ cup chopped green onions

½ cup pitted and chopped green olives

½ cup crumbled feta cheese

1 cup ripe tomatoes, cut into large dice

3 tablespoons chopped parsley

DRESSING

1 cup olive oil

2 tablespoons mayonnaise

2 cloves garlic, crushed

½ tablespoon dillweed

Salt and freshly ground black pepper to taste

Prepare the pasta and the lamb. Sauté the onions in the oil just until clear. Toss all ingredients together with the mixed dressing. Taste for salt and pepper and chill.

RUSSIAN SALAD, GREEK STYLE

SERVES 8–10
AS A SALAD COURSE

This is very popular in Greece and you will find it in all the large restaurants in downtown Athens. It is a milder form of the famous Salad Olivier offered in Russia. It is actually just a potato salad with peas and carrots added. I am convinced that the Greeks are to be credited with the invention of mayonnaise, given their affection for and early use of lemon whipped with olive oil. It is no wonder that this dish is common in the tavernas of Athens. No mustard is used in this dish and very little chopped pickle. I do add hard-boiled eggs to mine.

3 *pounds potatoes, cooked,*
  peeled, cut, and chilled for
  salad

8 *green onions, chopped*

4 *eggs, hard-boiled, chilled,*
  and peeled

1 *10-ounce package frozen*
  peas and carrots, defrosted
  and drained

DRESSING

1 *cup mayonnaise*

½ *cup olive oil*

1 *dill pickle, chopped*

1 *tablespoon drained and*
  chopped capers

Salt and freshly ground
black pepper to taste

GARNISH

Additional mayonnaise for
a decorative garnish

Parsley or celery leaves,
whole

Place all the salad ingredients in a large mixing bowl. In a small bowl blend the dressing. Toss with the salad and then place in a smooth mound on a serving dish. Pipe the mound with a bit of mayonnaise in an interesting pattern and garnish with whole parsley or celery leaves.

POTATO SALAD, GREEK STYLE

When in Athens you must eat at Monastiraki Square in a taverna called Sigalas. It is a wonderful old joint that serves everything in the classic Greek kitchen buffet. This salad is often on the menu. Note that it is typical of regular Greek potato salad in that it contains no mayonnaise and the main flavor is provided by good olive oil and celery leaves.

The quantity of the ingredients is simply decided according to your taste.

Potatoes, cooked and cut for salad, chilled

Green onions, chopped

Parsley, chopped

Celery leaves, chopped (I like lots!)

Greek Salad Dressing (page 144)

Oregano, whole, hand-crushed, to taste

Toss all with the mixed dressing. At Sigalas they just heap it on a plate. It is delicious and simple.

VEGETABLE SALAD, GREEK STYLE

Since eating in Greece I have taken to offering salads in this wonderful style. Cold, cooked vegetables, such as green beans, asparagus, artichoke hearts, cabbage, cauliflower, okra, spinach, tomatoes, are tossed with olive oil, fresh lemon juice, oregano, and salt and pepper. That's it! You prepare any mixture you like and it will hold up well on your buffet.

SALAD MYKONOS

I spent a few days on the island of Mykonos, and it was in the middle of February, a rather cold time of the year. There were no tourists about and most of the hotels and restaurants, which catered to the tourists, were closed. A resident, a bricklayer that I met in one of the back streets, took me to a tiny eating place that stayed open all year round for the local fishermen. It is called Kouneli or "The Rabbit." There is no menu but fish is always served. The cook is charming, though she speaks no English at all. This is the salad that comes with dinner. It is simple, elegant, and just wonderful.

Lettuce: green-leaf, red-leaf, or butterhead lettuce

Green onions, chopped

Dillweed, fresh, chopped

Greek Salad Dressing (page 144)

Salt and freshly ground black pepper to taste

Toss and serve. To tell the truth I think she also throws in a shot of good white wine vinegar.

VARIATION: You might just try a shot of crushed garlic in this salad. Though my friend in Mykonos did not use it, I think the blend of garlic and dill is basic and you should try it!

ITALY

CELERY AND MUSHROOM SALAD SAVINI

Savini's is a very fancy restaurant in the Galleria in Milan. Yes, it is expensive, but you must at least have coffee in the middle of the most beautiful shopping "mall" you have ever seen. It has been there for one hundred years. Savini's serves a salad very close to this one. The secret is the cheese. Don't use cheap cheese or cheap olive oil in this dish.

8–10 *ribs celery, cleaned and sliced as thin as possible*

¼ *pound fresh white mushrooms, sliced thin*

½ *cup thinly shaved Pecorino cheese*

¾ *cup good olive oil*

Juice of 1 lemon

Salt and freshly ground black pepper to taste

Toss all together and marinate 1 hour before serving. See page 151 for a hint on shaving cheese.

FENNEL SALAD, ROMAN STYLE

This is a common item on Roman restaurant menus, but you must not think it is common food. It raises a green salad to new heights.

Prepare a green salad of lettuce, cucumbers, celery, and thinly sliced fresh fennel bulb. Toss with a dressing of olive oil, lemon juice, salt and pepper, and perhaps a bit of grated Parmesan or Romano cheese. Wonderful, and you can tell the children that you are making "Licorice Salad" since fennel does have that wonderful light licorice flavor.

ITALIAN FLAG SALAD
(Insalata alla Bandiera)

This one is fun to prepare. For each guest, cut a few ripe tomato wedges, a few sweet green bell pepper wedges, and some white onion wedges. Use just a few leaves of the onion wedges on each plate and arrange a circle of the three colors of the Italian flag. The dressing is just good olive oil, lemon juice or wine vinegar, and salt and pepper. This is fun to serve and very colorful.

ROASTED PEPPER SALAD, ROMAN STYLE

One of the most refreshing salads that you can find in Rome consists simply of roasted red sweet bell peppers, peeled and dressed with lemon juice, olive oil, a pinch of oregano, and salt and pepper.

Sweet bell peppers are easily roasted and peeled. The process is the same for red, green, yellow, or orange sweet peppers. Place them on a baking sheet and broil in your electric oven, close to the top element, watching closely until small black and brown spots appear on the skin. Turn the peppers to roast them evenly. Place the peppers in a baking pan and place in a preheated 375° oven uncovered. Bake for about 35 minutes. Remove from the oven and cover the pan with a kitchen towel, thus allowing the peppers to cool in the midst of their own steam. When cool enough to handle, the skin will come right off. Seed and core the peppers and proceed with the production of your pepper appetizer salad.

You also might try the roasting method in the hint below.

> **HINT: ROASTING SWEET BELL PEPPERS** on an *asador* grill (page 19) is simple. Place the grill over your burner and roll the peppers on the top of the heated grill. Watch closely so that they do not burn. This method gives you a much more "toasted" flavor than the oven-broiler method.

↓ Bake at 375° for a few min. Take out &
cover w/ towel. Can scrape skin off easily.

OLIVE AND PEPPER SALAD

SERVES 6–8
AS A FIRST COURSE

This is the kind of dish that you will find in a good trattoria in Rome. I have put together a version that is a compilation of various similar salads I tasted in the Eternal City. This is simple to prepare and terribly rich.

1 *cup olive oil*

3 *cloves garlic, crushed*

5 *anchovies, flat fillets*

1 *medium yellow onion, peeled and sliced*

3 *red sweet bell peppers, cut into large julienne strips*

3 *green sweet bell peppers, cut into large julienne strips*

1 *cup pimiento-stuffed small green olives, drained*

Juice of 1 lemon

1 *teaspoon dry oregano, crushed by hand*

¼ *cup chopped parsley*

Salt and pepper to taste

Heat a large frying pan and add 4 tablespoons of the oil. Add garlic and anchovies, and mash the anchovies to form a paste. Add onion, peppers, olives. Sauté just until the peppers are barely tender but still bright in color. Allow mixture to cool. Make a dressing with the remaining oil, lemon juice, oregano, parsley, and salt and pepper to taste. Toss with the cooled olive and pepper mixture. Allow to marinate 1 hour before serving.

I like to serve this on a bed of iceberg lettuce or in a lettuce cup.

Seafood

FISH

Someday it would be fun to have a food anthropologist answer my question. Have more people in the world been kept alive on fish or on meat? I think the answer is fish. The Chinese have always been great fish eaters, with fresh fish being the primary protein source in the southern regions and dried and salted fish being a major food source in the northern regions.

Two thousand years ago, at the time of the Roman Empire, the Chinese were raising fish in ponds and tanks, some right outside the kitchen window. Carp, a member of the goldfish family, will eat almost anything, and it does not need a lot of fresh water. You could throw leftover food or scraps right out the window and into the tank . . . and a few weeks later harvest a wonderful big fish. The Chinese must be credited with the invention of the fish farm, a method of raising food that is just beginning to become popular in our culture.

The Chinese insist on fresh fish, and I mean alive, whenever possible. I have seen women in Hong Kong reject a fish because they can tell that it was killed several hours ago. And they waste nothing; even the bones can be steamed over bean curd or the cheeks and heads used in a fine casserole. To this day the fish as a symbol means plenty and fulfillment. That is why I wear an antique Chinese jade fish around my neck.

The peoples of the Mediterranean have always enjoyed fish, from the beginning of recorded history. In the fourth century B.C. Aristotle, the great Greek philosopher, wrote exhaustive biological studies on fish that overshadowed any other work done on fish until the sixteenth or seventeenth century. Even the art of the time used fish in common daily decoration, a time that predated the Roman Christian use of the fish symbol. There is good evidence to prove that the Greeks actually taught the Romans how to catch and appreciate fish. The Romans had shown little interest in fish until their armies returned to Italy from Greece in 185 B.C. Eventually, Apicius, the great Roman gourmet of the first century, learned to love fish so much that he offered an entire chapter on sauces for fish in his ancient cookbook.

When you go to Rome remember that one of the reasons the Italians have always loved fish is that there is no single spot in all of Italy that is more than one hundred miles from the seacoast. You will eat very well in the Roman fish houses.

You may also wish to consider:

Shrimp Chowed with Water-Chestnut Flour and Gin *(page 429)*
Hot and Spicy Squid *(page 109)*
Steamed Pork with Mushrooms and Dried Squid *(page 339)*

FISH WITH CELERY IN A HOT PLATE

The history of certain foods is *so* interesting. In ancient Rome an herb called lovage was used constantly. It is a member of the celery family and celery leaves can be used in place of the older herb. In China a special type of celery has always been appreciated, and it looks and tastes very much like the Roman version. Who got which from whom? We simply do not know, but the following recipe will show how the celery leaf is used to flavor something as delicate as a very fresh fish. I will simply give the ingredients and method for this dish. It is really quite simple and yet it makes a very grand presentation in Hong Kong restaurants such as the Chiu Chow Garden. Frank Yuen, one of the managers of Maxim's, the group that owns this restaurant, gave me one of the special pans that they use in the final cooking of this dish. You can use a simple pan, though in Hong Kong a fish-shaped aluminum pan is placed on a burner at your table. The result is simple and terribly elegant.

A whole fish is cleaned and marinated in light soy, dry sherry or Chinese rice wine, and a tiny bit of grated ginger. The fish is then steamed (page 19) until it is just barely tender, about 20 minutes. A small amount of chicken broth is seasoned with sherry, white pepper, and salt and placed in the fish-shaped cooking pan. The pan is placed on a burner at your table and filled with the fish and the seasoned broth. Celery leaves are heaped about the fish and it is allowed to cook while you watch and anticipate. The time of cooking at the table is only about 10 minutes, but the resulting meal will be remembered for years.

FISH FILLETS
STIR-FRIED WITH CELERY

SERVES 4 AS
PART OF A CHINESE MEAL

I tasted this dish for the first time in Hong Kong. The utter simplicity and the refreshing flavor of the celery make for a blend that we seldom see in Chinese restaurants in this country. We Americans always seem to go for fish dishes that are much more complicated than they need be.

Chinese celery looks very much like thick parsley and the leaves are the source of the flavor. If you use American celery in this dish be sure to find stalks with lots of leaves.

½ pound whitefish fillets, boneless and sliced thin (cod, sea bass, or flounder will work well)

MARINADE

2 egg whites, beaten

2 tablespoons cornstarch

⅛ teaspoon salt

4 cups peanut oil for deep-frying

1 tablespoon peanut oil

1 large clove garlic, crushed

⅛ teaspoon salt

½ teaspoon fresh ginger, cut into paper-thin slices and then into sticks

1 cup celery, cut julienne, very fine, leaves and all

¼ cup chicken broth or Chinese Chicken Soup Stock (page 113)

Pinch of ground white pepper

Pinch of sugar

1 tablespoon cornstarch mixed with 1 tablespoon water

GARNISH

Carrot, finely grated

Green onion, chopped

Cut the fish and mix the marinade. Mix it well. Soak the fish in the marinade for 20 minutes, or longer, in the refrigerator.

In the meantime, cut up and prepare all other ingredients.

Heat the peanut oil to between 280° and 300°, no hotter. Deep-fry the drained fish just until it turns white—a couple of minutes. It will not brown.

Heat a wok and add the tablespoon of fresh peanut oil, garlic, salt, and ginger. Chow for a moment over high heat and add the celery. Cook just until hot and add the chicken broth, pepper, and sugar. Bring the sauce to a boil and thicken with the cornstarch and water mixture. Add the drained fish fillets and stir-fry just until hot. Garnish and serve.

This delicate dish is great with rice.

VARIATION: You may wish to dip the fresh pieces in a dipping sauce. See pages 201–202 for some possibilities. Soy and vinegar are very good with this dish.

STEAMED FISH WITH SOYBEAN CONDIMENT AND BEAN CURD

SERVES 4 AS
PART OF A CHINESE MEAL

In this simple and profound dish the bean curd picks up the wonderful flavors of fish, ginger, and the soybean condiment. It is a favorite among the Chinese and if you enjoy bean curd as I do, it will be a favorite with you as well.

½ pound whitefish, boneless fillet, cut into thin slices (cod or sea bass will be fine)

1 cake bean curd, cut into ½-inch slices

SAUCE

1 clove garlic, crushed

¼ teaspoon finely grated fresh ginger

2 tablespoons peanut oil

1 tablespoon Chinese rice wine or dry sherry

2 tablespoons light soy sauce

Pinch of sugar

Pinch of MSG (optional)

1 tablespoon soybean condiment (mein see)

3 green onions, sliced Chinese style (page 142), for garnish

So simple. Cut the bean curd and arrange on a large steaming plate. Arrange the fish on the top of the bean curd. Mix the sauce and pour over the top. Garnish with the green onions and place in a bamboo steamer (page 19). Steam for 20 minutes or to your taste.

BRAISED FISH
OI MANN

SERVES 4 AS
PART OF A CHINESE MEAL

Oi Mann is a wonderful restaurant in the Lau Fau Shan fishing village. It is in the New Territories, on the mainland just west of Hong Kong. You can make the trip for just a day and you will find a superb meal in this restaurant. The fish for sale is arranged in tanks in front of a long alleyway of restaurants and peddlers. You pick out what you want and the owner carries it, live, into his restaurant. The place is rather plain but the food will be unforgettable.

½ pound whitefish fillets, boneless and cut into 1-inch-square pieces

FRYING BATTER

1 egg

1 teaspoon baking powder

¾ cup cornstarch

4 cups peanut oil for deep frying

SAUCE

1 tablespoon peanut oil

1 large clove garlic, diced very fine

½ teaspoon fresh ginger, cut into fine julienne twigs

1 teaspoon soybean condiment (mein see)

1 tablespoon oyster sauce

1 tablespoon light soy sauce

1 tablespoon Chinese rice wine or dry sherry

¼ cup Chinese Chicken Soup Stock (page 113)

Pinch of sugar

1 tablespoon cornstarch dissolved in 1½ tablespoons water

GARNISH

Green onion, sliced, or celery leaves, chopped

Heat the oil for deep frying in a wok to 360°.

Mix the egg with the baking powder and add the fish to the batter. Put the cornstarch on a plate and remove the fish pieces from the batter and dredge each in the cornstarch. Deep-fry, in two batches, until the fish is golden brown, about 5 minutes. Be sure to keep your oil up to temperature. Drain the fish pieces on paper towels.

Heat another wok and add the 1 tablespoon of fresh peanut oil. Chow the garlic and ginger together for a moment and then add the soybean condiment. Chow for a moment and add the remaining ingredients for the sauce. Thicken with the cornstarch. Add the fish to the sauce and toss just until all is hot. Garnish and serve.

HINT: IF YOUR DEEP-FRYING OIL SMELLS OF FISH simply deep-fry a few slices of fresh ginger in the oil for a few minutes. You will be amazed at how the ginger will clean up the flavor and odor of the oil.

STEAMED FISH WITH BLACK BEANS

SERVES 6 AS PART OF A CHINESE MEAL

I never tire of the flavor of fermented black beans, *dow see*. Black beans and garlic are just the thing for fish of any kind, and I think you will be surprised at how easy this classic Chinese dish really is.

1 *pound whitefish or other fish fillets* or *1 pound of fish cut into steaks*

SAUCE

1 *tablespoon peanut oil*

2 *cloves garlic, chopped very fine or crushed*

¼ *teaspoon fresh grated ginger*

1 *tablespoon fermented black beans* (dow see)

2 *green onions, cut Chinese style (page 142)*

Pinch of sugar

1 *tablespoon Chinese rice wine or dry sherry*

2 *tablespoons light soy sauce*

Pinch of MSG (optional)

Place the fish in a steaming plate. Heat a wok and add the oil, garlic, and ginger. Rinse the black beans in a bit of water and add to the wok. Chow for just a moment, then add the rest of the sauce ingredients, and pour this sauce over the fish. Place in a bamboo steamer (page 97) and cook for about 15 minutes, or until the fish flakes and is done to your taste.

FISH WITH OLIVES
AND BEAN CURD

SERVES 4–6

The heavy sweet flavor of dried Chinese olives gives this dish a most interesting richness. This is not for lovers of Chinese Dinner #1 on the menu. The flavors are strictly Chinese!

4 *tablespoons peanut oil*

1 *teaspoon salt*

2 *pounds fish fillets, cut into 1-inch-square pieces (whitefish, cod, salmon, or a mixture of these)*

SAUCE

4 *slices fresh ginger root, cut julienne*

2 *tablespoons light soy sauce*

2 *teaspoons dry sherry or Chinese rice wine*

⅓ *cup dried olives (lom see), soaked in water for 2 hours, drained, and rinsed in fresh water*

¼ *pound bean cake, deep-fried (page 28)*

GARNISH

2 *green onions, chopped*

1 *tablespoon Chinese parsley (cilantro), coarsely chopped*

Heat a wok and add the oil and salt. Stir-fry the fish fillets for a few minutes. Add the sauce mixture and stir until hot. Add the drained olives and bean curd, cover, and cook a few more moments, stirring occasionally. Garnish with the green onions and Chinese parsley.

FISH FILLETS
WITH SESAME

SERVES 6–8
AS A CHINESE MEAL

This is a very tasty way of preparing fish, a way that even your children will enjoy. It is not uncommon to see whole families in Hong Kong restaurants enjoying this dish late in the evening.

1½ pounds whitefish fillets, boneless, cut into pieces 1 inch by 3 inches

Salt and pepper to taste

1 tablespoon light soy sauce

1 tablespoon sesame oil

1 cup flour for dredging

2 egg whites, beaten

4 tablespoons white sesame seeds

4 tablespoons black sesame seeds

4 cups peanut oil for deep frying

Soy, Ginger, and Vinegar Dip Sauces (page 201)

Marinate the fish pieces in the salt and pepper, soy, and sesame oil for about 15 minutes. Drain. Dust each piece with flour, then dip into the egg white, then sesame seeds.

Deep-fry the fish pieces in oil at 360° until done to taste, about 5 minutes. Serve with the dip sauce.

GREECE

SMALL FISH DEEP-FRIED IN OLIVE OIL

I had never thought of deep-frying fish in olive oil until the family and I had lunch at a wonderful restaurant in Piraeus, the waterfront of Greece. The place has been taken over by the son now and is inferior to the old man's version, but you might like to visit Kokkina Varka, "The Red Boat," nevertheless.

The old cook would dust small fish in flour seasoned with salt and pepper. Then he would deep-fry the fish in a big frying pan of hot olive oil on the top of the stove. The result was just delightful. Try the same thing at home. Buy decent olive oil by the gallon at any Middle Eastern or Italian market and use it for deep-frying. Keep it refrigerated in between fryings and keep it clean. Strain it after each use and remove the sediment from the container before the next use.

Olive oil is much better for you for deep-frying than most other vegetable oils, with the exception of peanut oil. Either of those two oils will do you well.

GREEK FISH CHOWDER

T he proper name for this Greek dish is *kakkavi*, meaning "pot."

¼ *cup olive oil*

3 *medium yellow onions, peeled and chopped*

2 *cloves garlic, chopped fine*

2 *1-pound cans peeled tomatoes, coarsely chopped*

4 *ribs of celery, chopped*

2 *teaspoons salt*

⅛ *teaspoon cayenne pepper*

1 *bay leaf*

½ *cup dry red wine*

4 *cups water*

1 *pound whitefish, boneless fillets*

½ *pound each of any or all of the following: Clams, rinsed; Mussels, scrubbed clean and rinsed; Crabs; Scallops; Shrimp; Squid, cleaned and cut into ½-inch circles (page 188)*

Heat a 6-quart heavy stockpot and add the oil, onion, and garlic. Sauté until they are clear, about 5 minutes. Add the remaining ingredients, except the seafood, and simmer, uncovered, until the sauce is rich and full-flavored, about ½ hour. Add the fish and shellfish in the order given, giving each variety a moment to cook. The clams will take longer than the squid.

Serve in bowls with Old Greek Bread (page 475) or French bread, and a Greek Village Salad (page 144).

NOTE: In some Greek communities the *kakkavi* is served with *avgolemono* sauce stirred in. The older dishes, however, are plain, as above, with the exception of the tomatoes. I like this version.

BAKED FISH ARCHESTRATUS

SERVES 4–5

Archestratus was a Greek from Syracuse who wrote one of the earliest known cookbooks about 330 B.C. His recipe for baked fish gives the following advice:

"Buy the best fish you can find, preferably from Byzantium. Sprinkle with marjoram. Wrap the fish in fig leaves and bake. Have slaves serve it on silver platters."

1 *pound whitefish*
½ *teaspoon marjoram*
Salt and pepper
Juice of 1 lemon
4 *green onions, sliced the long way into 2-inch pieces*

12 *fig leaves or 1 small jar grape leaves, drained and rinsed*
1 *cup dry white wine*

Cut fish into 1-inch-square pieces. Sprinkle with marjoram, salt and pepper, and lemon juice. Pour hot water over the fig leaves to soften, or rinse the canned grape leaves in cold water.

Spread leaves out one by one. Place a piece of fish and a bit of green onion on a leaf and wrap it up, tucking in the sides as you roll. Place the rolls side by side in an oiled baking pan and pour the wine over all. Bake in a preheated over at 350° for 20 minutes, uncovered.

FISH GRILLED GREEK STYLE

I was so amazed by this simple process that when I returned to Tacoma from Greece I immediately learned to duplicate the equipment. Since the equipment is the critical matter here, I shall just explain the process. The ingredients are easy.

In Piraeus, the waterfront in Athens, a chef used to heat up a piece of sheet steel, about $\frac{1}{4}$-inch thick, until it was very hot indeed. The long and narrow metal grill would cover 2 burners of his restaurant gas range. He would then place a whole cleaned fish, head on, in a wire fish-shaped grilling rack, brush it with an olive oil and garlic mixture, and place the rack *on top of* the murderously hot piece of sheet steel. The fish oil, combined with the garlic and olive oil, would drip onto the sheet steel and smoke like mad. He would turn the fish now and then and check for doneness by simply poking it with his finger. When the fish was served at the table the skin was removed and the whole doused with fresh lemon juice. The flavor was just spectacular.

I do this on my commercial gas range in my restaurant, with all the fans going. *I do not suggest* that you try this on your home gas range as it cannot take the terrific heat buildup under the sheet steel. Instead, try this process on your barbecue. Put the steel on the barbecue rack and get it as close to the coals as possible. Heat it until it is very hot and then proceed as above. By the way, this method does cause wonderful little dark-brown toasty spots to form on the fish . . . causing one to call this the earliest version of "blackened fish."

ITALY

ASSORTED FRIED SEAFOOD
(Fritto Misto di Mare)

*MAKES 2½ CUPS BATTER,
ENOUGH FOR 3 POUNDS OF FOOD*

You will see this dish all over Rome. The Romans eat less seafood than you might expect, given the fact they are only thirty miles from the sea. But they do love *Fritto Misto di Mare*. You can make an excellent one at home, far better than you will find in most American restaurants. I picked up this recipe in Rome. It is very typical.

THE DEEP-FRYING BATTER	Shrimp, cleaned of their shells
3 eggs, beaten	Squid, cleaned and cut into ½-inch circles (page 188)
1 cup water	
1 teaspoon baking powder	Artichoke hearts (page 400) (optional)
1 cup flour	
1 teaspoon salt	Zucchini sticks (optional)
Ample oil for deep-frying	Lots of lemon wedges for garnish
Whitefish fillets of any kind	

Mix all for the batter and let it rest for a few minutes while you bring the cooking oil up to 400°. The secret to this dish and to having a coating that is not greasy or soggy is the temperature of the oil. Fry just a few things at a time and keep the oil up to 400°. It is very easy to do, but remember, deep-frying is dangerous. Be sure you use every safety precaution.

Garnish with lots of lemon wedges

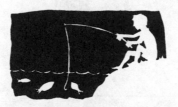

FISH STEW FOR CHRISTMAS EVE

SERVES 6
AS A MAIN COURSE

Christmas Eve in Italy is very much like Lent in America in that you are not expected to eat meat. To solve the problems of this difficult red-meat-abstinence rule, the Italians invented a wonderful fish stew for the eve of the birth of the Christ. It calls for up to eight or nine different kinds of fish and seafood put together in a wonderful stew. The result makes abstinence a blessing!

½ cup olive oil

3 cloves garlic, chopped fine

1 quart Fish Stock
(page 126)

1 cup dry white wine

2 cups Italian Tomato Sauce
(page 208)

THE EIGHT OR NINE DIF-
FERENT KINDS OF FISH:

½ pound baccalà, soaked for
2 days as per instructions
(page 342)

2 pounds of either or a
combination of both:

Clams, rinsed

Mussels, scrubbed clean

2 pounds of any one or a
combination of all:
Shrimp;
Squid, cleaned and cut
into ½-inch circles (page
188);
Baby octopus, cleaned
(page 198);
Crab, in the shell;
Lobster;
Cod, fresh fillets

Salt and freshly ground
black pepper to taste

GARNISH

Italian bread, sliced and
toasted

Italian parsley, chopped

You had best prepare the fish before you do much more with this recipe as the salt cod (baccalà) must soak for 2 days.

Heat a 12-quart heavy stockpot and add the olive oil and garlic. Barely brown the garlic and then add the Fish Stock, wine, and Italian Tomato Sauce. Bring to a simmer and cook for about 15 minutes, uncovered. Begin adding the seafood, in the order listed. It is important not to overcook or undercook the various kinds of fish.

When the clams are open and the fish barely tender, the stew is ready to serve. Taste the stew first to see if you desire salt and pepper.

Serve with a toast slice in each bowl and a bit of parsley garnish.

PAN-FRIED FISH WITH OIL AND LEMON JUICE

The simplest method of frying fish is used throughout Rome, and I expect this has been going on for a long time. We do too much to our fish in this country. Sometimes the simple method is the best one.

Pan-fry any fish fillet you wish in olive oil. Use no salt or pepper until you serve it at the table. Garnish the fish with a great deal of fresh lemon juice and you will need little salt or anything else, for that matter.

SHELLFISH

Shellfish have been popular with all three of our ancient cultures for hundreds of years. You simply cannot think of the cuisine of China without thinking of shellfish, even in those areas inland where fresh fish is impossible to obtain. The shrimp, scallops, abalone, and oysters are dried and relished by people far from the sea.

Shellfish were of particular importance to the Greeks in ancient times, but not just for eating. In democratic Greece the shells of oysters or mussels, called *ostraka,* were used as ballots. Voters would inscribe their choice of candidates in the mother-of-pearl lining of the shell and then cast their ballots. And a purple dye, the imperial color, was made from a sea snail.

Apicius, the great Roman gourmet, loved shellfish and advised pickling them in a vinegar brine, a dish that we still enjoy today. Certainly the Seafood Salad, Roman Style (page 185) is a descendant of Apicius's ingenuity.

The Shrimp and Oyster Sauce (page 173) and the Shrimp in Greek Tomato Sauce with Feta (page 182) will become favorites for you, I am sure.

You might also consider:

Shrimp Chowed with Water-Chestnut Flour and Gin (page 429)

CHINA

‖ LIVE DRUNKEN SHRIMP ‖

I hesitate to tell you about this dish, but I have decided I can chance it with you. By this time we understand one another and you know that I will try anything, any food anywhere at any time, at least once.

In Hong Kong a very strange dish is offered. I do not think it really worth the effort, but it is good. A large glass casserole is brought to your table with quite a bit of Chinese rice wine in the bottom of the dish. The lid is removed and live shrimp are dumped into the heavy wine. They sit still for a moment and then, as the wine intoxicates them, they begin jumping about. They then begin banging themselves on the lid, jumping about in such a violent manner that it is amusing. They are drunk! The shellfish are then removed from the wine bath and dropped into rapidly boiling Chinese Chicken Soup Stock. They die instantly, of course, but when they are served you can certainly taste the wine that they imbibed. A light dipping sauce accompanies this very Hong Kong dish.

There are two reasons why I expect that you will not try this dish in this country. First, your children will think you heartless, though they will eat a hamburger, never having met the cow. Second, it is very difficult to find fresh lively shrimp in this country. So . . . go to Hong Kong. It is one of the most fascinating cities in the world.

VELVET PRAWNS

SERVES 3–4 AS
PART OF A CHINESE MEAL

The process of "velveting" a food is a Chinese invention of great importance. The flavor of the food is preserved, the texture is enhanced by the process, and the end result will just blow your socks off! It is very easy to do.

½ *pound large prawns,*
30–35 count per pound

THE BATTER

2 *egg whites*

2 *tablespoons cornstarch*

⅛ *teaspoon salt*

4 *cups peanut oil for deep-frying*

Peel the shrimp, leaving the tail attached. Cut the shrimp down the back side so that they can be opened and "butterflied."

Mix well the ingredients for the batter. Marinate the prawns in this mixture, refrigerated, for ½ hour. Heat the oil to between 280° and 300° and deep-fry the shrimp. When the shrimp turn white and float they are cooked. Do not overcook them as they will not turn the least bit brown at this temperature. Drain well and serve or quickly chow with a favorite sauce.

PRAWNS WITH CHILI SAUCE

SERVES 4 AS
PART OF A CHINESE MEAL

The seafood in Hong Kong is just unbelievable. Craig, my cooking assistant, and I tried a new restaurant every night for two weeks and took our camera crew with us most of the time. It is hard to get a bad meal in this city since the competition is so severe and the seafood so fresh.

This dish is from the Peking Garden in Hong Kong.

½ pound large prawns,
30–35 count per pound

MARINADE
3 eggs, beaten
⅛ teaspoon baking powder
¾ cup cornstarch

4 cups peanut oil for deep-frying

THE SAUCE
1 tablespoon fresh peanut oil

1 large clove garlic, diced very fine
1 teaspoon garlic and red chili paste (page 30)
Pinch of sugar
1 teaspoon rice wine vinegar or Chinese red vinegar
2 tablespoons Chinese rice wine or dry sherry
1 tablespoon light soy sauce

Peel the prawns and slice them halfway through down the back in order to butterfly them. Mix the marinade and add the shrimp. Refrigerate for 15 minutes.

Heat the oil for deep-frying to 360° and deep-fry the shrimp for 3 to 4 minutes. Drain and set aside.

Heat another wok and add the fresh peanut oil for the sauce. Chow the garlic for a moment and then add all remaining ingredients. Toss until the sauce is hot and then add the shrimp. Toss until all is hot again and serve.

STEAMED SHRIMP WITH SPECIAL SAUCE

*SERVES 6–8 AS
PART OF A CHINESE MEAL*

The shrimp used in this dish at the Oi Mann restaurant in Lau Fau Shan, Hong Kong, are fresh, of course. You can see them alive in a tank outside as you go in to enjoy your meal. In this country shrimp are hard to find live but do not pass up this dish simply because you must use frozen shrimp. Just be sure that they smell fresh and still have the shell on.

1 *pound large prawns or shrimp, shell on, 30–35 count per pound*

THE SAUCE
(THIS IS WHAT DOES IT!)

2 *small red or green fresh hot peppers,* or both, *seeded and sliced* very thin

2 *tablespoons light soy sauce*

1 *tablespoon* hot *peanut oil*

Place the shrimp, shell still intact, in a bamboo steamer rack (page 19). Have the water in the steamer boiling before you put the shrimp rack in the steamer. Steam until the shrimp change color and are hot all the way through, about 6 minutes.

In the meantime, clean the peppers for the sauce by removing the seeds and slicing the pods. Place the slices in a small dish and add the soy. Heat the peanut oil in a wok until it is just smoking hot. Pour the oil into the peppers. Be careful with this as it will spit at you!

Serve the shrimp on a large platter with the sauce in a dipping dish in the center of the platter. Each guest will shell the shrimp and dip them in the sauce. Then each guest will give you a hug! This is powerful stuff.

SHRIMP AND OYSTER SAUCE

SERVES 4–5 AS
PART OF A CHINESE MEAL

This is a regular dish on the menu of really good Chinese restaurants in this country, and it is just as popular in Hong Kong. You may have seen this dish with the title "Shrimp and Lobster Sauce," since the sauce can also be used on lobster. Who can afford lobster? Try this one with good shrimp or prawns.

1 *pound shrimp, 30–40 per pound count*

1 *tablespoon dry sherry or Chinese rice wine*

1 *tablespoon light soy sauce*

1 *tablespoon peanut oil for chowing*

¼ *pound pork, coarsely ground*

2 *cloves garlic, chopped fine or crushed*

2 *slices fresh ginger, each the size of a 25-cent piece, cut julienne*

2 *teaspoons fermented black beans* (dow see), *rinsed*

3 *green onions, chopped*

Dash of MSG (optional)

¼ *teaspoon sugar*

2 *tablespoons oyster sauce*

½ *cup Chinese Chicken Soup Stock (page 113) or canned chicken stock*

1 *teaspoon cornstarch mixed with 1 tablespoon water*

1 *egg, beaten*

Peel the shrimp and marinate in the soy and wine for 15 minutes.

In the meantime, heat a wok and add ½ tablespoon of the oil. Chow the pork and remove the meat to the serving dish, leaving the oil in the wok. Heat the wok again and add the rest of the oil. Chow the garlic, ginger, and black beans for a moment and then add the shrimp, drained of the marinade. Chow on high heat until the shrimp have changed color and are just barely tender, about 3 minutes. Add all remaining ingredients, including the cooked pork, with the exception of the egg. Stir until a sauce forms and then stir in the egg. Serve immediately.

SHRIMP AND PEPPERS ON AN IRON PLATE

SERVES 6 AS
PART OF A CHINESE MEAL

The rage, it's the rage, in Hong Kong, New York, and San Francisco. Actually, sometimes the rage is quite delicious. The principle behind this dish is a round iron plate that is heated and brought to the table; then the cooked food is dumped on this murderously hot plate. The steam, the sizzling of the food on the metal, the hot oil from the peppers now in the air . . . the whole production is very dramatic. This is a delicious seafood version of the Hong Kong "in" dish.

1 *pound whole shrimp, 25 to 35 per pound, peeled*

MARINADE

2 *tablespoons Chinese rice wine or dry sherry*

2 *tablespoons light soy sauce*

¼ *teaspoon ground white pepper*

1 *egg white, beaten*

1 *teaspoon cornstarch*

2 *tablespoons peanut oil for chowing*

¼ *teaspoon salt*

2 *cloves garlic, chopped fine or crushed*

1 *slice ginger, the size of a 25-cent piece, cut julienne*

4 *small green or red hot peppers, seeded and sliced*

Hot red crushed pepper flakes to taste or *hot red pepper oil*

4 *green onions, chopped Chinese style (page 142)*

8 *water chestnuts, sliced*

Sesame oil for garnish

Mix the marinade and soak the shrimp in this for 20 minutes.

Put the iron plate on the stove to get very hot. (You can use a black frying pan for this and later just set it on a piece of wood on the table.)

Heat the wok and add the oil, salt, garlic, and ginger. Add the peppers and pepper flakes or oil, and chow for a moment. Throw the shrimp, drained, into the wok. Chow until the shrimp are done to taste and then add the green onions and water chestnuts. Garnish with the sesame oil and remove to a serving plate. Quickly take the serving plate to the dining room while someone else brings in the iron plate or frying pan. Pour the shrimp into the pan *after* warning everyone to hold up their cloth napkins in front of them to prevent the hot gases from the oil from getting in their eyes. Hold the napkins high and peek over the top so that all can see the shrimp sizzle on the iron plate.

This is fun to serve!

SCALLOPS WITH GARLIC CHIVES

SERVES 5–6 AS
PART OF A CHINESE MEAL

I love scallops and I love garlic chives. When I tasted this dish in Hong Kong I decided that I was in heaven. You may have trouble finding garlic chives in this country unless you live in a city with a large China-town. Otherwise, use regular chives, or even green onions, and the dish will still be most delightful.

2 *tablespoons peanut oil*

2 *cloves garlic, diced very fine*

1 *slice fresh ginger the size of a 25-cent piece, cut very thin julienne*

¾ *pound large scallops, cut in half through the middle*

1 *cup garlic chives, cut into ½-inch pieces,* or regular *American chives or green onions*

THE SAUCE

1 *teaspoon rice wine vinegar or Chinese red vinegar*

½ *teaspoon salt*

2 *tablespoons Chinese rice wine or dry sherry*

¼ *teaspoon ground white pepper*

¼ *cup Chinese Chicken Soup Stock (page 113)*

1 *tablespoon cornstarch mixed with 1 tablespoon water*

Unless you are really fast in the kitchen I suggest you cut the scallops and mix the sauce before you do anything else. You must not overcook this dish. Cut the chives as well.

Heat a wok and add the oil. Chow the garlic and ginger for just a moment and then add the scallops. Chow for 2 minutes or so and add the chives. Stir the sauce and then add it to the wok. Stir-fry until all is thick and hot.

This light and flavorful dish is great as the focal point of a Chinese meal, or it is delicious served with rice as a regular Chinese meal.

VELVETED SCALLOPS IN CELERY

SERVES 4–6 AS
PART OF A CHINESE MEAL

We tasted this dish in Hong Kong, and I cannot remember where. It sounds complex, but, as is typical of most Chinese cooking, it is not. The rules are always the same. Have the wok hot and do not overcook.

MARINADE

2 egg whites

2 tablespoons cornstarch

⅛ teaspoon salt

¾ pound large scallops, cut in half through the middle

SAUCE

⅛ teaspoon salt

2 tablespoons Chinese rice wine or dry sherry

¼ cup Chinese Chicken Soup Stock (page 113)

1 tablespoon cornstarch mixed with 1 tablespoon water

4–5 cups peanut oil for deep frying

1 tablespoon peanut oil

1 clove garlic, chopped very fine

⅛ teaspoon grated fresh ginger

3 green onions, chopped

1 cup chopped Chinese celery leaves, or regular celery leaves

Mix the ingredients for the marinade and add the scallops. Refrigerate for 20 minutes while preparing the other ingredients.

Mix the ingredients for the sauce and set aside.

Heat the oil to between 280° and 300°. Deep-fry the drained scallops for just a few minutes, until they turn white and begin to float. Drain and set aside.

Heat a wok and add the oil, garlic, and ginger. Chow for a moment and then add the green onions and celery leaves. Stir-fry for just a moment and then add the drained scallops. Toss for a moment until all is hot and add the mixed sauce. Stir until all is thickened and hot. Serve immediately.

SCALLOPS IN SZECHWAN SPICY SAUCE

*SERVES 4–5 AS
PART OF A CHINESE MEAL*

The Maxim's restaurants in Hong Kong just amaze me. Normally, when you find out that a restaurant is a part of a chain, you are prepared for a rather "chain" meal. This is not so with this company. I can recommend them over and over again, though they have restaurants offering several different kinds of Chinese cuisine.

This dish is from the Szechwan Garden in Hong Kong.

4–5 *cups peanut oil for deep-frying*

¾ *pound large scallops, cut in half through the middle*

SAUCE

1 or 2 *dried red chile peppers, seeded, soaked for 1 hour in water, then drained and chopped*

2 *tablespoons light soy sauce*

Pinch of sugar

½ *tablespoon rice wine vinegar or Chinese red vinegar*

1 *tablespoon dry sherry or Chinese rice wine*

2 *tablespoons fresh peanut oil*

½ *teaspoon finely grated fresh ginger*

2 *cloves garlic, chopped fine*

6 *green onions, cut Chinese style (page 142)*

Heat the deep-frying oil to 360° and deep-fry the scallops for just a few minutes. Drain and set aside.

Mix the ingredients for the sauce and set aside. Heat a wok and add the oil, ginger, and garlic and chow for a moment. Add the green onions and the scallops. Toss for a few seconds and add the sauce mixture. Stir-fry until all is hot and serve immediately.

CRAB IN BLACK BEAN SAUCE

SERVE 3–5 AS PART OF A CHINESE MEAL, DEPENDING ON THE SIZE OF THE CRAB

Jason will not eat most shellfish. When he was very little he told me that he was not interested in shellfish, not interested at all. So I cooked this dish for him one day and I had him hooked. He is convinced that this is the best crab dish possible. I think I agree.

1 large fresh Dungeness crab

THE SAUCE

2 tablespoons peanut oil

2 cloves garlic, chopped fine

1 tablespoon fermented black beans (dow see)

2 tablespoons Chinese rice wine or dry sherry

2 tablespoons light soy sauce

Pinch of sugar

1 tablespoon sesame oil

6 green onions, sliced Chinese style (page 142)

1 egg, beaten

If the crab is alive, plunge it into boiling water and simmer for 15 minutes. If the crab has been precooked, you may omit this step.

Remove the shell and clean out the crab by removing the long spongy gray gills. Leave the rest of the roe and liquid in the crab. Break the legs off the crab, leaving them whole, and then break the body into 4 pieces.

Heat a wok and add the oil and the garlic. Rinse the black beans quickly and add them to the wok. Chow this for just a moment and then add the rest of the sauce ingredients. Chow until all is hot and then add the crab pieces. Stir-fry for a couple of minutes and add the green onions. Chow until all is hot and stir in the egg. Stir until the sauce thickens a bit. Serve immediately.

GARLIC-STEAMED LOBSTER OR CRAB

This is a dish that I can only describe. It is just wonderful and terribly simple, and comes from the Oi Mann restaurant in the Lau Fau Shan fishing village that I described earlier.

The dish is easy to prepare and the results are spectacular. One need simply have a very fresh or a live lobster. Plunge it into boiling water to kill it quickly. Remove and drain. Cut the lobster in half the long way and drench it with peanut oil mixed with as much garlic as you wish, or can stand. Place the halves in a bamboo steamer (page 19) and steam until very tender, about 15 minutes.

Garnish with green onion slivers and chopped Chinese parsley.

CRAB WITH SOYBEAN CONDIMENT

SERVES 3–5 AS PART OF A CHINESE MEAL, DEPENDING ON THE SIZE OF THE CRAB

I found this recipe in San Francisco. The Chinese food in San Francisco rivals any Chinese food anywhere, except Hong Kong. And that includes mainland China, as far as I can tell.

This is a simple dish to prepare and therefore "frugal." I simply will not discuss the cost of Dungeness crab. Whatever it is when you go to get one, it will be worth it.

1 large Dungeness crab

SAUCE

1 tablespoon peanut oil

1 clove garlic, chopped fine

½ teaspoon grated fresh ginger

2 tablespoons soybean condiment (mein see)

3 green onions, cut Chinese style (page 142)

Pinch of sugar

2 tablespoons light soy sauce

2 tablespoons Chinese rice wine or dry sherry

1 teaspoon cornstarch mixed with 1 tablespoon water, for thickening

Prepare the crab for chowing just as you would for the recipe for Crab in Black Bean Sauce, above.

Heat a wok and add the peanut oil, garlic, and ginger. Stir-fry for just a moment or two and then add the remaining ingredients for the sauce. Add the crab pieces and chow until all is hot. Thicken with the cornstarch and water mixture and serve.

FRIED MILK WITH CRABMEAT

SERVES 4 AS PART OF A CHINESE MEAL

I cannot tell you enough about the glories of Hong Kong. On my first visit a few years ago, I wandered into the Jade Palace Restaurant, at the Star Ferry Dock Terminal. I could not imagine what they could do with fried milk and crab, so I ordered the dish. This is as close as I can come to this great delicacy, and my rendition is pretty close. You will enjoy this.

5 egg whites

½ teaspoon salt

1½ tablespoons cornstarch

¾ cup cold milk

½ pound fresh crabmeat, cleaned

¼ cup peanut oil for cooking

SAUCE

1 teaspoon sesame oil

1 teaspoon light soy sauce

Pinch of ground white pepper

GARNISH

1 tablespoon Virginia ham slivers or Italian ham slivers

1 tablespoon chopped Chinese parsley

Whip the egg whites by hand until they are frothy. Add the salt. Blend the milk and cornstarch together and combine with the crabmeat. Gently fold in the egg whites.

Heat the oil in a SilverStone-lined 12-inch frying pan to normal scrambled-egg cooking temperature. Pour in the crab and egg mixture and cook over a medium flame, stirring gently until the mixture sets up. Add the sauce ingredients as the dish comes to completion. Do not brown.

Put on a serving platter and add the garnishes.

GREECE

SHRIMP ANANIUS

SERVES 2 FOR DINNER
OR 4 AS A FIRST COURSE

In about 550 B.C. there lived in Greece a poet named Ananius. He was a great lover of shrimp and he described a recipe he called his favorite. Theresa Karas Yianilos, in her wonderful little book, *The Complete Greek Cookbook,* has worked out the directions. It is interesting to see what the Greeks were eating 2,500 years ago. It sounds to me very much like yuppie food from the Upper East Side of Manhattan.

1 *pound large shrimp,*	1 *cup dry white wine or*
unpeeled, 30–35 count per	*beer*
pound	$\frac{1}{2}$ *teaspoon marjoram*
1 *cup water*	$\frac{1}{2}$ *teaspoon salt*

Bring the water, wine or beer, and seasonings to a full rolling boil. Plunge in the shrimp. Allow the liquid to come to a boil again and boil the shrimp for 2 minutes. Drain the liquid and serve.

SHRIMP IN
GREEK TOMATO SAUCE
WITH FETA

SERVES 4–6

When I first saw the old cook preparing this dish in Athens I was fascinated. He used small Greek clay casseroles and placed them directly on a high gas burner. The flames would leap about the casserole and thus bring everything to temperature in just a short time. It is one of the finest shrimp dishes that I know, and it is actually very easy to prepare.

By the way, I think you need to know that the term "casserole" comes from the Greek word *katsarola,* which simply refers to a baking pot. The Greeks invented the concept of the casserole . . . another one of the things for which they have not been given proper credit.

You will like this dish. I demonstrated this method of cooking shrimp before two thousand chefs and eaters in New Orleans. Coals to Newcastle! They loved it . . . and we were doing the demonstration in order to raise funds for a wonderful school for retarded children. Sister Lillian runs St. Michael's School, and I am convinced she must be one of God's favorite people. So, when you eat this dish think of St. Michael's . . . or just send them a check. They need it.

2 cups Greek Tomato Sauce
   (page 204)
½ cup clam juice or Fish
   Stock (page 126)

1½ pounds large shrimp in
   the shell, 30–35 count
   per pound
½ pound imported feta
   cheese, sliced ¼ inch thick

Mix the clam juice with the tomato sauce. Place the shrimp, shells intact, in the bottom of a 12-inch SilverStone-lined frying pan or casserole. Cover with the sauce and top with the sliced cheese. Place the pan on high heat and bring to a rapid simmer, covered. Reduce the heat and cook until the shrimp are done to your liking, about 7 to 10 minutes. Stir in the cheese and serve. Many people eat the shell and all!

NOTE: If you are preparing this dish on an electric stove rather than gas, have the burner preheated to High before placing the pan on the burner.

VARIATION: You may also bake this dish in a 475° oven, uncovered, for about 15 minutes or until all is very hot and bubbly.

BABY SNAILS IN GREEK TOMATO SAUCE

The Greeks call them snails but we call them periwinkles, or tiny snails. They are served as a first course in Greece and they are wonderful. Don't worry about the distressing sound that you must make in order to suck them out of the shell. Everyone else will either understand or be jealous!

Buy the tiny snails in a good fish market or in Chinatown. The Chinese love these as well. Rinse them several times by rubbing them together a bit in order to get rid of the mud. Place some Greek Tomato Sauce (page 204) in a saucepan and bring it to a simmer. Add a few tablespoons of olive oil and pour in the drained snails. Simmer until they are tender, about 6 minutes.

This is a first course that will stop your guests in their tracks, though they are a bit of an effort to eat. Just suck out the meat and have a sip of good Greek wine.

FRIED SHRIMP PIRAEUS

This is how they do it at the famous harbor in Athens. It is so simple that it is embarrassing, but you must remember that olive oil is the secret. Do not substitute vegetable oil. Blah!

Dust whole shrimp with flour. Fry in deep pan with 2 inches of olive oil for 3 minutes. Drain and serve.

That is it. Cook as much as you like and you will certainly compliment your guests.

ITALY

BABY SNAILS IN ITALIAN TOMATO SAUCE

When you go to Rome you must eat at the Da Franco seafood restaurant. Every course is fish and the price is fixed. It is not at all expensive and the place is delightful. You might have such a dish on your visit there.

Cook small snails just as you do in the Greek recipe above, but use Italian Tomato Sauce (page 208) instead. And NO, don't put grated cheese on fish of any kind, at least not for me.

SEAFOOD SALAD, ROMAN STYLE
(Vecchia Roma)

SERVES 8–10
AS A FIRST COURSE FOR AN
ITALIAN MEAL

When the owner of the wonderful Vecchia Roma restaurant near the Jewish Ghetto of Rome told me that he put mayonnaise in his seafood salad, I was a bit curious. But when Antonio Palladino told me that I would love it, I watched closely. He makes his own mayonnaise and uses just a touch. This recipe is superb!

2½ pounds octopus, pounded, washed, simmered until tender (about 2 hours and 15 minutes, covered)

24 mussels

½ pound bay scallops

½ pound medium shrimp

1½ pounds squid, cleaned and cut into ½-inch circles (page 188)

1 white onion, peeled and sliced

1 cup chopped celery

½ cup chopped parsley

DRESSING

½ cup olive oil

⅓ cup white wine vinegar

3 tablespoons mayonnaise

1 teaspoon whole, crushed oregano

Freshly ground black pepper to taste

Salt to taste, if necessary

Cook the octopus in water to cover. Remove from the water and let cool, reserving the liquid. Clean the tentacles by washing off the membranes. Save the suction cups for the salad. Then slice the tentacles and set aside.

In the same liquid simmer the mussels until they just open. Remove and cool, then take them from the shells. Set aside.

To the same pot add enough water to poach the scallops, shrimp, and cleaned squid. Poach these separately, using the same water. Remove and allow to cool. Peel the shrimp.

Allow all seafood ingredients to cool and then place in a large bowl with the onion, celery, and parsley. Toss with the mixed salad dressing.

SQUID

Yes, I will admit that they are ugly. Squid do not look attractive on the plate if you are serving them whole, but please understand that squid has been extremely popular in all three of our ancient cuisines since the seventh century. If you had been raised eating these creatures you would cease to call them ugly. They are delicious!

The Chinese dry them and then restore the meat during the wintertime. The Greeks stew them, make salad with them, and deep-fry them. When fried squid come to the table with Garlic Sauce (page 206) I am overjoyed. And when I have a cold squid salad in Rome I begin to feel sorry for Americans who demean this unattractive cephalopod.

Squid is probably the most underutilized seafood in American waters. But there seems to be some hope for us as we, as a people, are beginning to enjoy this creature, an enjoyment that our three ancient cuisines have celebrated for as long as they can remember.

You might also like to consider:

Hot and Spicy Squid *(page 109)*
Steamed Pork with Mushrooms and Dried Squid *(page 339)*

CHINA

SQUID BALLS

SERVES 6–8 AS
PART OF A CHINESE MEAL

Squid is a marvelously versatile food product, and it is not expensive. Americans feel a bit squeamish about eating one of the great denizens of the deep but we are being silly. Squid, like shrimp, may not look attractive when they are live in a basket, but they certainly are when cooked and ready to eat.

This is a wonderful way of getting into squid. It takes little time to prepare and it will certainly convince your squid skeptics that they must convert and join us squid lovers.

1 *pound squid, cleaned and drained*

1 *tablespoon pork fat, chopped*

¼ *teaspoon freshly grated ginger*

1 *teaspoon Chinese rice wine or dry sherry*

½ *teaspoon salt*

¼ *teaspoon MSG (optional)*

1 *egg white*

1 *tablespoon cornstarch*

4–6 *cups peanut oil for frying*

Place all of the ingredients except the cooking oil in a food processor and work to a smooth paste. Form into small balls ¾ inch in diameter. Heat oil to 350° and fry the balls in 3 batches, cooking them until they float. Remove and drain in a colander and bowl. Increase the temperature of the oil to 375° and fry all of the balls a second time, all at once, until light and golden.

These may be served with Szechwan Pepper and Salt Dip (page 202) or with the following sauce:

THE SAUCE
1 *tablespoon peanut oil*
1 *teaspoon fresh ginger, cut julienne*
Pinch of sugar
3 *tablespoons light soy sauce*

1 *tablespoon rice wine vinegar or Chinese red vinegar*
½ *teaspoon garlic and red chili paste (page 30)*

Chow all of the above ingredients together and then throw in the squid balls. Chow until the balls are hot. Serve immediately.

HINT: HOW TO CLEAN SQUID. Squid is probably the most maligned creature from the sea. You remember the great stories from Jules Verne's classics about gigantic squid that swim under the sea. What a horrible fright to put upon the squid lovers of the world. While it is true that squid grow to great length, the kind that you and I buy in a fish market, either frozen or fresh, are little rascals, being about 5 or 6 inches long total. They are easy to clean. You simply cut the head off each and remove the filling from the tube, or body. Don't forget the plasticlike backbone of the squid. You will find it within the tube of the fish while digging around. Rinse the tubes, and you are ready to begin. I also save the tentacles, though not the head, for other dishes.

HINT: ON COOKING SQUID. The rule is simple. Never sauté the squid *more* than three minutes . . . and never stew or simmer the fish *less* than twenty minutes.

Two Squid, Chowed

SERVES 6–8 AS
PART OF A CHINESE MEAL

You see dried squid waving in the breeze all over the harbor in Aberdeen, in Hong Kong. It is a staple for the wintertime but it can be enjoyed at other seasons, of course. In this case you cook dried squid along with fresh squid, thus giving the name to the dish.

¼ pound dried squid, soaked for 24 hours (Change the water at least twice)

1 pound fresh squid, cleaned but not cut (page 188)

2 tablespoons peanut oil

½ teaspoon salt

2 cloves garlic, chopped fine

1 teaspoon finely grated fresh ginger

2 tablespoons light soy sauce

3 green onions, cut Chinese style (page 142)

½ teaspoon garlic and red chili paste (page 30)

1 teaspoon sesame oil

2 tablespoons Chinese rice wine or dry sherry

Pinch of sugar

½ teaspoon MSG (optional)

White pepper, ground, to taste

½ tablespoon cornstarch mixed with 1 tablespoon water

Rinse the soaked dried squid and clean. Be sure to remove the cuttle-bone in the bag. Remove the head and score the back side of the squid by cutting just into the skin with a cleaver. Make long cuts and then angled cuts so that you have a trellis pattern cut into the skin. Do not cut all the way through. (See illustration.) Cut the squid into 1-inch-wide pieces, cutting across the squid body. Set aside.

Clean the fresh squid and slit the creature down the belly so that you can open it into one piece. Cut a trellis pattern as above and then into 1-inch-wide pieces. Set aside.

Heat a wok and chow the oil, salt, garlic, and ginger. Chow for just a moment and then add the dried squid pieces. Chow for 2 minutes and add the fresh squid. Chow for 2 minutes and add the remaining ingredients except the cornstarch and water. Chow until all is hot and then thicken with the cornstarch mixed with water.

This is great served with a vegetable course and lots of rice. You can make it much hotter by adding more garlic and red chili paste.

DEEP-FRIED SQUID WITH SPICED SALT

This is a terrific dish and a bit different from the usual deep-fried squid that everyone is eating in the Greek restaurants.

Clean the squid and cut it into ½-inch circles (page 188). Dust with flour and deep-fry at 360° until barely golden. Do not overcook as it will get tough.

Serve with Szechwan Pepper and Salt Dip (page 202).

ITALY

SQUID SALAD

SERVES 6
AS A FIRST COURSE

The secret to this great delicacy is not to cook the squid too long. If it is undercooked it is rubbery, and if it is overcooked it is rubbery. So, either quickly blanch it or cook it for 20 minutes. There is no middle road.

Many Americans say that they do not like squid. I had this dish in several places in Rome, as well as in San Francisco, and I still contend that anyone who likes seafood will love this dish.

I picked up the allspice addition from the Plaza Café on the corner of Thirty-fourth Street and Eighth Avenue in New York. A very nice place for lunch!

1½ pounds fresh squid, cleaned and cut into ½-inch circles (page 188)

1 cup chopped celery

1 yellow onion, medium, peeled and sliced

DRESSING

⅓ cup olive oil

¼ cup white wine vinegar

1 teaspoon whole oregano, crushed

¼ teaspoon allspice

½ cup chopped parsley

Salt and freshly ground black pepper to taste

Lemon wedges for garnish

Clean and cut the squid. Blanch in ample boiling water just until the circles curl, about 30 to 60 seconds. Drain and place the squid, along with the celery and onion, in a salad bowl. Mix the dressing and toss. Garnish with the lemon wedges and chill for a short time before serving.

SEAFOOD SALAD DA FRANCO

Da Franco restaurant in Rome is a scene! All the courses are seafood and the price is set. Not at all expensive and you will have one of the most enjoyable meals in Rome. Why am I telling you this when I probably will never be able to get into the place again!

The seafood salad consists of the following:

Octopus, cooked and sliced

Squid, cleaned and blanched

Shrimp, peeled and cooked

The flavors that make this salad so wonderful come from fresh fennel bulb, yellow onion, and celery, all sautéed in olive oil and chilled. These are tossed with the chilled seafood along with a good deal of parsley and a nice olive oil and lemon juice dressing, with just a shot of wine vinegar. The result is delicious.

DEEP-FRIED SQUID, ITALIAN STYLE
(Calamari Fritti)

Clean the squid and cut into ½-inch circles. Dust with seasoned flour and deep-fry at 360° until the pieces are barely golden, about 3 minutes. Serve with ample fresh lemon wedges and you have the dish, Roman style. They have been eating it this way for a long time.

SQUID IN ITALIAN TOMATO SAUCE

The ease with which you can prepare this dish will amaze you. Just remember that you must not overcook this dish. Taste often!

Clean and cut the squid into ½-inch circles (page 188). Place the squid in a saucepan and add a bit of Italian Tomato Sauce (page 208) and a few shots of dry red wine. Bring to a simmer and cook for a few minutes until tender. Taste regularly so that you do not overcook this dish.

GREECE

SQUID PILAF
(Kalamaria Pilafi)

SERVES 6
AS A DINNER

This is a wonderful dish that is common throughout the Greek Islands. It is easy to prepare and the results are just short of spectacular.

1½ *pounds squid, cleaned*
and cut into ½-inch circles
(page 188)

½ *cup olive oil*

3 *cloves garlic, crushed*

½ *cup chopped yellow onion*

¼ *cup finely chopped celery*

¼ *cup dry red wine*

½ *cup Greek Tomato Sauce*
(page 204)

¼ *cup chopped parsley*

¼ *cup finely chopped green*
onion

1 *teaspoon salt*

Freshly ground black
pepper to taste

2¼ *cups boiling water*

1 *cup long-grain rice*

Clean and cut the squid and chop the tentacles into small pieces. Heat a 12-inch frying pan and add the oil, garlic, onion, and celery, and sauté until the onion is clear. Add the prepared squid and the remaining ingredients except the water and rice. Bring to a simmer and cook for 20 minutes, covered.

Stir in the rice. Add the water, bring to a boil, and turn to a simmer. Cook, covered, for 25 minutes or until the rice is done. Additional salt may be added if needed.

SQUID WITH LEMON AND OIL

It is very common for Greek cooks to simply clean squid and cook it, unsliced, in a hot frying pan with a bit of olive oil. Salt and pepper are added when served, along with a good deal of fresh lemon juice. This is the easiest of favorites!

SQUID AND SPINACH

How easy can a dish be? This is a common way of serving squid in Greece and I enjoyed it several times. The recipe need only be described.

Clean the squid and cut into ½-inch circles (page 188). Wash 2 bunches of spinach and chop. Drain well.

Cook squid in olive oil and garlic for just a few minutes. Add spinach, cover pot, and cook down. Add lemon juice and salt before serving.

STUFFED SQUID, GREEK STYLE

SERVES 4–6
AS A REGULAR MEAL

After eating so much squid in Greece one has to ask what the Greeks would eat if squid did not exist. I am flabbergasted by the variations on a common theme that the Greek cook has managed to create. This one is a jewel.

12 squid, cleaned (page 188), with tentacles removed

3 tablespoons olive oil

2 cloves garlic, chopped fine

1 medium yellow onion, peeled and chopped medium fine

⅔ cup long-grain rice

2 medium tomatoes, ripe, chopped medium fine

1 bunch spinach, carefully washed and chopped medium

½ cup Fish Stock (page 126) or Basic Chicken Stock (page 129)

SAUCE

½ cup additional Fish Stock or Basic Chicken Stock

¼ teaspoon oregano

⅛ teaspoon dried mint

Juice of 1 lemon

Salt and freshly ground black pepper to taste

Clean the squid and chop the tentacles (page 188). Heat a large frying pan and add the olive oil, garlic, and onion. Sauté until the onion is clear, and stir in the rice. Add the chopped tomatoes, spinach, and tentacles, and the ½ cup stock, and simmer, covered, for 8 minutes. Allow this mixture to cool a bit. Stuff the squid tubes with the rice mixture and place them in a stove-top casserole.

Mix the sauce and pour over the squid. Cover and bring to a simmer. Cook until tender, about 20 minutes.

VARIATION: You might try adding a bit of dill to this dish as well. It is typical of the Islands.

OCTOPUS

I am always amused by the look on the face of a person who is tasting octopus for the first time. It is a wonderful food, if it is cooked properly, and it is not difficult to prepare.

The Chinese seem to ignore these creatures, except in a dried form, but the Romans and Greeks have eaten them fresh since ancient times. The Greeks pound the meat on a rock in order to tenderize it a bit and then grill it. It is wonderful. And the Romans still make wisecracks about the octopus being an aphrodisiac . . . . a belief they have held since the first century.

Try these recipes and you will be converted into an octopus lover. If you have trouble finding the meat, come and see me in Seattle. I have scuba-diving friends who love to "wrestle" octopus in the bay in front of my office. What some people will do for kicks!

GREECE

OCTOPUS SPAGHETTI ZORBA

SERVES 4–6 AS A MAIN COURSE

There is a restaurant in Delphi run by a strange fellow named Niki. His mother is behind most of the recipes in the place but he does a very decent job. This dish is excellent.

$1\frac{3}{4}$ *pounds octopus tentacles*

$\frac{1}{2}$ *teaspoon salt*

$\frac{1}{2}$ *cup olive oil*

1 *yellow onion, peeled and chopped*

2 *cloves garlic, chopped fine*

2 *cups Greek Tomato Sauce (page 204)*

$\frac{1}{4}$ *cup dry red wine*

Salt and pepper to taste

$\frac{1}{2}$ *pound dry pasta (I like fettucini for this dish)*

Juice of 1 lemon

Place the octopus in a stockpot along with about $3\frac{1}{2}$ cups of water. Add the teaspoon of salt and bring to a simmer, covered. Cook for about 1 hour. You may need to add more water as it cooks away. When the octopus is tender, remove from the pot, reserving the broth. Allow the tentacles to cool and wash off the purple membrane. Cut the tentacles up into pieces about $\frac{1}{2}$ inch thick. Chop the suction cups and return the meat to the broth and add the remaining ingredients, except the pasta and lemon juice. Simmer for an additional hour. Drain the broth from the pot and measure to be sure that you have 4 cups of liquid. If not, make up the difference with water. Return the liquid to the pot and add the pasta and cook, covered, just until tender. Add the fresh lemon juice and serve immediately.

OCTOPUS IN WINE
AND TOMATO SAUCE

SERVES 6–8

This is the easy way to enjoy a dish that is very common, but very much appreciated, in the Greek tavernas. It is rich and tender, none of that rubbery texture that you are so nervous about.

¼ cup olive oil

2 cloves garlic, chopped fine

1 medium yellow onion, peeled and chopped

3 pounds octopus tentacles, washed and sliced into ½-inch pieces

1 cup dry red wine

4 very ripe tomatoes, chopped

½ cup Greek Tomato Sauce (page 204)

1 cup water

Salt and freshly ground black pepper to taste

Heat an 8-quart covered stove-top casserole and add the oil and garlic. Sauté for a few minutes and then add the onions and cook until they are transparent. Add all remaining ingredients and cover. Simmer until the octopus is tender, about 2 hours or so. You may need to add additional water during the cooking process.

Check for salt and pepper before serving.

Generally this is served over rice and it makes a fine meal.

OCTOPUS SALAD,
GREEK STYLE

This is a colorful and delicious dish, and it will shock guests who think they do not like octopus.

*Cold cooked octopus, sliced thin
(Simmer in salted water for 1½
hours and cool)*

Cucumber, sliced

Ripe tomatoes, ½-inch dice

Greek olives

Greek Salad Dressing (page 144)

Parsley for garnish

I think the best dressing for this dish is made simply from good olive oil, lemon juice, a shot of white wine vinegar, and some oregano. A little salt and pepper will help, of course.

Serve this as a main course in the summertime and as a first course during the winter.

ITALY

BABY OCTOPUS SALAD

This is one for those strong of stomach and dull of eye. These little creatures are rather cute if you are into that sort of thing, but for many they might be a little too much. This is a common salad in both Rome and Greece.

You can find the baby version of the great octopus in very large fish markets or in markets that cater to people from the Far East. Clean by pinching out the little beak that is to be found in the mouth, surrounded by the legs. Also, if you wish, you can make a tiny slit in the back of the head and squeeze out the insides. Generally this is already done on the frozen variety.

Simmer them in salted water for about 30 to 45 minutes, or until done to your taste. Drain and cool them a bit and then serve lukewarm with a good olive oil and lemon juice dressing. You might add some parsley and fresh basil as well. This is a delicious dish and I do hope you will try it.

Sauces and Condiments

SAUCES

When most Americans think of a sauce, they think of a heavy topping that often covers the food, thus dramatically changing the flavor of the main ingredient. That is not the case with our three ancient cuisines. In each of these cultures a sauce is seen as a supporter of flavor, not the flavor itself. Our habit of saucing has certainly given rise to our use of much too much sauce on pasta. We seem to think that more is better so we heap it on, thus covering the delicate flavor of the pasta itself. Not so in Rome, China, or Greece.

CHINA

The Chinese do not use sauces in the way that the Greeks or Romans, and eventually the French, used them. In good Chinese cooking you bring each food to its own point of fulfillment, and then blend it, if you wish, with other foods. Thus, each food should taste like what it is. To put it bluntly, it is considered almost immoral to cover the flavor of a food with the flavor of something else. Sauces therefore support, they do not flavor.

DIP SAUCES

One of the most common ways sauces are used in Chinese cuisine is for dipping. A food, most often meat or fish, is completed and brought to the table and one may choose to dip it in any one of the following.

These sauces are not used for actual cooking, though they could be. Instead, they are placed in little dishes on the table.

SOY AND GINGER

Just that. Grate some ginger into light soy.

JULIENNED GINGER, SOY, AND VINEGAR

The vinegar adds a wonderful touch. Try a rice vinegar or a red Chinese vinegar.

GINGER, SOY, VINEGAR, AND SESAME OIL

The sesame oil adds a great deal of depth and would therefore be used with foods stronger in flavor.

GREEN ONION SAUCE

I tasted this sauce for the first time at the Peking Garden in Hong Kong.
It is a fine place and this sauce is light and delicious.

6 *green onions, chopped*

1 *clove garlic, chopped fine*

¼ *teaspoon salt and ¼*
teaspoon pepper cooked
together (Pan-fry for a
moment or two until it
just begins to smoke)

2 *tablespoons very hot*
peanut oil poured over the
whole

Coriander, chopped, might be a nice addition.

PEPPER SAUCE FOR SEAFOOD

This is one from the wonderful Oi Mann seafood restaurant in the Lau
Fau Shan fishing village.

2 *small red or green hot*
peppers, seeded and sliced thin

1 *tablespoon light soy sauce and*
1 tablespoon dark soy sauce

3 *tablespoons hot peanut oil*
poured over the whole

SZECHWAN PEPPER AND SALT DIP

This is not actually a sauce but a dry dip. It is delicious with meats,
particularly fowl.

2 *tablespoons salt*

1 *teaspoon coarsely ground*
black pepper

1 *teaspoon Szechwan*
peppercorns (page 40)

Heat all in a frying pan until it barely begins to smoke, shaking the pan
as you heat the mixture. Remove and cool and then grind in a small
electric coffee grinder or with mortar and pestle.

CHOWING SAUCE

A real Chinese chef would probably not approve of what I am offering here since the Chinese would be more apt to mix the sauce at the
last minute, and every time. This sauce holds up well, however, and

you can keep it in the refrigerator. Just give it a shake and slosh some into the wok when you are chowing. Mix as much as you wish, given these proportions, and keep it sealed and refrigerated.

I was given this sauce by Sharon at the wonderful Mandar-Inn in Chicago's Chinatown. She would always mix it fresh, for each dish, of course, but you and I can get away with this.

1 *tablespoon dark soy sauce*	1 *tablespoon dry sherry*
1 *tablespoon light soy sauce*	½ *teaspoon white pepper*
1 *tablespoon oyster sauce*	½ *tablespoon sugar*

LOOING SAUCE

This is often called a "master sauce" since it is used in one of the major methods of cooking in China, simmering in a very rich sauce. This sauce can be used over and over again, as long as you keep it refrigerated and bring it up to boiling temperature before each use. As the flavors change and mellow you can add more of this or that and thus develop your own special master sauce.

4 *cups water*	5 *tablespoons sugar*
1 *cup light soy sauce*	4 *slices fresh ginger*
1 *cup dark soy sauce*	
1 *star anise*	GARNISH
½ *cup Chinese rice wine or* *dry sherry*	*Sesame oil*
	Green onion, chopped

Mix all together in a stainless-steel pot and bring to a boil. You can simmer any kind of meat in this that you wish, and the sauce just gets better with each use. Do not put fish of any kind in this sauce as it will be ruined, but chicken, duck, goose, quail, pork, beef, and even lamb will do nicely. A bit of sesame oil and green onion garnish are added just as the dish is served.

Remember that now and then you must add more of the ingredients to the sauce.

GREECE

The Greeks love good sauces and use them often, but they are generally cooked into the dish rather than put on top. The most famous sauce is Egg-Lemon, or *Avgolemono*. You will see it with meats, vegetables, even with pasta. The other important cooking sauces are a good tomato sauce, and of course, Basic White Sauce.

‖ GREEK TOMATO SAUCE ‖

MAKES ABOUT 6 CUPS OF SAUCE

This wonderful sauce is basic to the Greek kitchen. It is used with vegetables, fish, meats, shellfish, and even with rice. The cinnamon and allspice certainly point to the Middle Eastern or Turkish influence on Greek cooking. Make a batch of this and have it in the refrigerator at all times and you will always be ready for Greek cooking.

3 *tablespoons olive oil*

1 *yellow onion, peeled and coarsely chopped*

1 *clove garlic, chopped fine*

5 *very ripe tomatoes, cored and coarsely chopped (about 4½ cups)*

2 *tablespoons chopped parsley*

2 *teaspoons whole oregano*

1 *cup dry red wine*

1 *8-ounce can tomato sauce*

¼ *teaspoon ground cinnamon*

Pinch of ground allspice

Salt and freshly ground black pepper to taste

Heat a large SilverStone-lined frying pan and add the olive oil. Sauté the onion and garlic until clear. Add the tomatoes, parsley, and oregano. Simmer, covered, until the tomatoes are very tender, about 25 minutes. Add remaining ingredients and cook an additional 20 minutes.

NOTE: The sauce will keep well in the refrigerator for several days. Use it for any of the foods mentioned in the explanation to this recipe.

EGG-LEMON SAUCE
(Avgolemono)

I love this stuff and it is a great invention of the Greeks. It probably is the ancestor of mayonnaise and is very useful in the kitchen. Use fresh lemon juice, always . . . always.

1 cup Basic Lamb Stock (page 128) or Basic Chicken Stock (page 129)

2 tablespoons butter and 2 tablespoons flour cooked to form a roux

2 eggs

Juice of 1 lemon

2 tablespoons water

Salt and pepper to taste

Heat the Lamb or Chicken Stock and prepare the roux. Thicken the stock with the roux.

In a separate bowl whip the eggs, lemon juice, and water together until frothy. Add the egg to the thickened stock, stirring constantly. Bring to temperature but do not boil, stirring all the time until thick. Salt and pepper.

BASIC WHITE SAUCE

The more common term for this sauce is Béchamel, named for a Frenchman. However, this sauce was in use in Greece 150 years before it appeared in France so I hesitate to use the French name. One Greek writer claims that this sauce was invented in Greece three thousand years ago by a chef named Orion. In any case, the Greeks have received so little credit for what they have given the food world that even *they* call this sauce by the French name. Enough of this!

2 cups milk	Cayenne pepper to taste
3 tablespoons peeled and chopped yellow onion	½ stick (⅛ pound) butter
	3 tablespoons flour
1 bay leaf	Salt to taste

Bring the milk to a simmer. Add the yellow onion, bay leaf, and cayenne. Simmer for a few minutes and then strain the onion and bay from the milk. In another pan melt the butter, and stir in the flour. Cook for just a moment and stir this into the hot milk. Return the milk to the heat, stirring constantly until it is thick, about 10 minutes. Add salt to taste.

VARIATION: The Greeks very often add just a touch of cinnamon and/or allspice to this sauce. It is just great for meats, vegetables, or even fish.

GARLIC SAUCE
(Skorthalia)

MAKES ABOUT 2½ CUPS

This is not a cooking sauce but a dipping sauce, and believe me, when you dip into this you will know that you have eaten some garlic. It is great with fish, especially fish that has been deep-fried. I also enjoy it on vegetables, such as Eggplant Slices Baked (page 443).

1 large head garlic	½ cup white vinegar
10 slices white bread	2 tablespoons lemon juice
1 cup olive oil	3 tablespoons water

Peel and crush the garlic, the entire head. Remove the crusts from the white bread, and place the crustless bread in a mixing bowl. Add the garlic along with the olive oil and vinegar. Let this soften for 1 hour.

Beat with an electric mixer until all is smooth. Don't try this with a food processor as it will be *too* smooth. I use my KitchenAid mixer with the wire whisk. Add the lemon juice, and slowly add the water while the mixer is running so that you will have a thick and fluffy sauce.

BASIC BROWN SAUCE

MAKES 1 QUART

Many Americans think only of tomato sauce when they think of Italian food. Not so! The tomato did not arrive in Italy until the 1600s and it came from the Americas. Cheeses and oils were commonly used for sauces in Italy prior to the tomato, and they still are. A good brown sauce is also common in many regions, though this sauce will look a bit French to you. The use of thyme goes back to the early Roman Empire.

This sauce takes some doing but it is well worth it and it will keep several days in your refrigerator.

1 stick (¼ pound) butter or ½ cup olive oil

1 cup peeled and chopped yellow onion

1 cup unpeeled and chopped carrots

⅓ cup chopped parsley

1 bay leaf

1 teaspoon whole, dried thyme

½ cup flour

2 cups dry red wine

2 quarts Basic Brown Soup Stock (page 132)

2 tablespoons tomato paste

¼ teaspoon freshly ground black pepper

¼ cup dry sherry

Salt to taste

Heat a 4-quart heavy stockpot and add ½ of the butter or olive oil. Add the onions, carrots, and parsley. Sauté until the vegetables begin to lightly brown. Add the bay leaf and thyme and turn to a low simmer.

In a small frying pan melt the remaining butter or oil. Add the flour and cook, stirring, until it is light brown. Stir this roux into the vegetables. Add the remaining ingredients to the pot, except for the sherry and salt. Bring to a boil, turn to a heavy simmer, and cook the sauce, uncovered, for about 2 hours, or until it has reduced by half. Add the sherry and simmer for 5 minutes. Add salt to taste. Strain before serving or using.

ITALIAN TOMATO SAUCE

MAKES 3 QUARTS

This one is easy to prepare and very versatile in your kitchen. You will be surprised at how quickly you will use up this flavorful sauce.

This one is made without meat so that you can use it in all sorts of dishes, meat dishes included.

2 28-ounce cans tomato purée

1 6-ounce can tomato paste

1 quart Basic Chicken Stock (page 129) or 1 quart Basic Brown Soup Stock (page 132)

2 cups dry red wine

¼ cup olive oil

2 yellow onions, peeled and minced

6 large cloves garlic, chopped fine

2 ribs of celery, with leaves, minced

1 carrot, unpeeled, grated

½ cup chopped parsley

½ pound fresh mushrooms, chopped

½ teaspoon crushed red pepper flakes

1 tablespoon oregano

1 teaspoon dried rosemary

2 bay leaves, whole

1 tablespoon dried basil or 2 tablespoons fresh basil

2 cloves, whole

½ tablespoon freshly ground black pepper

2 tablespoons salt, or to taste

1 teaspoon sugar

Place the tomato purée, tomato paste, chicken or beef stock, and wine in a large pot. Heat a frying pan and add the olive oil. Sauté the onions, garlic, celery, and carrot until they just begin to brown a bit. Add to the pot along with all remaining ingredients. Bring to a light boil and then turn to a simmer. Simmer for 2 hours, partly covered. Store in the refrigerator in plastic, glass, or stainless steel containers . . . *never aluminum* as the acid in the tomato will "eat" the aluminum. The sauce will keep for a week in the refrigerator.

SAUCE BOLOGNESE

MAKES 3 CUPS

This is a cheater's method, I suppose, but it is just terrific. I tasted a pasta dish with a sauce very close to this one at dinner one night in Bologna and I was totally content. You prepare this sauce from two other sauces that you already have in your refrigerator . . . and I contend the result will be better than the usual recipes for such a dish.

1 *cup Italian Tomato Sauce (page 208)*

1 *cup Basic Brown Sauce (page 207)*

¼ *cup whipping cream*

¼ *cup freshly grated Parmesan or Romano cheese*

Salt and pepper to taste

1 *cup Pot Roast Shredded (page 318)*

Mix all ingredients together and simmer for a few minutes. Serve over pasta, gnocchi, or polenta.

GREEN SAUCE FOR BOILED MEATS

MAKES ABOUT 2½ CUPS

The Cesarina Restaurant in Rome serves some wonderful food. It is actually not Roman style at all, but Bolognese. This sauce is served with the boiled meat cart, a heated trolley filled with *bollito*. It is just a wonderful event, what with six or seven boiled meats heaped on your plate . . . and then this sauce.

I have omitted the cooked tongue that is usually used in this dish in this particular restaurant.

3 cups chopped Italian
  parsley, clean but very
  dry

1 small yellow onion,
  coarsely chopped

3 cloves garlic, crushed

2 stalks celery, coarsely chopped

½ cup drained giardiniera
  (These Italian pickled
  vegetables can be found
  in any Italian market)

¼ cup capers

3 flat anchovies

¼ teaspoon dry red pepper
  flakes

½ lemon peel, grated

1½ cups olive oil

3 tablespoons white wine
  vinegar

Salt and pepper to taste

Place all of the ingredients in a food processor and process just until it is rather coarsely ground. It should not be smooth.

Serve with boiled meats such as beef, chicken, tongue, pig's feet, pork, and sausages.

TUNA SAUCE FOR MEATS
(Tonnata)

MAKES 1½ CUPS

This is the famous *tonnata* sauce of Italy. It is really quite simple and I found an interesting variation in Rome. The chef put a shot of brandy in the sauce and it took on a whole new possibility. This is very close to a tuna mayonnaise, and since it keeps for several days sealed in the refrigerator, you are ready to use leftover meats or precooked meats in a very creative way.

1 7-ounce can of tuna,
  drained

8 flat anchovies, drained on
  a paper towel

¼ cup fresh lemon juice

2 tablespoons brandy

¾ cup olive oil, at room
  temperature

1 tablespoon chopped capers

Place the tuna, anchovies, and lemon juice in a food blender. Blend for a few moments and add the brandy. Slowly pour in the olive oil as the machine runs. Remove the sauce from the container and stir in the capers.

Serve over meats and salads. Traditionally this is served with cold veal but I love it over chicken.

PESTO SAUCE

MAKES ABOUT 2 CUPS

This uncooked sauce originally came from Genoa, where it is still prized. You will find it useful in Italian cooking and it keeps for several days in the refrigerator. Or you can buy a prepared sauce, but buy one packed in glass, not in a tin. Christopher Ranch in California makes a fairly decent pesto.

4 cups tightly packed fresh basil leaves

½ cup olive oil

2 cloves garlic, crushed

6 sprigs parsley

Salt and freshly ground black pepper to taste

¼ cup pine nuts, walnuts, or almonds

½ cup freshly grated Parmesan or Romano cheese

Place the basil in a food blender, not a processor. (Don't bother trying this with dried basil; it won't work.) Add the oil, garlic, parsley, salt, pepper, and nuts. Blend until all are chopped very fine but not smooth. Remove from the blender and stir in the grated cheese.

Use in soups and on pasta.

CONDIMENTS

The proper definition of a condiment is simply a seasoning for food, such as mustard or spices. Each of our three ancient cuisines uses condiments in a very different way and the background of some of these differences is most interesting.

The most famous condiment in China, and the most common, is soy sauce. This is made from fermented soybeans, a bit of wheat, and salt. The time of the invention of this luscious liquid was probably during the Chou dynasty, which means the sauce is at the very least 2,600 years old. It is one of the oldest condiments we have in the world.

The Romans were very fond of a heavy condiment made of fermented anchovies and salt, along with water. It is called *garum,* and I expect that it was very close to what the Vietnamese call *nuc moom,* or fish sauce. The Romans mixed this with reduced wine, making *oenogarum,* and used this to flavor many dishes . . . too many as far as I am concerned. The flavor does not go well with our contemporary palates. It is interesting to note, however, that the Romans took this sauce with them to India via the spice and silk route. The Indians added a bit of tamarind and some additional spices. The sauce became very popular with the British when they hit India during the nineteenth century. The sauce was taken back to England and we know this ancient Roman banquet sauce, with some changes, as Lea & Perrins or Worcestershire. Funny how far this sauce traveled before we tasted it in America!

The Greeks do not really have a special mixed condiment but we must mention the use of lemons in Greece. The lemon came to Greece during pre-Christian times, probably from Babylonia. The shape of the lemon appeared in the art of the time though the Greeks did not seem to use them much in food preparation. By the fifth century A.D. the Greek cook began using the fruit in the kitchen and in our time it is impossible to think of the cuisine of Greece without thinking of the lemon. People buy them in Athens in great bags, just as we buy five or ten pounds of potatoes. The lemon is now a most serious condiment in the land of Athena.

I have listed some of the condiments that are common in each of our cuisines. A more detailed explanation of the more complex items will be found in the glossary.

These lists are to help you in your planning and shopping.

China

Soy sauce *(page 33)*

Fermented black beans *(dow see)* *(page 29)*

Soybean condiment *(mein see)* *(page 31)*

Foo yee *(page 29)*

Oyster sauce *(page 31)*

Ginger, fresh

Garlic

Rice vinegar *(page 32)*   Five-spice powder *(page 39)*
Red vinegar *(page 32)*   Star anise *(page 40)*
Chinese rice wine *(page 32)*   Szechwan peppercorns *(page 40)*
Sugar   Dried hot chili peppers
MSG *(page 40)*   Chinese parsley *(page 42)*
Pickles

Greece

Mint and oregano   Tomato sauce   Lemon juice
Cinnamon and allspice   Onions   Vinegars
Dill   Garlic   Cheeses *(pages 35–36)*
Olive oil   Wine

Rome

Garlic   Basil   Onions
Olive oil   Tomato sauce   Dried hot chili peppers
Lemons   Wine   Cheeses
Mint   Vinegars

Ancient Rome

Garum (Try *nuc moom* from the Vietnamese grocery)
Reduced wines (boiled)
Lovage (Use celery leaves)
Coriander, both fresh and in seed form

PINZIMONIO

This is a contemporary bit that is common in Rome.

Salt and pepper, mixed with a little good olive oil. Eaten with raw vegetables such as fava beans or fresh fennel.

OENOGARUM

I doubt that you will enjoy this in your food but the old Romans thought it was great!

1 cup red wine, reduced to
  ¾ cup

2 tablespoons fish sauce
  (nuc moom *from
  Vietnam or Thailand)*

SESAME

The sesame seed is an Old World wonder, and it is a common food in all three of our ancient cuisines.

The seed probably originated in the subtropics of Asia, and it has been important there as a food and oil for thousands of years. The Chinese were using the plant as early as the third millennium B.C. and the Greeks and Romans used it very early in their cooking. The Greek soldiers considered the seeds so typical of their culture that they carried little bags of the product with them to battle so that they might have a small reminder of home when they were far away.

The seeds come from a rough and gummy sort of plant. When the pod dries in the fall it pops open with such force that the tiny explosion scatters the seeds all over the place. This is probably what Ali Baba was referring to in the Arabian Nights when he stood before the locked door at the cave and shouted, "Open sesame!" He was literally saying, "Open up like an exploding sesame pod!" Oh, where do I get this stuff?

The seed offers 55 percent of its weight in oil, an oil that has been used in cooking since Biblical times. The seeds and oil are used in cooking candy, salads, breads, seasoning, coatings, and a thousand other dishes.

You might also consider:

Shredded Chicken Sesame *(page 84)*

Fish Fillets with Sesame *(page 161)*

Sesame Dragon Mouths *(page 473)*

Sesame Almond Chicken Wings *(page 241)*

Chinese Sesame Chicken *(page 242)*

Chinese Sesame Cookies *(page 494)*

Greek Sesame Bread *(page 477)*

Sesame Circles *(page 478)*

Breadsticks, Italian Sesame *(page 481)*

Tahini Bean Dip *(page 88)*

GREECE AND CHINA

TAHINI, HOMEMADE

MAKES 1½ CUPS

If you cannot find tahini or sesame paste in a Middle Eastern grocery or a Chinese grocery, you can certainly make your own. It is very simple, but I think that you should remember that in ancient times there was no such thing as a food processor. This paste was ground by hand with a mortar and pestle, both in China and in Greece.

| $\frac{3}{4}$ pound sesame seeds | Salt, very little (optional) |
| 2 teaspoons plus 3 tablespoons peanut oil | |

Place seeds on baking sheet and toast in 350° oven for 20 minutes or until lightly roasted. Process in medium-sized food processor for 3 minutes. Add 2 teaspoons peanut oil and process on high for 30 seconds. Add 3 tablespoons peanut oil and process until very smooth, about 2 minutes. Add the optional salt.

OLIVES AND OLIVE OIL

The olive is a holy symbol, one of the most ancient foods in the world, and it is delicious! Archaeological evidence indicates that the earliest use of olives dates as far back as 6000 B.C., and this was probably in what is now called Syria, Palestine, and Crete. And it was an olive branch that was brought to Noah by the dove, signaling his deliverance from the Flood. For all of the peoples of the Mediterranean region, the olive branch is a superb symbol of life, of cuisine, of joy.

While the Chinese have eaten olives since ancient times, they did not seem to get into olive oil. Greece, on the other hand, has lived by the olive since the olive tree thrives in difficult terrains, as does the other symbolic biblical plant, the grape. The goddess Athena bestowed the olive on the city of Athens, and the people of Greece have been making use of the tree ever since. They had markets for their wonderful olive oil all about the Mediterranean, and thus they had to develop a navy to protect their sea-lanes, a navy that became the greatest sea power in its day. And the Romans are to be credited with the invention of the screw press, which meant that the rich oil could be more easily extracted from the fruit. The oil of the olive has been basic to life in Rome since before the Christian era.

There are many types of olives in the world, as the following list will show. Green olives are simply that, olives picked before they ripen.

California black olives	Green Spanish
Calamata, Greek	Green stuffed
Greek: several varieties and qualities	Chinese dried olives (*lam see*)
	Preserved Chinese olives, sweet
Dried Italian	Licorice-flavored salty Chinese olives
Tiny French Niçoises	Licorice-flavored sweet Chinese olives

Olive oils vary a great deal in their richness, color, and flavor. The reason the Chinese have never used olive oil in their cooking is because the oil has a bright flavor all its own and it will impart that flavor to any dish. The Chinese traditionally used lard since it adds less flavor to the food. They now use peanut oil. The Greeks and Romans, however, used the oil not only as a cooking lubricant but as a flavoring in itself.

Don't be confused by the grades of olive oil. There is really quite a simple system.

The first pressing of the olive gives us an "Extra Virgin" grade, one that was not produced with undue pressure or heat. The oil is light and flavorful, the kind you want for your very best salad dressings.

"Superfine Virgin Olive Oil" is next in quality, with "Fine Virgin Olive Oil" being next. "Virgin Olive Oil" is still a very good product and certainly suitable for most of your kitchen needs.

Products labeled simply as "Pure Olive Oil" are just that, and generally the oil comes from the last of the pressings, which means heat has been applied in order to get the last drop out of the pulp and seed. Generally the oil is a bit more bitter but certainly fine for cooking. Buy it by the gallon. You can find some very good brands from Greece that are very reasonable.

The country of origin also has something to do with the flavor. Generally the Italian, Spanish, and Greek oils are bright in flavor and usually affordable. I love oil from Sparta, in Greece, since it has a flavor that reminds me of herbs and of the Greek sun. This is strictly for salads since it is expensive.

Do not worry about buying large amounts of olive oil; it will keep better than any other oil you can buy. I keep a quart each of two or three different kinds on my cooking counter. The rest of the gallon can I store in the refrigerator, though some people tell me that even that is not necessary.

We now know that olive oil is really quite good for us. It contains no cholesterol, of course, since it is not an animal fat. As a matter of fact, the heart people now believe that olive oil helps break down cholesterol that has already built up in your system. That's the best news I've had all year!

You will find many recipes in this book that include olive oil. Among them are:

Greek Salad Dressing *(page 144)*

Greek Duck with Olives *(page 261)*

Olive and Pepper Salad *(page 152)*

Olive Rolls *(page 483)*

Olive Bread *(page 483)*

Green Olive Soup *(page 134)*

Fish with Olives and Bean Curd *(page 161)*

Steamed Pork with Chinese Olives *(page 301)*

Rice Congee *(page 378)*

Chinese New Year Noodles with Olives *(page 356)*

HINT: WHEN BUYING OLIVE OIL consider the use. You should probably buy a good extra virgin oil for salads, and a medium grade for pasta. For deep-frying and normal cooking buy the stuff by the gallon at a good Italian or Greek grocery. The merchant will help you so that you do not feel obligated to use the wrong oil at any time. Oil by the gallon for pan-frying is not at all expensive. On the other hand, fine extra virgin for salads is expensive. Boy, is it expensive! But it makes the difference between making a really fine salad and just playing around with lettuce.

Eggs

The egg is a most ingenious package. Architecturally it is a near miracle, and in terms of food content and flavor it is a great gift to the cook. It is also one of the most versatile foods that we have.

While the fact that the egg is a religious symbol of new life is well known to most of us, we are not aware of the many kinds of eggs that are eaten. The Chinese domesticated chickens around 2000 B.C. and thus we have enjoyed the chicken egg. But the duck egg is also very common in China and these are the eggs that are preserved in mud and ashes and called "100-year-old eggs." They are only a few weeks old, at the most. The Chinese also salt eggs, a method of preservation that results in a wonderful concentration of flavors. While the egg has always been a common food in China, it is nevertheless associated with wealth because of its richness.

The Romans ate all kinds of eggs, and the more exotic they were, the more they were desired. Peacock eggs, ostrich eggs, and quail eggs, as well as the more common duck and chicken eggs, were all enjoyed by the Roman citizen.

The Greeks are probably responsible for our image of Easter eggs, though they have always dyed their eggs one color, red, for the blood of the Christ. The colored eggs are braided into Easter breads and offered as gifts on that highest day of the Greek Church year, Easter.

You might also want to consider:

Egg, Artichoke, and Tuna Pizza *(page 487)*

Asparagus with Cheese and Eggs, Italian Style *(page 413)*

CHINA

TEA EGGS

MAKES 12 EGGS

This is one of the most beautiful food products that I know. The process leaves the egg looking like alabaster, a very rich and old alabaster. Your guests will be delighted with both the appearance and the taste since the anise is very plain. Channing and Jason used to call these "Licorice Eggs."

12 *eggs*

2 *tablespoons salt*

2 *tablespoons dark soy*
sauce

3 *star anise, whole*

2 *tablespoons dark tea such*
as oolong or black tea

Using an egg poker put a hole in the *large* end of 12 eggs. Place in a stainless-steel pan and cover with water. Add 1 tablespoon salt. Bring to a simmer and cook for 20 minutes, the lid off. Cool the eggs under running water. Using the back of a dinner spoon, gently crack the eggs so that there are many hairline cracks in the shell.

Replace the eggs in the pan. Add 1 tablespoon salt, the dark soy sauce, star anise, and the very dark tea. Bring to a simmer, uncovered, and cook for 2 to 3 hours. Let cool in the broth for 8 hours. Gently peel the shells from the eggs and serve whole or wedged.

You might like to serve these with a splash of light soy and sesame oil.

SALTED EGGS

Thisis obviously a very old method of preserving eggs and giving additional flavor, all in the same operation. What you will have is an uncooked pickled egg and the eggs must be cooked eventually. Do not be concerned about the fact that they are not refrigerated. The salt solves the problem of preservation.

4 *cups water*

1¼ *cups kosher salt*

1 *dozen eggs*

⅛ *cup black tea, such as po*
nay or dark oolong

Boil the water and add the salt, stirring until it dissolves. Allow the water to cool completely. Place the eggs in a bowl and add the tea. Cover with the salt solution, being careful not to add any salt that did not dissolve. Place a saucer on top of the eggs so that they remain under the solution at all times. Cover and allow to sit for 20 days. Then refrigerate. They can actually be used after the first ten days, but a brighter flavor will develop if you wait the longer time.

The eggs can be hard-boiled, peeled, and served just as they are, along with a little light soy sauce and some sesame oil. Or they can be used in cooking other dishes such as the Steamed Pork with Salted Eggs (page 226).

Do not be alarmed when you break the shell of the uncooked egg and find that the yolk is firm, almost as if cooked. The salt does that and preserves the egg for a long time.

BABY CORN AND QUAIL EGGS

SERVES 6–8 AS
PART OF A CHINESE MEAL

This dish is fun, and very easy. Both of the main ingredients come from China canned. The blending offers a dish of color, texture, and excellent flavor.

2 tablespoons peanut oil

1 slice ginger, the size of a 25-cent piece, cut julienne

1 clove garlic, chopped fine

1 15-ounce can baby corn, drained

1 15-ounce can quail eggs, drained

¼ cup Chinese Chicken Soup Stock (page 113) or ¼ cup Basic Chicken Stock (page 129)

2 tablespoons oyster sauce

1 teaspoon cornstarch mixed with 1 tablespoon water

Pinch of sugar

½ tablespoon sesame oil

GARNISH

Chinese parsley

Shredded iceberg lettuce for a bed

Heat the wok and add the oil. Chow the ginger and garlic for just a moment and add the drained corn. Chow just until the corn is hot and add the drained eggs. Be careful from here on that you do not break or tear up the eggs. Add the remaining ingredients, except the garnishes, and chow until the dish is hot and thick. Place on a bed of shredded iceberg lettuce and garnish with the Chinese parsley.

STEAMED PORK WITH SALTED EGGS

SERVES 6 AS
PART OF A CHINESE MEAL

This is a favorite of mine. Chinese friends tell me that they remember the days of their youth, when their parents were short on money, and Mama would have to divide the salted yolk very carefully to see that each was served the fair amount. Such is the history of this dish.

1 *pound pork, finely ground*

10 *water chestnuts, coarsely chopped*

2 *tablespoons dry sherry or Chinese rice wine*

2 *tablespoons light soy sauce*

½ *teaspoon grated fresh ginger*

1 *tablespoon cornstarch*

1 *fresh egg*

1 *teaspoon sesame oil*

½ *teaspoon freshly ground black pepper*

1 *green onion, chopped*

2 *Salted Eggs (page 224)*

Place all ingredients, except the salted eggs, in a mixing bowl and mix vigorously until smooth. Place the meat in a 9-inch-square stainless-steel cake pan or dish. Make two indentations in the top of the meat and break the salted eggs over the meat, placing the yolks in the indentations. Steam in a bamboo steamer (page 97) for 20 minutes. Be sure the steamer is hot before beginning to time the cooking process.

ITALY

RICOTTA FRITTATA

SERVES 6

The omelet goes back to ancient times. The Greeks loved eggs, but I think that the classic frittata, an omelet partially cooked and then broiled, must be credited to the Romans. Apicius had several dishes that he called "custards," which were really closer to a frittata. This is a good one, and it is rich and filling.

1 *pound ricotta*
Salt and freshly ground
black pepper to taste

6 *eggs*

3 *tablespoons grated*
Parmesan or Romano
cheese

2 *tablespoons olive oil*

Using an electric mixer, cream the ricotta with the salt and pepper until smooth and fluffy. In a separate bowl beat the eggs with the grated cheese. Add eggs to the ricotta and blend well.

Heat a 10-inch SilverStone-lined frying pan and add the oil. Add the egg and cheese mixture and cook over low heat until the bottom is golden and the eggs begin to set. Place under a heated broiler until lightly browned on top.

Place on a serving platter and cut into wedges to serve.

Poultry
and Game

CHICKEN

Chicken is so common to our Western table that we think the chicken is ours. It is not. What we know as the common fowl is probably the descendant of the wild red jungle fowl of South Asia and we should most likely credit the Chinese with domesticating the bird around 200 B.C. And what a job of domestication! There are now more chickens in the world than human beings and the meat of the old hen is the most universally eaten by humans. This is due to the fact that the chicken is willing to acclimate to all but the coldest regions on earth. Only the dog can live in a wider range of climates.

Actually I should not give all of the credit for spreading the bird to the Chinese. The Greeks also raised chickens for their eggs, and by the time the Chinese were commonly raising the fowl for food, the Greeks began to eat them as well. The Greeks spread the good word of the good bird and the Romans, who had eaten chickens during their tours in Asia Minor, went to Greece to learn new techniques for breeding and raising the flavorful and versatile creature. The bird increased in popularity in Rome, with both poor and wealthy citizens, and some of the high-class crowd did strange things with chickens. Horace loved the taste of a chicken that had been drowned in wine prior to cooking!

All three of our ancient cultures still enjoy this ancient bird, but you must go to a Chinese community to understand which of the three cultures is the most concerned about freshness. The Chinese buy the creatures live, and you witness a great deal of poking and pushing at the bird so that one can be sure the chicken is young. I saw one old woman pick up the live chicken, turn him over, and blow on his tail! My Chinese friend, Ken Hom, later explained that she simply wanted to see how large the tail oil sack was, since the younger the bird, the smaller the sack. Oh!

You might also like to consider:

Chicken with Leek Belts *(page 450)*
Chinese Chicken with Chestnuts *(page 428)*

CHINA

CHINESE POACHED CHICKEN

I did this dish for you a few years ago when we first began the shows in Chicago. It is the most simple chicken recipe I know. It is so simple that some people have called to say that they doubt it will work. Everyone who has tried it, however, loves it. The final product is moist and flavorful. Since there is no salt in this dish you must add whatever seasoning you like when serving.

Read the instructions carefully and you will be very pleased. The dish was given me by my adopted Chinese aunt, Mrs. Mary Young. Please try it.

Fill a 12-quart kettle almost full of water and bring it to a boil. Place 1 whole chicken, about 3 pounds, in the boiling water. The water will stop boiling in just a moment or so. Using wooden spoons so that you do not tear the skin, remove the chicken from the water and place it on a tray. Cover the pot and bring the water back to the boiling point. Put the chicken back into the pot, cover, and turn off the heat. Leave the bird in the pot and the pot on the burner, but you will need no more heat. The water will be hot enough to cook the bird. After 1 hour the chicken is done. Remove, cool, and debone the chicken.

I save the skin and bones for a later soup stock. I use some of the poaching water for covering the meat, which is then refrigerated. Some of the poaching water can be used for the soup stock. It has no flavor of its own.

This chicken can be used in the preparation of several other dishes. It is also great for chicken salads, chicken with pasta, etc.

ROAST SALT CHICKEN

SERVES 4–6 AS
PART OF A CHINESE MEAL

I know, I know. This is too much salt. But, strangely enough, the juices from the chicken are sealed in the chicken by the salt. The result is not as salty as you might think. It is a classic method of preparation and it is certainly easy. The salt falls right off!

1 *3-pound chicken*

MARINADE
3 *tablespoons dark soy sauce*
3 *tablespoons sesame oil*

3 *cloves garlic, crushed*

2¼ *cups rock salt (for pickling)*
1 *green onion, chopped*
Aluminum foil

Mix the marinade and rub the chicken inside and out. Put ¼ cup of the salt inside the bird, along with the chopped onion. Place 1 cup of the salt on a large piece of aluminum foil and set the bird in the salt. Cup the foil up around the bird and pour the remaining cup of salt on top. Seal up with more foil if necessary and place on a baking pan. Bake at 375° for 1 hour, or until done to your taste.

Brush the salt from the chicken before serving. Hack (page 24) the chicken up into small serving pieces. Serve warm or cold.

CHICKEN BAKED WITH HONEY AND SOY SAUCE

SERVES 4–6 AS
PART OF A CHINESE MEAL

The point behind this book has something to do with the interesting connections among the "old cuisines"—China, Greece, and Rome. This recipe was given me one evening while eating at an informal Roman fish house, Da Franco. I was eating dinner with . . . I hope you understand and believe this story . . . a prince of Rome, one Prince Ugo. He traces his ancestry back to the Caesars, and I found him fascinating. He has an old family castle right in the middle of the city of Rome. The man has been everywhere and knows everybody, and we began to talk food. When I told him about this book, he blurted out this recipe. I say "blurted out" because we both had had too much Roman wine. The dish is simple. The dish is delicious. The dish should be cooked by your children while *you* drink the Roman wine.

1 *3-pound chicken, whole*

MARINADE

2 *tablespoons honey*

2 *tablespoons dark soy sauce*

2 *tablespoons sesame oil*

Mix the marinade ingredients and rub the chicken inside and out. Allow the bird to marinate for about ½ hour, turning now and then. Save the marinade for basting. Tie the legs and place the chicken on a roasting rack and pan. Bake at 350° for 15 minutes and then 325° for 20 minutes. Then, turn the heat down to 300° for 30 minutes. Baste with the remaining marinade a few times during cooking.

Watch the bird closely as it cooks. You want it to be golden brown and certainly not burned.

BEGGAR'S CHICKEN

SERVES 6–8 AS
PART OF A CHINESE MEAL

There are many legends behind this famous Chinese dish. The most common story claims that a famished pauper stole a chicken and wrapped the feathered bird in wet clay and placed it in a fire. He certainly did not have any cooking equipment! When the clay had dried out, the bird was removed from the fire. The feathers stuck to the clay so the final result was a moist and lovely dish. One story goes so far as to claim that a beggar brought this dish to the Empress during a famine in China. She was so impressed that she declared it one of the great dishes of China. You can make up any story you like when you serve this dish, and we will assume that your creativity will add to the joy of the evening.

No, I do not use a feathered chicken for this dish. One cleaned at the supermarket will do just fine.

1 3½ pound chicken, washed and patted dry

MARINADE

2 tablespoons dark soy sauce

1 tablespoon sesame oil

1 tablespoon dry sherry or Chinese rice wine

1½ teaspoons five-spice powder (page 39)

1 teaspoon freshly grated ginger

1 teaspoon salt

2 cloves garlic, crushed

Parchment paper (or make your own, page 101)

1 paper lunch bag

12 pounds clay from a local potter

Mix all of the marinade ingredients together and rub the bird with this mixture, inside and out. Tie the legs together and place the bird on a roasting rack in a pan. Roast in a 450° oven, breast side up, for 20 minutes, or until the bird browns a bit. Remove from the oven and allow to cool slightly. Place the chicken, breast side up, on a large piece of parchment paper and wrap up. Slip the wrapped bird into the paper lunch sack and fold up the ends of the bag.

Roll out the clay on a dish towel on a breadboard to about ⅜ inch thick, 16 inches wide, and 21 inches long.

Place the bagged chicken in the middle of the clay and bring the sides of the clay slab up to meet across the top, shaping close to the bird.

Press the ends down and secure by pinching the clay. Do this carefully so that you have a kind of clay envelope with about a 1-inch edge of clay on the top and the ends. Trim off the excess. Pinch together decoratively if you like.

Place the clay-covered chicken in a large baking pan and bake at 350° for about 2½ hours. Transfer the bird to a large shallow tray or basket and invite your guests to watch the cracking of the clay. Use a wooden mallet. The clay will crack readily and you can lift off the pieces. Return the chicken to the kitchen and remove all the clay. Pull off the paper bag and hack (page 24) the chicken into serving pieces.

CHICKEN WITH TWO ONIONS IN SAND POT

SERVES 4–6 AS
PART OF A CHINESE MEAL

This dish will have an unusual flavor due to the use of the wonderful five-spice powder. If you do not have a sand pot (page 19), you can certainly use a stove-top casserole.

1 3-pound chicken, hacked (page 24) into 2-inch pieces

MARINADE

2 tablespoons light soy sauce

2 tablespoons dry sherry or Chinese rice wine

1 teaspoon ginger, either cut julienne or grated

4 tablespoons peanut oil

2 cloves garlic, finely chopped

¼ teaspoon salt

1 cup Chinese Chicken Soup Stock (page 113)

2 yellow onions, peeled and cut into 8 wedges each; divide the wedges into leaves

6 green onions, cut Chinese style (page 142)

Pinch of brown sugar

¼ teaspoon five-spice powder (page 39)

½ head iceberg lettuce, torn up

Cut the chicken and mix with the marinade. Allow to sit for 15 minutes.

Heat the wok and add ½ of the oil. Chow the garlic and salt for just a moment. Add the chicken, drained of the marinade. Reserve the marinade.

Brown the chicken well on all sides and add the broth. Cover and cook until the chicken is done to your taste. Remove the cover and allow the broth to reduce a bit. Remove all from the wok and set aside.

Heat the wok and add the remaining oil. Chow the onions until the yellow ones begin to brown a bit. Return the chicken to the wok along with all remaining ingredients except the lettuce but including the marinade. Chow for a few moments so that all is hot.

Place the lettuce in a 4-quart sand pot or stove-top casserole. Top with the chicken and onions and cover. Place on the stove and heat until the pot is very hot. Serve immediately.

CHICKEN CHOWED WITH BLACK BEANS

SERVES 4–6 AS
PART OF A CHINESE MEAL

This is a favorite of all serious Chinese food freaks. If the chicken is not overcooked the result will be spectacular. It looks like a lot of work but it is not.

1 *3-pound chicken, hacked (page 24) into 2-inch pieces*

MARINADE

2 *tablespoons light soy sauce*

2 *tablespoons cornstarch*

1 *egg white*

1 *teaspoon salt*

2 *tablespoons peanut oil*

4 *tablespoons peanut oil*

3 *cloves garlic, chopped fine*

1 *yellow onion, peeled and cut into 1-inch pieces*

3 *tablespoons fermented black beans (dow see) rinsed in plain water and mashed with 2 tablespoons dry sherry or Chinese rice wine*

2 *green sweet bell peppers, cored and cut julienne*

FINAL SAUCE

1 *tablespoon light soy sauce*

2 *tablespoons dry sherry or Chinese rice wine*

1 *cup Chinese Chicken Soup Stock (page 113)*

1 *teaspoon brown sugar*

Cut the chicken and soak in the marinade for 15 minutes. Heat a wok and add 2 tablespoons of the oil. Drain the marinade from the chicken and reserve. Brown the chicken pieces well in the wok, then remove and set aside. Drain the oil from the wok and discard. (Too much chicken fat in it!)

Heat the wok again and add the remaining 2 tablespoons of oil. Chow the garlic for a moment and add the onions and the *dow see* mashed with the sherry. Chow for a moment and add the green peppers. Return the chicken to the wok along with the reserved marinade. Add the ingredients for the final sauce. Stir well and cover. Simmer the dish until the chicken is tender but not overcooked, about 20 minutes.

VARIATION: You may wish to thicken this dish with 1 tablespoon of cornstarch mixed with an equal amount of water. Add it after the final sauce is hot. Stir well and serve.

CHICKEN WINGS IN FIVE SPICE

MAKES 24 PIECES

The Chinese have always been fond of chicken wings. The reason is that the wing is very moist and filled with gelatin, thus creating a wonderful bite, but only a bite. It takes a pile of these to fill a family but they make a wonderful addition to a Chinese meal of several courses.

12 *chicken wings, whole*

    MARINADE

½ *teaspoon freshly grated ginger*

⅛ *cup light soy sauce*

⅛ *cup dry sherry or Chinese rice wine*

½ *teaspoon five-spice powder*

1 *cup water-chestnut flour (page 35)*

4 *cups peanut oil for deep-frying*

Cut each wing into 3 logical pieces. Save the tips for soup and use only the 2 meatier parts for this recipe.

Prepare the marinade and marinate the wing pieces for ½ hour. Drain and toss in the water-chestnut flour. Deep-fry at 360° until golden brown, about 5 minutes.

FRIED GARLIC CHICKEN BALLS

SERVES 8–10 AS
PART OF A CHINESE MEAL

Ground chicken is now available in most supermarkets. It is a good product and these chicken balls put a good product to good use. The kids will prefer these to chicken nuggets, I'm sure.

2 pounds ground chicken meat

½ teaspoon white pepper

½ teaspoon salt

2 tablespoons cornstarch

1 tablespoon dark soy sauce

2 egg whites

½ teaspoon freshly grated ginger

2 tablespoons dry sherry or Chinese rice wine vinegar

4 cloves garlic, crushed

COATING

1 cup cornstarch

1 cup water-chestnut flour (page 35)

4 cups peanut oil for deep-frying

Mix the chicken with all of the seasonings and egg whites. Mix it very well. Form into balls about the size of large walnuts and set on waxed paper. When all are formed, mix the cornstarch with the water-chestnut flour and roll each ball in this mixture. Deep-fry, in several batches, in 360° oil until the balls float and are golden brown in color, about 5 minutes. Taste one to be sure they are done to your liking.

CHICKEN STEAMED WITH CHINESE SAUSAGE

SERVES 4–6 AS
PART OF A CHINESE MEAL

The sweetness of wonderful Chinese sausage, *lop chong*, adds a most interesting dimension to this dish. It is easy to prepare since there is no browning of meat involved. The only problem you will have is finding the sausage, unless you are in a large city that has Chinese markets. If you cannot find the *lop chong*, try the dish using julienned ham instead.

1 *3-pound chicken, hacked (page 24) into 2-inch pieces*

MARINADE

1½ *teaspoons salt*

2 *tablespoons light soy sauce*

1 *tablespoon cornstarch*

1 *tablespoon dry sherry or Chinese rice wine*

1 *tablespoon peanut oil*

6 *large Chinese mushrooms, soaked for 3 hours and sliced; drain, but save the liquid*

3 *Chinese sausages* (lop chong), *diagonally sliced into thin pieces*

Hack the chicken and place in a bowl with the marinade ingredients. Mix well and let marinate for 2 hours.

Slice the mushrooms and sausages and add to the bowl. Also add 2 tablespoons of the mushrooms' soaking water.

Place in a steamer pan or bowl and steam for 45 minutes or until the chicken is tender but not dry.

CHICKEN AND PORK IN LETTUCE

SERVES 6 AS
PART OF A CHINESE MEAL

This dish is akin to mu-shu pork, though the addition of chicken pleases my palate. If you have never had such a dish in lettuce leaves you are in for a treat. Of course you can use Peking Pancakes (page 474) or even wheat tortillas, but for me the lettuce does the job!

½ pound pork, coarsely chopped

½ pound chicken, skinless and boneless, coarsely chopped

MARINADE

2 tablespoons light soy sauce

1 egg white, beaten

1 tablespoon cornstarch

1 tablespoon dry sherry or Chinese rice wine

½ teaspoon freshly grated ginger

3 tablespoons peanut oil

1 teaspoon salt

2 tablespoons peanut oil for chowing

3 eggs, beaten

1 ounce black tree-ear fungus (page 29), soaked in fresh water for 1 hour

1 tablespoon oyster sauce

1 tablespoon sesame oil

3 green onions, chopped

1 head iceberg lettuce, separated into whole leaves

Chop the meats and marinate *only the pork* in the marinade mixture for 15 minutes.

Heat the wok and add the oil and salt. Chow the chicken first, just until barely done, and remove. Add the pork, along with the marinade, and chow until done to taste. Remove.

Heat the wok again and add the oil for the eggs. Beat the eggs and chow over medium heat so that they become scrambled but not dry. Chop them up in the wok with the wok paddle and remove to a plate.

Add the remaining ingredients, except the lettuce, to the wok and chow until the fungus is hot. Add the pork, chicken, and eggs to the mixture and toss until all is hot. Remove to a serving bowl.

Serve by wrapping a few tablespoons of the meat mixture in a lettuce leaf, just like a burrito.

VARIATIONS:

1. Add some garlic and red chili paste (page 30) to this dish. Serve as above. Wonderful!

2. Substitute Peking Pancakes (page 474) for the lettuce leaves.

3. See the Dried Oysters and Pork in Lettuce recipe (page 338) for another version of this dish.

ROAST "LUNG KONG" CHICKEN

SERVES 4–6
FOR A CHINESE DINNER

The wonderful Peninsula Hotel in Hong Kong makes a dish very much like this. At least this is as close as I can come to the dish that I had there. It is not complicated and the results are moist and delicious.

1 3-pound chicken, cut in half the long way

Looing Sauce (page 203)

6 cups peanut oil for deep-frying

Blanch the chicken halves in boiling water for 2 minutes. Drain. Place the bird halves in a pot of Looing Sauce and bring to a boil. They should be covered with the sauce. Turn the heat to a simmer and cook lightly for 15 minutes, then allow the halves to cool in the sauce.

Remove and place on a rack on the counter. Pat dry with paper towels and dry the meat using an electric fan. Aim the fan at the bird halves for about 3 hours, or until the skin is dry to the touch.

Deep-fry one half at a time in oil at 350°. Be very careful when sliding the half into the hot oil. A wok lid will be helpful in protecting your hands and face in case the oil should pop and spit at you.

Deep-fry each half until the skin is crispy and golden. Drain on paper towels before cutting up to serve.

LOOED CHICKEN

SERVES 6
AT A CHINESE-STYLE DINNER

Prepare a basic Looing Sauce (page 203) or use one that you have reserved in your refrigerator. Place enough of the sauce in a 6-quart stove-top covered casserole to cover 1 whole chicken. Bring the sauce to a boil and add the chicken. Cover and turn to a simmer. Cook for 30 minutes and turn off the heat, allowing the chicken to cool in the sauce for 1 hour.

My favorite method of serving this simple and tasty peasant dish is to simply hack up the bird (page 24) and arrange on a platter. Garnish with a bit of sesame oil and chopped green onions.

SESAME ALMOND CHICKEN WINGS

SERVES 6 AS
PART OF A CHINESE MEAL

I love chicken wings, and so do the Chinese. The wing has a great deal of flavor so it is moist and wonderful eating. This is a quickie recipe using the ancient sesame seed as well as the almond.

12 *chicken wings*

MARINADE

1 *tablespoon light soy sauce*

1 *tablespoon Chinese rice wine or dry sherry*

½ *teaspoon freshly grated ginger*

2 *egg whites, beaten*

COATING MIXTURE

2 *tablespoons ground almonds*

2 *tablespoons rice flour*

2 *tablespoons cornstarch*

½ *tablespoon wheat flour*

2 *tablespoons sesame seeds*

4 *cups peanut oil for deep-frying*

Chinese Dip Sauce (page 201) (Choose your favorite)

Cut each of the wings into 3 logical pieces, setting the wing tips aside for soup stock. Prepare the marinade and soak the wing pieces in this for 15 minutes. In the meantime, blend the coating mixture and heat the oil. Drain the marinade from the wings and dip each in the egg whites. Then dredge in the coating mixture. Deep-fry at 360° until each piece is golden brown, about 5 minutes. Serve hot with any of the dip sauces.

QUICK CHINESE
ROAST CHICKEN

You can throw this recipe together in nothing flat, and it really does taste very much like the roast chicken you will find in a good Chinese takeout house.

1 3½ pound chicken, whole, cleaned

MARINADE

2 tablespoons dark soy sauce

2 tablespoons Chinese rice wine or dry sherry

¼ teaspoon grated fresh ginger

½ teaspoon five-spice powder (page 39)

2 tablespoons honey

Salt and freshly ground black pepper to taste

Mix marinade and rub chicken inside and out. Allow to marinate in bowl for 1 hour. Place on a poultry rack and bake at 375° for about 1 hour, or to taste.

CHINESE SESAME
CHICKEN

SERVES 8 AS PART
OF A CHINESE MEAL

This is so simple that you must not tell anyone about it. Just prepare the dish and let them compliment you . . . and leave it at that.

8 chicken thighs

MARINADE

2 tablespoons light soy sauce

2 tablespoons Chinese rice wine or dry sherry

½ teaspoon freshly grated ginger

¼ teaspoon ground white pepper

1 egg white, beaten

½ cup flour

½ cup cornstarch

½ cup sesame seeds

6 cups peanut oil for deep-frying

Marinate the thighs in the marinade mixture for 15 minutes. Dip each thigh into the egg white and then dredge in the flour and cornstarch mixed with the sesame seeds. Deep-fry at 360° until golden and tender, about 15 minutes. You will have better luck with this dish if you fry 4 pieces at a time and keep your oil up to temperature.

GREECE

ROASTED CHICKEN, GREEK STYLE

SERVES 4

The wonderful thing about Greek cooking is that it is rarely complex. You can bake this chicken or cut it in half to place on the barbecue. Either way is most enjoyable and the olive oil helps keep it moist.

1 *3-pound chicken*
½ *cup olive oil*
   Juice of 2 lemons

1 *tablespoon oregano*
   Salt and pepper to taste

Marinate the chicken in the above mixture for 1 hour, being sure to rub some inside the chicken. Bake at 375° for 1 hour or until done. If you wish to do this on a barbecue, it is best to cut the bird in half the long way and then marinate. Cook to your liking over medium-hot coals.

CHICKEN ROLL, GREEK STYLE

SERVE 6–8

Prepare two chickens just as for the Chicken Roll, Roman Style (page 247) but omit the marjoram and parsley and substitute 1 tablespoon whole oregano. Roast, and serve with a good Greek salad (pages 144–149) and a dry white wine.

ITALY

FRICASSEE OF CHICKEN, ROMAN STYLE

SERVES 4

This has got to be one of the best Italian chicken dishes I know. I added a bit with the artichokes and the result is delightful. It is a chicken stew that has a sauce so rich that you can save the sauce and get another entire meal out of it. Just serve it over pasta. Period!

2 tablespoons olive oil

1 3-pound chicken, cut into
8 pieces

3 cloves garlic, chopped

1 cup red wine

2 cups Basic Brown Soup
Stock (page 132)

½ cup coarsely chopped
pancetta or bacon

1 cup coarsely chopped ripe
tomatoes

2 teaspoons whole marjoram

1 14-ounce can artichoke
hearts, quartered,
drained well

1 tablespoon each butter
and flour, cooked together
to form a roux (page 26)

Salt and freshly ground
black pepper to taste

Heat a large frying pan and add the oil. Brown the chicken pieces well. Remove to a 6-quart covered stove-top casserole. Add the garlic to the pan and sauté just a moment. Deglaze (page 24) the pan with the red wine and add to the casserole. Add all remaining ingredients except the artichokes, roux, and salt and pepper. Bring to a boil and cover. Turn to a simmer and cook for 40 minutes. Add the artichokes and simmer another 10 minutes, uncovered. Stir in the roux and taste for seasoning. Careful with the salt as the pancetta is salty itself.

DEVIL'S CHICKEN
(Pollo alla Diavola)

SERVES 4

This dish has a wonderful name that will tickle your children. The dish will probably also tickle their throats since chicken of the devil is supposed to be *very hot*! You can calm it down for the kids and spice it up for your mate. Either way it is easy and delicious. I like this dish cooked on the charcoal barbecue.

1 3–4-pound chicken

½ cup olive oil

2 tablespoons hot pepper
sauce (Tabasco) or to taste

Juice of 2 lemons

1 tablespoon freshly ground
black pepper to taste

1 teaspoon salt

Using poultry shears, cut the bird open by cutting down the backbone. Flatten a bit by pounding with your hand so that the chicken is "butterflied."

Mix the remaining ingredients in a large bowl and marinate the bird for 2 hours.

Grill on a medium-hot charcoal barbecue, skin side down, for 25 minutes. Turn and cook until the juices run clear, about another 20 minutes. Keep basting with the remaining marinade.

CHICKEN WITH SWEET BELL PEPPERS

SERVES 4

P lease don't use canned pimientos for this dish. Find good fresh peppers and you will have a wonderful meal.

1 *3-pound chicken, cut into serving pieces*	4 *sweet red bell peppers, cored and cut into 2-inch squares*
½ *cup olive oil*	3 *large ripe tomatoes, cored and chopped very coarsely*
Salt and freshly ground black pepper to taste	3 *tablespoons chopped parsley*
3 *cloves garlic, diced fine*	
6 *flat anchovies, rinsed*	1 *cup dry white wine*
	1 *teaspoon whole marjoram*

Cut up the chicken. Pan-brown in ½ of the oil. Place in stove-top casserole. Add salt and pepper to taste.

Sauté the garlic and anchovies in remaining oil. After about 2 minutes you can mash the anchovies and mix with the oil. Add peppers and sauté a bit. Put all in a casserole along with remaining ingredients. Cover and simmer until tender, 40 minutes.

CHICKEN ROLL, ROMAN STYLE

SERVES 6–8

No, you do not prepare this after you have gotten home late from the office and have a friend to entertain. On the other hand, if you made this dish in front of your friend, he/she would certainly be entertained! It is a bit more difficult than a stew but not as tough as you think.

2 *chickens, each 3 pounds*

4 *tablespoons olive oil*

Juice of 1 lemon

3 *cloves garlic, crushed*

2 *teaspoons whole marjoram*

1 *tablespoon chopped parsley*

Salt and freshly ground black pepper to taste

Debone one chicken, leaving the skin and meat intact. This is not as difficult as it sounds. Simply use a very sharp paring knife and start at the neck of the bird. Gently pull the skin back and begin cutting the meat from the bone and carcass, being careful not to puncture the skin. Remove the wings and the legs, just where they join the thigh. Once you have cut the meat away from the carcass halfway down the bird, do the same from the other end. The carcass will come right out! Remove any meat from the bones that you may have missed. Skin and remove the meat from the second chicken, this time in large pieces. Do the same with the legs from both birds. Save the bones from both birds for soup stock. You can throw in the skin from the second bird as well.

Mix the meat from the second chicken with the remaining ingredients. Stuff the whole boneless bird with the seasoned meat and tie with string into a long, round loaf. You will need some help with the tying; someone needs to hold the thing as you wrap it.

COOKING: You may either poach the chicken roll in Basic Chicken Stock (page 129) made from the bones or you can bake it at 350° until the center registers 180° on a meat thermometer. This will take about 1 hour 30 minutes, or less.

Cool and slice. I like to serve this with Tuna Sauce (page 210) and a pasta dish such as Pappardelle (pages 370 or 371). A green salad is a necessity.

GOOSE

I wish Americans better understood the goose. He is easy to cook and I think he is the greatest of the fowl for feasting.

We know that people have been enjoying goose for thousands of years. It is believed that geese have been domesticated since neolithic times and we know that the ancient Egyptians loved goose. In classical Greece geese were treated to special diets of moistened grain to fatten them up and the people of Gaul did the same for the geese marketed in Rome.

Geese are mentioned in early Chinese texts and were highly valued through the ages. Marco Polo reported that the Chinese were raising huge geese! They still do. And while the bird is seen on the tables of the rest of Europe and America, I believe that the most creative uses of the bird come from China. You will love these two recipes, as they are neither fatty nor difficult to prepare.

LOOED GOOSE

SERVES 10–12 AS
PART OF A CHINESE MEAL

I love the name of the dish . . . and the flavor of the dish is even better. "Looing" refers to simmering in a soy-based sauce, so cut the wisecracks about this bird being lewd! It is tender and moist, and actually very simple to prepare. The fattiness of the goose can be removed easily since it cooks into the sauce. When you chill the sauce prior to the next use, the fat can be removed.

1 8–9-pound goose

BASIC LOOING SAUCE

1½ cups dark soy sauce

1½ cups light soy sauce

2 star anise, whole

½ cup sugar

½ cup dry sherry or Chinese rice wine

6 slices fresh ginger, each the size of a 25-cent piece

3 quarts water

Cut the goose into quarters. Rinse well and drain.

Place all the ingredients for the looing sauce in a 12-quart kettle and bring to a boil. Add the goose pieces and add additional water just so that the pieces are barely covered. Bring to a simmer, cover, and gently cook for 30 minutes. Allow the bird to cool in the broth, covered, for 1 hour. Remove and slice for dinner.

You can serve the meat as it is with a bit of sauce or try it with Roasted Salt and Pepper (page 266).

SAVE THE LOOING SAUCE FOR ANOTHER USE. REFRIGERATE.

GOOSE, CHIU CHOW STYLE

This is just a wonderful mixture of flavors . . . and very rich flavors indeed. I had this dish the first time in a Chiu Chow restaurant in Hong Kong. It is in the Ocean City Building in Kowloon and called Ocean City Chiu Chow. You would do well to try the original version. The following is simply a guess, and it is delicious.

Use the full breast of a Looed Goose (page 249). Pan-fry the breast until the skin is golden brown. Place the meat, sliced thin, on a platter. Debone the breast before slicing.

PEPPER SAUCE

1 tablespoon Szechwan peppercorns (page 40)

1 teaspoon black peppercorns

3 tablespoons peanut oil

1 clove garlic, crushed

1 tablespoon sesame oil

Pinch of salt

Prepare the pepper sauce by crushing both types of peppercorns with a mortar and pestle or in a small electric coffee grinder. Do not pound or grind too fine. Heat the peanut oil in a small frying pan and add the peppercorns. Stir a bit until the oil barely begins to smoke. Remove from the heat and add the remaining ingredients.

Pour the pepper sauce over the sliced goose and serve.

Servings depend on how much goose you slice! Prepare plenty as this will be very popular at your Chinese table.

DUCK

In 1873 one of the famed Yankee Clippers delivered a cargo of nine Peking ducks to Long Island, New York. From these nine creatures have descended all the millions and millions of domestic ducks of this species in the United States. Known today as "Long Island Duckling," they remain in this country an underrated and underconsumed food, despite their rich and distinctive flavor. In contrast, our three ancient cuisines have always appreciated ducks, and have eaten them in great numbers.

Duck is particularly prized in China and has been for centuries. After pork, duck and chicken are considered the most important meats in China. I am amused by the fact that the duck is respected by the Chinese not just because he is delicious to eat but because he can take care of himself! You let him out in the morning and he returns home having fed himself . . . though you do not, of course, ask him what he has been eating. Most of the recipes in this section are indeed Chinese, as they are the wisest of cooks when it comes to duckling.

Although their preparations were far more mundane and straightforward, the ancient Greeks and Romans were very fond of duck. As a matter of fact the famous French dish Duck à l'Orange was actually invented in ancient Rome . . . and Apicius was very fond of the dish.

Read these recipes and maybe I will be able to convince you that you should enjoy duck much more often. You might also wish to consider:

Duck and Jellyfish Salad (page 138)

CHINA

||| CHINESE ROAST DUCK |||

SERVES 6 AS
PART OF A CHINESE MEAL

When I was a boy of about fourteen I began to hang around Seattle's Chinatown. Roast duck was expensive and I decided that I should learn to make my own. Some arrogance! I asked a woman in a Chinese grocery, Wa Sang Market, to help me. Florence has been a friend ever since and I still ask her advice on recipes.

1 duck, approximately 4 pounds in size, completely defrosted if frozen, washed and dried with paper towels

1 tablespoon salt

2 cups water

*2 packages George Washington Brown Broth

2 pieces orange peel—1 inch wide, the length of the orange

2 teaspoons five-spice powder

2 teaspoons MSG (optional)

2 star anise flowers

1 tablespoon sugar

1½ tablespoons soybean condiment (mein see)

2 cloves garlic, sliced thin

2 tablespoons dry sherry or Chinese rice wine

1 medium-size onion, peeled

½ cup honey

1 tablespoon vinegar

¼ teaspoon ground dry ginger

Chinese plum sauce for dipping (can be purchased in a can in any Chinese grocery)

Salt the duck completely inside and out. Allow the duck to sit for 1 hour and then, using paper towels, wipe the bird down completely.

Bring the water to a boil and add the Brown Broth, orange peel, five-spice powder, optional MSG, star anise, sugar, soybean condiment, garlic, and the sherry or rice wine. Boil for a few minutes and allow the sauce to cool to lukewarm.

Put the onion inside the bird and sew up the neck and open body cavity, leaving just an opening into which you pour the sauce. Then, close up the opening completely. We do not want the sauce to run out of the bird during the baking. Tie the legs together and place, breast side up, on an oiled roasting rack. Put the rack in a roasting pan and roast the bird, uncovered, at 400° for 20 minutes. Lower the heat to 375° and continue roasting, allowing 25 minutes per pound total roasting time. Include the first 20 minutes in the total time. Do not overcook the bird. You may have to turn the heat down to 350° during the last ⅓ of the total roasting time so that he does not brown too quickly.

Mix the honey, vinegar, and ground ginger together and baste the bird with this mixture about every 20 minutes during the roasting process.

NOTE: I have good luck using small poultry wires for the closing-up process. You can find them in almost any kitchen-gadget store.

Cut the duck up into serving pieces and serve the plum sauce on the side as a condiment.

*George Washington Brown Broth is available in most fancy grocery stores and delicatessens. It is an excellent product.

PEKING DUCK

SERVES 8 AS
PART OF A CHINESE MEAL

The Lee Gardens Hotel in Hong Kong has a duck oven on the roof! It is still heated with charcoal in contrast to most restaurants, which now use gas. The chef, head of the Rainbow Dining Room, was most gracious in showing me the whole process involved in the proper preparation of this dish, the most famous duck recipe in the world. It is not at all complicated, nor will you need any special equipment.

1 4½-pound duck, defrosted and patted dry

INSIDE SEASONING

¼ tablespoon salt

½ teaspoon Chinese five-spice powder

¼ teaspoon MSG (optional)

½ teaspoon sugar

2 quarts boiling water for blanching

BASTING SYRUP

*1 cup malt sugar (dry or liquid) (page 40)

1 cup hot water

2 tablespoons Chinese red vinegar or red wine vinegar

3 slices lemon, peel and all

GARNISH

Peking Pancakes (page 474) or wheat tortillas

Hoisin sauce (page 30)

Green onions or scallions

Mix the inside seasoning together and rub the mixture into the inside of the duck. Sew up the duck, both head and end. You might use poultry pins for this.

Make a large loop of string and place it under the wings of the bird so that you can hang him over a very large bowl. Use a kitchen-cabinet knob for the hanger. Pour the boiling water over the duck and continue ladling the hot water over the bird—about eight times. Allow to drain 10 minutes.

In the meantime, mix the ingredients for the basting syrup together. Drain the bowl beneath the duck of the water. Now, repeat the pouring process, this time using the basting syrup. Allow the duck to dry for about 3 hours. I use an electric fan for this process.

*Malt sugar or syrup can be found in any Chinese grocery.

Place the duck on an oiled poultry rack and place the rack in a pan. Roast at 400° for 20 minutes. Then, turn the oven down to 375° and cook 25 minutes per pound, total cooking time. Include the first 20 minutes in the total time.

Serve the thinly sliced duck, along with the skin, which is the best part, in the pancakes, along with a bit of hoisin and green onions. Make "brushes" of the onions or simply slice them the long way into nice slivers.

DUCK LIKE A MANDOLIN

SERVES 8 AS
PART OF A CHINESE MEAL

This recipe is basically the same as the Peking Duck above, but it is a bit easier. The duck will actually look like a mandolin only if you can find a bird that still has the head on. The head is left on the bird to resemble the top of the neck of the mandolin.

Cut the bird down the breastbone, using poultry shears. Open, or "butterfly," the duck and pat dry. Season with the inside seasoning just as in the recipe above. Place the bird, inside down, on a roasting rack and allow to sit while you boil 2 quarts of water and prepare the basting sauce, as in the above recipe. Place the broiling-pan rack, along with the bird, over the sink. I put mine on a large bowl in the sink. Using a ladle, gently pour the boiling water over the skin side of the bird only. Allow to dry for 20 minutes and then pour the sauce over the bird. Return the rack to the broiling pan. Discard the boiling water and basting syrup that flowed into the bowl in the sink.

Allow the bird to dry on the rack for 3 hours. I use an electric fan for this, just as in the above recipe.

Bake 20 minutes at 400° and then turn down the heat to 350° and bake 1 hour. Serve as Peking Duck, above, or simply cut up into serving pieces and then restore the shape of the "mandolin" on a large platter for serving.

STEWED DUCK WITH MUSHROOMS

SERVES 6 AS
A PART OF A CHINESE MEAL

When you prepare a Chinese meal you want to have several courses, and often cooking too many at the last minute can be a chore. This one is a casserole dish and it waits on the top of the stove or in the oven until you are ready to serve. Easy and a mushroom lover's paradise.

- 1 4-pound duck cut into 6 pieces
- 3 tablespoons peanut oil for pan-frying
- 3 cloves garlic, sliced thin
- 2 slices fresh ginger, size of a 25-cent piece, cut julienne
- 2 whole green onions, cleaned
- 8–10 whole dried Chinese mushrooms, soaked for 3 hours
- 3 cups Chinese Chicken Soup Stock (page 113) or regular Basic Chicken Stock (page 129)
- ½ cup Chinese rice wine or dry sherry
- ¼ cup light soy sauce
- ½ tablespoon sugar
- ½ tablespoon soybean condiment (mein see) or 1 star anise (I prefer the soybean condiment in this dish)

Pan-brown the duck pieces in a few tablespoons of oil in a large frying pan. Remove the pieces to a 6-quart covered stove-top casserole. In the same frying pan sauté the garlic and ginger for a few moments. Add the green onion and sauté for just a moment. Place *all* ingredients in the casserole and mix well. Bring to a boil and lower the heat. Simmer, covered, until the duck is very tender, about 1¼ hours.

STEAMED DRIED DUCK AND PORK

*SERVES 6 AS
PART OF A CHINESE MEAL*

The richness of the dried duck invades the pork in this dish. It is common food in Hong Kong, but very uncommon in this country. You might have to get used to the "cured" flavor of the dried duck.

¼ *dried duck, hacked
(page 24) into
¼-inch-wide pieces*

1 *pound lean
ground pork*

8–10 *water chestnuts,
coarsely chopped*

2 *tablespoons Chinese
rice wine or dry sherry*

2 *tablespoons light soy sauce*

½ *teaspoon grated fresh
ginger*

1 *tablespoon cornstarch*

1 *egg*

1 *teaspoon sesame oil*

⅛ *teaspoon freshly
ground black pepper*

1 *green onion,
chopped fine*

Cut the duck and soak it in fresh water for 2 hours. Change the water and bring to a simmer. Immediately turn off the stove and leave the duck, covered, in the water for ½ hour. Drain and discard the water.

Place all ingredients, except the duck, into a bowl and mix well. Place in a steaming bowl or glass pie plate. Top with the duck slices. Steam in a bamboo steamer (page 97) for 30 minutes.

TEA-SMOKED DUCK

SERVES 6–8 AS
PART OF A CHINESE MEAL

This is probably the second most famous Chinese method of preparing duck. In terms of Hong Kong popularity it stands right behind the famous Peking Duck.

1 *4-pound duck,*
split in half

1 *teaspoon salt*

¼ *teaspoon freshly ground*
black pepper

3 *tablespoons dry sherry or*
Chinese rice wine

2 *tablespoons sesame oil*

FOR SMOKING

½ *cup alder or hickory*
sawdust

¼ *cup black tea leaves*

2 *teaspoons sugar*

4 *cups peanut oil for deep-*
frying

Split the duck, using poultry shears and a cleaver, and pat dry. Marinate the halves in the salt, pepper, wine, and sesame oil for 2 hours. Blanch in boiling water for 2 minutes. Allow to dry on a rack for 1 hour.

Smoke in a wok or a Cameron smoker (page 19) using the wood, tea, and sugar. If you use a wok simply line the bottom with heavy aluminum foil and put the wood, tea, and sugar on the foil. Place a cake rack or steaming rack into the wok and put the duck on the rack. Bring the temperature up until you get some smoke, then turn it down a bit and watch it carefully, whether using the Cameron or the wok. Smoke for 20 minutes.

Place each half in a glass pie plate or steaming dish and steam for 45 minutes. Allow to cool and deep-fry in peanut oil until golden brown and crispy.

NOTE: This dish may also be done with chicken.

CHINESE DUCK SALAD

I developed this dish one night since I had a bit of roast duck left over. That does not happen very often. This salad is so good, however, that it would be worth your time to roast a duck just for this dish.

½ *pound cooked boneless duck meat, cut julienne (I prefer the smoked duck)*

¾ *pound bean sprouts*

¼ *cup fresh chopped coriander*

DRESSING

¼ *cup rice wine vinegar (Japanese)*

2 *tablespoons light soy sauce*

2 *tablespoons sesame oil*

½ *teaspoon sugar*

2 *tablespoons freshly toasted sesame seeds*

Black pepper, freshly ground, to taste

Iceberg lettuce, shredded, for base

Place the ingredients for the salad in a bowl. Mix the dressing separately and toss with the salad. Serve over shredded iceberg lettuce.

DUCK SOUP, CHINESE STYLE

This sounds like an old Groucho Marx movie, I know. Realize, however, that the Chinese are very frugal cooks. Little or nothing is wasted. When the Peking Duck is finished, the bones go into soup and it is not uncommon to see a restaurant advertise its Peking Duck "Cooked Three Ways." This means that the duck skin and pancakes are served first. The meat of the duck is then served with vegetables, and finally, the carcass comes back as soup.

This is easy and delicious, so don't throw out those duck bones.

2 quarts Chinese Chicken Soup Stock (page 113)

6 dried Chinese mushrooms, soaked in 1 cup warm water, the water reserved

Pinch of ground white pepper

1 cup Chinese greens (bok choy, Napa)

Bones from 1 roast duck

3 green onions, chopped

1 teaspoon sesame oil

1 cup cooked duck meat, cut julienne

Salt to taste

1 ounce cellophane noodles (sai fun) (page 29)

GARNISH

1 raw egg

1 tablespoon chopped Chinese parsley

Bring the stock to a simmer and add the mushrooms and the water in which they were soaked. Add the pepper, greens, and bones. Simmer for 1 hour.

Drain the stock and discard all solids except the mushrooms. Cut the mushrooms julienne and return to the stockpot. Add the green onions, sesame oil, and cooked duck meat and taste for salt. Drop the noodles into the pot and simmer until they are just tender, about 5 minutes.

Place the soup in a tureen and add the shelled raw egg, whole. It will cook on the way to the table. Add the parsley garnish. Stir the egg into the soup at the table.

LOOED DUCK FEET

SERVES 8, AT LEAST, AS PART OF A CHINESE MEAL

I told you that the Chinese never waste food. The feet of the duck are blanched and peeled. You can buy them in Chinatown all ready to be cooked. When Mary Young, my adopted Chinese aunt, and I go to a dim sum lunch in San Francisco, we always have this great delicacy. You simply chew the gelatinous meat off the bone and spit out the toes. Are you still with me?

8 duck feet, peeled	1 teaspoon sesame oil
2 cups Looing Sauce (page 203)	for garnish

Soak the duck feet overnight in water in the refrigerator. Prepare the feet for cooking by cutting off the toenails, if this has not already been done. Blanch the feet in boiling water for 3 minutes and drain. Place in a stove-top casserole and add the looing sauce. Bring to a simmer and cook, covered, until the feet are very tender, about 2 hours. Remove from the sauce to a serving plate and garnish with the sesame oil.

NOTE: You can prepare these ahead of time and simply reheat them either in the sauce or put them in a bowl with very little sauce and reheat them in your bamboo steamer (page 97).

GREECE

GREEK DUCK WITH OLIVES

SERVES 6

Duck is not as common in Greece or Rome as it is in China. This dish, however, is a smash. I tasted it the first time in a fine restaurant on the outskirts of Athens and the recipe is simple to duplicate. You will have no problems with this one.

1 4-pound duck, cut into 6 pieces	2 cups Greek Tomato Sauce (page 204)
3 tablespoons olive oil	½ cup dry red wine
1 yellow onion, peeled and sliced	1 cup green olives
	Salt and freshly ground black pepper to taste

Heat a 6-quart stove-top casserole and add the oil. Brown the duck pieces and remove from the pan. Sauté the onion and then add all ingredients to the pot. Cover and bring to a simmer. You may need to add a bit of water. Simmer until tender, about 1½ hours. Watch that it does not dry out, in which case you must add a bit more water.

DUCK GRILLED GREEK STYLE

This one is typical of the whole concept of Greek grilling. You split a duck down the middle, rub it with olive oil, garlic, oregano, and salt and pepper, and put it on the grill. Or you can broil it carefully in the oven.

Do not overcook the duck. The inside should be very moist and tender. Garnish the duck with fresh lemon juice just prior to serving.

ITALY

In Roman times the duck was prized by the wealthy, who thought up all kinds of ways to serve this bird.

DUCK WITH TURNIPS APICIUS

The most interesting duck dish that I found in early Western recipes comes from Apicius, around the first century. Craig, my cooking assistant, tried one of these and we both thought it was interesting, but you have to be a serious lover of turnips to get into this one.

The recipe is described in this way:

The duck is simmered in water and aniseed for 30 minutes. It is then stuffed with a bread dressing seasoned with leeks and coriander. Turnips are boiled, mashed, and spread over the stuffed duck, which is then roasted for 1½ hours. A sauce is made, using the popular herbs of that time, mixed with a bit of wine vinegar and the pan gravy. The herbs were cumin, coriander, pepper, and fennel.

The result is rather strange-looking by contemporary standards, but it is moist and tasty.

Give me a Peking Duck any day!

SMALL BIRDS

In the ancient world small birds were considered great delicacies. They were enjoyed in China, and still are, a fried quail, Chinese style, being one of the finest bird dishes I know.

We Americans do not relish small birds much since we seem to think that they are too much work to eat. We want big chunks of meat so we will enjoy a chicken or turkey more than a pigeon or squab. But we are missing a flavor, albeit in a small quantity, that was celebrated at the great banquets of ancient Rome. Apicius, the first-century cookbook author, loved figpeckers, small birds with a very funny name, and squabs and pigeons of all kinds. His Roman friends loved them as well and went from these small birds to a great deal of ostentatious nonsense, serving flamingo tongues and brains with eggs, and even roasted canary. How many of those creatures would you have to kill before you had a luncheon platter? And the ancient Greeks used to enjoy roasted peacock!

I prepared and taped a whole show on small birds in ancient cuisines . . . but you will never see it. I realized after the taping that even though we raise all kinds of quails, pigeons, squabs, and game hens for public consumption, I would never get away with chopping up little birds on the air. I have too many children in my audience who would think me evil. I wish I could make them understand that we all must subsist on the resources of the world, and there is little difference between enjoying a small bird and a hamburger. The cow felt no better about the meal than did the bird. I hope you will try these dishes; they are some of the finest foods that I have ever found.

CHINA

BROWNED SQUAB WITH ROASTED SALT AND PEPPER

SERVES 4 AS
PART OF A CHINESE MEAL

Squab, a fancy name for pigeon, is very popular with the Chinese. The meat is dark and moist and will respond to several methods of cooking. In ancient China these birds were eaten by rich and poor alike.

2 squabs

Salt and freshly ground
black pepper to taste

1 teaspoon dark soy sauce

3–4 cups peanut oil
for deep-frying

Cut each squab in half. Rub with the salt, pepper, and soy. Deep-fry in the hot oil, at 375°, until lightly browned, about 15 minutes. Do not overcook.

Hack (page 24) the squab into bite-sized slices and arrange on a heated platter.

Serve with Roasted Salt and Pepper (below). The pieces of bird are lightly dipped into the salt and pepper mixture.

ROASTED SALT AND PEPPER

Heat a wok and add 3 tablespoons kosher salt, 2 tablespoons freshly ground coarse black pepper, and 1 tablespoon Szechwan peppercorns. Heat until the aroma is bright and the salt begins to brown a tiny bit, stirring all the time. Cool and grind in a food blender. Serve with poultry.

FRIED QUAIL, CHINESE STYLE

SERVES 6–8 AS
PART OF A CHINESE MEAL

This is a delicious dish. Since the bird is simmered first in the looing sauce, it is very moist, even after a quick deep-frying.

3 *cups Looing Sauce (page 203)*   4 *cups peanut oil*
4 *quails, split in half*   *for deep-frying*

Bring the looing sauce to a boil and put in the quails. Bring back to a simmer and cook for 4 minutes. Remove from the sauce, drain, and pat dry with paper towels. Deep-fry in oil at 375° until golden, about 3 minutes. Do not overcook.

BROWNED QUAIL, CHINESE STYLE

The quail is generally a bit smaller than the squab, but each responds to cooking in the same way. This is a delicious dish, though given the price of quail it is a tad expensive.

Prepare the quail just as you do the squab in the recipe on page 265. Serve with Roasted Salt and Pepper (page 266) and a lemon squeeze.

FRIED SQUAB, CHINESE STYLE

The squab is cooked in exactly the same manner as the quail on page 265, but it will need a bit more time at each step since the bird is a little larger. Simmer in the looing sauce for 8 minutes and then deep-fry for 5 minutes.

TEA-SMOKED GAME HEN

SERVES 3–4 AS
PART OF A CHINESE MEAL

Game hens are a relatively recent bird, a development of modern agricultural science. However, in old China similar birds were common and this method of cooking remains a classic.

1 1½-pound game hen

Salt and freshly ground black pepper to taste

2 tablespoons dry sherry or Chinese rice wine

2 tablespoons sesame oil

3 tablespoons jasmine tea leaves

4 tablespoons alder or hickory sawdust

6 cups peanut oil for deep-frying

Cut the bird in half, using poultry shears or a Chinese cleaver.

Rub the halves with the salt and pepper, wine, and sesame oil. Allow to marinate for 2 hours.

Dip the halves into boiling water for 1 minute. Remove and place on a rack for drying.

Smoke the halves in a Cameron smoker (page 19) for 15 minutes using the tea leaves and the alder or hickory sawdust.

Place the halves on a plate and steam in a bamboo steamer (page 97) for 20 minutes. Allow the pieces to cool and then deep-fry in hot peanut oil, at 375°, until golden brown and crispy, about 4–5 minutes.

GREECE

Quail in Tomato Sauce, Greek Style

The great thing about always having a bit of Greek Tomato Sauce in your refrigerator is that you can prepare Greek meals in a hurry. This is a simple method of cooking quail that is common in the tavernas of Athens.

6 *quails, each split in half*

¼ *cup olive oil*

1½ *cups Greek Tomato Sauce (page 204)*

½ *cup dry red wine*

Salt and freshly ground black pepper to taste

Heat a large covered frying pan or *sauteuse*. Cut the quails in half and pan-brown in the olive oil. Add the tomato sauce and wine. Cover and simmer 45 minutes to 1 hour, or until the legs move easily. Add salt and pepper to taste.

ROASTED QUAIL APPETIZERS HOMER

SERVES 6

In ancient Greece small birds were very popular at a formal feast. Homer, the great poet, was particularly fond of thrushes and he sang an epic poem about them, a poem entitled "Epikichlides." This recipe is probably as close as we can come to the object of his affection.

¼ *pound butter*	½ *teaspoon thyme*
6 *quails*	½ *teaspoon oregano*
2 *slices toasted bread, cut into cubes*	*Salt and freshly ground black pepper to taste*
½ *pound crumbled feta cheese*	1 *clove garlic, crushed*

Heat the butter in a large frying pan. Roll the birds in the hot butter. Butter a baking dish with some of the melted butter and spread the bread cubes in the dish. Stuff the birds with the feta and place them on top of the bread. Stir the herbs, seasonings, and garlic into the remaining butter and baste each bird. Bake, uncovered, in a preheated oven at 375° for 40 minutes to 1 hour, depending on your taste.

GRILLED SQUAB, GREEK STYLE

SERVES 3–6, DEPENDING ON HOW YOU WISH TO FINALLY CUT THE BIRDS!

Another example of the brilliant background of Greek grilling. Remember that the Greeks invented the grill as we know it and they still use rather simple and basic ingredients. The results are always delicious.

3 squabs, ¾ to 1 pound each, split down the back and "butterflied" or flattened out

3 tablespoons olive oil

2 cloves garlic, crushed

½ teaspoon whole oregano, crushed by hand

Juice of 1 lemon

Salt and freshly ground black pepper to taste

Mix all the ingredients together in a large bowl. Allow the birds to marinate for 1 hour. Place the birds on a barbecue grill, at low heat, and grill 15 minutes bone side down. Turn each and grill 20 minutes on the skin side.

Be careful not to allow fires to start when the fat begins to drip on the charcoal.

Cook a total of 35 minutes or until the juice of the bird is clear and not pink or bloody.

ITALY

ROAST QUAIL EDMONDO

T rattoria Edmondo is a wonderful place to eat. To say it is informal is putting it mildly! The place is a collection of people who look like character actors for wild Italian movies and the owner, Edmondo, stands beside your table and slices the bread on his chest. Plates of olives, sausages, and pepperoni come as you sit down. It is in the style of a very old Roman establishment. His quail is just outstanding and this recipe is somewhat close to what he does. The treatment is really quite simple.

The birds are split in half and pan-browned in olive oil and garlic, along with a bit of salt and pepper. A small amount of dry red wine is added to the pan along with some Italian Tomato Sauce (page 208). The pan is then covered and gently simmered until the birds are tender.

They can be served with a side of pasta, the sauce becoming the glory of the evening.

GAME HENS WITH ROSEMARY AND GARLIC

The smell of rosemary and garlic in the air always makes me think of the back streets of the villages on the edge of Rome. You can have a fine Roman party with this dish and you can even urge your guests to place themselves on their sides on cushions and eat only with their fingers. Slaves had to eat sitting upright in Rome, but free citizens reclined. This would be a great dish for such an eating method.

3 *game hens, split in half*
¾ *cup olive oil*
4 *cloves garlic, crushed*
3 *tablespoons dry sherry*
3 *dashes Tabasco*

1 *tablespoon finely chopped fresh rosemary*
Juice of 1 lemon
Salt and freshly ground black pepper to taste

Split each bird in half, using either a Chinese cleaver or poultry shears. Set aside.

Using a very large bowl mix the remaining ingredients together. Marinate the bird halves in this mixture for 1 hour, turning often.

Broil in an electric oven, 7 or 8 minutes on a side, or on a charcoal barbecue. I prefer the charcoal, but be sure not to have the coals too hot. Cook to your preference.

VARIATION: You can use this same recipe for squab or quail. Just remember to cut down on the cooking time according to the size of the bird.

HINT: WHEN CUTTING POULTRY OR LARGE FISH with a Chinese cleaver, save your hand by placing a piece of rubber garden house, cut along one side, over the top of the cleaver. In this way you can use your hand for pounding on the cleaver without hurting yourself.

QUAIL OR
SQUAB IN CREAMED
ITALIAN SAUCE

This dish is done in the same style as Roast Quail Edmondo (page 270). Instead of the red wine use a little white wine along with the Italian Tomato Sauce. Just before serving remove the halves to a serving platter and add a few tablespoons of whipping cream to the sauce remaining in the pan. Bring to a simmer and pour over the birds. This is just delicious!

Meats

LAMB

W e are talking ancient food here. Men and women have eaten lamb
for thousands and thousands of years. Sheep bones have been found
in the caves Peking Man inhabited half a million years ago, although
domestication of the sheep probably did not begin until about 12,000
years ago. At that time wild goats and sheep were attracted to the fields
of wild grain that began to grow as the world climate changed. Domes-

tication eventually followed as the villagers moved to protect this generous grain supply. The first hard evidence of sheep raising dates from 8920 B.C. in Iraq and Romania, and sheep appear to have been raised in prehistoric China on the loess plateau, a region where the ancient winds had deposited rich soils.

Italy and Greece still have their own ancient traditions of eating lamb. Lamb was raised in Greece from prehistoric times and remains the favorite meat of its people. Today about three million lambs are eaten annually in Greece, and they are cooked according to recipes that go back to the earliest days of recorded history. I spent time in Greece during the Eastertide and feasted on lamb that was cooked the way the Greeks have always cooked it, and I do mean always. Olive oil, lemon juice, oregano, and thyme. The result is just wonderful.

Lamb in the Roman kitchen has always been important. To this day the Romans claim that they have the best pastureland in Italy, and thus the best lamb. I shall not argue. Every part of the animal is celebrated in the Eternal City, and the innards seem to have an especially high place in the celebration. The Romans would rather eat a slice of lamb than a piece of fish, though they are only thirty miles from the sea.

I expect the Chinese were the first to couple lamb with its best seasoning, garlic. In the *Book of Songs,* a volume from around 600 B.C., lamb is offered with garlic, and to this day in the northern regions of China the dish is made the same way . . . the very same.

I wish Americans would stop overcooking lamb so that it could be enjoyed more in our culture. We still seem to be suffering from the argument common in the Old West. It was the cattleman against the sheepherder. Lamb is, I believe, the finest of the red meats.

You might also wish to consider the following recipes:

Greek Lamb and Pasta Salad *(page 146)*
Chinese Lamb and Leeks *(page 448)*

LAMB HOT POT, MONGOLIAN STYLE

T he first time I tasted this dish was in Beijing. I enjoyed my time there but I was surprised . . . no, I was somewhat hurt by the quality of the food. I tried to get into good restaurants, but that is hard for a Westerner unless you have a local with you. I finally managed to get into the most famous Lamb Hot Pot restaurant in Beijing. When I left I was filled, content, and yet still disappointed. I believe the problem with quality stems from the fact that there is very little refrigeration in China and to make matters worse, much of the good-quality food is shipped out of China to Hong Kong and America. China needs the money, and Chinese eaters suffer for it. I think you can get the best Chinese food in Hong Kong and, secondly, in San Francisco. New York and Seattle do very well, too.

In any case, here is the dish. You can do it at home with little effort as long as you have a Hoko or Hot Pot.

Lamb, boneless and lean, sliced into strips, very thin

Chinese Chicken Soup Stock *(page 113) or* Basic Lamb Stock *(page 128)* for the Hoko Pot

Napa cabbage, chopped as for coleslaw, *or* bok choy, chopped

Bean curd, cut into ½-inch cubes

Bean thread or cellophane noodles, soaked for 20 minutes

The lamb is sliced very thin and cooked in a Hot Pot filled with bubbling chicken or lamb broth. Each guest is to have his own plate of thinly sliced lamb. Napa and bean curd may also be added to the pot and removed when you will. The noodles can be added at any time, but they are generally added as one of the last ingredients. Small brass strainers can be provided for each person to use in claiming his/her portion of the pot.

Each guest cooks his lamb and then dips it into a sauce. The dip sauces vary and several recipes are given on page 202. You may wish to create your own, given any of the following ingredients:

Light soy sauce

Sesame oil

Ginger, freshly grated

Hot pepper oil

Chinese rice wine or dry sherry

Worcestershire sauce

Sugar, just a pinch

Green onions, chopped

Chinese parsley, chopped

The meal is concluded with the consumption of the soup.
For full instructions on using the Hoko Pot, see page 116.

MONGOLIAN LAMB

SERVES 6 AS
PART OF A CHINESE MEAL

Great grills are used for this dish in famous Mongolian restaurants in China. You may want to use a tabletop grill of some sort and cook this at the table in front of your guests. I think the dish is just fine straight from the kitchen wok. It is rich!

1 pound lean, boneless lamb
shoulder, sliced thin in
1-inch-wide strips

MARINADE

2 tablespoons oyster sauce *light soy*

3 green onions, chopped *1" pieces*

1 tablespoon chili sauce *hoisin sauce*
(from catsup department)

Freshly ground black
pepper to taste
(I like lots)

FOR CHOWING

2 tablespoons peanut oil

½ teaspoon salt

3 cloves garlic, diced fine

GARNISH

2 cups iceberg lettuce,
shredded as for tacos

3 green onions, chopped

1 tablespoon sesame oil

*or
soy sauce
fresh ginger
sherry
hoisin*

*P.Y. 116 th St.
Wong Lee Ok*

I often freeze the lamb just a bit so that I can slice it very thin. Mix the marinade and soak the meat in same for 30 minutes.

Heat a wok and add the oil, salt, and garlic. Chow just until the garlic begins to change color and then add ½ of the marinated meat. Chow over very high heat until done to your taste. Remove to a warm plate and chow the second half. Serve over the lettuce and add the onion and sesame oil garnish.

VARIATION: You might want to serve the meat along with lettuce leaves that can be rolled like burritos instead of the chopped lettuce. Peking Pancakes (page 474) are also just delicious filled with the meat and shredded lettuce.

GREECE

LAMB AND TOMATO SAUCE, GREEK STYLE

SERVES 6–8

This is a very common way of serving the favorite meat of Greece. Since it uses tomato, we can assume the recipe is rather recent, only about four hundred years old, but this same dish can be found throughout Greece.

3 tablespoons olive oil

3 pounds lean lamb
shoulder, bone in, cut into
serving pieces

Salt and freshly ground
black pepper to taste

2 cups Basic Lamb Stock
(page 128) Basic Chicken
Stock (page 129)

1 cup dry red wine

3 cloves garlic, finely chopped

2 yellow onions, peeled and
coarsely chopped

1 cup chopped parsley

¼ teaspoon allspice

¼ teaspoon cinnamon

½ teaspoon oregano

2 cups coarsely chopped
ripe tomatoes

Salt and freshly ground
black pepper to taste

Heat a large frying pan and add the olive oil. Brown the cut-up pieces of lamb, in 2 batches, on both sides. Season with the salt and pepper. Place the meat in a 6-quart casserole, along with the broth and wine, leaving the oil in the frying pan. Reheat the frying pan and sauté the garlic and onions until clear. Add the remaining ingredients, except the final salt and pepper, and sauté just until the tomatoes cook down a bit. Add this mixture to the casserole, along with salt and pepper to taste. Bring to a simmer, cover, and cook until the meat is very tender, about 1½ hours.

LAMB WITH CHEESE AND PASTA

SERVES 4
AS A MAIN COURSE

This is a tasty way to use up a little leftover lamb, providing you have not overcooked the lamb in the first place.

½ pound fettucine (dry)

½ cup olive oil

3 cloves garlic

¾ to 1 pound medium-rare
lamb, cut julienne

1 cup grated kefalotyri
cheese (page 36)

¼ cup chopped parsley

Salt and pepper to taste

Bring a pot of water to boil for the pasta.

Heat a frying pan and sauté the garlic in the oil. Just as the pasta is finishing, add the cooked lamb to the hot garlic oil and sauté for just a moment. Toss the meat with the drained pasta, along with all other ingredients.

LAMB WITH ORZO PASTA, GREEK STYLE

SERVES 6–8
AS A MAIN COURSE

This is another dish that I first tasted at Taverna Sigalas, in Monastiraki Square, in Athens. The food that they serve is not complex, and while it is typical of taverna food it is of very good quality and seasoned nicely. I think it is better than most of the fancier eating houses in the city.

This is an exceptionally good dish that is just great for entertaining.

3 pounds boneless lamb shoulder

3 tablespoons olive oil for pan-browning

Salt and freshly ground black pepper to taste

6 cups Basic Lamb Stock (page 128) or Basic Chicken Stock (page 129)

½ cup olive oil

2 cups orzo pasta (page 36)

1½ cups peeled and chopped yellow onion

2 large ripe tomatoes, chopped

2 teaspoons dried dillweed

¼ cup chopped parsley

Juice of 1 lemon for garnish

In a stove-top Dutch oven brown the boneless lamb shoulder in the olive oil. Add the salt and pepper. Add enough stock to come halfway up the side of the meat, and simmer, covered, until very tender, about 2 hours.

Remove the meat from the pot and set aside, covered to keep warm. Remove the fat from the stock in the pan and add additional stock, if necessary, to make up a total of 4 cups. Remove the stock from the pan and set aside.

Heat the Dutch oven again and add ½ cup olive oil. Add the orzo pasta and toss for a minute. Add the chopped yellow onion and sauté until the onion is clear. Stir in the tomatoes, dillweed, and parsley.

Return the meat to the pot, along with the 4 cups of stock. Cover and simmer until the broth is absorbed and the pasta is tender, about 30 minutes. Add the juice of 1 lemon just before serving.

NOTE: If the dish is too wet when the pasta is tender, continue to cook for a few more minutes with the lid off to reduce the sauce.

Serve with the lamb on top of the pasta.

ROAST LAMB, GREEK STYLE

SERVES 4–6

Nothing can equal the scent of a lamb roasting on Easter Day in the back streets of a Greek village. I suppose that lamb on Easter is the annual culinary highlight of the Greek diet. I have added a bit of olive oil to keep this roast moist, but you would not have to do this with a whole lamb.

1 5–6-pound leg of lamb
½ cup olive oil
3 cloves garlic, crushed

1 teaspoon whole oregano, crushed by hand
Salt and freshly ground black pepper to taste

FOR RARE LAMB: Allow the lamb to come to room temperature. Heat your oven to 400°. Mix the oil, garlic, and oregano together and rub the leg completely. Season with salt and pepper and place on baking rack in a pan. Insert a meat thermometer in the thickest part of the leg, being careful not to touch the bone. Bake at 400° for 40 minutes, so that the meat can brown. Turn the oven down to 325° and bake for an additional 40 to 50 minutes, or until the thermometer registers 140°.

Remove the meat from the oven and allow it to sit ½ hour before slicing. It will continue to cook during this time.

FOR MEDIUM LAMB: Follow the above instructions but cook a bit longer so that the thermometer registers 145° to 150°.

Slice thin and serve with some of the pan juices.

Lamb Rib Chops, Broiled Greek Style

Lamb recipes do not have to take long to prepare. This recipe is very quick, and flavorful as well. Just don't overcook the meat.

Remove the bone from lamb rib chops or lamb shoulder steak. I prefer the shoulder steak as it is a bit more moist.

Pound the meat fairly thin, using a metal meat pounder (page 21). Brush with olive oil and garlic, and sprinkle with salt and pepper, and oregano. Grill or broil quickly so that the meat remains tender. Use high heat for this.

Souvlaki

MAKES 8 SANDWICHES

This is an old Athenian dish that will make you wonder about who invented the first takeout food. These lamb-laden skewers are for sale all over the major Greek cities, and the flavor is made even more exciting by the grilled bread with the yogurt dripping down the sides.

2 *pounds of lean lamb cut into 1-inch-square cubes*

MARINADE

½ *cup olive oil*

1 *cup red wine*

1 *teaspoon salt*

Freshly ground black pepper to taste

1 *teaspoon oregano*

1 *teaspoon whole dried mint, crushed by hand*

3 *cloves garlic, crushed*

8 *loaves of Pita Bread with Olive Oil, Grilled (page 479)*

GARNISHES

Purple onions, sliced paper thin

Tomatoes, ripe and sliced thin

Plain yogurt

Marinate cubes of meat in a large bowl. Mix two or three times during a 2-hour period.

Place on wooden skewers and broil, turning once, until tender but still a bit pink on the inside.

Serve in a grilled pita loaf with onions, tomatoes, and yogurt on top.

NOTE: This dish is also just great with pork.

BARLEY PUDDING
WITH LAMB

SERVES 6
AS A MAIN COURSE

This dish goes back to the second century B.C. The flavors are unusual for us but this kind of food was evidently very common in ancient times. I have added a bit of garlic to the old recipe and I think that you will love the result.

- 6 *cups water*
- 2 *teaspoons salt*
- 2 *pounds boneless lamb,*
  cut into serving chunks
- 3 *cloves garlic, crushed*
- 1 *cup barley*
- 2 *tablespoons olive oil*

Place the water, salt, lamb, and garlic in a 4-quart heavy covered saucepan. Bring to a boil, turn to a simmer, cover, and cook for 2 hours. Remove all from the pots, reserving the broth. Remove the fat from the broth and add enough additional water to make 6 cups.

Place the barley in a grain grinder and grind very coarsely. You want something like groats or bulgur wheat, in terms of texture. Stir the olive oil into the barley groats and place in the pan. Return the meat and measured broth to the pan and bring to a light boil. Simmer, covered, for 25 minutes, or until the barley is soft and tasty and the liquid is absorbed.

Serve this with crusty Italian bread or with pita bread. Eat the pudding with the bread for a rather heavy but simply delicious meal.

GROUND MEAT
ON SKEWERS

SERVES 8

This is a very creative version of meat on a stick. Just off Monastiraki Square in Athens is a place that puts ground meat on metal skewers and then broils it. The result is delicious, very close to the famous "gyros'' sandwiches that are made from ground meat that is grilled upright on a rotating spit. This is just great for a party as you can prepare everything ahead of time and then cook these for your guests at the last minute. Use the firebrick grill (page 285).

1 *pound ground pork*

1 *pound ground lamb*

1 *teaspoon each salt and pepper*

3–6 *cloves garlic, crushed, to taste*

Juice of 1 lemon

1 *teaspoon whole oregano, hand-crushed*

2 *tablespoons ouzo*

4 *loaves Pita Bread with Olive Oil, Grilled (page 479)*

GARNISHES

Tzatziki (page 86)

Purple onions, peeled and sliced paper thin

Parsley, chopped

Cherry tomatoes, broiled on metal skewers until tender

Mix all and mold on flat metal skewers. The skewers will have to be about ⅜ inch wide and 18 inches long in size. You may have to have these made for you at a sheet-metal shop. Thin skewers just will not work as the meat will fall off. Put about ¼ pound of meat on each oiled skewer and sort of press it until it is the shape of a sausage. Place the meat sticks on an oiled baking sheet and bake for 20 minutes at 375°. Brush with olive oil and garlic for final grilling over the firebrick grill.

Pull the metal skewers from the meat as you serve them in the grilled pita bread. Fill each loaf with the garnishes of tzatziki, sliced purple onions, parsley, and tiny broiled tomatoes.

GRILLED LAMB CUBES, GREEK STYLE

This is a simple dish that one sees in the villages outside of Athens and on the islands. It is easy to prepare, and the flavors will be very close to what you would find in beautiful Greece.

Lamb cubes, about 1 inch square, are marinated in olive oil, garlic, oregano, and fresh lemon juice for about 3 hours. The meat cubes are then put on sticks and grilled over charcoal fires. Your barbecue will do well. Add a bit of salt and pepper before serving. Do not overcook the meat. This can be avoided by not creating too hot a fire. Just cut down a bit on the number of charcoal briquets that you use.

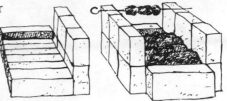

ITALY

ROAST LAMB, ITALIAN STYLE

Young roast lamb is the expected dish for Easter in Rome. While the Romans have loved lamb since the time of the Empire it still seems to be most popular on holidays. It can be purchased regularly in the many fine restaurants, but it does not seem to find its way to the family table as often as I would expect. I cannot explain this, but I would eat lamb three times a week if I lived in Rome. It is just wonderful!

LAMB RIB CHOPS, BROILED ROMAN STYLE

The Romans have loved mint since ancient times. A typical bit of grilling genius can be accomplished by using the Lamb Rib Chops, Broiled Greek Style (page 282), and using dried mint in the recipe instead of oregano. The flavor is refreshing . . . and now you know why the rest of us began using mint sauce or jelly on our lamb. It is an old Roman custom.

PORK

The story is absurd! When Charles Lamb was asked how people first came to realize that roast pork is delicious, he spun a charming tale—though historically it is out of whack. He told of a child in ancient China who returned to his home after a serious fire. The family's pet pig had been burned in the blaze and the boy tasted roast pork for the first time. Come now . . . are you going to tell me that architecture, the building of houses, developed before the discovery of cooking? It could not be, since people were roasting meat while living in caves. No, the simple truth is that pork has been popular since ancient times, and each of our three cultures learned to cook the piggy in the early days.

To this day pork is so prized in China that it is listed among the "Eight Marvels" of food, and it is listed not once but *twice,* as pork and as ham. In Italy there is an old phrase that refers to the pig as having "thirteen flavors," simply because the animal is so versatile in the kitchen.

Please remember that everything on or in the pig is used. Nearly every morsel is turned into food or some other product. The skin becomes leather and can be used for skin grafts for human burn victims. The glands go into pharmaceuticals, the stomach for pepsin, and the inedible fat for lubricants. The hair goes into hairbrushes, paintbrushes, insulation, and upholstery. No wonder 400 million pigs live on this good earth. We need them!

The pig was probably the second animal to be domesticated, the dog being the first. The meat is easy to preserve and the results are delicious. It is no wonder that the ancient Chinese began to domesticate pigs as early as 5000 B.C., and while a pork taboo began in ancient Egypt and Israel, the Chinese and Greeks have never wavered from their culinary commitment to the porker.

While you enjoy the following recipes you might also consider:

Pork with Leeks and Black Beans *(page 449)*
Spareribs with Black Beans and Pepper Sauce *(page 105)*
Garlic Ribs with Green Pepper and Black Beans *(page 106)*
Steamed Pork with Salted Eggs *(page 226)*

BARBECUED PORK STRIPS
(Cha Shao)

*SERVES 6–8 FOR A
DIM SUM SNACK OR A COURSE
IN A CHINESE DINNER*

This is the most commonly known Chinese pork dish in America, and I do not know why. Usually American-Chinese restaurants use very lean cuts of pork and the result is a dry and tasteless version of the real Chinese delight. That's why you put all that mustard and sesame seed on the pork. It is too dry to eat otherwise. (Boy, am I talking American heresy here!) A little fat in the meat is necessary for good flavor, according to the Chinese.

For this version choose pork butt that has little streaks of fat in it and the result will be juicy and flavorful.

2 *pounds boneless pork butt*

MARINADE

2 *tablespoons Chinese
Chicken Soup Stock
(page 113)*

2 *tablespoons dark
soy sauce*

1 *tablespoon soybean
condiment* (mein see)

1 *tablespoon Chinese rice
wine or dry sherry*

1½ *tablespoons honey*

¾ *teaspoon salt*

1 *large clove garlic, crushed*

2 *tablespoons hoisin sauce
(page 30)*

*A few drops of red
food coloring*

Cut the pork into long strips 1½ to 2 inches square. Mix all for the marinade and marinate the meat for 3 hours, unrefrigerated, or 6 hours in the refrigerator. Turn the strips every hour or so.

Preheat the oven to 350°. Place a large cake pan half filled with water on the lowest shelf of your oven. This will catch drips from the meat and prevent smoking. Place the meat strips directly on an oven rack and put in the top position of the oven. Be sure that all of the meat is over the dripping pan. Roast for 45 minutes without disturbing the meat. Then, turn the heat up to 450° and roast for an additional 15 minutes or until the pork strips are crisp and a rich brown color. Slice the meat and serve it hot or cold . . . or use in other dishes as directed.

> **HINT: TO MAKE HOT CHINESE MUSTARD** simply purchase a can of Colman's English dry mustard. Boil a bit of water and allow it to cool. Mix the water with dry mustard to the desired consistency. Keep stirring the mustard until it is as hot as you like it. The longer you stir the hotter it will get!

BARBECUED SPARERIBS

SERVES 4–6 AS A
COURSE IN A CHINESE DINNER

In Hong Kong you can purchase these ribs already prepared, and still warm, just as you have been able to do for one thousand years in China. Since pork has been popular almost since the beginning of Chinese history we can bet that a lot of these ribs have been consumed.

MARINADE

2 cloves garlic, crushed

3 tablespoons dark soy sauce

2 tablespoons dry sherry or Chinese rice wine

1 teaspoon freshly grated ginger

½ tablespoon brown sugar

½ tablespoon sesame oil

½ teaspoon five-spice powder (page 39)

1 tablespoon hoisin sauce

1 teaspoon pepper sauce, such as Tabasco or Mexican Hot Sauce

1 tablespoon catsup

1 2-pound side of pork spareribs, cut into 2 or 3 pieces

Mix all for the marinade and pour in a bowl over the ribs. Coat the ribs well by rubbing in the sauce and marinate, turning now and then, for 3 hours, unrefrigerated.

Bake on a preheated roasting pan in a 400° oven for 35–40 minutes. Serve hot or at room temperature.

If you wish to have a bit more "crunch" on the ribs broil them a bit after baking. Broil them just until they are nicely browned.

CRISPY ROAST PORK

SERVES 8–10 AS
PART OF A CHINESE MEAL

This is the richest pork dish I know in terms of the Chinese table. It is rich because it is very fatty. I love this meat, sometimes called *litchen*, though I do not allow myself this fatty luxury very often. I hope, once you taste this, that you will be as disciplined. It may be hard to stop eating!

I found this recipe in a cookbook published in the Chinese community in Seattle. It is called *Flavors of China* and has many recipes that are very typical of Chinese home cooking.

2–2½ *pounds fresh side of pork, lean, with skin on*

1 *teaspoon salt*

MARINADE

1 *tablespoon soybean condiment* (mein see)

1 *tablespoon dark soy sauce*

¼ *teaspoon salt*

1 *teaspoon sugar*

1 *clove garlic, crushed*

1 *teaspoon fresh ginger, grated*

Lay pork on a board, skin side up, and pierce it all over with an ice pick. Rub salt into the pork on both sides. Mix all of the ingredients for the marinade together. Place the meat on a broiling-pan rack, skin side down, and rub the meaty side with the marinade. Let stand for 1 hour.

Heat the oven to 350°. Turn the meat skin side up and place the pan on the middle rack in the oven. Roast, uncovered, for 1½ hours, piercing the skin in many places with an ice pick. Do this 3 or 4 times during the baking. Then, turn the oven on broil and broil the meat for 15 to 20 minutes, or until the skin is crisp. Be careful that you do not burn the meat at this point. You want it to be a dark golden brown.

Chop into bite-size pieces and garnish with green onions. Or use the meat in other recipes.

SMOKED SIDE OF PORK

Smoke the raw side of pork in a Cameron smoker (page 19) for about 20 minutes and then proceed as on page 176. The results are absolutely delicious! The meat is eaten as is or it can be chowed with other ingredients as in the recipe below.

SMOKED SIDE OF PORK WITH HOT BLACK BEAN SAUCE

SERVES 6 AS PART OF A CHINESE MEAL

The Smoked Side of Pork can be sliced and chowed Hunan style. Your guests will probably consider this one of the best Chinese dishes that you have learned to prepare. Yes, it takes some time, as you must smoke it, roast it, and then chow it. The flavors are so delectable that you will not mind the work.

2 *tablespoons peanut oil*

1 *tablespoon fermented black beans* (dow see), *rinsed in warm water and drained*

1 *tablespoon finely chopped garlic*

1¼ *pounds Smoked Side of Pork (above), cooked and cut into ¼-inch slices, and then into ½-inch pieces*

1 *green sweet bell pepper, cored and seeded, cut into ½-inch squares*

2 *tablespoons light soy sauce*

½ *teaspoon garlic and red chili paste (page 30)*

½ *cup Chinese Chicken Soup Stock (page 113) or regular chicken soup*

3 *green onions, cut Chinese style (page 142)*

½ *teaspoon salt*

Heat a wok and add the oil, black beans, and garlic. Chow for a moment, mashing them together, and then add the pork slices. Chow for a moment and add the remaining ingredients. Chow until all is very hot.

SLOW-SIMMERED PORK ROAST

SERVES 8 AS
PART OF A CHINESE MEAL

I have not seen Ann Gelow for years. She is a charming woman from Taiwan who married a fellow who was running our University Church draft-counseling center, years ago, when I was a college chaplain. She worked during the day and offered me this dish for dinner one evening. It had been slowly cooking all the time she had been at work. It is simple to make and just heaven to eat.

3 green onions, cut Chinese style (page 142)

1 teaspoon fresh ginger, cut julienne

2 star anise, whole

2 tablespoons soybean condiment (mein see)

2 tablespoons light soy sauce

2 teaspoons brown sugar

½ cup dry sherry or Chinese rice wine

2 cloves garlic, sliced thin

½ teaspoon ground white pepper

2 cups water (More may be needed)

2¼ pounds boneless pork roast (I prefer pork butt)

Mix all the ingredients together, except the pork. Place the meat in a ovenproof casserole that is just large enough to hold it. Pour the sauce over the top, cover the dish, and bake at 275° for anywhere from 5 to 8 hours, depending on your taste.

PORK AND GARLIC CHIVES

SERVES 3–4 AS
PART OF A CHINESE MEAL

There is a vegetable in China that looks like pale green chives but has the wonderful flavor of garlic. If you are near a Chinatown you can find this ingredient; otherwise try this tasty dish with regular chives.

2 tablespoons peanut oil

2 cloves garlic, chopped fine

1 slice fresh ginger, cut into tiny julienne sticks

2 green onions, sliced Chinese style (page 142)

1 tablespoon light soy sauce

⅛ teaspoon ground white pepper

Pinch of MSG (optional)

1 tablespoon Chinese rice wine or dry sherry

½ pound lean pork cut into julienne strips

1 cup chopped garlic chives or regular chives

Sesame oil, just a splash, for garnish

Heat a wok and add 1 tablespoon of the oil, the garlic, and ginger. Chow for a moment and add the green onions, soy, pepper, the optional MSG, and the wine. Chow for a minute and remove from the wok.

Reheat the wok to smoking. Add the remaining tablespoon of oil and the pork. Chow just until the pork is tender and remove from the wok, leaving the oil in the wok. Add the chives and chow until tender, then return the sauce and the pork. Toss for a moment until all is hot. Add the sesame oil, toss, and serve.

HINT: FOR PROPER CHINESE CHOWING remember these simple rules.

1. Always have everything totally prepared, chopped, mixed, sliced, before you turn on the wok.

2. Heat the wok first, and then add the oil and ingredients. "Hot wok, cold oil, foods won't stick." If using an electric stove rather than gas leave the burner on high and control the heat by moving the wok off and on the burner.

3. Use fresh ingredients as much as possible.

4. Do not overcook the food.

5. Serve the dish the moment it is done, no matter what is going on at the table. An old Chinese proverb says, "A man should wait for the dish. The dish should never wait for the man."

PORK AND PEPPERS
ON IRON PLATE

SERVES 3–4 AS
PART OF A CHINESE MEAL

This type of dish is the current rage in Hong Kong. It hit San Francisco a few years ago and everyone seems to get a bang out of a dish coming to the table that positively spews hot pepper oil all over the guests. The iron plate, which can be purchased in large Chinese communities, is heated on the stove and then placed on a wooden plank and brought to the table. The server pours the cooked dish, hot from the wok and filled with hot peppers, on the hot iron plate. Everything sizzles and bubbles and brings out a most marvelous flavor. Of course, most of the guests have to hide behind a big cloth napkin in order to protect their eyes and clothing from the pepper oil. You can try this with a black frying pan that has been heated very hot and placed on a board. Great fun and very dramatic! The taste of this dish can also be very hot. Adjust it to your own taste.

¾ pound boneless pork butt, cut julienne

1 tablespoon dark soy

1 tablespoon dry sherry or Chinese rice wine

½ teaspoon julienne-cut ginger

3 tablespoons peanut oil

3 cloves garlic, finely chopped

½ teaspoon salt

½ cup green onions, cut Chinese style (page 142)

½ cup julienne-cut green sweet bell peppers

6 dried small red peppers, soaked in ¼ cup water

½ cup julienne-cut bamboo shoots

1 teaspoon ground white pepper

1 tablespoon sesame oil

1 teaspoon garlic and red chili paste or to taste

Marinate the cut pork in the soy, wine, and ginger for about 15 minutes. Heat the wok and add 2 tablespoons of the oil, along with the garlic, and salt. Chow the pork over high heat just until barely done to taste. Remove. Heat the remaining tablespoon of oil and add the vegetables and pepper to the wok and chow for a moment. Add the remaining ingredients and return the pork to the wok. Toss until all is hot and bring to the table. Pour on the preheated iron plate or black frying pan and stand back!!!

SIDE OF PORK AND OYSTERS IN SAND POT

SERVES 4 AS
PART OF A CHINESE MEAL

While this dish takes some doing, it is a classic. You will need to have some leftover Crispy Roast Pork for an opener, and then you are on your way.

The sand pot is explained on page 19 and can be found in Chinatown. Otherwise, use any good stove-top casserole.

½ cake firm bean curd

4 cups peanut oil for deep-frying

1 tablespoon peanut oil

Pinch of salt

¼ teaspoon freshly grated ginger

1 clove garlic, chopped fine or crushed

½ tablespoon light soy sauce

3 green onions, cut Chinese style (page 142)

⅛ teaspoon sugar

1 tablespoon oyster sauce

Pinch of MSG (optional)

Pinch of ground white pepper

1 cup of Crispy Roast Pork (page 290) sliced ¼ inch thick and then into 1-inch pieces

½ cup Chinese Chicken Soup Stock (page 113) or Basic Chicken Stock (page 129)

1 teaspoon cornstarch mixed with 1½ teaspoons water

1 medium head iceberg lettuce, torn up

1 cup small oysters

Slice the bean curd into squares ½ inch thick, and then cut each square into 2 triangles. Place bean curd slices on paper towels to drain a bit of the moisture.

Heat the deep-frying oil to 360° and deep-fry the bean curd slices until golden, about 10 minutes. Be careful with this as the bean curd will "spit" at you when you put it in the hot oil. Remove and drain the slices.

Heat a wok and add the tablespoon of peanut oil. Chow the salt, ginger, and garlic for just a moment. Add the soy sauce, green onions, sugar, oyster sauce, the optional MSG, and the white pepper. Stir for just a moment and add the cooked pork. Chow just until the pork is hot and then add the chicken broth. When the broth begins to boil, stir in the cornstarch and water. Cook until thickened. Place the lettuce in the bottom of a sand pot or stove-top casserole. Stir the oysters into the pork and sauce and pour all over the lettuce. Cover and place on high heat until all is hot. Serve from the casserole.

SIDE OF PORK WITH COD AND BEAN CURD IN SAND POT

SERVES 4–6 AS PART OF A CHINESE MEAL

This one is similar to the dish above in that it uses seafood, bean curd, and Crispy Roast Pork. A dish that is similar to this one, but superior, I am afraid, is served at the wonderful Sea Garden Restaurant in Seattle's Chinatown. This is as close as I can come to the delicate flavors that they can create in this fine Hong Kong–style seafood house.

$\frac{1}{2}$ cake firm bean curd

4 cups peanut oil for deep-frying

1 cup Crispy Roast Pork (page 290), sliced $\frac{1}{4}$ inch thick and then into 1-inch pieces

THE FISH

$\frac{1}{2}$ pound codfish fillets, skinless and boneless, cut into 1-inch by 1-inch pieces

$\frac{1}{2}$ tablespoon Chinese rice wine or dry sherry

$\frac{1}{2}$ tablespoon light soy sauce

$\frac{1}{8}$ teaspoon baking powder

1 egg white, beaten

$\frac{1}{4}$ cup each cornstarch and flour, mixed

FOR CHOWING

1 tablespoon peanut oil

1 clove garlic, chopped fine

$\frac{1}{8}$ teaspoon freshly grated ginger

3 green onions, cut Chinese style (page 142)

$\frac{1}{2}$ tablespoon light soy sauce

Pinch of sugar

1 tablespoon oyster sauce

Pinch of MSG (optional)

Pinch of ground white pepper

½ cup Chinese Chicken Soup
Stock (page 113) or Basic
Chicken Stock (page 129)

1 teaspoon cornstarch mixed
with 1½ teaspoons water

1 medium head iceberg
lettuce, torn up

Slice the bean curd into squares ½ inch thick, and then cut each square into 2 triangles. Place bean curd slices on paper towels to drain a bit of the moisture.

Heat the deep-frying oil to 360° and deep-fry the bean curd slices until golden, about 10 minutes. Be careful with this as the bean curd will "spit" at you when you put it in the hot oil. Remove and drain the slices.

Prepare the cod and marinate in the sherry and soy for 10 minutes. Heat the deep-frying oil again to 360°. Mix the baking powder with the egg white. Drain the fish of the marinade and mix with the egg white. Dredge each piece of fish in the cornstarch/flour mixture and deep-fry until golden, about 5 minutes or less. Drain and set aside.

Heat the wok and add the oil for chowing. Chow the garlic and ginger for a moment and add the green onions. Add the soy, sugar, oyster sauce, optional MSG, and white pepper. Chow for a moment and add the chicken stock. Bring to a quick boil and stir in the cornstarch/water mixture. Stir to thicken. Add the bean curd, pork, and fish to the wok.

Put the torn lettuce in the bottom of a sand pot (page 19) or stove-top casserole. Pour the sauce and meat mixture over the top. Heat on a high burner until all is steaming hot.

SPARERIBS WITH BLACK BEANS

SERVES 6 AS
PART OF A CHINESE MEAL

I suppose all of us love to chew on bones when we can get away with it. This dish, popular even at formal Chinese dinners, *must* be chewed on, and the flavor is wonderful. You cannot make too much of this dish for me!

1 pound pork spareribs, cut into 1-inch-long individual pieces (Have your butcher run them through his bandsaw!)

3 tablespoons light soy sauce

2 tablespoons dry sherry or Chinese rice wine

3 cloves garlic, chopped fine

1 tablespoon fermented black beans (dow see), rinsed and mashed

Pinch of brown sugar

½ teaspoon MSG (optional)

1 teaspoon sesame oil

1 teaspoon garlic and red chili paste (page 30), or to taste

2 tablespoons cornstarch

2 green onions, chopped

½ green pepper, cut into julienne strips

Place the sparerib pieces in a colander and pour 2 quarts of boiling water over them. Do this in the sink. Drain them well and chow, or pan-fry, until lightly browned. Drain the fat and place them in a bowl. Add all other ingredients except the onions and green pepper. Mix well and then add the onions and pepper. Place in a steaming dish and steam for 1 hour 15 minutes. They will be very tender and delicious.

SPARERIBS WITH BLACK BEANS IN SAND POT

SERVES 2–3 AS A MAIN COURSE, 4 AS PART OF A CHINESE MEAL

The secret behind sand-pot cooking is to put the casserole on a very high burner and almost burn the lettuce, which is used as a base in the dish. The almost smoky flavor that results will completely change the nature of the spareribs. It is luscious!

Prepare the above recipe. Place a medium-sized head of iceberg lettuce, torn up, in a 2-quart sand pot (page 19) or stove-top casserole. Place the cooked ribs on top of the lettuce. Cover and place on high heat. When the whole is hot and bubbling, serve. This is great on rice, and yes, I eat the lettuce as well.

Deep-Fried Pork Balls

SERVES 4–6 AS
PART OF A CHINESE MEAL

These are easy! Even the kids will love to make them, and yet they are a real delicacy. This same meat mixture can be used for other dishes as well, as you will see from the following recipes.

1 *pound lean pork, finely ground*

1 *green onion, finely chopped*

1 *teaspoon freshly grated ginger*

1 *teaspoon light soy sauce*

1 *tablespoon dry sherry or Chinese rice wine*

1 *egg, beaten*

¼ *teaspoon salt*

Pinch of MSG (optional)

2 *tablespoons cornstarch*

1 *teaspoon sesame oil*

¼ *teaspoon ground white pepper*

6 *cups peanut oil for deep-frying*

Mix all of the ingredients together and stir, using your hand, until the mixture is smooth and holds together. Moisten your hands with a bit of water and form the meat into balls about the size of large walnuts. Fry ½ of the meatballs in oil at 360° until they float. Remove and fry the other half. Allow the oil to return to temperature and fry the whole batch a second time, just until they are nicely browned and crispy, about 5 more minutes.

Drain and set aside.

These can be served just as they are, or with Szechwan Pepper and Salt Dip (page 202). You can also simply chow them with a bit of garlic and red chili paste along with a bit of soup stock.

Bird's Nest Meatballs

SERVES 4–6 AS
PART OF A CHINESE MEAL

No, there is no bird's nest in this dish. However, these are easy to prepare and great fun to eat. The noodle fries and curls up a bit to resemble the tiny twigs of a bird's nest. Great flavor is imparted by the noodle.

resemble the tiny twigs of a bird's nest. Great flavor is imparted by the noodle.

Prepare a batch of meatballs as directed on page 299, adding some chopped yellow onion and some grated carrot to the meat mixture. Do not cook. Cut 3 ounces of *sai fun* noodles (page 29) into 1-inch lengths. I use kitchen scissors for this. Roll the meatballs in the small noodle pieces and then deep-fry ½ batch at 375° for 4 seconds, or until the noodles puff up. Remove and do the other half. Let the oil cool to 325° and cook the whole batch a second time until done to taste, about 6 minutes. Drain and serve hot.

PEARL MEATBALLS

SERVES 4–6 AS
PART OF A CHINESE MEAL

The wonderful name for this dish comes from the fact that the sticky-sweet rice in which you roll the meatballs takes on a pearly color and appearance when steamed. This dish is great served right from the steamer. It certainly adds some class to meatballs! Yes, you can do this with lean ground beef. It will work well.

⅔ cup sticky sweet rice

1 pound pork, ground fine

2 tablespoons light soy sauce

1 tablespoon dry sherry or
Chinese rice wine

1 clove garlic, crushed

6 water chestnuts, peeled
and chopped coarsely

½ ounce dried Chinese mushrooms,
soaked in water 2 hours,
drained and chopped coarsely

1 teaspoon salt

1 teaspoon sugar

3 tablespoons cornstarch

1 green onion, chopped

¼ teaspoon MSG (optional)

¼ teaspoon ground white
pepper

Lettuce leaves for steaming
or waxed paper (3-inch
squares) for steaming

Rinse the rice until the water is clear and soak in cold water for 6 hours. Place rice in colander and drain very well.

Mix all together except the rice and lettuce. Form into 1-inch meatballs and roll each to cover in the soaked rice.

Cut the lettuce leaves into 2-inch squares or circles and place a meatball on each, then into the steamer. Or, you can use waxed paper. Steam for 30 minutes or until the rice is glossy and tender.

STEAMED PORK
WITH CHINESE OLIVES

The flavor of the dried Chinese olive, *lam see*, is very rich and rather heavy. The *lam see* resemble dried Italian olives, though when you buy them in Chinatown they will be pitted.

Soak ½ cup *lam see* olives in warm water for 1 hour. Drain. Prepare a batch of Steamed Pork with Salted Eggs (page 226), omitting the salted eggs. Mix the olives with the meat and steam as directed. Be prepared for a very interesting but rather strong flavor.

SPARERIBS WITH
LOTUS ROOT

SERVES 6–8 AS
PART OF A CHINESE MEAL

The lotus plant, a wonderful waterlily, provides China with leaves in which to wrap and cook food, a starch for thickening dishes that is much older than cornstarch, and a root vegetable that is simply a piece of art. As you slice the root or tuber you find a lovely lace pattern in the vegetable. Since it is so attractive, the Chinese love to use it in special dishes. This is such a dish.

2 pounds pork spareribs, cut
  into 1-inch pieces
  (Have the butcher do this
  for you)

MARINADE
2 tablespoons light soy sauce
2 tablespoons Chinese rice
  wine or dry sherry
½ teaspoon freshly grated
  ginger

¼ teaspoon sugar
¼ teaspoon ground white pepper

1 tablespoon peanut oil
  for chowing
2 cloves garlic, chopped fine
  or crushed
3 green onions, chopped
1 cup lotus root, sliced thin
  (Fresh is best, but hard to
  find; canned will do nicely)

Bring 3 quarts of water to a boil and dump in cut ribs. Blanch for 1 minute. Drain the ribs well and soak in the marinade for ½ hour.

Heat a wok and add the oil and garlic. Chow for a second and add half the ribs, drained. Chow until lightly browned and remove to a steaming bowl. Chow the second half of the ribs in the same oil. Place in another steaming bowl. Top each with the onions and sliced lotus root. Steam in a bamboo steamer (page 97) until tender, about 1 hour.

GREECE

PORK WITH CELERY, GREEK STYLE

SERVES 4–6 AS A MAIN COURSE

Taverna Sigalas, on Monastiraki Square in Athens, served this dish one night to Craig, my cooking assistant, and me. We were both very taken by the utter simplicity of the dish and the brightness of the flavors.

Celery leaves have been common in cooking since the very early days of all three of our cultures, China, Greece, and Rome. In Rome, during the first century, lovage would have been used in such a dish. It is a member of the celery family and the flavor is very sharp. In our time you can simply use celery leaves.

Don't be cool to this dish just because it is so simple. The best of Greek cuisine is not necessarily complex.

2 *tablespoons olive oil for browning*

2 *pounds boneless pork roast, cut into several large pieces*

COOKING LIQUID

2 *cups Basic Chicken Stock (page 129)*

½ *cup dry white wine*

5 *tablespoons olive oil*

2 *cloves garlic, chopped fine*

Salt and freshly ground black pepper to taste

4 *cups chopped celery leaves and stalks (The more leaves, the better)*

In a 6-quart Dutch oven, heat the oil for browning and brown the meat on both sides. Add all of the ingredients for the cooking liquid. It should come up about halfway on the side of the meat. If it does not, add more chicken stock or wine. Bring to a simmer and cover. Cook for 1¾ hours or until tender. Add the celery and simmer ½ hour more until the celery is very tender. Uncover the pot for the last 15 minutes to reduce the sauce.

This can be served with rice pilaf or pasta, but I love it just plain in a bowl with crunchy Greek bread and a good glass of retsina wine.

PORK SOUVLAKI

The Greeks have been cooking meat on little sticks for thousands of years. You can make Pork Souvlaki, an old dish, just the same way you make lamb Souvlaki (page 282). The pork makes a wonderful change.

ITALY

ROAST PORK, ROMAN STYLE

SERVES 5–6 FOR DINNER

In Italy, particularly in Rome and Bologna, you can find stands that sell pork roast already cooked. It is roasted in such a beautiful way that it is very hard to resist the urge to simply buy a chunk and eat it on the street, the crunchy pork fat sticking to your beard and fingers. This is as close to the Roman style as I can come. It sounds like a lot of work when you read the recipe but it is really quite simple.

1 *2-pound piece fresh side of pork, skin left on*

1 *2-pound boneless pork butt roast*

Salt and freshly ground black pepper to taste

1 *tablespoon dried, whole rosemary*

1 *tablespoon olive oil*

2 *cloves garlic, crushed*

Place the side of pork skin side down on the counter and, using a good butcher knife, cut off enough meat so that only ¾ inch remains attached to the skin. Place the knife parallel to the counter and do this carefully. It is not a big job at all. Reserve the removed meat and fat for another dish.

Cut the boneless roast open so that you can add all of the additional seasonings and then roll up the roast. Encase it in the side of pork, skin side out, and tie with several pieces of string. You should wind up with a nice long, shaped roast encased by the pork skin. The ends will be open, of course.

Place the meat in a roasting rack, skin side up. Prick the skin thoroughly, using an ice pick. Place in the upper third of an oven preheated to 325°. Place a meat thermometer in the roast and roast until the thermometer hits 170°. Then, turn the oven on to BROIL and cook until the skin is bubbly and crunchy. Be careful, as this should take only a few minutes. You need to watch this.

The whole cooking process will take about 35 minutes per pound, total time.

Remove and slice the roast for serving. The skin is the best part . . . although I think that the roast served cold the next day is almost as good. What decisions!

BEEF

W e can understand why beef was not popular in the ancient world
if we understand that beef is the most costly meat in the world.
That is to say, it costs more to produce a pound of beef than of any
other meat that we normally eat. More grain, more grass, more fresh
water, more space, more of everything. So, in the old days it was simply
not popular. We Americans still insist on our beef, each of us eating

nearly eighty pounds a year. We have the room to raise the animal, but the rest of the world does not.

The Greeks did raise oxen, but they were roasted only on very special occasions. One occasion, in 400 B.C., called for the public roasting of three hundred oxen. Some barbecue! But in general Greece was simply not suited to keeping those animals on the little land that they had. And as the development of agriculture moved from raising meat to growing more grain, the land available for cattle shrank. By A.D. 1000 the developments in food and diet due to the advancement of agriculture had converted men and women from a diet in which meat was dominant to one in which grains were dominant. In the days of Peking Man, about 300,000 years ago, people lived on a diet that was about 70 percent meat. That is not the case now, and it can never be again. Nevertheless, our three ancient cultures do enjoy beef, but it is generally used as a flavoring rather than as a whole course, as the following recipes will show.

You may also wish to see:

Chinese Beef and Chestnut Stew *(page 427)*

CHINA

MONGOLIAN BEEF

SERVES 4 AS
PART OF A CHINESE MEAL

Channing and Jason, my sons, always order this dish when we go to a favorite Chinese restaurant. It is not a complex dish but it uses both the deep-frying method of cooking and the chowing method, and all of this for beef. You would think that after the meat is cooked twice, it would be dead. It is not, and you will love the flavors that these two cooking methods create.

1 *pound beef flank steak,*
sliced thin across the grain

MARINADE

1 *tablespoon light soy sauce*

1 *tablespoon dry sherry or*
Chinese rice wine

½ *teaspoon freshly grated*
ginger

4 *cups peanut oil*
for deep-frying

FOR CHOWING

1 *tablespoon peanut oil*

2 *cloves garlic, sliced thin*

4 *green onions, sliced*
Chinese style (page 142)

1 *teaspoon hoisin sauce*
(page 30)

Pinch of MSG, (optional)

¼ *teaspoon ground white*
pepper

Marinate the cut meat in the soy, wine, and ginger. Mix well and let sit for 15 minutes. Drain the marinade well. Separate the meat into individual pieces.

In a wok or deep pan heat the deep-frying oil to 375°. Add the meat all at once and stir a bit to separate. Remove after 1 minute and allow the meat to drain in a colander.

Heat the wok again and add the oil for chowing. Add the garlic and green onions and chow for just a moment. Add the hoisin, optional MSG, and the pepper. Add the meat. Stir-fry until all is hot, and serve.

VARIATION: You may wish to serve this dish over deep-fried cellophane (*sai fun*) noodles (page 29). It is very dramatic.

HINT: USE THE SERVING PLATE WHEN CHOWING Chinese food. It is silly to dirty lots of little dishes when you are simply organizing the chopped meat and vegetables for a chowed dish. Since some ingredients must be cooked separately, you can just arrange these on the platter, cook them as you go, return them to the platter, and then finish the dish. In the end the whole works goes on the same plate anyhow!

PEPPER ONION BEEF

SERVES 4 AS
PART OF A CHINESE MEAL

Your mouth should burn a bit from all of the black pepper that you are to put in this dish. I know that nothing but green onions and black pepper sounds strange to you . . . but the flavor is just wonderful.

1 *pound beef flank steak, sliced thin across the grain*

MARINADE

1 *tablespoon light soy sauce*

1 *tablespoon dry sherry or Chinese rice wine*

½ *teaspoon freshly grated ginger*

4 *cups peanut oil for deep-frying*

FOR CHOWING

1 *tablespoon peanut oil*

2 *cloves garlic, sliced thin*

8 *green onions, cut Chinese style (page 142)*

Pinch of MSG (optional)

Pinch of sugar

Freshly ground black pepper to taste (Use lots of pepper for this dish. That is what makes it so terrific!)

Marinate the cut meat in the soy, wine, and ginger. Mix well and let sit for 15 minutes. Drain the marinade well and separate the meat into individual pieces.

In a wok or deep pan heat the oil for deep-frying to 375°. Add the meat all at once and stir a bit to separate. Remove after 1 minute and drain the meat in a colander.

Heat the wok again and add the oil for chowing. Add the garlic and green onions and chow for just a moment. Add the drained meat and all remaining ingredients, using plenty of black pepper. Chow until the meat is hot, and serve.

> **HINT: AVOID THE HIGH COST OF FLANK STEAK** for Chinese cooking by purchasing lean chuck roast. Remove any large chunks of fat. Cut it into thick strips and place it in a freezer until it is very firm. Slice thin and proceed with the recipes.

OYSTER BEEF

This is a fine beef dish, and the lettuce cooked with the meat makes an interesting change from the normal restaurant version.

1 *pound beef flank steak,*
sliced thin across the grain

1 *tablespoon light soy sauce*

1 *tablespoon Chinese rice*
wine or dry sherry

Pinch of sugar

Black pepper, freshly
ground, to taste

2 *tablespoons oyster sauce*

3 *tablespoons peanut oil*

½ *teaspoon sesame oil*

2 *green onions, sliced*
Chinese style (page 142)

½ *head iceberg lettuce,*
shredded

⅛ *cup Chinese Chicken Soup*
Stock (page 113)

Marinate the beef in the soy sauce, wine, sugar, black pepper, and oyster sauce for 15 minutes. Heat a wok and add 1½ tablespoons of the peanut oil. Chow the meat quickly on high heat, about 3 minutes. Remove from the pan to a serving bowl. Heat the wok again and add another 1½ tablespoons peanut oil. Add the sesame oil and green onions, and chow for a moment. Add the lettuce and return the meat to the wok. Add the chicken stock and cook for a moment while a sauce forms.

GINGER BEEF

Some people claim they dislike the flavor of fresh ginger in Chinese food. Generally that is because the cook is using too much ginger. In this dish it is impossible to put in too much of that wonderful root. Go to it and enjoy!

1 pound beef flank steak,
 sliced thin across the grain

1 tablespoon dry sherry
 or Chinese rice wine

1 tablespoon light soy sauce
 Pinch of sugar

2 tablespoons peanut oil

2 cloves garlic,
 chopped fine

5–6 thin slices fresh
 ginger, cut julienne
 (page 25)

2 teaspoons oyster sauce

⅛ cup Chinese Chicken
 Soup Stock (page 113)

2 green onions,
 cut Chinese style
 (page 142)

2 eggs, well beaten

Marinate the meat in the wine, soy sauce, and sugar for 15 minutes. Heat a wok and add the oil. Chow the garlic and the ginger for 1 minute. Remove the garlic and ginger from the wok, reserving them, and leaving the oil in the pan. Chow the beef on one side for 1 minute and then add the removed ginger and garlic. Add the oyster sauce, chicken broth, and green onions and chow for a moment. Stir in the beaten eggs and cook just for a moment, until the mixture thickens.

SMOKED MEATBALLS

SERVES 10–12
AS PART OF A CHINESE MEAL

These are very flavorful little numbers that can be served in several ways. They are also rich and therefore go a long way at the table.

1¼ pounds ground beef

1¼ pounds ground pork

1 egg

1 teaspoon freshly grated
 ginger

2 tablespoons dry sherry or
 Chinese rice wine

2 tablespoons dark
 soy sauce

1 tablespoon sesame oil

3 tablespoons chopped
 green onion

2 tablespoons cornstarch

I place all of the ingredients above in my KitchenAid and then let the machine beat it into a smooth mixture. If you do not have such a machine you will need to mix this by hand very well.

Form meatballs just a bit bigger than 1 inch in diameter. Place them on plates and steam them in your bamboo steamer (page 97) for about

20 minutes. Then place them in a Cameron smoker (page 19), or some other smoker, and smoke them for about 15 minutes, using either alder or hickory sawdust.

The meatballs can be served just as they are or you can offer Szechwan Pepper and Salt Dip (page 202) as a dip. You might also try one of the various dip sauces on page 201. They can also be chowed with a sauce or with vegetables, as in the next recipe.

NOTE: These meatballs freeze very well, either cooked or raw.

MEATBALLS WITH BLACK BEANS AND GREEN PEPPER

SERVES 5 AS PART OF A CHINESE MEAL

If you have some leftover smoked meatballs, try serving them in this manner. This is the kind of food that keeps the Hunan farmers alive during those bitterly cold winters. The hot chili paste keeps the system aware of reality!

1 tablespoon peanut oil

2 cloves garlic, chopped fine

2 teaspoons fermented black beans (dow see) (page 29), rinsed

½ green sweet bell pepper

½ teaspoon garlic and red chili paste (page 30)

1 teaspoon light soy sauce

½ cup Chinese Chicken Soup Stock (page 113) or Basic Chicken Stock (page 129)

1 teaspoon cornstarch mixed with 1 tablespoon water

½ batch cooked smoked meatballs (above)

4 green onions, cut Chinese style (page 142)

Heat a wok and add the oil, garlic, and black beans. Smash them together a bit as you chow for a moment. Add the bell pepper, chili paste, soy, and soup stock. Bring to a quick boil and stir in cornstarch and water mixture. Cook until thick. Add the cooked meatballs and green onions and chow until all is hot.

LOOED BEEF

SERVES 4–6 AS PART
OF A CHINESE MEAL AND 6–8
AS AN APPETIZER COURSE

I just love the name of this dish, and you can be assured that your kids will have fun throwing the name around the neighborhood. The name refers to a style of cooking, a slow simmering in a dark sauce or looing sauce. The result is delightful and a wonderful way to do a pot roast.

2 tablespoons peanut oil

2–3 pounds boneless
chuck roast

5 cups Looing Sauce
(page 203)

Heat a large frying pan and add the oil. Brown the meat on both sides, and brown it well. Place the meat in a heavy stove-top covered casserole and add enough looing sauce to cover. Bring to a boil and turn to a simmer. Simmer covered for 1 hour and 20 minutes, or until the meat is tender. Serve the meat hot with a bit of the sauce or turn off the heat and allow the meat to cool in the sauce and then slice it for an appetizer course.

Save the sauce for other uses.

LOOED BEEF IN SAND POT

SERVES 4 AS
PART OF A CHINESE MEAL

This is a typical winter casserole dish in China. The cooked lettuce adds a nice refreshing flavor to the meat.

2 cups iceberg lettuce

1 pound Looed Beef (above),
cooked and cut
into ½-inch cubes

½ cup Looing Sauce
from the meat

2 tablespoons thinly sliced
yellow onion

GARNISH

2 green onions, chopped

Place the lettuce in the bottom of a 2-quart sand pot (page 19) and top with the meat and sauce. Place the yellow onions on top and place the dish on a heat diffuser over high heat. When all is hot serve with the green-onion garnish.

You can do this dish in any kind of stove-top casserole.

GREECE

POACHED MEATBALLS IN EGG AND LEMON SAUCE
(Youvarlakia)

SERVES 6

Every taverna in Athens has a variation on this dish, but the version offered at Taverna Sigalas, in Monastiraki Square, is particularly delicious. The restaurant is behind an Orthodox Church, which is one thousand years old, at least. Somehow this adds to the delight of a lunch in the courtyard.

1½ *pounds lean ground beef*
½ *cup long-grain rice (uncooked)*
½ *cup finely chopped yellow onion*
2 *eggs, separated*
3 *tablespoons chopped parsley*

¼ *teaspoon allspice*
Salt and freshly ground black pepper to taste
½ *cup olive oil*
Juice of 2 lemons

Place the meat in a mixing bowl and mix in the rice, onion, eggs (whites only), parsley, allspice, and salt and pepper. Mix very well and form into small meatballs, about 1 inch in diameter. Place the oil in a large covered frying pan and add the meatballs in a single layer. Barely cover with water and put on the lid. Simmer the meatballs until the rice is tender, about 40 minutes. Remove the meatballs to a heated plate.

Leave ¾ cup of the remaining liquid in the pan and discard the rest. (If you are short of liquid, add chicken broth to make up the difference.) Beat the egg yolks in a bowl and add the lemon juice. While stirring, add the broth from the pan. Return this mixture to the pan and heat and stir until it is thick. Return the meatballs to the sauce and gently heat for serving.

FRIED MEATBALLS
(Keftedes)

SERVES 6

If you are tired of hamburger dishes, American style—and who isn't?—then try these Greek meatballs. They are simple to make and just wonderful served cold—with yogurt, of course.

- ¾ cup bread crumbs, soaked in ½ cup water
- 1½ pounds lean ground beef
- 1 large yellow onion, peeled and chopped fine
- 3 tablespoons chopped parsley
- 1 teaspoon mint leaves
- 1 teaspoon oregano
- 2 cloves garlic, peeled and crushed
- 1 tablespoon olive oil
- 2 eggs
- 1 tablespoon fresh lemon juice
- Salt and freshly ground black pepper to taste
- Flour for dredging
- 1 cup olive oil for frying

Squeeze the water from the bread crumbs and place in a mixing bowl along with the beef. Add all other ingredients except the flour and oil for frying. Mix well and form into small oblong meatballs. Dredge each in flour and pan-fry in the olive oil until lightly browned and done to your taste. Do not dry them out!

These are great hot or cold.

MEATBALLS
IN TOMATO SAUCE
(Keftedes me Saltsa)

Prepare the meatballs as above. Reheat them in a bit of Greek Tomato Sauce (page 204).

HAMBURGERS, GREEK STYLE

This is for Channing, my hamburger lover, but I will share it with you as well. Niki, the owner and cook at Zorba's Taverna in Delphi, told me that he makes a terrific hamburger and he used to sell them from a canteen truck in the States. He gave me the recipe, a recipe that only a crazed Greek could think up. It is delicious.

Try adding a bit of dried mint and oregano, along with crushed garlic and olive oil, to your hamburger meat, along with some salt and pepper, of course. Now, here is the crazed part. Add a stiff shot of ouzo, that wonderful Greek anise liquor, to the meat as well. Mix this all up and grill or pan-fry just as you normally do. You may become crazed as well!

ITALY

BEEF, ROMAN JEWISH STYLE

SERVES 6

The Jewish Ghetto in Rome, a place you must visit, still has a few restaurants that serve food that has been typical of these people for the last few hundred years. You will find kosher bakers and kosher butchers. And you will find a few dishes like the following.

2 pounds boneless beef pot roast,
cut into 1-inch cubes

4 tablespoons olive oil

3 cloves garlic, chopped fine

Salt and freshly ground
black pepper to taste

½ cup Basic Brown Soup
Stock (page 132)

½ cup dry red wine

2 cups Italian Tomato Sauce
(page 208)

In a large frying pan brown the meat pieces very well in the olive oil
and garlic. You may have to do this in 2 or 3 batches. See the **HINT** on
page 317.

Place the meat in a suitable stove-top covered casserole and add the
remaining ingredients. Simmer, covered, until the meat is very tender,
about 2 hours. You may have to add some water to the pot now and
then. Do not let the dish dry out.

This can be served in a bowl with a great deal of bread or with pasta.

BEEF SLICES WITH ROSEMARY

SERVES 6 AS
PART OF AN ITALIAN MEAL

Beef is quite expensive in Rome, at least by our standards. I expect
this has always been the case, given the fact that Rome was literally at
the crossroads of the world for so long. Foods came in from all over the
Mediterranean, but meat had to be local. If you were not a free citizen,
I expect you saw few dishes like the following.

The butcher in Rome, who may very well operate from a mobile truck
shop in the middle of the market square, will slice meat for you very
thin. You buy just a few slices for the family and grill them in this way.

3 tablespoon olive oil

2 cloves garlic, chopped medium

1 pound lean beef roast,
sliced quite thin

Salt and freshly ground
black pepper to taste

1 tablespoon chopped fresh rosemary

¼ cup dry white wine

Heat a large heavy frying pan and add the oil and garlic. Pan-fry the
meat on both sides quickly over medium-high heat. Salt and pepper the
meat and remove it to a heated serving platter. Add the rosemary to the
pan along with the white wine. Deglaze the pan (page 24) and pour the
sauce over the meat.

HINT: WHEN BROWNING MEATS use a very heavy frying pan and small batches of meat. If you put all the meat in a thin pan at once, the little heat available in the thin metal of the pan will be absorbed quickly and you cannot sear the meat, only slowly cook it, thus toughening the meat. Proper browning means that you sear the meat quickly, thus sealing in the flavorful juices and coloring the natural sugar that is in the meat.

MEATBALLS, ROMAN STYLE

MAKES 20 MEATBALLS; SERVES 6-8 PERSONS

I suppose I could live on meatballs: Swedish meatballs, Chinese meatballs, German meatballs, Polish meatballs, Greek meatballs, Hungarian meatballs, Jewish meatballs, and certainly Italian meatballs. This version from Rome has a very deep flavor due to the pancetta and prosciutto that are aded to the beef. You can substitute our bacon and ham, if you must, but the flavor will not be as rich.

THE MEATBALLS

2 pounds lean ground beef

½ pound ground pork

6 ounces pancetta, diced very small

6 ounces prosciutto, sliced thin and chopped

3 eggs

1 cup chopped parsley

3 cloves garlic, crushed

1 cup bread crumbs, soaked in 1 cup milk

Salt and freshly ground black pepper to taste (Careful with the salt as the pancetta and prosciutto will also add salt to the dish)

¼ cup olive oil for browning

THE SAUCE

1 cup dry red wine

2 cups Italian Tomato Sauce (page 208)

1 cup Basic Brown Sauce (page 207) or substitute brown gravy

1 ounce dried mushrooms, soaked in 2 cups water (Reserve the water)

Additional parsley for garnish

Mix the meatball ingredients together, with the exception of the oil for browning. Form into 20 balls and pan-brown in the olive oil. Do this in 2 or 3 batches.

Place the meatballs, along with the oil, in a 6-quart stove-top casserole. Deglaze (page 24) with the wine the frying pan in which you cook the meatballs. Add the wine to the pot along with the 2 sauces and the mushroom water. Chop the mushrooms and add to the pot.

Cover and bring to a simmer. Leave the lid ajar so that the sauce will reduce a bit. Cook for about ½ hour. Place meatballs on a platter and serve the gravy separately. It is great on pasta or polenta.

POT ROAST SHREDDED

I cannot figure out any other way of getting a fresh-tasting beef flavor into a dish, as they do in Rome. The beef must be cooked separately and then blended with the sauce at the last minute so that it does not have that "cooked forever" flavor. In any case you will find it helpful to have a cooked and shredded pot roast sitting in your refrigerator. It will add depth to many dishes such as a Bolognese sauce or a meat salad.

1 *boneless pot roast, 3 to 4 pounds*

1 *tablespoon olive oil*

1 *cup dry white wine*

2 *cups water*

Salt and freshly ground black pepper to taste

Pan-brown the roast in a large frying pan with the olive oil. Place in a stove-top covered casserole and add the wine and water. Cover and simmer for about 2½ hours. It should be very tender. Add the salt and pepper to taste. Cool and shred the meat, saving the juice. Store in the refrigerator with the juice on the meat.

BEEF ON A
STICK, ROMAN STYLE

The fancy meat shops in Rome are just astoundingly beautiful. Many meats are prepared, seasoned, tied, put on sticks, rolled into special shapes . . . and put in a butcher's case that becomes a mosaic of tidbits all ready to take home and quickly finish in your broiler or oven. It is important to note that none of these offerings contains a great deal of meat, at least not by American standards. Meat is expensive in Rome and the dishes are prepared in a careful, artistic, and frugal manner.

An example of such shop preparation is a stick of beef cubes separated alternately by whole, fresh bay leaves, onion wedges, and sliced mushrooms. Dress this with a bit of olive oil and salt and pepper, perhaps some basil and thyme, and dinner is ready for the broiler.

INNARDS

F rom prehistoric times innards have been an important part of mankind's diet. In America we have largely rejected these meats since we seem to feel that they are symbols of poverty. In our three ancient cuisines, however, they were symbols of delight and joy at the table.

In classic Rome innards were offered at the most exclusive banquets. To this day the Romans love innards and they are served in the oldest of the city's trattorias. My favorite, Trattoria Edmondo, serves pasta with lamb intestines and deep-fried lamb brains along with vegetables. Now be careful with your rejection of these dishes as they are just delicious. *Frattagli,* or innards, have been enjoyed since the early days of the empire when these cheap cuts of meat were all that the lower classes could afford. They were sold, already cooked, in stalls in the streets of Rome. The peasants rarely got their hands on the better cuts of meat and thus the affection for innards lingers on in Rome as a profound culinary memory.

You will find some wonderful Greek dishes for innards in this section as well. When you have been raised on tripe soup, or on innard soup that is served after the Easter Mass at midnight, then you continue to long for these dishes for the rest of your life. Liver cooked Greek style may very well change your opinion of liver!

Finally, the most experienced cooks in the world, the Chinese, have prized tripe and tongue since before recorded history. I had wonderful innards in Hong Kong, and I shall never forget a big plate of braised duck tongues that was served me at the Great Shanghai Restaurant.

Please calm down and give me a chance to convince you that Americans are going without some of the best flavors in the animal. We prefer our innards ground up and stuffed into a hot dog so that we cannot tell the contents. Enough! Cook tripe, tongue, and lamb brains and taste flavors that go "back to the beginning" of cooking.

You might also wish to consider:

Spicy Pork Tripe *(page 104)*   Headcheese Appetizer *(page 92)*

CHINA

LOOED BEEF TONGUE
(Ngow Lay)

SERVES 8–10 AS A
FIRST COURSE AT A CHINESE MEAL

If you do not care for tongue, so be it. For those of us who do, it is a premium food. This recipe is great served warm, sliced thin, as a part of a Chinese appetizer plate. Served cold, with a bit of hot mustard and horseradish sauce, it is even better.

1 *fresh beef tongue, around*
  3 pounds

SEASONINGS

2 *teaspoons salt*
½ *cup light soy sauce*

¼ *cup sugar*
2 *slices ginger, each the size*
  of a 25-cent piece
2 *cloves garlic, sliced thin*
3 *star anise, whole*

Place the tongue in a 4-quart stove-top casserole and add water just to cover. Bring to a boil and discard the water. Add the ingredients for the seasonings and enough fresh water to come halfway up the tongue. Bring to a boil, turn to a simmer, cover, and cook for 1 hour and 15 minutes, turning 3 times during the process. Remove the tongue from the pot but save the juices. Allow the meat to cool and remove the skin. Just pull it off! Put the tongue back in the pot and simmer again for about 45 minutes more. Remove, cool a bit, and slice.

LOOED PORK TRIPE
(Hog Maws)

This is very popular as a dim sum or as a first course. John Young, my beloved adopted Chinese uncle in San Francisco, brought this dish home one evening for a snack before our dinner. It was served at room temperature along with a glass of Scotch. The flavor was mild and a bit sweet, and I was surprised at the difference between pork tripe and beef tripe, which is much tougher and takes much longer to cook. Colonel Young smiled at my appreciation. He always seemed to enjoy exposing me to a new and wonderful Chinese delicacy. How I wish he could sit with me now and review this book.

Clean the tripe by removing all fat. Just pull it off. Rinse well and cut the tripe into ¼-inch strips. Drain well and place in a saucepan or stove-top casserole. Add Looing Sauce (page 203) just to cover. Simmer until tender, about 1 hour.

Steam to reheat, if you wish. Garnish with sesame oil and chopped Chinese parsley.

Serve as a first course or at a dim sum feast.

PORK TRIPE
IN HOT SAUCE

SERVES 4
AS A FIRST COURSE

While this is commonly served as a dim sum course it is just great for dinner, if you have the right crowd. Pork tripe is very mild in flavor, not like beef tripe at all. Please try this one. Please. And write me and tell me what you think. I love it!

2 *pounds pork tripe (hog maws)*

3 *tablespoons peanut oil for chowing*

3 *cloves garlic, chopped fine*

1 *teaspoon salt*

SAUCE

3 *tablespoons light soy sauce*

2 *slices ginger, the size of a 25-cent piece, cut julienne*

¼ *cup Chinese rice wine or dry sherry*

2 *teaspoons chili sauce with fermented black beans (page 29)*

½ *teaspoon ground white pepper*

6 *green onions, cut Chinese style (page 142)*

1 *tablespoon cornstarch mixed with 1 tablespoon water for thickening*

Remove as much fat as possible from the tripe. Blanch the tripe in boiling water for 2 minutes. Drain. Cut the meat into ¼-inch-wide strips.

Heat a wok and add the oil, garlic, and salt. Chow the tripe for a few minutes and add the ingredients for the sauce. Cover and simmer until all is very tender, about 15 minutes. If you wish to thicken this dish, stir in the cornstarch mixed with water.

A favorite trick in the restaurant dim sum business is to make a large batch of this and keep it in the refrigerator. When someone orders a bit simply steam it and serve. So easy . . . and just delicious.

STEWED OXTAIL, CHINESE STYLE

SERVES 5–6

This is a very rich dish. I prefer to make a batch of this the day ahead and then chill it so that I can remove much of the fat. It is then easy to reheat for a dinner. I do hope you like oxtail. No, of course it is not from an ox. Oxtail in our time comes from a steer.

3 pounds oxtails, cut at each joint

4 tablespoons peanut oil

2 cloves garlic, sliced thin

1 teaspoon salt

2 tablespoons fermented black beans (dow see), rinsed and drained

½ yellow onion, peeled and coarsely chopped

3 slices ginger, the size of a 25-cent piece, cut julienne

2 tablespoons dark soy sauce

2 tablespoons Chinese rice wine or dry sherry

1 teaspoon sugar

Trim the oxtail pieces of excess fat. Heat a large wok or frying pan and add the peanut oil. Add the garlic and salt and chow for just a moment. Add the oxtails and brown on both sides. Remove the oxtails from the wok and drain the oil, reserving the oil. Set the oxtails aside.

Heat the wok again and add 2 tablespoons of the oil. Add the black beans and chow for a moment. Add the remaining ingredients on the list and then add the reserved oxtails. Toss and remove the whole to a stove-top casserole. Add water to not quite cover. Cover the pot and simmer until the meat is very tender, about 2 hours, or longer to taste. The pieces should be very tender and certainly flavorful.

Serve with rice or noodles as a main course for a Chinese dinner.

GRILLED LIVER, GREEK STYLE

While we were in Delphi for Greek Easter, friends we had just met served us this dish in the streets, along with much too much wine. It is simple and will give you a new image of liver.

Lamb or beef liver, cut thin

MARINADE
Olive oil
Garlic, crushed

Oregano, crushed
Salt and freshly ground black pepper to taste

Marinate the slices of liver and then cook them on a hot grill, turning once. Do not overcook liver as it will be tough.

TRIPE SOUP WITH EGG-LEMON SAUCE
(Skembe Avgolemono)

SERVES 4–6

The first time I ever tasted this wonderful soup I was in the home of Mrs. Koustela Stergachis. She came to America from the Isle of Rhodes, and she is a wonderful cook. While making pastries for my delicatessen she offered me a bowl of *skembe* or *patsas*. It is just superb. And if you are too lazy to make it, you can have it at the Parthenon Restaurant in Chicago, but "only on Sundays." I make my own.

1 *pound tripe, lamb or beef*	½ *cup dry white wine*
1 *medium yellow onion, peeled and quartered*	1 *rib celery, chopped medium fine*
2 *bay leaves*	*Salt and freshly ground black pepper to taste*
2 *cloves garlic, peeled and cut in half*	
4 *cups Basic Chicken Stock (page 129) or Basic Lamb Stock (page 128)*	EGG-LEMON SAUCE
	3 *eggs, at room temperature*
½ *pound boneless lamb, trimmed and cut into very small pieces*	½ *cup fresh lemon juice*

Rinse the tripe and place in a 6-quart kettle. Add the onion, bay leaves, and garlic. Barely cover with water and bring to a boil. Cover and simmer for 2 hours. Drain and discard the broth. Cut the tripe into small sticklike pieces and return to the kettle. Add the remaining ingredients, except the eggs and lemon juice, and bring to a boil. Cover and simmer until both meats are tender, about 45 minutes.

Whip the eggs well and stir in the lemon juice. Add 1 cup of the broth from the kettle to this mixture and stir well again. Remove the kettle from the burner and stir in the egg-lemon sauce. We do not want the eggs to curdle. Check for seasoning and serve immediately.

LAMB INNARDS ON A SPIT
(Kokoretsi)

I do not expect you to run out and buy the makings for this dish for two reasons. You are not used to eating a whole dish of innards and you would have a very difficult time buying them even if you wanted to. We use innards in "meat products," but they are often hard to find on the fresh market.

I just want to describe this dish for you because it is very old and, as far as I am concerned, a classic dish.

The liver, heart, kidneys, sweetbreads, and spleen of the lamb are cut into pieces and placed on a large skewer. The whole is wrapped with the intestines of the lamb and then seasoned with salt and pepper, olive oil, and a bit of oregano. This is roasted, turning the skewer over a charcoal fire, until the whole thing is wonderfully golden and crunchy. The skewer is removed and the dish served in thick slices.

When you are in Athens you can go to the Pelopenese Grill just behind Omonia Square. They have this traditional dish all the time, and I hope you will try it. Buy a beer and a side of roast pork or chicken, and eat until you cannot move. The bill will be tiny.

HINT: PUT FRESH ANISE OR FENNEL IN INNARDS.
When you are cooking a boiled tongue, or perhaps a tripe dish, just add the cut-up fresh vegetable to the pot. It has a wonderfully cleansing and flavoring effect.

LAMB INNARD SOUP FOR EASTER
(Mageiritsa)

SERVES 10

This is a bowl of memories, of traditions, more than it is a soup. The Easter lamb, the Paschal lamb, is purchased by each Greek family just a day or so before Easter. The head is removed, along with all of the innards, and with these a special soup is made for midnight on Easter Eve. It is the moment of the breaking of the Lenten fast, the moment of the Resurrection, the moment of excitement and joy in every city in Greece. Christmas Eve is the closest thing we have to the great Easter celebration of the Orthodox Church, and we do very little with Easter. Just as a turkey or ham is necessary to the Western Christmas, so this soup is necessary to the midnight meal on Easter Eve.

I have eliminated the use of the lamb head for stock as I am quite sure you will have a tough time finding one in any case.

2 quarts Basic Lamb Stock
(page 128)

½ cup olive oil

1 medium yellow onion,
peeled and chopped

1 bunch green onions,
cleaned and chopped

½ cup chopped parsley

2 or 3 lamb hearts, cut in half

2 lamb kidneys, cleaned of
extra fat and cut in half

3 or 4 lamb tongues, whole

½ pound boneless lamb (shoulder
steak, etc.), diced

1 tablespoon flour

½ cup white wine

¼ pound lamb liver

1 tablespoon dried dillweed

Salt and pepper to taste

½ cup rice

EGG-LEMON SAUCE

3 eggs, at room temperature

½ cup fresh lemon juice

Parsley, chopped, for
garnish

Prepare the stock.

Heat a large frying pan or stove-top casserole and add the olive oil. Sauté the onions and parsley for just a moment and then add the heart, kidneys, and tongues, along with the boneless lamb. Sauté for 15 minutes or so and stir in the flour. Stir it well. Add the white wine and stock, stirring all the time, and cook until the mixture thickens a bit. Cover and simmer until the meats are tender, about 2 hours. Add additional water now and then to keep the soup up to the same level.

When the meats are tender add the liver, dillweed, salt and pepper to taste, and the rice. Simmer, covered, for 20 minutes or until the rice is tender. Turn off the heat and remove the meats from the pot. Peel the tongue and dice fine. Chop the heart, kidney, and liver as well. Return to the pot and bring to a simmer once again.

Whip the eggs with the lemon juice in a 2-cup measuring glass. Quickly stir in 1 cup of the broth. Add this mixture to the pot and stir until it thickens a bit. Taste to see if salt and pepper are needed. Garnish with the parsley and serve.

TRIPE, ROMAN STYLE
(Trippa alla Romana)

SERVES 6 AS
A MAIN COURSE ON PASTA

I gave you a recipe like this in my first cookbook, years ago. This one is much better. But I must tell you that a man once approached me in a large airport, just after I had published the first book . . . in 1984. He did not introduce himself . . . he did not tell me he watches the shows . . . he just said, "Hey, Frugal! How long do you have to cook that damn tripe before you eat it. Mine is now at a week on the stove." I laughed very hard but you understand that cooking tripe is not at all difficult. Just be patient. This is a very good recipe, and typical of Rome.

3 *pounds beef tripe*

6 *tablespoons olive oil*

3 *cloves garlic, sliced thin*

1 *yellow onion, peeled and coarsely chopped*

½ *pound boneless pork, cut into medium dice*

1 *cup red wine*

2 *cups Basic Brown Soup Stock (page 132) or canned stock, not bouillon cubes!*

2 *cups Italian Tomato Sauce (page 208)*

Peel of ¼ fresh lemon in very large pieces

1 *tablespoon fresh rosemary needles or 1 teaspoon dried rosemary needles*

¼ *cup chopped parsley*

Salt and freshly ground black pepper to taste (I like LOTS of black pepper in this dish)

½ *cup freshly grated Parmesan cheese*

1 *cup whipping cream*

Rinse the tripe and place in a 12-quart pot. Cover with water and bring to a boil. Drain and rinse the tripe in cold water. Cut the tripe into small pieces about ½ inch wide and 2 inches long. Set aside.

In a large frying pan heat the oil and add the garlic. Sauté for just a moment and then add the onion and pork. Cook until the onion is clear.

Return the tripe to the pot. Add all other ingredients except the cheese and cream and simmer until the meat is very tender, about 2 hours. You may wish to leave the lid off the pot for part of this time so that the sauce will reduce a bit. Watch carefully that the liquids do not evaporate too quickly. If this should happen, simply add a bit of water so that all can continue to cook properly.

Just before serving stir in the cheese and cream. Reheat, test for seasonings, and serve.

This is great with polenta, rice, or pasta. I just eat it from a bowl with French bread and some dry red wine.

OXTAILS, ROMAN STYLE

SERVES 6–8, ALONG WITH PASTA, FOR A MAIN DISH

Simple is the word and wonderful is the dish. The Jews in Rome, who still live around the Jewish Ghetto, love meat cooked in this way. The secret is to brown the meat severely and then simmer it slowly in tomato sauce and wine. There is a wonderful restaurant in the Ghetto that serves food in this manner, but it has no name and is known only to the locals. I don't know how to explain the location since an address will not help you. The locals won't tell you where the place is located!

4 *pounds oxtails,*
   cut at the joint

Salt and freshly ground
black pepper to taste

2 *tablespoons olive oil*

2 *cloves garlic, sliced thin*

1 *cup dry red wine*

2 *cups Italian Tomato Sauce (page 208)*

Season the oxtails with salt and pepper. Heat a 6-quart stove-top covered casserole and add the oil and garlic. Sauté for just a moment and add one third of the meat. Brown well on both sides and remove. Brown the next third and then the last. Drain the fat from the pot and return all of the meat, along with all other ingredients. Cover and simmer until very tender, about 2½ hours. You may need to add a bit of water now and then if the mixture dries out.

Serve with pasta as a main course. Salad and bread will complete a very "old-fashioned" Roman meal. The sauce is so rich you won't believe it!

NOTE: See **HINT: WHEN BROWNING MEATS** (page 317)

PASTA WITH LAMB INTESTINES
(Rigatoni con Pagliata Edmondo)

Now, I ask you. Are you not surprised that I would include such a dish in this collection? I have already explained in the opening section to this chapter that Romans traditionally have eaten and enjoyed innards. This one, however, threw me. The lamb intestines are to be from a young lamb, thus they are not available at all seasons. I did have a chance to taste this Roman classic at Edmondo's, in Rome. He simmers the lamb intestines very gently and then cooks them a second time in a light Italian tomato sauce with a bit of cream. This mixture is served over rigatoni, along with cheese and pepper on top. I really was not sure what to expect, but I can tell you now that when you are in Rome you must go to his restaurant and try this dish. It is unusually good and certainly Roman!

Try this dish using the beef tripe recipe above instead of the lamb intestines. It will work well.

FRIED INNARDS, ROMAN STYLE EDMONDO
(Fritto Misto)

I love this restaurant, really a trattoria, a wonderful neighborhood joint. Edmondo specializes in Roman innards and his deep-fried dishes, a mixture of lamb brains, lamb cutlets, artichokes, and vegetables, are just the best imaginable. This is his method of frying these wonders, as far as I can understand it.

THE BATTER

See the recipe for Assorted Fried Seafood (page 165)

Ample peanut oil for deep-frying

THE MEATS

Lamb brains, cut into 3-inch lengths

Lamb cutlets (I use thin pieces of boneless lamb steak)

Lamb heart, boiled in broth a bit until it is tender, then cut into strips

THE VEGETABLES

Artichoke hearts (page 400)

Zucchini sticks

Prepare everything completely before you begin. Be sure that your deep-frying oil is at 400° before you start frying. Fry the assorted foods in small batches so that the oil stays hot. Be sure to reheat the oil to 400° between batches. Drain the food well on paper towels before serving.

‖ HEADCHEESE SALAD ‖

SERVES 6
AS A FIRST COURSE

You will enjoy this excellent dish only if you can buy headcheese from a good Italian delicatessen. Don't buy that inferior product that is sold in a plastic container in your supermarket. It is not the genuine article. If you have an Italian deli in your town, you will find yourself making this easy dish often.

1 pound Italian headcheese, cut into julienne strips

1 cup Pot Roast Shredded (page 318)

1 tablespoon of the broth in which the beef was cooked

1 medium yellow onion, peeled and sliced thin

$\frac{1}{4}$ cup olive oil

Juice of 1 lemon

Salt and freshly ground black pepper to taste

1 tablespoon parsley

6 lettuce-leaf ''cups'' for garnish

Julienne the headcheese and place in a bowl along with the beef and broth. Sauté the onion in a bit of the oil just until it is limp, not discolored. Add all ingredients, except the lettuce, to the meat bowl and toss. Marinate for 1 hour and serve at room temperature in the lettuce cups.

TONGUE IN SWEET AND SOUR SAUCE, ROMAN STYLE
(Lingua in Agrodolce alla Romana)

SERVES 6–8

This is another wonderful dish from my friend in Rome, Mrs. Jo Bettoja. She reminded me that the presence of the raisins and pine nuts, along with the sweet dressing, points directly back to earlier times in Rome. I think this is one of the best tongue dishes I have ever tasted . . . and I thank her for it. You will too!

1 beef tongue, about 2 pounds	Juice of 2 fresh lemons
2 bay leaves	$\frac{1}{3}$ cup white raisins
1 medium yellow onion, peeled and quartered	3 cloves garlic, crushed
1 clove, whole	$\frac{1}{4}$ teaspoon dried red pepper flakes
10 black peppercorns, whole	3 tablespoons finely chopped parsley
1 tablespoon kosher salt	$\frac{1}{4}$ cup pine nuts, lightly toasted (page 38)
3$\frac{1}{2}$ tablespoons sugar	
3 tablespoons white wine vinegar	

Clean the tongue by trimming off a bit of the part where the tongue was attached. Wash and place in a 4-quart kettle with lid. Cover with water and add the bay leaves, onion, clove, peppercorns, and salt. Bring to a boil and simmer, covered, for 2 hours. Drain, cool enough to handle, and peel the tongue.

Dissolve the sugar in the vinegar over low heat, stirring. Add all the remaining ingredients except the pine nuts.

Slice the tongue thinly and arrange on a serving dish. Pour over the sauce, taking care to cover all the meat. Sprinkle over the pine nuts. Leave for a night to marinate in a cool place, preferably not in the refrigerator.

NOTE: I would suggest that you make this dish early in the day and allow it to marinate a few hours before serving.

Garnish with additional parsley, if you wish.

Dried Foods

S ometimes a discovery becomes so commonplace in our lives that we forget about its implications. Consider how life was changed with the realization that foods could be dried. This oldest method of preserving food was probably discovered during the arid windstorms some 30,000 years ago. Preservation of food for the winter was the most important result of this process, but consider that this discovery also allowed people to travel with a food supply in their bags. Finally, dried food gave us possibilities for trade since the food would not spoil en route. Life was seriously changed when we learned to dry foods.

The first food to be dried was probably fish. Why do we continue to dry it when freezing and refrigeration now allow us to keep the fish for a time and yet still maintain fresh flavor? We continue to dry certain foods because the process changes and enriches the flavor. The Chinese still dry fish and enjoy the concentration of the original taste even though fresh fish is sold in the same shop.

Almost any food product can be dried, and many actually improve in flavor during the process. Chinese black mushrooms are a good example. Fresh Chinese mushrooms, now available in many American supermarkets, simply do not have that wonderful rich flavor that you find in the dried ones. And leave it to the Chinese to continue to enjoy the flavors of the Old World. They dry almost every vegetable and fish product available and then reconstitute them in dishes that are hardly to be considered peasant style. They are the wisest of the food driers, and perhaps the oldest.

The Greeks were fond of drying fruits of all kinds and they brought this appreciation with them when they were taken into Rome as cooks. The Romans enjoyed the dried figs and citrus fruits from Greece to such an extent that they gave their traveling armies a fruit allotment when they went off to conquer. Is it too farfetched to believe that they took these delights with them on their invasions of England, and that we now credit the English with the invention of fruitcake when it is actually a very old Roman dish? Go to the Jewish Ghetto in Rome and buy some fruit bars. And you thought English fruitcake was heavy! Craig, my assistant, saw the clerks selling the cakes by weight, and I replied that it was just like selling pound cake. After tasting one he exclaimed, "This is no pound cake. This is ton cake!"

You might also wish to consider:

Two Squid, Chowed *(page 189)*   Jellyfish Salad *(page 137)*
Steamed Dried Duck and Pork   Duck and Jellyfish Salad
  (page 257)   *(page 138)*

DRIED ABALONE WITH MUSHROOMS

SERVES 4–6 AS PART OF A CHINESE MEAL—A VERY EXPENSIVE PART

The flavor of dried abalone is heavy and rich . . . absolutely delicious. However, it is not what you would call "tender" in the normal sense. The richness makes up for the nice, rather chewy, texture.

Don't put this book back on the shelf just because this dish takes several hours to cook and dried abalone costs over $30 a pound. Hey, I didn't ask you to buy a whole pound! Just look at this as one of those dishes that you do once . . . for very important guests. I expect that for those of you who are closet cookbook readers, this is the only taste you will have of this dish . . . just reading about it. That is fine with me, but you must know that such a thing exists.

6 ounces dried abalone (available in good Chinese markets), soaked for 24 hours

3 green onions

2 ginger slices, each the size of a 25-cent piece

Chinese dried mushrooms, soaked for 2 hours

1 tablespoon peanut oil

2 cloves garlic, chopped fine

2 tablespoons light soy sauce

1 tablespoon Chinese rice wine or dry sherry

Pinch of sugar

2 tablespoons oyster sauce

$\frac{1}{2}$ cup Chinese Chicken Soup Stock (page 113) or Basic Chicken Stock (page 129)

$\frac{1}{4}$ teaspoon sesame oil

Pinch of ground white pepper

1 teaspoon cornstarch and 1 tablespoon water mixed together (optional)

Soak the dried abalone in warm water for 24 hours, changing the water several times. Drain, and place in a 1-quart saucepan. Add the green onions and ginger slices and cover with water. Simmer, covered, until tender, about 5 or 6 hours. You will need to add a little more water now and then. Test for tenderness by poking with a skewer. Slice thinly and set aside in the cooking broth.

Soak the mushrooms, remove the stems, and slice the caps into ¼-inch-wide pieces. Set aside.

Heat the wok and add the oil. Chow the garlic for just a moment and add the drained abalone and mushroom slices. Chow until they are hot and add the remaining ingredients. Thicken if you wish with the cornstarch and water mixture.

DRIED SCALLOP AND CHIVE SOUP

SERVES 8–10

I tried a dish close to this one at the wonderful Sun Tung Lok Restaurant, in Kowloon, Hong Kong. The place is terribly expensive but they serve wonderful food, and many are fancy variations on old dried foods. This such a dish.

4 *ounces dried scallops, soaked*

8 *cups Chinese Chicken Soup Stock (page 113)*

2 *dried Chinese mushrooms*

2 *tablespoons Chinese rice wine or dry sherry*

1 *tablespoon light soy sauce*

Salt to taste

¼ *cup Chinese Poached Chicken (page 230), shredded*

Pinch of ground white pepper

1 *tablespoons sesame oil*

1 *tablespoon Chinese garlic chives or Western chives*

3 *egg whites, beaten*

Slivers of Chinese or Southern ham for garnish (Substitute boiled ham if necessary)

Soak the dried scallops overnight, changing the water twice. Place the chicken stock, along with the mushrooms and the drained scallops, in a Chinese double boiler (page 123) or regular double boiler, and cook, covered, for 3 hours.

Remove the soup from the double boiler and place it in a 4-quart saucepan. Bring to a light boil and add the remaining ingredients, except the chives, egg whites, and ham-sliver garnish, and cook for 10 minutes. Stir in the chives and the beaten egg whites and garnish with a few slivers of ham. Serve immediately.

DRIED OYSTERS AND PORK IN LETTUCE

SERVES 4 AS
PART OF A CHINESE MEAL

This is wonderful fun to prepare and even more fun to eat. You will begin to wonder if the Chinese also invented the burrito! I think they did!

- 4 ounces dried oysters, rinsed and soaked for 2 hours
- 6 Chinese dried mushrooms, soaked for 2 hours
- ½ pound lean pork coarsely ground
- 1 tablespoon light soy sauce
- ⅛ teaspoon freshly grated ginger
- 1 tablespoon Chinese rice wine or dry sherry

- 2 cloves garlic, crushed
- 1 teaspoon cornstarch
- 2 tablespoons peanut oil for chowing
- 8 water chestnuts, chopped coarsely
- 1 tablespoon oyster sauce
- ½ teaspoon sesame oil
- 6 green onions, chopped
- 8 lettuce-leaf cups (iceberg lettuce)

Soak the oysters and mushrooms, drain, and grind together, coarsely. Mix with the ground pork. Add the soy sauce, ginger, rice wine, garlic, and cornstarch. Mix well and place in a steaming dish. Steam for 20 minutes (page 97).

When ready to serve dinner, add the peanut oil to a hot wok. Chow the steamed mixture, along with the water chestnuts, oyster sauce, sesame oil, and green onions, breaking up the mixture as it cooks for about 3 minutes.

Drain any excess fat from the cooked meats and serve in a bowl along with the lettuce cups on the side. Place a bit of meat in each cup and roll up and eat like a burrito.

> **HINT: TO PREPARE LETTUCE CUPS** simply remove the core of the iceberg lettuce by banging the bottom core of the head on the counter. The core can then be easily and quickly removed. Hold the head under running cold water and remove the leaves gently, letting the water do much of the work. Drain and chill.

STEAMED PORK WITH MUSHROOM AND DRIED SQUID

SERVES 4–5 AS
PART OF A CHINESE MEAL

In the early days of the Chinatowns in America, many staff members of a shop or market would eat at least 2 meals a day in the shop itself. Kitchens were built in the back of the store and the boss would often do the cooking. In a few places in Seatttle and San Francisco, Chicago and New York, you can still see such a practice. This recipe was given me by my friend Mr. George Foo Yee of the Wah Young Company, located in Seattle's Chinatown. He recited the ingredients *after* he had fed his staff.

2 *ounces dried squid, soaked overnight, drained and chopped*

4 *Chinese dried mushrooms, soaked for 2 hours*

1 *pound lean pork coarsely chopped*

8 *dried red dates, soaked for 4 hours*

2 *cloves garlic, crushed*

¼ *teaspoon freshly grated ginger*

2 *tablespoons light soy sauce*

1 *tablespoon Chinese rice wine or dry sherry*

½ *tablespoon cornstarch*

1 *tablespoon peanut oil*

White pepper, ground, to taste

Pinch of MSG (optional)

Drain all the soaked items well. Mix all together and place in a steaming dish. Steam in a bamboo steamer (page 97) for 30 minutes.

Serve as a course in a Chinese meal. The liquid remaining in the steaming dish is just great over rice.

CHINESE SAUSAGE, DRIED DUCK, AND ROAST PORK SAND POT

SERVES 4 AS
PART OF A CHINESE MEAL

The flavors of these meats, each already very rich because they are dried, combine in this dish to offer a distinct and wonderful blend. It is very typical of the "hot sand pot" dishes that you find in Hong Kong.

½ pound dried duck, cut into 1-inch-square pieces (Use a cleaver for this), soaked in ample water overnight

3 Chinese sausages (lop chong), whole

1 tablespoon peanut oil

1 clove garlic, chopped fine

1 medium yellow onion, peeled and sliced

⅛ teaspoon freshly grated ginger

½ pound Crispy Roast Pork (page 290), sliced, or ½ pound Barbecued Pork Strips (page 288)

4 green onions, cut Chinese style (page 142)

1 tablespoon light soy sauce

Pinch of brown sugar

½ teaspoon sesame oil

White pepper, ground, to taste

1 medium head iceberg lettuce, torn

Simmer the soaked dried duck, along with the sausage, for 20 minutes. Cut the sausage into 1-inch pieces. Chow the duck and sausage quickly in the wok along with the remaining ingredients except the lettuce. Drain the fat. Place in a sand pot (page 19) over the lettuce and place on a heat diffuser over a hot burner. When all is piping hot, serve.

SALTED COD, GREEK STYLE
(Bakaliaros)

It is interesting to note how common dried fish was in the ancient world. Many early citizens knew only this kind of fish, as they lived inland and shipment of fresh fish was impossible. For an old-timer these flavors bring forth wonderful memories of a youth in Greece.

During the holidays that call for fasting beforehand, such as Christmas and Easter, this dried cod becomes a major menu item. I have talked with so many young Greeks who say, "No, I don't really care for the stuff. My mother practically raised us on *bakaliaros!*" Then I asked them what they now eat on Christmas Eve or during the fasting times in Lent. Well, it is *bakaliaros*, of course. There is something to remembering who you are through certain foods. The Romans also loved this dish and Italian variations follow in the next series of recipes.

Soak the salted cod just as in the recipe for Salted Cod in Cream Sauce (page 342). Cook in just the same manner but omit the cream sauce and serve the hot fish with any of the following:

*Greek Salad Dressing
(page 144)*

Yogurt, plain or with dillweed

Garlic Sauce (page 206)

SALTED COD IN CREAM SAUCE
(Baccalà)

SERVES 4–6 AS A FISH
COURSE FOR AN ITALIAN MEAL

The secret to refreshing this dried salt cod is lots of water. It is soaked for days and you can find it ready to go in Roman fish markets. They use wonderful old marble tanks that sit out on the street, filled with *baccalà* and with a stream of fresh water running into the tank all the time. You can find this dried fish in any Italian market. Don't buy the stuff imported from Canada in tiny boxes. It is much too expensive.

I should also tell you that there is a restaurant in Rome, between Campo de' Fiori and the Jewish Ghetto, that has this on its menu . . . and it is the *only* item on the menu. You cannot get into the place!

1 *pound dried salt cod fillets, soaked and refreshed for 2 days*	3 *tablespoons flour*
	½ *cup dry white wine*
1 *yellow onion, peeled and chopped*	1 *cup milk*
	½ *cup cream*
1 *carrot, unpeeled, sliced*	1 *teaspoon capers, rinsed and chopped*
1 *bay leaf, whole*	
6 *peppercorns*	*Salt and freshly ground black pepper to taste*
CREAM SAUCE	1 *tablespoon pine nuts, toasted (page 38), for garnish*
1½ *tablespoons butter*	
1½ *tablespoons olive oil*	

Buy pieces of salt cod that are fairly thick and fresh-looking. Cut them into 1½-inch pieces, across the grain of the fish. Rinse well and place in a large bowl. Cover with water and allow to soak, changing the water 2 or 3 times each day, for 48 hours. You do not have to refrigerate.

Drain the cod and place in a 4-quart soup pot. Add fresh water to cover and the onion, carrot, bay leaf, and peppercorns. Bring to a simmer and cook for 20 minutes or until the fish is tender.

While the fish is cooking, prepare the sauce. Heat the oil and butter in a small frying pan and add the flour. Cook just a few minutes to prepare a roux. Do not discolor. In a saucepan heat the wine, milk, and cream. Add the roux, stirring constantly. When the sauce thickens, remove from the heat and add the capers. Taste, and adjust pepper. I doubt that you will want any salt.

Drain the pieces of cod well and place on a serving platter. Top with the sauce and garnish with the pine nuts.

SALTED COD IN TOMATO SAUCE

SERVES 4–5
AS A FIRST COURSE

This one is easy, providing you are keeping some Italian Tomato Sauce in the house.

Soak 1 pound of salt cod fillets as instructed above. Drain and simmer in Italian Tomato Sauce (page 208) just to cover. You may need to add a little water as it cooks. It should be tender in about 20 minutes.

Serve with pasta or salad, and a very dry white wine. This is also great for a first course, chopped and served directly over spaghetti.

Pasta

W ho did it? Who invented pasta? Food lovers have argued about this issue for hundreds of years, and I certainly intend to get in on the debate.

The Italians claim that pasta was invented in Italy. The Chinese claim that they invented pasta and prove their case by pointing out that Marco Polo brought pasta or noodles from China back to his beloved Venice. He also brought back coal and gunpowder, but there is good evidence that indicates pasta was being enjoyed in other areas of Italy prior to Polo's trip, though the dish was not known in Venice at the time. There is an ancient macaroni maker depicted on the frescoes of an Etruscan tomb. There are other references to pasta dishes, including that of a Greek, one Hesychius, who wrote during the eighth century. All of these events predate the trip by Mr. Polo.

Reay Tannahill, in her terrific volume, *Food in History* (see Bibliography), points out that prior to Polo's trip people in both India and the Arab lands were eating noodles. They called them *sevika* or *righta*, meaning "threads." Tannahill hypothesizes that pasta was introduced to Italy via the Arab–Venice/Florence/Genoa trade connections and then spread gradually throughout Italy. In support of this theory she notes that the word *spaghetti* is derived from *spago*, "string," a word and item not dissimilar to the "thread" noodles of the Arabs.

It appears that the argument as to who invented which is not an argument at all. The Chinese and the peoples of Arabia and Italy knew of pasta quite independently of one another, though the Chinese probably had it first. So much for that!

Grains were cooked into pastes or pulses in ancient Rome, and the term "polenta" probably comes from *puls*. The mush was eaten with a sauce of some sort and was enjoyed by both the peasants and the city dwellers. The trip that the grain took from a mush to noodles of a thousand different shapes was a profound trip, indeed. My dear friend Carlo Middione says in his wonderful book, *The Food of Southern Italy* (see Bibliography), that for southern Italians in our time "pasta is as necessary as water and air for survival." After tasting some of the following recipes you will understand why.

The Greeks have some wonderful pasta dishes, though they are not as complicated or as varied as the Italian ones. There are some theories that the Italians introduced pasta into Greece during the fourteenth century, but I think it is just as likely that the Middle Eastern peoples brought pasta into Greece at a much earlier date. In any case, you must make *pastitsio*. And when you prepare such a dish, you will realize that the Greeks invented what the Italians call *lasagne*.

There are major differences between Italy and China when it comes to the celebration of the noodle. Italy has at least one hundred shapes of pasta, but all are made from wheat. China, on the other hand, has only two shapes, long noodles and flat noodles, but they are made from all kinds of foods such as wheat, rice, beans, tapioca, and buckwheat, thus giving us few shapes but many textures. Some cook up to look like glass; others have a rich dark brown color with a flavor to match. The importance of the noodle for the meal is also different in the two cultures. In China the meal can consist of noodles, long thin noodles to symbolize longevity, or noodles with fish to represent plenteousness. In Italy pasta is never a main course but rather one part of the whole meal.

China has always been a hungry nation, and the invention of the noodle was a great blessing. We know that noodles were commercially prepared as early as A.D. 100 and sold on the streets. The peasants seemed to enjoy them from the first, with the upper classes not catching up until the sixteenth century. After all, the noodle provided the peasant kitchen with good nutrition and endless possibilities for variation, and the noodle cooked quickly, not a small matter for a people short on fuel.

There is one more difference between the noodle makers of China and those of Italy. In Italy pasta is either rolled and then cut, or it is extruded from machines. The Chinese use both of these methods, but they also "pull" noodles. A large piece of dough is pulled and then floured, pulled again and floured, and each time the number of strands doubles. Finally, and in just a minute or two, the noodle maker has a thousand strands in his hands. It is one of the most fascinating food-preparation techniques that I know of anywhere in the world. You can see it done when you go to Hong Kong. Wonderful fun!

You might also wish to consider:

Lamb with Orzo Pasta, Greek Style *(page 280)*
Greek Lamb and Pasta Salad *(page 146)*
Octopus Spaghetti Zorba *(page 196)*
Pasta with Mushrooms Natalie *(page 464)*

CHOW MEIN, CANTONESE STYLE

SERVES 6 AS
PART OF A CHINESE MEAL

This is surely the most famous Chinese noodle dish in America. The only problem is that the deep-fried noodle dish most Caucasians think of as Chinese is not a Chinese dish at all. Real chow mein is not deep-fried. *Chow* means "to pan-fry," and *mein* means "noodle." Pan-fried is what is going on here. So, here is my favorite version. Your kids will think you are a genius, though you may have to call this something other than its real name . . . otherwise your children will probably be expecting the old deep-fried noodle bit.

$\frac{3}{8}$ *pound Chinese dried egg noodles*

1 *cup pork, cut julienne*

MARINADE

1 *tablespoon dry sherry or Chinese rice wine*

2 *tablespoons light soy sauce*

$\frac{1}{2}$ *teaspoon freshly grated ginger*

6 *tablespoons peanut oil for pan-frying*

1 *yellow onion, peeled and sliced*

2 *ribs celery, chopped thin*

3 *Chinese dried mushrooms, soaked (page 31), drained, and chopped*

$\frac{1}{2}$ *cup sliced water chestnuts*

3 *ribs bok choy (page 28), sliced*

SAUCE

1 *tablespoon light soy sauce*

$\frac{1}{8}$ *teaspoon sugar*

$\frac{1}{4}$ *teaspoon salt*

Pinch of MSG (optional)

1 *tablespoon sesame oil*

1 *cup Chinese Chicken Soup Stock (page 113) or Basic Chicken Stock (page 129)*

1 *tablespoon cornstarch*

2 *cups fresh bean sprouts*

THE NOODLES

Bring an 8-quart pot of water to a boil and add the noodles. Carefully stir. When they begin to float freely, drain and rinse in cold water. Drain well again. Spread the noodles out on a large oiled broiling rack and allow them to dry for two hours. I use an electric fan to help them along.

Heat a large wok and add 3 tablespoons of peanut oil. Place the noodles in the wok, all in a big nest, and gently pan-brown them on one side. Get them good and brown. Turn the nest and brown it a bit on the other side. Remove from the wok and allow to cool.

THE MEAT AND VEGETABLES

Marinate the cut pork for 15 minutes. Drain the marinade and reserve. Heat the wok and add 1 tablespoon oil. Chow the meat for a few minutes until tender. Remove to the serving plate.

Heat the wok again and add 2 tablespoons oil. Chow the onion, celery, and mushrooms until the onions are clear. Add the water chestnuts and bok choy. Remove all to the serving plate.

Mix the sauce, adding the reserved marinade. Place the noodles in the heated wok and add the sauce. Toss just to cover the noodles and add the meat and vegetable mixture. Gently toss and stir-fry all together until the noodles are tender but still a bit firm.

Add the bean sprouts and toss just until they are hot, not cooked. Serve immediately.

HINT: TO FREEZE CHOW MEIN NOODLES you need simply boil, dry, and then pan-fry them. This is a lot to do on a day when you want chow mein. Do a double or triple batch one day and freeze the rest in seal-tight freezer bags. They defrost in a very short time and you simply refresh them with a bit of oil in a hot wok. Then, add the soup stock and vegetables as per your recipe.

CHOWED NOODLES WITH PORK AND SESAME SAUCE

SERVES 4 AS
PART OF A CHINESE MEAL

This dish is old, popular, easy, and frugal. If you have put some chowed noodles in the freezer you can prepare this dish in very little time and everyone will love it. It is just the perfect blend of pork and sesame!

½ pound dried Chinese egg noodles, chowed or pan-fried (page 348)

2 tablespoons peanut oil

1 clove garlic, crushed

⅛ teaspoon salt

½ pound lean pork, cut julienne

½ cup Chinese Chicken Soup Stock (page 113) or Basic Chicken Stock (page 129)

THE SAUCE

Prepare 1 batch of Sesame Garlic Dressing from Chicken Shredded with Sesame Garlic Paste (page 84)

Green onions, chopped, or Chinese parsley, chopped, for garnish

Pan-fry or chow the noodles as instructed. Remove them from the wok. Reheat the wok and add the oil, garlic, and salt. Chow for a moment and add the pork. Chow the pork to your taste and remove from the wok. Return the noodles to the wok and heat them for a few moments, tossing all the time. Add the broth and cooked pork and chow until the noodles absorb the liquid. Remove from the heat and add the sesame sauce. Toss and place in a bowl. Add the garnish and serve.

CHOW FUN NOODLES

MAKES 8–10
10-INCH-ROUND NOODLES

This is one of the most wonderful and versatile noodles that I know, but I cannot tell you how to make it of rice. This one is made with wheat flour—strictly a home version of a Chinese classic—but it is very close to the original. The actual rice noodle involves grinding rice flour while trickling water onto the mill. The batter simply dribbles out the bottom of the mill. You can see this being made in San Francisco and New York, but once you see the enormous old stone mill needed for this dish you will trust me and try this wheat-flour version. Make a few batches and then use them in the recipes that follow.

1¼ cups cold *water*

2 tablespoons peanut oil

1 cup unsifted Swans Down cake flour

1 *tablespoon cornstarch*

1 *teaspoon salt*

Place the above ingredients, *in the order given,* in a food blender. The order is important as you must have the liquids in the blender first. Blend for a moment and then scrape down the sides of the blender with a rubber spatula. Blend again at high speed for 30 seconds. Pour into a small bowl and cook.

TO COOK THE NOODLES

I use 10-inch stainless-steel cake pans. They work beautifully. Oil each pan with a bit of peanut oil and a paper towel. Place 2 ounces of batter in each pan and steam (see page 97) for 3 minutes. Remove from the steamer and allow the pans to cool a bit. Pull the noodles from the bottoms of the pans and place on waxed paper. Oil the pans again and continue. I do 3 at a time.

Be very careful to see that your steamer is level so that the noodles will be even all the way across. Also, remember that the steamer must be good and hot, with a great deal of boiling going on. A quiet steamer will not do the job!

You will need to make more than one batch of this if you are serving more than 2 people. You will catch on to this very quickly.

NOTE: You will have poor luck with this recipe if you use a cake flour other than Swans Down. I have tried several others but they are not milled as fine as is this particular product. Stick to this flour and you will have good luck with all of the noodle and dumpling recipes in this book.

VARIATION: You can also just go ahead and buy these noodles premade in any city that has a large Chinatown. I know they are available in New York, San Francisco, Seattle, Chicago, Portland, Vancouver, B.C., Los Angeles, and Boston.

COLD CHOW FUN AND PORK ROLL

*SERVES 8 AS A
DIM SUM OR APPETIZER COURSE*

This is just a delicious cold dish. It can be served as part of a dim sum meal or as an appetizer for a formal Chinese meal. In either situation everyone will love this one.

4 *Chow Fun Noodles (page 349)*

¾ *cup Barbecued Pork Strips (page 288), cut in julienne strips*

1 *cup fresh bean sprouts*

3 *tablespoons chopped Chinese parsley*

DRESSING

2 *tablespoons light soy sauce*

2 *tablespoons sesame oil*

⅛ *teaspoon sugar*

1 *teaspoon rice vinegar*

Prepare a batch of Chow Fun Noodles.

Mix the pork, beans sprouts, and parsley in a bowl. Prepare the dressing and toss with the vegetable and meat mixture. Divide the filling among the 4 noodles and roll up. Chill a bit before serving. Cut each roll into 4 pieces.

BEEF CHOW FUN

SERVES 6 AS PART OF A CHINESE MEAL

The first time I ever tasted this dish I was with my friend Mary Young. It was 1967, in San Francisco, and this dish was very popular there. I don't believe that at that time you could get it anywhere else in the country . . . but San Francisco, yes. Mary took me to a particular restaurant and we enjoyed this dish. When I returned to San Francisco I asked her to take me to the same restaurant for the same dish. No, we had to go to a different restaurant to get the same version. The chef had moved to a different restaurant and his fans moved with him. Such is San Francisco . . . and, I suppose, the restaurant business.

1 batch Chow Fun Noodles (page 349)

1 pound beef flank steak, sliced thin across the grain

MARINADE

1 tablespoon dark soy sauce

1 tablespoon cornstarch

1 egg white

1 tablespoon peanut oil

7 tablespoons peanut oil for pan-frying

2 cloves garlic, chopped fine

1 slice ginger, the size of a 25-cent piece, cut julienne

1 tablespoon fermented black beans (dow see), rinsed

1 tablespoon Chinese rice wine or dry sherry

½ medium yellow onion, peeled and sliced

½ green sweet bell pepper, cored and cut julienne

SAUCE

¼ teaspoon MSG (optional)

1 tablespoon dark soy sauce

¼ teaspoon sugar

1 tablespoon Chinese rice wine or dry sherry

Pinch of white pepper

1 tablespoon oyster sauce

1 cup fresh bean sprouts

Chinese parsley for garnish (optional)

Prepare the Chow Fun and slice into noodles about ½ inch wide. I usually oil the noodle a bit before cutting it so that the strands will not stick together.

Slice the meat and mix the marinade. Marinate the meat for 15 minutes.

Heat the wok and add 2 tablespoons of the peanut oil. Toss the noodles about in the oil until they are very hot and begin to color just a bit on the edges. Remove to the serving platter and set aside.

Heat the wok again and add 3 tablespoons of the peanut oil, along with the garlic and ginger. Chow for a moment and add the rinsed black beans and the sherry. In this chow the onion and green pepper, just until very hot. Remove to the serving platter.

Heat the wok a third time and add 2 tablespoons of the peanut oil and the meat. Chow on one side only until it begins to brown. Return the vegetables, the noodles, and the sauce to the wok and toss with the meat until hot. Add the bean sprouts, toss just a minute or so, and serve.

You might like to offer a Chinese parsley garnish.

MEAT-STUFFED CHOW FUN ROLLS

This dish is usually served in a formal dim sum house. I have seen patrons get up from their chairs and simply march across the dining room to take this dish from a cart. They do not want to miss out should the cart be empty by the time it gets to their table. The dish is that popular.

Prepare a batch of Chow Fun Noodles (page 349).

Choose a cooked meat filling, such as chopped barbecued pork, chowed beef, or chowed shrimp. Roll a bit of the meat filling into each noodle and place on a small oiled plate. Steam until the noodle is heated through and then add a bit of the following sauce just as you serve.

SAUCE FOR CHOW FUN
ROLLS

2 tablespoons dark soy sauce

⅛ teaspoon sugar

¼ teaspoon freshly grated
   ginger

¼ teaspoon crushed garlic

Pinch of MSG (optional)

2 tablespoons peanut oil

½ teaspoon Worcestershire
   sauce

2 green onions, chopped

Blend all together in a small saucepan and warm a bit. Allow to cool before serving over the rolled chow fun.

NOODLES IN OYSTER SAUCE

(Gon Lo Mein)

*SERVES 4 AS A
LUNCHEON DISH OR 6 AS PART
OF A CHINESE MEAL*

My friend Mary Young first explained this dish to me because she knew I was feeding a goodly number of college students during my days as a chaplain. "You can't afford to feed students unless you know about this dish. It is delicious and cheap!" She was right . . . as she always has been.

2 *chicken breasts, skinned, boned, and cut julienne*

MARINADE

1 *tablespoon light soy sauce*

1 *tablespoon dry sherry or Chinese rice wine*

½ *teaspoon freshly grated ginger*

2 *tablespoons peanut oil*

1 *ounce Chinese dried mushrooms, soaked (page 31), drained, and cut julienne*

½ *pound dried Chinese egg noodles*

1 *tablespoon sesame oil*

3 *tablespoons oyster sauce*

3 *green onions, chopped*

Chinese parsley, chopped, for garnish

Have all prepared before starting this dish. Bring a pot of water to boil for the noodles. Cut the chicken and marinate for 15 minutes. Heat a wok and add the peanut oil. Chow the chicken and mushrooms together just until the chicken is tender. Remove to a plate. Boil the noodles in the salted water just until they float and are soft but still quite firm, about 4 minutes. Drain. Heat the wok again and add the chicken, noodles, and remaining ingredients, except the parsley. Gently toss and stir-fry until the dish is hot throughout.

Top with the parsley and serve immediately.

CHINESE NEW YEAR NOODLES
(Jai)

SERVES 6 AS
A PART OF A CHINESE MEAL.

*J*ai is a classic method of preparing *sai fun* (mung bean noodles). This vegetarian dish is eaten on the New Year to remind all of the necessity of a simpler and more contemplative life-style. The Buddhist monks still practically live on this dish, and I love it. My dear friend John Young, my adopted Chinese uncle, used to eat this dish with so much garlic and red chili paste (page 30) that I was amazed. His theory was: "The hotter, the better." You adjust this dish to your own desired level of heat.

2 *tablespoons peanut oil*

½ *teaspoon salt*

3 *cloves garlic, chopped very fine or crushed*

¼ *teaspoon freshly grated ginger*

VEGETABLES

6 *Chinese dried mushrooms, soaked for 2 hours, cut julienne*

1 *cup Chinese celery cabbage (Napa), sliced as for coleslaw*

*¼ *cup dried lily buds, soaked for 1 hour (optional)*

2 *ounces dried bean-curd skin, soaked for 1 hour (optional)*

½ *cup bamboo shoots, cut julienne*

THE SAUCE

2 *tablespoons* foo yee *(page 29)*

1 *tablespoon light soy sauce*

⅛ *teaspoon sugar*

2 *teaspoons sesame oil*

½ *teaspoon ground white pepper*

1 *teaspoon garlic and red chili paste (page 30), to taste*

4 *ounces cellophane (sai fun)* noodles, soaked for 1 hour

2 *cups Chinese Chicken Soup Stock (page 113) or Basic Chicken Stock (page 129)*

Green onions, chopped, or Chinese parsley, chopped, for garnish

*Lily buds, dried, can be found in Chinese markets. They offer a fragrant blessing to the dish.

Remember the basic rule for chowing: Have everything ready before you light the wok. Soak and prepare the vegetables, mix the sauce, and then go to it.

Heat the wok and add the oil, salt, garlic, and ginger. Chow for a moment and then add the vegetables. Chow until hot and tender and then add the sauce, the drained noodles, and the chicken stock to the wok. Stir and simmer uncovered until the noodles are clear and tender and have absorbed most of the broth. Taste for salt and place in a serving bowl. Garnish and serve.

CHINESE NEW YEAR NOODLES WITH OLIVES

Most of us in this country are surprised to hear that the Chinese enjoy dried olives, and have for a long time. The olives are called *lam see* and can be purchased in most Chinese markets. They are similar to an Italian dried olive, and very rich. Soak them in water for an hour or so, drain them, and then add them along with your vegetables during the preparation of *jai* for the New Year. This makes the dish very special but you may be surprised by the taste as it is a bit sharp.

GLASS NOODLES WITH PEANUT SAUCE

SERVES 4–6 AS AN APPETIZER COURSE, 4 AS PART OF A CHINESE MEAL

Sai fun, the thin noodles made from mung beans, are often called "cellophane" or "glass" noodles since they become almost transparent when cooked. This is a very tasty cold salad that will tickle your youngsters. When Channing and Jason were little we called this dish "Peanut Butter and Worms." Such fun!

1 4-ounce package of sai
   fun *noodles*

2 cups *Chinese Chicken Soup
   Stock (page 113) or Basic
   Chicken Stock (page 129)*

THE SAUCE

2 tablespoons peanut butter

4 tablespoons hot tap water

3 tablespoons light soy sauce

Pinch of sugar

½ *teaspoon sesame oil*

*Shot of Tabasco or garlic
and red chili paste (page
30) to taste*

GARNISH

Green onions, chopped

1 *tablespoon dry roasted
   peanuts, chopped*

Soak the noodles for 1 hour and drain. Place in a saucepan with the
soup stock and simmer until they are tender but not mushy, about 10
minutes. Drain the stock from the noodles, reserving it for another use.
Place the noodles on a tray and refrigerate them for 1 hour.

Mix the sauce by putting the peanut butter in a 2-cup measuring glass
and adding the hot water. Stir with a fork until it is the consistency of
whipping cream. Add the remaining ingredients for the sauce and mix
with the chilled noodles. Place the noodles on a serving dish and garnish with the green onions and peanuts.

GREECE

‖ PASTA WITH MIZITHRA ‖

SERVE 6 AS A
FIRST COURSE OR SIDE DISH

This is a very basic dish. It can be found on the menu of most tavernas
in Athens and it makes a wonderful side dish for just about anything. It
is simply macaroni and cheese, Greek style. The flavor of the Mizithra
cheese is what makes you remember beautiful Greece.

½ cup olive oil

4 cloves garlic, chopped fine

1 pound dry pasta, cooked and drained

½ cup freshly grated Parmesan cheese

½ cup freshly grated Mizithra cheese

Salt and freshly ground black pepper to taste

¼ cup chopped parsley for garnish

Bring the water for the pasta to boil and prepare everything else. It is important never to overcook pasta.

Heat the olive oil in a small frying pan and add the chopped garlic. Sauté for just a moment and set aside. Boil the pasta until just barely tender. Drain and toss with all ingredients. Serve as a side dish in the place of another starch.

PASTITSIO

SERVES 6–8

The Greeks seem to have been into baking things long before the rest of us. I think they are to be given credit for the invention of baked pastas, this particular dish being the most famous of the many regional varieties. It is a splendid invention, and predates what the Italians were later to call *lasagne*.

When you see this dish in Greece it is not made with what we call macaroni. The hollow tubes of pasta are very long and very thin and much closer to what an American Italian would call long ziti. In any case, do not use elbow macaroni. The Greeks think that would verge on heresy!

You must prepare this dish in 3 different stages. It will go together beautifully and is not as complicated as a properly made lasagne. This version is from the women at St. Demetrios Greek Orthodox Church in Seattle. Their terrific cookbook is called *Greek Cooking in an American Kitchen* (see Bibliography).

THE MEAT MIXTURE

6 *tablespoons butter*

¾ *cup peeled and finely chopped yellow onion*

2 *cloves garlic, crushed*

1¼ *pounds lean ground beef*

1 *16-ounce can peeled tomatoes, mashed*

½ *cup canned tomato sauce*

½ *cup water*

1 *teaspoon salt*

⅛ *teaspoon freshly ground black pepper*

½ *teaspoon cinnamon*

⅛ *teaspoon cloves*

THE MACARONI

4 *quarts water*

Salt

¾ *pound Greek macaroni or Italian ziti (Use long, medium size, not elbow or short pasta)*

¼ *cup butter, melted*

6 *eggs, beaten*

1 *cup grated Parmesan or Romano cheese*

THE WHITE SAUCE

6 *tablespoons butter*

6 *tablespoons flour*

2 *cups warm milk*

3 *eggs, beaten*

2 *tablespoons dry sherry (optional)*

½ *teaspoon nutmeg*

½ *cup grated Parmesan cheese*

½ *teaspoon salt*

Dash of white pepper

Prepare the meat mixture by heating a large skillet and adding 2 tablespoons of the butter. Sauté the onion and garlic until golden. Add remaining butter and the crumbled ground beef. Add remaining ingredients for the meat mixture and simmer, uncovered, for 20 minutes, or until most of the most of the liquid has been absorbed. Mixture should be thick. Set aside.

Prepare the macaroni by bringing the water to a boil in a large stockpot. Add the salt and the macaroni. Stir gently and cook uncovered until tender, about 7 to 8 minutes. Drain and rinse with cool water. Drain well and place in a large bowl. Add the melted butter, beaten eggs, and grated cheese. Put half of this mixture into a greased 9 × 9 × 2-inch baking pan and top with the meat mixture. Cover the meat with the remaining half of the pasta.

NOTE: I like to arrange the pasta in straight rows so that when you cut and serve the dish the pasta is even and beautiful. That is how they do it in Greece!

Prepare the white sauce by melting the butter in a medium saucepan. Stir in the flour and cook for a moment. Gradually add the heated milk, stirring constantly, and cook until thickened and smooth. Beat the eggs in a separate bowl and stir in ½ cup of the sauce. Blend and stir the egg mixture into the saucepan. Continue to stir and cook over low heat until all is thickened. Add remaining ingredients for the sauce. Pour the sauce over the macaroni and bake at 350° for 25 minutes, or until the top is delicately browned.

PASTITSIO BAKED WITH PHYLLO

SERVES 6–8

Generally I stay away from hotel dining rooms when I travel. I find the food neither good nor bad . . . it just sits there on the plate and bores me. However, the Amalia Hotels in Greece offer good quality in terms of service and the food is most often quite good. The Hotel Amalia in Delphi, a well-run hotel indeed, offered this dish to us on Easter Day, along with the roast lamb, of course. It makes a smashing presentation since it looks like a beautiful baked cake but it is really filled with pastitsio.

Prepare all of the ingredients for a Pastitsio (page 358) but do not construct the final dish.

Brush an 11-inch-diameter tube pan (3 inches deep) with melted butter. Brush 5 or 6 sheets of phyllo (page 36) with butter and line the pan with the sheets, leaving a bit to hang over the edges so that you can fold the excess over the top when the construction is completed.

Mix the meat sauce and the pasta together and lay this in the pan, with a bit of the white sauce, in 2 or 3 layers. Fold the excess phyllo over the top and brush with a bit more butter. Bake at 350° until the phyllo is golden brown, about 50 minutes or so. To serve, place a large serving plate over the top of the pan. Turn both pan and plate over at once so that the pastitsio comes out upside down on the serving platter.

ITALY

PASTA WITH ZUCCHINI

SERVES 6
AS A DINNER COURSE OR 8
AS A PASTA COURSE

This dish is not supposed to save you from the neighbors who will leave that eighteen-pound zucchini on your porch. You will not need that much for this recipe. However, during the winter you will begin to long for this dish . . . once you have tried it . . . and once zucchini has risen high in cost. This is all a Roman plot!

½ cup pancetta (Bacon will work, but the flavor is very different)

¼ cup olive oil

3 cloves garlic, chopped fine

1½ pounds zucchini, cut julienne and well drained

½ cup whipping cream

⅓ cup freshly grated Parmesan cheese

Salt and pepper to taste

1 pound dry pasta (I prefer penne with this dish)

Heat a large frying pan and sauté the pancetta until clear. Remove the meat and fat from the pan. Drain and discard the fat and set the meat aside. Add the olive oil to the pan and sauté the garlic for just a moment. Add the well-drained zucchini and sauté over high heat until the zucchini is hot but not mushy. Add the cream and stir.

Toss the above with the cooked pasta (page 368), adding the pancetta, cheese, and salt and pepper to taste.

PASTA ALL' AMATRICIANA

SERVES 4
AS A FIRST COURSE

The name sounds so complicated . . . but this is simply pasta with tomatoes and Italian bacon. It is very popular in Rome and has been for many generations. It is simple to prepare and obviously one of those dishes that Romans depend upon when in a hurry.

SAUCE

⅓ pound pancetta, coarsely chopped

1 medium yellow onion, coarsely chopped

2 tablespoons olive oil

¼ teaspoon dried red pepper flakes, or to taste

1 cup Italian Tomato Sauce (page 208)

Salt and pepper to taste

½ pound dry pasta (I prefer penne with this dish)

4 tablespoons freshly grated Pecorino or Parmesan cheese for garnish

Sauté the pancetta and onion until transparent. Add the oil, red pepper, Italian Tomato Sauce, and salt and pepper to taste. Simmer for a few minutes and toss with the cooked pasta. Top with the cheese.

CANNELLONI

SERVES 8
FOR A PASTA COURSE,
4 FOR A MAIN DISH

I have made this dish before, of course. It is a classic in the pasta world. However, I was not prepared for the delicious version served in Bologna. I was invited to the home of friends of Carlo Middione, the chef at Vivande Porta Via, in San Francisco. The couple have lived in Bologna for many years and they are just charming. Mrs. Nasi prepared a dish very close to this one for lunch. I have attempted to duplicate her wonderful flavors and I think the presence of mortadella, the wonderful cold prepared meat of Bologna, will change your mind about any previous versions of this dish that you may have tasted.

NOODLES

3 eggs

1 cup water

1 cup flour

Salt to taste

Olive oil for oiling the pan

FILLING

2 tablespoons olive oil

½ pound lean pork, coarsely ground

½ pound lean veal or beef, coarsely ground

½ pound mortadella, coarsely ground

1 egg

2 tablespoons chopped parsley

2 tablespoons freshly grated Parmesan cheese

Fresh chopped basil or dried basil to taste

Salt and freshly ground black pepper to taste

SAUCE

2 cups Sauce Bolognese (page 209)

1 cup Basic White Sauce (page 205)

GARNISH

3 tablespoons freshly grated Parmesan cheese

Prepare the noodles. Place the eggs in a food blender. Add the water, flour, and salt. Blend until smooth, scraping down the sides of the blender once, using a rubber spatula. Heat a 10-inch SilverStone-lined crepe or omelet pan and oil with a tiny bit of olive oil. I use a small paper towel for this. Add 2 ounces of batter to the hot pan and turn the pan to spread out the batter evenly. Cook on one side only until the noodle is dry on top. These should not be at all browned or too dry, so the pan should not be too hot. Separate the cooked noodles with waxed paper. You should have 8 noodles.

Prepare the filling. Heat a frying pan and add the olive oil. Sauté the pork for a few minutes and then add the beef or veal. Cook until the meat falls apart. Remove from the pan and drain the fat. Allow the meat to cool and then add the remaining filling ingredients. Mix well.

To finish: Lay out a noodle on waxed paper, cooked side up. Place filling in the center and roll it up. Place seam side down in a baking dish and top with the two sauces. Just pour one on top of the other. Sprinkle the cheese on top and bake at 375° until the dish browns and all is hot, about 15 to 20 minutes.

VARIATION: You might want to mix the white sauce with the meat filling and proceed as above.

PASTA WITH GARLIC AND EGGS

SERVES 4–6
AS A FIRST COURSE

Garlic, eggs, and cheese. It is not a complex dish to prepare but the flavors simply belong together. Another dish that is very typical of the Roman trattorias, and if you have not been there yet you must go. You will eat *so* well!

- ½ *pound dry pasta of your choice*
- 2 *eggs, beaten*
- ½ *cup olive oil*

- 4 *cloves garlic, crushed*
- 2 *tablespoons freshly grated Parmesan cheese*
- *Salt and pepper to taste*

Put the pasta on to boil in plenty of salted water. In the meantime, heat the oil in a small frying pan and add the garlic. Sauté just for a moment. Drain the pasta and toss all ingredients together. Salt and pepper to taste.

PASTA WITH SWEET RED PEPPERS AND ANCHOVIES

SERVES 6

When I think of the pasta dishes of Rome I rarely think of a tomato sauce. Peppers and anchovies are really more typical. This dish can be found in many fine trattorias and it is a snap to prepare. No, the anchovy flavor will not be too strong for you since you are going to soak the salty little fishes in milk first.

1	2-ounce can anchovies, rinsed and drained	1	pound dry penne pasta, cooked
¼	cup milk		Freshly ground black pepper to taste
3	cloves garlic, diced fine or crushed		
¾	cup olive oil		Salt to taste
2	sweet red bell peppers, cut in a ¼-inch dice		Parsley, chopped, for garnish

Drain the anchovies and soak them in the milk for 15 minutes. Drain and discard the milk.

Sauté the garlic and the anchovies in the olive oil. Cook just for a few minutes so that you can mash the anchovies into a paste. Add the chopped peppers and sauté just until they are tender but not soft. Toss with hot pasta. Add salt and pepper to taste. Careful with that salt as the anchovies will probably add enough. Top with the parsley garnish. No cheese with fish, please.

PASTA EARS WITH CAULIFLOWER

SERVES 6–8
AS A FIRST COURSE

I had so much fun with the kids when I did this show. I told my younger fans—and we have a wonderful flock of children watching the shows—that this dish had a funny name. Well, they remembered the time that I cooked tortellini and claimed that the noodle was modeled after Venus de Milo's belly button. Actually, that is supposed to be true. I showed them this dish, a dish made with tiny little balls of pasta pressed into ear shapes, and served it with cauliflower, thus giving us cauliflower ears! They booed and hissed and ate the whole works.

This dish comes from Sicily, where the grandmas still stand about and press out the tiny pasta ears. You can buy them already prepared in any Italian grocery. Ask for *orecchiette*, "little pasta ears."

1 1½-pound head of
   cauliflower, broken into
   little flowerets

½ cup olive oil

¾ pound dry pasta ears
   (orecchiette)

3 cloves garlic, chopped
   fine or crushed

16 anchovies, flat, soaked in
   ½ cup milk for 1 hour
   and then drained,
   discarding the milk

½ teaspoon dried red
   pepper flakes or to taste

Salt and freshly ground
black pepper to taste
(Careful with that salt!)

Bring a pot of 4 quarts of water to a boil and blanch the flowerets of cauliflower for just a few minutes. Add 1 tablespoon of the olive oil to the water during this process. Drain the vegetable, reserving the water, and plunge the flowerets into cold water. Set aside.

Bring the water in which the cauliflower was cooked to a boil again and cook the pasta, just until it is barely tender.

In the meantime, heat the remaining oil and sauté the garlic, drained anchovies, and pepper flakes until the anchovies can be mashed with a wooden fork. Drain the pasta and the cauliflower and mix all together, heating until the dish is hot. Serve *without* cheese. They tell me that's how they do it in Sicily.

PASTA CARBONARA, ROMAN STYLE

SERVES 8–10
AS A FIRST COURSE

Pasta Carbonara is one of the great inventions of the food world. It is an old dish and reminds us of times when people had to live on a few pieces of dried Italian bacon and an egg or two . . . but with pasta you could survive, and survive very well.

I had this dish one night at Trattoria Edmondo, a wonderful and basic Roman joint. The dish was filled with pancetta, that great Italian bacon that is not smoked at all but hung to age until it has a musty and heavy flavor. Talk about flavors of the Old World! We want everything fresh and therefore lose those ancient tastes. Drying and curing were terribly important not just for preservation but also for flavor. Our American bacon will just not do in this dish.

¼ pound pancetta (You can
use regular bacon for this
dish but it is just not the
same, nor as good)

¼ pound butter

1 cup milk

2 tablespoons white wine vinegar

1 pound pasta, dry

2 eggs, whipped

⅓ cup grated Parmesan or
Romano cheese

Salt and pepper to taste

Cut the pancetta into little pieces ¼ inch square and sauté in the butter
until the bacon is clear. Heat the milk in a small saucepan and add the
bacon and butter. Add the vinegar; this will turn the milk to cheese.
Simmer gently for about 15 minutes, or until the sauce cooks smooth.

Boil your favorite pasta al dente. Drain and return to the pan. Immediately throw in the eggs, the bacon sauce, and the grated cheese.
Add salt and pepper, toss, and serve immediately.

PASTA CARBONARA WITH MUSTARD

Add 1 tablespoon of Dijon mustard to the above sauce, just as you
are tossing the pasta. A very delicious addition!

PENNE CARBONARA
(La Carbonara Restaurant)

SERVES 6–8
AS A FIRST COURSE

I don't know if they named this restaurant after this dish but both the
restaurant and its version of this pasta are classics!

The eating house is located on the edge of the market square in Rome,
Campo de' Fiori. You will be treated very well and you will have trouble
passing up their exceptionally beautiful antipasto table. Try this dish as
well.

½ pound pancetta, chopped

1 pound penne pasta, dry

4 eggs, beaten

⅓ cup grated Pecorino cheese

⅓ cup grated Parmesan cheese

Salt and freshly ground
black pepper to taste

Sauté the pancetta until transparent. Set aside. Cook the pasta al dente. Drain and return to the pot. Add the bacon, along with its fat, the eggs, both cheese, and pepper. Cook over very low heat, stirring constantly. Keep the pasta moving in the pot so that the eggs do not scramble. You may have to take the pot off the heat now and then. A thin sauce should form on the noodles. Serve immediately

---

HINT: ON COOKING PASTA AHEAD OF TIME. If you have a large party and intend to serve pasta, you may want to consider cooking the pasta before and heating it up at the last minute. This can be done, if you are careful, by boiling the pasta until it is not quite done to your taste and then draining it and plunging it *immediately* into cold water. Drain the pasta and keep it cold until dinner. Heat it up by throwing it into a pot of boiling water for just a moment and then draining it and serving it immediately. This will work only if you do not overcook the pasta in the first place!

FRESH PASTA

Now, away with the fancy shapes of pasta and let us get down to serious eating. I do not believe that fresh pasta is necessarily superior to the dried product. Some is better, some is not. When you desire a very thin pasta, however, as I do in these next few dishes, it must be made fresh. It is worth the effort and if you have a hand-crank pasta machine it is little effort. I do not care for pasta from those electric "extruder" machines. Pasta must be rolled for me.

1½ *cups unbleached white flour*   3 *eggs*

1 *cup semolina flour*   1 *tablespoon olive oil*

½ *teaspoon salt*   1 *tablespoon water*

Place the flours and salt in a large bowl. Mix well and form a well in the center. Add the remaining ingredients and pinch all together with your fingers to form a dough. Knead for a few minutes until the dough is smooth and elastic. Place the dough on the counter and cover with the bowl. Let rest ½ hour.

Knead a few times again and form into any shape desired.

Remember to allow your pasta to dry for about an hour before cooking. Or, most pasta forms freeze very well. Dry a bit first and then freeze on covered trays or in boxes.

PASTA TIES WITH CABBAGE

SERVES 6
AS A FIRST COURSE

The Italians have done a wonderful thing with pasta. The shapes they have thought up are just fascinating, what with the wheels, ears, corkscrews, tubes, pens, angel hair, ribbons, horns, conchs, stars, snails, little hats, little tubes, rice shapes, butterflies, and bow ties. We are talking about a culture that has fun with pasta!

You will like this dish. I stole it from a street restaurant in Rome.

½ pound pasta ties

½ cup olive oil

3 tablespoons butter

3 cloves garlic, crushed

6 anchovies, flat

⅛ teaspoon dried red pepper flakes

¾ cup peeled and chopped yellow onions

3 cups thinly sliced green cabbage

2 cups thinly sliced radicchio or 2 cups thinly sliced red cabbage

¾ cup cream

Salt to taste

¼ cup grated Parmesan or Romano cheese

Heat a large frying pan and add the oil, butter, garlic, anchovies, and red pepper flakes. Sauté for a few minutes so that you can mash up the anchovies.

Add the onions and sauté until transparent. Add the cabbage and sauté over low heat just until tender. Add the radicchio and continue cooking until all is tender and the water cooked out.

In the meantime, cook the pasta to taste.

Add the cream to the vegetable sauce and simmer lightly. Salt to taste.

Toss this mixture with the cooked and drained pasta and stir in the cheese.

PAPPARDELLE WITH PESTO

SERVES 4
AS A FIRST COURSE

Felidia's, on the corner of East Fifty-eighth Street and Second Avenue in New York, makes wonderful pappardelle. This version that Lydia, the charming owner, served me on my last visit was simply prepared but with very fine ingredients. Oh, recording this recipe for you is making me hungry for my friends at Felidia's. Call ahead for a table or you'll never get near the place. It is very fine.

½ batch Fresh Pasta (page 368), rolled into very thin sheets and cut into 1-inch-wide noodles.

1 cup coarsely diced tomatoes, very ripe

3 tablespoons Pesto Sauce (page 211)

3 tablespoons freshly grated Parmesan or Romano cheese

Salt and freshly ground black pepper to taste

Boil pasta until barely tender. Toss with remaining ingredients, but toss gently. You don't want to tear the noodles. Heat to table temperature and serve immediately.

GARBANZO POLENTA

SERVES 6 AS A SIDE
DISH AT AN ITALIAN MEAL

Normally, polenta is made with cornmeal, corn that came from America. In the very old days a polenta was made from garbanzo beans, sometimes called chick-peas, *ceci* to the Italians. They also made a lovely sweet polenta out of dried chestnut flour. Try this dish. It is unusually good, and you will have no trouble finding garbanzo flour in any Italian market.

1 *quart water*

2 *teaspoons salt*

1½ *cups garbanzo flour*
    Freshly ground black pepper to taste

½ *teaspoon whole thyme*

1 *cup freshly grated Parmesan or Romano cheese*

Bring the water to a boil and add the salt. Remove the pan from the heat and stir in the garbanzo flour, using a wire whip. Work fast and stir hard or you will get lumps. Return the pan to the burner and cook, stirring with a wooden spoon, until it is very thick, about 15 minutes. It should be as thick as hot breakfast cereal. Add the remaining ingredients and pour the mixture into an oiled bread pan. Chill overnight, covered. Slice the polenta ¼ inch thick and pan-fry in olive oil, just before dinner.

PAPPARDELLE WITH TELEPHONE WIRES

SERVES 4
AS A FIRST COURSE

The "telephone wires" in the name of this dish come from the strings that will form between your fork and the plate. They are from the mozzarella cheese, of course. This is fun to prepare for your children but you must be fair and tell them that all normal rules of polite eating are to be disregarded that night.

½ *batch Fresh Pasta (page 368), rolled into very thin sheets and cut into 1-inch-wide noodles*

SAUCE

2 *cups fresh tomatoes*

4 *tablespoons olive oil*

1 *tablespoon finely chopped garlic*

2 *tablespoons butter*

1 *teaspoon oregano*
    Salt and freshly ground black pepper to taste

3 *tablespoons cream*

2 *cups coarsely grated mozzarella cheese*

Prepare the pasta and let it dry for about ½ hour.

Place all the ingredients for the sauce in a pan and simmer until all is tender, about 15 minutes. Cook the pasta al dente and toss all ingredients together, beginning with the sauce and adding the cheese last. Be careful that you do not tear the pasta when stirring it.

GREEN TUBES
WITH MEAT SAUCE
(Bologna)

SERVES 8–10
AS A FIRST COURSE

This is too rich to believe, but I urge you cook it nevertheless. The use of mortadella in the dish indicates the source of the dish: Bologna. I ate so well in that city that I cannot wait to go back. No tomato in this dish, just heaven.

1 *cup Basic White Sauce (page 205)*

⅛ *teaspoon freshly ground nutmeg*

2 *tablespoons olive oil*

3 *cloves garlic, finely chopped or crushed*

¼ *pound pancetta, coarsely chopped*

½ *pound veal or very lean beef, coarsely ground*

½ *pound mortadella, coarsely ground*

¼ *cup freshly grated Parmesan or Romano cheese*

1 *pound green penne pasta*

Salt and freshly ground black pepper to taste

Prepare the white sauce and stir in the nutmeg. Set aside.

Bring 4 quarts of salted water to boil for the pasta.

Heat a large frying pan and add the olive oil. Sauté the garlic for just a moment and then add the pancetta, cooking it until it is clear. Add the veal and cook until done to your taste. Add the mortadella, cheese, and the white sauce. Keep the sauce warm.

Boil the pasta, drain, and toss with the sauce. Check for salt and pepper, though you will probably not need any salt at all due to the pancetta.

Rice

The Chinese have been eating rice for the past four thousand years, and they each eat nearly a pound a day. Approximately three out of five people in this world live on rice, the main item in their diet, and the ways in which they have learned to cook it, especially in China, are wonderfully creative. It is served in the form of noodles, made into soup, rolled in leaves and vegetables, fried, steamed, made into sausages, and finally into sweet desserts. You can eat rice three meals a day. In China they do just that. In the ancient writings of 2000 B.C. rice is listed as one of the "five sacred crops," the others being soybeans, wheat, barley, and millet.

Our other two ancient cultures did not see rice until they encountered the soldiers of Alexander the Great, and rice was not cultivated in Italy until the fifteenth century. While the Greeks and Romans do enjoy rice, especially in the regions around Milan, they do not eat nearly as much of this grain as do the Chinese. The Greeks roll it in grape leaves, and the Italians prepare creamy risotto, but the rice is generally seen as a side dish, even though the Italians do eat more rice than any other European nation.

In China a meal without rice is inconceivable. The term for *rice* literally means "food," and even a common greeting involves mention of the food product. In our culture we say "Hello, how are you?" The Chinese say, *"Chi fan le mei you?,"* which is literally translated, "Have you eaten rice yet today?" Rice, or *fan,* is so much a part of the Chinese mind-set that it has become a symbol of plenteousness, which explains why we throw rice at a newlywed couple. We wish for them rice and plenty forever.

There are several types of rice used in the following recipes. It is best not to attempt to replace one with another in a recipe. All can be found in supermarkets, Italian groceries, or Chinese groceries:

Long grain—Chinese common rice

Short-grain or pearl rice—Japanese. A bit more sticky than long-grain

Sticky sweet rice—Japanese. A fat round Chinese rice that becomes
    very sticky when cooked

Arborio—Italian rice that is rich in flavor and absolutely necessary to
    a good risotto

CHINA

FRIED RICE

SERVES 6 AS
PART OF A CHINESE MEAL

I did not think that I would see much fried rice in Hong Kong since the versions that we get in Chinese restaurants in this country are so poor. It is usually used as "filler" in Dinner No. 1. But in Hong Kong, even at a formal meal, the last course is very often a wonderful fried rice. The Chinese must be sure that you are absolutely stuffed before you leave the table. If by chance you should still have the least bit of room left in your tummy you are to fill it with fried rice. This is a most gracious and wonderful way of caring for your guests.

½ pound pork steak, chopped

MARINADE

1 teaspoon light soy sauce

1 teaspoon Chinese rice wine or dry sherry

⅛ teaspoon freshly grated ginger

3 tablespoons peanut oil for chowing

Additional meats, all optional: Add any or all of these in any amount you wish. lop chong sausage, sliced; cooked chicken; cooked shrimp; ham, cut julienne

2 eggs, beaten

1 cup dry long-grain rice, cooked and cooled

2 cloves garlic, chopped fine

2 ribs celery, sliced thin

1 medium yellow onion, peeled and chopped

1 cup chopped bok choy or Chinese celery cabbage

8 water chestnuts, sliced thin

1 cup defrosted frozen peas

3 Chinese mushrooms, soaked for 2 hours, drained and sliced thin

4 green onions, cut Chinese style (page 142)

SAUCE

1 tablespoon light soy sauce

¼ teaspoon MSG (optional)

¼ teaspoon salt

Pinch of sugar

1 cup fresh bean sprouts

Marinate the pork for 15 minutes. Heat a wok and add ½ tablespoon of the peanut oil. Chow the pork until done to your taste and then add the remaining cooked meats. Chow all for a few minutes and remove to a large serving bowl.

Heat the wok again and add another ½ tablespoon of peanut oil. Pour the beaten eggs into the wok and tilt the wok in circles over the heat causing a thin egg pancake to form in the wok. Using the metal wok paddle, cut the pancake into pieces and chow for just a moment. Remove to the serving bowl.

Add a tablespoon of the peanut oil and chow the cooked cold rice until hot. Remove to the serving bowl.

Add the last tablespoon of the peanut oil and chow the garlic. Add all the vegetables, except the bean sprouts, in the order given, chowing the celery and onions a moment before you add the remaining items. Add the mixed sauce and chow until all is hot. Return the ingredients in the serving bowl to the wok and chow until very hot. Stir in the bean sprouts, test for salt, and serve.

STICKY SWEET RICE WITH MEATS

SERVES 6–8 AS
PART OF A CHINESE MEAL

This is a very flavorful rice dish, and a great way to use up meats left over from your Chinese dinner party. In Hong Kong, and in many American Chinatowns, you will see lotus leaves or bamboo leaves stuffed with this rice mixture and then tied into neat little bundles. Another common way to serve this dish is steamed, in a bowl. It is nice and filling.

All meats must be cooked ahead of time. Use 1 cup total of any or all of the following:

Chinese Poached Chicken (page 230)

Chicken Baked with Honey and Soy Sauce (page 232)

Roast ''Lung Kong'' Chicken (page 240)

Chinese Sesame Chicken (page 242)

Quick Chinese Roast Chicken (page 242)

Crispy Roast Pork (page 290)

Barbecued Pork Strips (page 288)

½ cup sticky sweet rice *(page 34)*

1 cup long-grain rice

½ tablespoon peanut oil

2 lop chong *sausages, sliced*

1 tablespoon dried shrimp *(page 33), soaked for 1 hour and drained*

3 Chinese dried mushrooms, soaked *for 2 hours, drained and sliced*

½ tablespoon light soy sauce

½ tablespoon Chinese rice wine or dry sherry

1 tablespoon oyster sauce

½ teaspoon sugar

1 tablespoon chopped green onions, white part only

Place the 2 kinds of rice in a heavy pot with a tight-fitting lid and add 3 cups of water. Cover and bring to a boil. Turn down to a low simmer and cook for 40 minutes. Watch that you do not burn this.

In the meantime, heat the oil in a wok and chow the *lop chong* slices and the dried shrimp for just a moment. Add the mushrooms and chow for a moment. Stir this mixture into the cooked rice, along with the cup of cooked meats, chopped into bite-size pieces. Stir in all remaining ingredients and place in a suitable steaming bowl. Steam in a bamboo steamer (page 97) for 20 minutes and serve.

VARIATION: You can also wrap this mixture in lotus leaves or bamboo leaves. These leaves are found in Chinatown. Soak them for 1 hour in warm tap water and then wrap up about ½ cup of the above mixture in each leaf. Make a nice little bundle and tie with string in several places. Steam in a bamboo steamer (page 97) for 20 minutes and serve. This is the traditional method of serving but you might not be impressed with the work in tying and wrapping.

RICE CONGEE
(Jook)

SERVES 8–10

Westerners are often surprised to find that citizens in the south of China eat rice at three meals a day. Why should that surprise us? We eat bread at three meals a day! In any case, this is a very warming soup made by cooking rice until it simply turns to a thick liquid. It is most often served for breakfast, and the flavor can be different each time, depending on what kind of meats you add to the soup. I love this stuff and Mary Young, my adopted Chinese aunt, brews up a batch of it that will just amaze you.

1 *cup long-grain rice*	1 *slice fresh ginger*
12 *cups water*	2 *eggs, beaten (optional)*
½ *teaspoon MSG (optional)*	1 *teaspoon sesame oil*
1 *pound chicken bones or pork neck bones, or a bit of each*	1 *teaspoon white wine vinegar*
	Pinch of white pepper to taste
½ *roll preserved Chinese turnip, chopped and rinsed*	2 *green onions, chopped, for garnish*

This is very simple to prepare. Put the rice in a 6-quart heavy-lidded saucepan and add the water, optional MSG, bones, preserved turnips, and ginger. Bring to a boil and turn down to a low simmer, covered. Stir often and cook for 2 hours or more, until the mixture is thick and fairly smooth. Remove the bones and ginger slice. Pour the beaten eggs over the top of the soup in a thin stream and count to 10. Gently stir in the eggs, thus forming "egg flowers." Mix the sesame oil, vinegar, and white pepper together and add to the pot. Garnish with the green onions.

VARIATIONS: You can add almost any kind of cooked meat or fish to this. Mary Young's favorite addition is abalone. Try any of the following:

Abalone, canned, drained, and sliced thin (but very expensive)

Pork, chopped, and dried oysters, soaked for 2 hours, drained and chopped a bit. Add to the pot during the last 15 minutes of cooking.

Chicken, cooked, chopped

Chinese Roast Duck (page 252), chopped into bite-size pieces

Seafood: shrimp, scallops, etc. added during last 10 or 15 minutes of cooking

Olives, Chinese dried, called *lam see* (page 31) Add during last couple of minutes of cooking.

GARNISHES

Chopped iceberg lettuce	Green onions, additional
Chinese parsley	Chinese Fried Bread Strips (page 472)

CHINESE SAUSAGE ON STEAMED RICE
(Lop Chong)

This is a simple and delicious lunch. Cook 1 cup of rice according to the instructions in the hint on page 375. Just before you cover the rice with a lid, set 2 *lop chong* sausages on top of the rice. Cover and cook according to instructions. The flavor is wonderful and the sausages provide another course along with the rice.

Lop chong can be purchased in any Chinese market.

GREECE

STUFFED GRAPE LEAVES WITH EGG-LEMON SAUCE

SERVES 6–8 AS AN APPETIZER COURSE

I cannot think of a more frugal dish . . . providing you understand that "frugal" means that you waste nothing. There was a time in Greek history when certain people were so hungry that they took to eating the leaves from the grape vines. From that time of destitution comes this dish, one of the most famous dishes in Greece. It is flavorful beyond belief!

1 16-ounce jar grape leaves (California leaves are fine; they are not quite as sharp as the imported Greek variety)

FILLING

1 cup raw long-grain rice

½ cup olive oil

1 cup chopped yellow onions

¼ cup chopped Italian parsley

1 tablespoon dried dillweed

Juice of 1 lemon

1 pound lean lamb, coarsely ground or chopped

1 teaspoon allspice

2 cloves garlic, crushed

Salt and freshly ground black pepper to taste

BROTH

2 cups Basic Chicken Stock (page 129) or canned chicken broth

Juice of 1 lemon

SAUCE

1 batch Egg-Lemon Sauce (page 205)

Mix all the ingredients for the filling.

Pick out the smallest leaves in the jar and set aside. Use some of these leaves to place a single layer on the bottom of the pot.

Cut the stems off the grape leaves. Spread a leaf on the counter, bottom side up, stem side toward you. Place 1 teaspoon of the filling in the center of the leaf. Fold the stem end over the filling, then fold the sides over to secure the filling, then roll from you toward the tip of the leaf, forming a small cigar or cylinder. The size should be approximately 2½ inches long and ¾ inch wide.

Do not wrap these too tightly as the rice needs room for expansion when it cooks.

Using a 2-quart heavy-lidded kettle, place the rolled leaves on top of the single layer in the bottom. Place the rolls up against each other rather tightly so that they will not come undone while cooking. Cover them with a layer of unrolled leaves and then add another layer of rolled leaves. Continue until all rolled leaves are in the pot. Top with the remaining unrolled leaves.

Place a medium plate over the top of the leaves, as a weight. Mix the chicken stock and lemon juice for the broth and pour over the leaves in the pot. Cover and bring to a light simmer. I use a heat diffuser (page 18) for this. Cook 1 hour. Remove the pan from the heat and allow it to cool for 1 more hour. *Do not remove the lid* or the leaves will darken.

Serve warm with Egg-Lemon Sauce on top.

STUFFED TOMATOES HYDRA

SERVES 6

The day I tasted this dish was memorable because our family was drenched during bad weather in Greece. We were cold and hungry and on a boat trip to the island of Hydra. As we approached the island of white domed houses and *no cars* anywhere in the village, the sun broke forth and polished all the buildings, right before our eyes. "Look, Dad," young Channing shouted, "this is the *real* Greece!" It was, too, as this recipe, which I found in a local restaurant, will prove.

6 *large ripe tomatoes*

½ *pound lean lamb,*
coarsely chopped

4 *tablespoons olive oil*

2 *cloves garlic, crushed*

1 *medium yellow onion,*
peeled and coarsely
chopped

1½ *cups raw long-grain rice*

1 *tablespoon chopped parsley*

2 *teaspoons fresh*
chopped mint or
1 teaspoon dried mint

¼ *teaspoon allspice*

Salt and freshly ground
black pepper to taste

½ *teaspoon sugar (optional)*

2¼ *cups water*

Core the tomatoes and remove the center pulp, leaving a bowl for stuffing. I use a grapefruit spoon for this. Save the pulp and juice.

Heat a 4-quart stove-top covered casserole and add the lamb, olive oil, garlic, and onion. Cook until the onion is transparent. Add the rice, the pulp from the tomatoes, parsley, mint, allspice, salt and pepper, optional sugar, and water. Bring the mixture to a boil, cover with a lid, turn to low heat, and cook until the rice is just barely tender, about 15 to 20 minutes.

Salt the insides of the tomatoes and stuff with the rice mixture. Place them in a oiled baking dish and bake at 375° for about 20 minutes, or until the tomatoes are hot and tender, but not soggy.

Use the remaining filling to stuff green sweet bell peppers or zucchini, or simply serve it a day or two later as a side dish.

VARIATION: These can be prepared ahead of time, up to the baking point. Baking is no problem when your guests arrive.

ITALY

We most often think of pasta when we think of the starchy part of an Italian meal. Rice, however, is very popular in Italy and has been since ancient times. In Milan the rice dishes are so spectacular that they are more popular than the pasta!

The method of cooking rice in Italy is very different from the Chinese method, and certainly different from our own. It takes a bit of time and care and the rice must be served immediately, but the results will make you proud. Just be sure and always use Arborio rice for these Italian dishes. Everything else will just turn to mush.

RISOTTO WITH MUSHROOMS
(Risotto con Funghi)

SERVES 4–6
AS A FIRST COURSE

This is a classic and a favorite of the Milanese. I had a plate of rice with mushrooms in a rather inexpensive garden restaurant on a May day in Milan. I kept closing my eyes and relishing the flavor. The waiter finally told me I would have to order lunch as this dish was simply considered a pasta course. I really could have sat there for days eating *risotto con funghi*. Even the name is fun to say!

1 ounce dried mushrooms (page 37), soaked in 1 cup water, the water reserved

3 tablespoons butter

2 tablespoons olive oil

¼ medium yellow onion, peeled and coarsely chopped

1½ cups raw Italian Arborio rice

2 cups Basic Brown Soup Stock (page 132)

3 cups water (Include in this the water from soaking mushrooms)

¼ cup freshly grated Parmesan cheese

Salt and freshly ground black pepper to taste

Soak the mushrooms until very soft, about 1 hour. Drain, reserving the water for the dish, and chop the mushrooms.

Heat a 4-quart heavy saucepan and add the butter, oil, onions, and mushrooms. Cook until the onions are clear and then add the rice. Stir carefully so that each grain is coated with the oil. In a separate pan bring the stock and water, including the mushroom water, to a simmer and add 1 cup of this liquid to the rice. Stir as it cooks to ensure a nice creamy dish. Continue adding broth as it is absorbed until the rice is tender but still a bit chewy. Stir in the cheese and salt and pepper to taste. Serve immediately.

RISOTTO WITH MUSHROOMS AND HERBS
(Risotto con Funghi ed Erbe)

Follow the recipe on page 383 but add ¼ cup chopped, drained, cooked spinach. I use frozen. Also, add a bit of oregano and rosemary or basil, to taste. This makes a lovely change from your usual starches at dinner.

RISOTTO WITH CHAMPAGNE
(Risotto con Sciampagna)

SERVES 4–6
AS A FIRST COURSE

Shall we talk about rich foods? In Italy cream and champagne belong together, as this recipe proves. You can find such a dish in fancy Roman eating houses such as the wonderful Er Moccoletto.

1 ounce dried mushrooms (page 37), soaked in 1 cup water.

3 tablespoons butter

2 tablespoons olive oil

¼ yellow onion, peeled and coarsely chopped

1½ cups Italian Arborio rice, raw or precooked (page 37)

3 cups Basic Chicken Stock (page 129) or canned chicken soup

1 cup champagne or dry white wine

½ cup whipping cream

Salt

Soak the mushrooms until soft, about 1 hour. Drain and use the liquid for some other purpose, perhaps a soup stock. Do not use the mushroom water in the risotto as it will cover the flavor of the cream and wine. Chop the mushrooms.

Heat a 4-quart heavy saucepan and add the butter, oil, onions, and mushrooms. Cook until the onions are clear and then add the rice. Stir carefully so that each grain is coated with the oil. In a separate pan bring the chicken stock to a simmer. Add 1 cup of the stock to the rice, stirring to ensure a nice creamy dish. Continue adding broth as it is absorbed. When the stock is absorbed, add the champagne and continue to cook, stirring gently. When the rice is beginning to become tender, add the cream and cook until the rice is tender but still a bit chewy. Taste for salt and serve immediately.

RISOTTO WITH SEAFOOD
(Risotto con Frutti di Mare)

SERVES 6
AS A FIRST COURSE

This is a common dish in the great seaports of Italy. No, I should not use the word "common." It is anything but that, though the dish is not difficult to find. I had one in Venice that was just unbelievable. This is as close as I can come to the recipe.

2 tablespoons olive oil

3 tablespoons butter

¼ medium yellow onion, peeled and coarsely chopped

2 cloves garlic, chopped fine

1 pound small clams or mussels, scrubbed clean

¼ pound large shrimp, peeled

1 pound squid, cleaned and cut into ½-inch circles (page 188)

1 cup dry white wine

1½ cups Italian Arborio rice, raw or precooked (page 37)

Chicken broth to make up 5 cups, including the broth from the cooked seafood

1 tablespoon tomato paste

1 tablespoon chopped parsley

Salt and freshly ground black pepper to taste

Heat a large heavy-bottomed covered saucepan and add 1 tablespoon of the oil and the butter. Sauté the garlic and onion for a moment or two and add the cleaned seafood, along with the wine. Cover and cook until the seafood is barely tender. Drain the broth from the pot and set aside both the seafood and the broth.

Heat a heavy 6-quart stove-top covered casserole. Add the rice and the remaining tablespoon of olive oil. Stir to coat each grain of rice. Heat the 5 cups chicken stock and seafood broth combined and add 1 cup to the rice pot. Cook until almost absorbed and add a second cup, stirring constantly to ensure a creamy consistency. Add the tomato paste and continue to add the broth as it is absorbed until the rice is just tender but still a bit chewy. Return the seafood to the pot, and add the parsley and salt and pepper to taste. Serve immediately.

FRIED RISOTTO CAKES

Make small patties of leftover mushroom or herb risotto and fry them in a bit of olive oil. Serve in a puddle of Basic Brown Sauce (page 207). This will be a hit, I promise!

Dumplings

I have a dumpling addiction. I always have had. I have no intention of ever attempting to rid myself of this burden. Just the thought of a Chinese dumpling, filled with ginger, or an Italian ravioli sitting in truffle butter, or a Greek rice-filled grape leaf, sends me to the kitchen with the shakes! I am addicted, I confess it.

The dumpling was probably first seen in China, though at that time it was a crude food product. Around three thousand years ago grains were pounded coarsely and roasted before being mixed with tea or water to make a primitive type of dumpling. This may be the oldest surviving form of pasta. The dumpling, a ball of dough with some sort of filling, certainly predates cut pasta, and the Chinese seem to be the most creative at preparing these gems. They are used at celebrations of all kinds and seasons, and at regular daily meals as well. The flavorings and fillings, as well as the types of flour used for the casings, seem endless in China.

In Italy dumplings do not have such a wide range. Ravioli and tortellini seem to be the most popular, and that is enough for me. The Greeks use few stuffed-dough dumplings though I suppose that the stuffed grape leaf, and maybe even the phyllo dough filled pies must also be called dumplings.

Don't put these recipes aside due to the time involved in preparation. Chinese, Greek, and Italian grandmas have always known that a good dumpling will cure one thousand ills.

CHINA

CHINESE BOILED DUMPLINGS

MAKES ABOUT 36 DUMPLINGS

These are fun to prepare and, believe me, they stay with you. I always eat too many of these when I make them . . . and so does everyone else at the table.

DOUGH

2½ cups unsifted flour

½ teaspoon salt

1 cup boiling water

1 tablespoon lard, cut up into little pieces.

Mix the flour and salt. Add the boiling water and stir with chopsticks. Add the lard. Knead all and let rest on a plastic counter under a bowl for 20 minutes.

THE FILLING

Prepare a batch of Pork Shu-Mei Filling (page 99) and add 1 cup finely chopped cabbage, squeezed dry in a potato ricer. Also add a stiff shot of garlic and red chili paste (page 30) the amount to your taste. Careful, this stuff is hot!

THE CONSTRUCTION

Break off a piece of the dough the size of 1 teaspoon. Keep the rest of the dough under the bowl. Roll the dough into a ball and then roll out into a 3-inch circle. You may need extra flour for this. Or, use a tortilla press that has been very lightly oiled with peanut oil on a paper towel. This gets you going and the rest of the rolling is easy.

Place 1 teaspoon of filling in the middle of each dough circle and brush a tiny bit of water on the edge of half of each circle. Seal up into half-moons, being careful to work the air out as you go.

Drop into boiling water and simmer until they float. Cook another 5 minutes after they rise. Drain and place in a bowl.

THE GARNISH

Garnish with chopped Chinese parsley, sesame oil, and red pepper oil.

VARIATION: These may also be served in soup broth or they can be steamed in oiled bamboo racks just as you cook Pork Shu-Mei (page 99).

POT STICKERS

You know you are in an American-Chinese restaurant that is popular with the young and sophisticated set when you see these dumplings marked on the menu as a "House Special." They are also very popular in China and Hong Kong.

The name comes, I suppose, from the fact that they always stick a bit to the pan. They always stick to me, as well!

Prepare a batch of dumplings from the recipe on page 388 but do not cook them. Heat a large lidded frying pan (I prefer SilverStone lined for this one) and add 2 tablespoons of peanut oil. Place half the dumplings in the pan and lightly brown them, over medium heat, on one side. Pour in 1 cup of Chinese Chicken Soup Stock (page 113) or Basic Chicken Stock (page 129) and put the cover on the pan. Turn up the heat and cook for 5 to 10 minutes. When the liquid has been absorbed, the dumplings are done. Repeat, using the other half of the dumplings.

Do not overcook these as you do not want them to be soggy. Check the pan carefully as they cook so that they are still a bit firm and delicious.

Serve with the garnish as in the recipe above or with any of the Dip Sauces on pages 201–202.

ROLLED DUMPLINGS

A quick version of dumplings can be made by using wonton skins. Buy them at the supermarket, though you can probably get the thin skins down in Chinatown.

Place a teaspoon of Shu-Mei Filling in the center of the wonton skin and roll it up, starting with one corner and rolling it over the meat. Fold in the other two corners on each side and finish the roll. You will have a neat little sealed package. Moisten the final corner to seal. You can boil these or prepare them as in the pot-sticker recipe above. They are much easier than using the homemade fresh dough . . . but they will not taste quite as good. So what! Some nights you just have to cut down on kitchen time and give yourself a good meal as well as a break. I understand.

WONTON DUMPLINGS

MAKES ABOUT 50 WONTONS, ENOUGH FOR 8 HUNGRY PEOPLE

This is the basis of a very famous and simply delicious soup, but I have certainly had some cheap and disgusting versions of this classic little Cantonese dumpling. American-Chinese restaurants serve a cheap and precooked mess with this name, and always with Dinner No. 1, a sin which must be avoided at all cost. Make your own and then you will understand me. They are simple and the kids will get a bang out of the construction.

THE FILLING

1 *pound fresh-ground lean pork or beef (I prefer the pork, but you can try a mixture of both)*

2 *tablespoons light soy sauce*

1 *tablespoon Chinese rice wine or dry sherry*

½ *teaspoon sugar*

2 *green onions, chopped*

½ *teaspoon freshly grated ginger*

2 *cloves garlic, crushed*

8 *water chestnuts, chopped very coarsely*

1 *teaspoon sesame oil*

1 *egg*

1 *tablespoon cornstarch*

THE NOODLE

1 *pound fresh wonton wrappers from the Chinese market (I prefer the thin ones)*

THE SOUP

8 *cups Chinese Chicken Soup Stock (page 113)*

¼ *cup chopped Chinese bok choy or mustard green from the supermarket or 1 10-ounce package frozen peas*

Leftover sliced barbecued pork or roast side of pork (optional)

GARNISH

1 *tablespoon sesame oil*

2 *green onions, chopped*

Pinch ground white pepper

For the filling mix all together, and mix well! Place a teaspoon of the filling on each noodle and lightly moisten 2 joining edges of the noodle. Fold over on the wet edges, forming a triangle. Be sure to press out all the air so that there is a good seal on the noodle. Place the dumplings on waxed paper until all are filled. Do not stack them on top of one another.

Bring the soup stock to a boil and drop in the wontons. Boil for about 10 minutes, uncovered, or until they float and look a bit wrinkled on the outside. They should be tender but not mushy. Add the remaining ingredients to the pot, bring up to heat, and place in a serving bowl. Add the garnishes and serve.

VARIATION: You may wish to add some fresh shrimp, chopped, to the above filling. That is a classic form found in Hong Kong.

ITALY

CHICKEN AND SPINACH RAVIOLI

MAKES 60 RAVIOLI

I don't suppose that any dumplings from Italy are more famous than the wonderful ravioli. They can be made in any size, stuffed with any filling, and covered with just about any sauce. In Italy these dumplings form a first course . . . but I can make a whole meal of these little pillows of delight.

THE RAVIOLI DOUGH

3 *eggs*   4 *cups regular flour*

Equal amount of water   1 *teaspoon salt*

Crack the eggs into a 2-cup measuring glass and add an equal amount of water. Place the flour in a mixing bowl, stir in the salt, and mix in the egg-water mixture and flour, pinching and stirring until you have a dough that can be kneaded. Knead this for about 5 minutes. This is very easy to do in a good mixer such as KitchenAid. It will do the work.

Roll out the dough and prepare 2 sheets, each of the same size. The thickness of the dough is up to you, but I like mine rather light and thin. Don't worry about rerolling the dough that needs to be cut away in this process. It will work fine. Use about $\frac{1}{4}$ of the dough for this step and thus prepare 4 batches of ravioli for cutting. If using a ravioli press just follow the instructions. I always use a small watercoloring brush to brush a bit of water around the filling so that the dumpling will seal properly. I remind you that if you don't press the air out of the ravioli before sealing, they will blow up like the *Hindenburg* when you cook them. Dust each with flour and set on a cookie sheet while you prepare the rest of the dinner.

THE FILLING

- 2 *cups poached chicken (see Chinese Poached Chicken (page 230), skinless and boneless*
- 1 *10-ounce package frozen chopped spinach, thawed and the water carefully squeezed out (I use a potato ricer for this!)*
- 2 *eggs, beaten*
- $\frac{2}{3}$ *cup freshly grated Parmesan cheese*
- 2 *tablespoons finely chopped Italian parsley*
- $\frac{1}{8}$ *teaspoon freshly ground nutmeg*
- $\frac{1}{4}$ *teaspoon whole marjoram*

Salt and freshly ground black pepper to taste (I like lots of pepper in this filling)

TOPPING

Toss with as much melted butter and grated Parmesan cheese as you like. Italian parsley, chopped, is great on top. Or, you may use a tomato-based sauce.

Using the fine blade on your meat grinder, grind the chicken and spinach, which has been squeezed well to drain moisture. Add the remaining ingredients and mix well.

Fill the ravioli as above and seal. Boil for about 8 minutes in ample water and toss with the melted butter and cheese.

HINT: FREEZE YOUR OWN RAVIOLI. It is simple and makes the next meal a breeze. Freeze them raw and use self-sealing freezer bags.

CHEESE AND
SPINACH RAVIOLI

In the recipe on page 392 substitute 2 cups drained ricotta cheese for the chicken. Omit the marjoram and nutmeg and add the grated peel of ½ lemon. Mix and fill the ravioli. Serve with a bit of butter, grated Parmesan cheese, cream, salt, and black pepper. Garnish with toasted pine nuts (page 38).

BEEF-FILLED RAVIOLI,
ROMAN-JEWISH STYLE

This is a simple recipe, a simple explanation, and a wonderful dish. It is typical of the food that has been served in the Jewish Ghetto in Rome for hundreds of years.

Mix salt and pepper with good lean ground beef. Fill the ravioli, as on page 393, and boil. Drain and serve with olive oil and grated Parmesan cheese and a little more salt and pepper. That is it! An easy recipe, and one that the children will enjoy.

COTEGHINO-FILLED
RAVIOLI

Prepare the ravioli dough as on page 393 and stuff with coteghino sausage, a spicy pork sausage available in Italian delicatessens. Since the meat is raw, be sure that you give the ravioli ample time to cook.

Top with Italian Tomato Sauce (page 208) or with butter and grated Parmesan cheese, a little cream, and salt with lots of black pepper.

GNOCCHI WITH CHEESE

SERVES 8–10 AS
PART OF A REGULAR MEAL OR
AS A PASTA APPETIZER

This dish sounds so simple but it takes time to prepare. It reminds us again that in the Old World the cook spent a great deal of time preparing even the most basic and inexpensive dishes. This one is worth the time and the rest of your household crowd can certainly help. Then it will take very little time.

2 *pounds baking potatoes,*
  washed but unpeeled

1 *egg yolk*

3 *cups regular flour*

3 *tablespoons semolina flour*

½ *teaspoon salt*

SAUCE

¼ *pound butter, melted*

1 *cup freshly grated*
  Parmesan or Romano
  cheese

Boil the potatoes, skin on, until they are fork tender. Drain them well and allow to cool just so that you can touch them. Peel and run through a potato ricer.

Place the potatoes in the bowl from your electric mixer and beat in the egg yolk. Add the flour, semolina, and salt and mix just until you have a smooth dough.

Roll the dough into long cylinders the thickness of your finger. Cut into ½-inch-thick slices. Roll each piece a bit on the rough side of a vegetable grater to give the dumpling some texture. Roll each piece quickly and set on a tray to dry a bit. You can forget about the rolling if you wish and just allow the dumplings to dry a bit before you boil them.

Flouring the dumplings before you put each on a tray will help keep them separated when they cook.

Bring 8 quarts of water to a boil and add about ¼ of the batch. Boil gently until the gnocchi float to the top. Continue to boil for one minute and then, using a strainer, remove them from the pot to a warm bowl. Continue cooking until all are done and then toss the dumplings with the butter and cheese.

Serve as a pasta or starch dish with almost any meal.

> **HINT: FREEZE A BATCH OF GNOCCHI** in preparation for your dinner party. Just roll them and flour them. Place them in a plastic self-sealing bag and freeze. Boil them without even defrosting.

GNOCCHI WITH SAUCE BOLOGNESE

Prepare the gnocchi as on page 394 and serve with Sauce Bolognese (page 209). Wonderful!

GNOCCHI FRIED

Try deep-frying a batch of gnocchi. Fry them in oil at 360° until they are golden brown and float on the oil. You will need to cook them in several batches. These are delicious with Italian Tomato Sauce (page 208) or with butter and cheese.

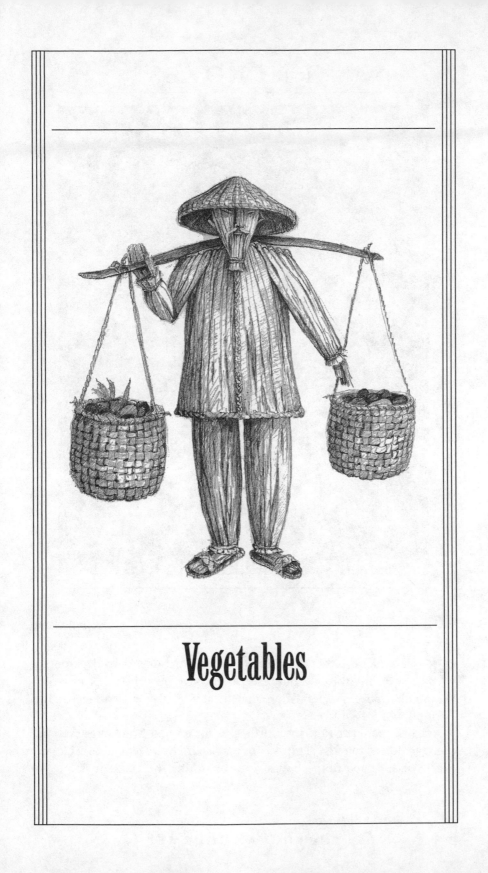

Vegetables

ARTICHOKES

W hat a wonder this old thistle is. The artichoke, a wild perennial herb of the thistle family, seems to have been first discovered in the Mediterranean region, more specifically, Sicily or Carthage. It has been popular ever since.

Apicius, the great Roman gourmet, reported that artichokes were all the rage during the first century A.D. Like so many vegetables, this lovely thistle disappeared from view in Europe during the Dark Ages only to make a spectacular reappearance in the late fifteenth century. It was reintroduced into Italy and traveled from Venice to Naples and on to Florence in the company of one Stozza family. During the sixteenth century Catherine de Médicis went from Florence to Paris to marry Henry II, and she brought with her not only her favorite Florentine chefs but also her beloved artichokes. The French were scandalized by her actions since all considered the vegetable to be a very powerful aphrodisiac, and Catherine's fondness for large quantities of this sensuous plant enhanced her notoriety—and, I might add, it certainly did not hurt the reputation of the artichoke.

We Americans are small-time artichoke eaters. Since the artichoke became familiar in America in the 1920s we have hardly made it a commonplace vegetable. About 70 million pounds of artichokes are raised each year, primarily in California, where Castroville is king in the artichoke kingdom, which means we eat about three quarters of an artichoke each year. In Rome everyone eats at least 175 artichokes a year. The Roman markets are just filled with them during the height of the season and you will see from the following recipes that the celebration of this vegetable is a grand feast.

The Greeks enjoy the artichoke in several ways and I was always surprised to see that the markets had this vegetable in its freshest form possible. If our markets did a better job at getting the thistle to us while it was still fresh I am sure we would consume more. The Greeks and Romans would simply not put up with artichokes in the condition in which we find them. One more dish from Greece . . . an artichoke moussaka. Place cleaned and sliced artichokes in your Moussaka (page 440) and cut down on the meat. This is just delicious.

You will want to remember that you should never cook artichokes in aluminum or iron; the metal will cause them to discolor. Use stainless steel or glass for best results.

You might also wish to consider:

Beans, Artichokes, and Peas *(page 423)*
Artichokes and Leeks *(page 452)*

ARTICHOKES, JEWISH STYLE

I had read about this dish but I could not quite understand what it would be. The first time that I tasted such a thing was at a restaurant called Trattoria "Da Giggetto," in the Roman Jewish Ghetto. The recipe itself is not complex, though you will find slight variations on the dish. If you have lots of money to spare, try this same dish at Piperno, in the same neighborhood. Be prepared to sell your luggage, your jewelry, and your mate in order to pay the bill.

The home version can be made in this way, and it is very good indeed.

6 artichokes, cleaned Roman style (see above)

Olive oil for deep-frying (Several cups will be necessary. Buy a brand in a large container. It need not be of expensive quality)

1 lemon

Salt to taste

In a heavy pot or wok heat the oil to 375°. Deep-fry the artichokes 2 or 3 at a time for 3 to 4 minutes. Remove from the oil and set aside. Restore the temperature of the oil and fry the chokes a second time until nicely browned, another 3 to 4 minutes. Remove and drain on paper towels. Season with a squeeze of lemon juice and a bit of salt to taste.

ARTICHOKES SAUTÉED IN WINE

SERVES 4–6 AS A VEGETABLE COURSE

This is the simplest of cooking methods, though you will have to catch on to how easily a choke can be cleaned. The flavor of this dish is clean and pure, and typical of the artichoke season in Rome.

6 artichokes, cleaned Roman style (page 400)	3 cloves garlic, peeled and crushed
Lemon juice	1 cup dry white wine
3 tablespoons olive oil	Salt and pepper to taste

Cut the cleaned artichokes in half lengthwise. With the flat side down slice the halves into ½-inch pieces. Place in a bowl and toss with lemon juice to prevent discoloring. Heat a large frying pan and add the oil and garlic. Sauté for just a moment and then add the artichoke slices. Sauté until very lightly browned, about 5 minutes. Add the wine, cover and simmer until tender, about 15 minutes. Salt and pepper to taste.

ARTICHOKES, CHILLED, ROMAN STYLE

SERVES 6 AS A FIRST COURSE

I saw artichokes cooked in this fashion all over Rome . . . and I ate them every chance I got. The methods that the Romans have thought up for cooking artichokes are just amazing, as is their affection for this blessed thistle.

6 artichokes, cleaned Roman style (page 400)

2 tablespoons olive oil for cooking

1 cup water

DRESSING

¾ cup olive oil

½ tablespoon whole oregano, crushed

¼ teaspoon salt

Juice of 1 fresh lemon

Black pepper, freshly ground, to taste

Place the cleaned artichokes upside down in a stove-top covered casserole. Add the 2 tablespoons of olive oil and about 1 cup of water. Cover and bring to a simmer. Cook for about 30 to 40 minutes, or until the chokes are tender. Chill, and pour the dressing over the dish. Serve with the stem upright, just as they were cooked.

ARTICHOKES STEAMED WITH PESTO

SERVES 6
AS A FIRST COURSE

I saw this dish on an antipasti table in Rome. I knew right away what it was and how it is to be prepared. This method is simple and the concept inspired.

6 artichokes, cleaned and trimmed (page 400)

2 tablespoons olive oil

6 tablespoons Pesto Sauce (page 211)

1 cup water

Cut the stems from the cleaned artichokes so that they will sit up in a *sauteuse* or deep SilverStone-lined frying pan. Add the oil to the pan. Rub a tablespoon of Pesto Sauce into the leaves of each choke and place it in the pan, along with a cup of water on the bottom. Cover and bring to a simmer. Cook until tender, about 45 to 50 minutes, or to your taste.

ARTICHOKES, STUFFED ROMAN STYLE

SERVES 6
AS A FIRST COURSE

The owner of Er Moccoletto, Hilda Bergonzi, is very proud of her excellent kitchens. When I was invited into these wonderfully clean and heavenly-smelling rooms, the cooks were preparing this dish. They were only too happy to tell me how to make it. The use of mint has been common in Rome since ancient times.

The Er Moccoletto restaurant is near the American Embassy in Rome. You can have a wonderful meal there.

6 artichokes, cleaned Roman style (page 400)

3 tablespoons chopped fresh mint

3 tablespoons chopped fresh parsley

2 cloves garlic, crushed

Salt and pepper to taste

$\frac{1}{2}$ cup olive oil

1 cup water

Cut the stems from the bottoms of the cleaned artichokes so that they will sit upright in a stove-top casserole or *sauteuse*. Mix mint, parsley, and garlic, along with salt and pepper to taste, with half of the olive oil. Place the remaining oil in the casserole and arrange the artichokes. Rub the leaves of each artichoke with the herb mixture. Cook over a low flame for a few minutes. Add the water and cover. Simmer until tender, about 45 to 50 minutes.

ARTICHOKES WITH HAM ON TOAST
(Crostini con Carciofi)

This elegant bit was served us in the midst of a Roman garden, in a restaurant not far from the great ruins of the old market. It is just lovely and a perfect dish for a light lunch.

Toasted bread slice

Italian Tomato Sauce
(page 208)

Ham slice, boiled

Artichokes Sautéed in
Wine (page 401), chopped
or sliced very thin

1 slice mozzarella or Swiss
cheese

Romano cheese for garnish

Put a bit of the tomato sauce on the toast. Add the ham slice and cover with the chopped or sliced artichokes. Top with the sliced cheese and then the grated cheese. Lightly broil until barely browned.

GREECE

ARTICHOKES WITH POTATOES, GREEK STYLE

SERVES 6
AS A VEGETABLE COURSE

When you walk into a Greek restaurant kitchen to look at the food, and you *are* expected to do this, you will very often find a great pan of artichokes and potatoes sitting in a steam table. The olive oil used is rich and aromatic, and the artichokes are fresh and tender. You cannot help but point at the pan and yell, "Yes!"

This dish is too good to limit to artichoke season. I make them with frozen chokes and the results are not bad.

1 medium yellow onion,
peeled and sliced

3 cloves garlic, peeled and crushed

3 tablespoons olive oil

½ cup coarsely chopped parsley

1 pound new potatoes,
unpeeled and quartered

2 cups Basic Chicken
Stock (page 129) or
canned broth

3 cups frozen artichokes,
defrosted

Salt and freshly ground
black pepper to taste

Sauté the onions and garlic in the oil until almost transparent. Add the parsley, potatoes, and chicken stock and cook, covered, for 10 to 15 minutes, or until the potatoes are just barely tender. Add the artichokes and simmer, covered, for another 10 minutes. Add salt and pepper to taste.

ARTICHOKES IN
GREEK TOMATO SAUCE

This common taverna dish need only be described. Cleaned artichokes (page 400) are sliced and sautéed for a moment in olive oil and a bit of garlic. A little Greek Tomato Sauce (page 204), along with a touch of dry white wine, is added to the pan. The pan is covered and brought to a simmer. Cook just until tender and serve.

ASPARAGUS

How our three ancient cuisines have loved asparagus, this distin-
guished and royal member of the lily family. The vegetable grows
in so many places now that it is hard to decide just where it first began.
We do know that it was commonly enjoyed in ancient Egypt, Greece,
and Rome. The Greeks loved the wild asparagus and the Romans began
to cultivate it around 100 B.C.

Apicius, the first-century Roman gourmet, loved asparagus and claims that it was enjoyed in Rome as early as 400 B.C. He took great care in the preparation of this vegetable and people who overcook it in our time would do well to read Apicius's recipe from two thousand years ago. We assume, from his and other writings, that asparagus remained a food of the wealthy until the fall of the Roman Empire in the fifth century. Julius Caesar, for instance, loved the stuff.

Following the fall of Rome, the vegetable disappeared from Europe. In China, however, mention was made of asparagus as early as the seventh century, and the food was finally reintroduced into Europe during the sixteenth century.

HINT: ON CLEANING ASPARAGUS. The old European method of peeling the stems in order to make them tender takes too much time for me. Besides, nothing is wasted if we save the broken ends for soup. Hold the bottom end of the stem in one hand and gently bend the stalk with the other. The stalk will break where it is tender, thus giving you a piece of asparagus that is entirely edible. With a little practice you will know exactly where to try to break the vegetable. Save the broken-off ends for soup. Slice and add to the soup stock and then drain well and discard the coarse stalks before serving.

CHINA

COLD ASPARAGUS, CHINESE STYLE

This is a lovely dish for a first course or a real hit when served later in the meal.

Clean the asparagus (see above) and leave it whole. Bring a pan of water to boil and add a tablespoon or so of peanut oil to help keep the color. Blanch the vegetable for about 4 or 5 minutes and then plunge into cold water. Drain and chill. When ready to serve, dress with Sesame Oil Salad Dressing (page 140).

ASPARAGUS WITH BEEF AND BLACK BEANS

SERVES 4–5 AS
PART OF A CHINESE MEAL

People are always asking me about my favorite recipe. I have too many! This one, however, is surely my favorite asparagus recipe.

1½ *pounds asparagus, cleaned (page 407)*

½ *pound beef flank steak, sliced thin across the grain*

3 *tablespoons light soy sauce*

½ *teaspoon grated fresh ginger*

2 *tablespoons dry sherry or Chinese rice wine*

1 *tablespoon cornstarch*

3 *tablespoons peanut oil*

2 *cloves garlic, sliced thin*

1 *tablespoon fermented black beans* (dow see), *rinsed (page 29)*

Pinch of salt

Pinch of sugar

¼ *cup Chinese Chicken Soup Stock (page 113)*

Slice the cleaned asparagus diagonally into ¼-inch pieces. Set aside.

In a small bowl marinate the sliced beef in 2 tablespoons of the light soy sauce, ginger, sherry or rice wine, and the cornstarch. Mix well and let sit for 15 minutes.

Heat a wok or large frying pan and add the oil. The oil should just begin to smoke. Quickly lay the meat on one side in the pan. Do not turn but cook over high heat for a moment until the one side begins to brown. Toss-stir the meat for a moment and remove from the pan, allowing the oil to drain back into the pan.

Heat the pan again and add the garlic. Chow for just a moment and add the rinsed fermented black beans. Chow for another moment and add the asparagus. Toss for a few seconds and then add the remaining soy sauce, salt, and sugar. Chow just until tender, about 5 minutes. Add the meat and chicken broth. Stir to make a sauce. Serve immediately.

GREECE

COLD ASPARAGUS, GREEK STYLE

This is so refreshing and so delicious and so utterly Greek! Asparagus is cleaned, blanched, and chilled, just as you do for the Cold Asparagus, Chinese Style (page 407). A dressing is prepared of 2 parts good Greek olive oil and 1 part lemon juice. Add a bit of salt and pepper to taste. The created sauce is called "Ladolemono." Dress the asparagus in plenty of this sauce and serve.

Please, don't be too Greek with this. I think both the Greeks and the Italians tend to overcook this wonderful vegetable. Don't you commit the same crime!

ASPARAGUS WITH OIL AND TOMATO, GREEK STYLE

*SERVES 4 AS
A VEGETABLE COURSE*

You are probably beginning to think that the Greeks cook everything in tomato sauce. Well, that is not far from the truth. The rule is simple.

Don't use much tomato sauce and you will have wonderful dishes, and dishes that are typical of the glorious and flavor-filled tavernas of Athens. In this case you will be making a fresh tomato sauce.

½ cup olive oil

2 cloves garlic, chopped fine

1 medium yellow onion, peeled and chopped

¼ cup chopped Italian parsley

1 cup chopped very ripe tomatoes

Salt and freshly ground black pepper to taste

1 pound asparagus, cleaned (page 407)

¼ cup dry white wine

Heat a 3-quart heavy stainless-steel or porcelain-lined stove-top casserole and add the olive oil. Sauté the garlic and onion until clear. Add the parsley and tomatoes and simmer for about 25 to 30 minutes, or until the tomatoes are very soft. Add salt and pepper to taste.

Cut the cleaned asparagus into 1-inch pieces and add to the pot, along with the white wine. Cook until done to your taste, which I hope will be a short time, just until tender and still a bit crunchy.

NOTE: I am convinced that the Greeks and the Italians both cook asparagus too long. Please do not be guilty of this crime!

PICKLED ASPARAGUS, GREEK STYLE

MAKES ABOUT 5 QUARTS

Theresa Karas Yainilos has written *The Complete Greek Cookbook* (see Bibliography). I hope you can find a copy as she loves pickles and vegetables. The basis for the following recipe came from her book, though I weighted the salad toward asparagus.

This is a good example of the taste of the Greek islands. As this recipe makes quite a bit, you should plan on preparing it when asparagus is cheap and you have some nice neighbors with whom you would like to share this delicious salad. It will keep for about 6 days in the refrigerator.

- 2 tablespoons salt
- 3 cups olive oil
- 2 carrots, peeled and sliced
- ½ pound small pearl onions, peeled
- ½ pound radishes, cleaned and cut in half
- 5 pounds asparagus, cleaned (page 407) and cut into 2-inch pieces
- 1 cup drained Calamata olives
- 1 cup drained green olives
- 8 cloves garlic, peeled and sliced
- 2 tablespoons mixed pickling spices
- 5 cups white wine vinegar (approximately)

Bring 3 quarts of water to a boil in a large stainless-steel or porcelain-lined kettle. Add the salt, 3 tablespoons of the olive oil, the carrot slices, and onions. Blanch for about 2 minutes and add the radishes and asparagus. Bring to a simmer and drain the liquid. Refresh the vegetables in cold water and drain again. Mix the olives with the vegetables.

Put the vegetable mixture in five 1-quart glass canning jars and divide the remaining ingredients among the jars, starting with the remaining olive oil and ending with the vinegar. Cap the jars and shake a bit to mix all. Store in the refrigerator for 2 days before serving, turning the jars upside down now and then to mix all. This will keep in the refrigerator for about 6 days, but it is best served on the second or third day.

ITALY

BLANCHING ASPARAGUS APICIUS

Apicius must have been some asparagus lover. He talks about this vegetable in the most tender manner and he urges us, in his cookbook from the first century, not to overcook the asparagus. His method is the one that we use today. He would peel the stems, though I just break them off (see **HINT: ON CLEANING ASPARAGUS,** page 407). They were then tied into bunches and cooked standing up in salted water, with the tender tips sticking out of the water. In this way the stem, the tougher part of the vegetable, is cooked without overcooking the tender top. There is no way that this ancient Roman method can be improved upon. Try it.

ASPARAGUS CUSTARD APICIUS

SERVES 3–4 AS
A SIDE DISH AT DINNER

It is exciting to realize that the Romans ate so well, at least some of them ate well. This dish goes back 2,000 years and needs little improvement, though you may find the flavoring from the fresh herbs a bit strange. Change them to suit your palate.

½ pound asparagus, cleaned (page 407), blanched, and coarsely chopped

½ cup chopped lovage (page 43) or chopped celery leaves

¼ cup medium-chopped fresh coriander

1 teaspoon savory

¼ medium yellow onion, peeled and chopped medium

Black pepper to taste

⅛ cup white wine

⅛ cup Basic Chicken Stock (page 129)

2 tablespoons olive oil

6 eggs, beaten

Chop the blanched asparagus, along with the fresh herbs and the onion. Mix this with the pepper, wine, chicken broth, and ½ tablespoon of the olive oil.

Heat a large frying pan or wok and add the remaining oil and the asparagus and herb mixture. Cook for a minute over high heat and then add the beaten eggs. Lower the heat and continue cooking, stirring occasionally, until the mixture begins to set up. Do not overcook. This should be very much like moist scrambled eggs.

ASPARAGUS WITH CHEESE AND EGGS, ITALIAN STYLE

SERVES 3–4 AS
PART OF A REGULAR MEAL

So what is new? If you will read the preceding recipe you will recognize the source of this contemporary dish, a dish from Florence and therefore called *Asparagi alla Fiorentina*. This is just a stupendous dish!

1 *pound asparagus, cleaned (page 407) and cut into 2-inch pieces*

½ *stick (⅛ pound) butter, melted*

½ *cup freshly grated Parmesan cheese*

Salt and freshly ground black pepper to taste

6 *eggs, beaten*

Blanch and drain the asparagus, being careful not to overcook it. In a bowl toss the asparagus with the butter, cheese, and salt and pepper. Remove to a platter and keep warm.

Scramble the eggs (do not overcook) and cover the asparagus with the eggs. Serve quickly!

Beans

In terms of subsistence the bean is almost as important in this world as is bread. From prehistoric times, beans, in one form or another, have kept people alive, and I suppose this is as true today as it was in early times.

There are three beans that lead the world: the soybean, the haricot bean, and the broad or fava bean. The soybean goes back to Asia about four thousand years ago and it is still a major food source there, though most soybeans are now grown in America. The fava bean is now popular everywhere, as is the haricot. There are many other types of beans, of course, and the following recipes will offer you a few new ideas for their use in your kitchen.

There were other uses for beans in earlier times. The Romans used beans as voting tokens in certain elections, giving rise to the saying, "Abstain from beans," meaning, stay out of politics. However, the primary use for beans in the Mediterranean has always been for food, and they are served with soup, rice, fish, as antipasto, with meat, and in many other ways.

The Chinese rarely serve a bean as a bean. They are the most accomplished among our three ancient cuisines at using the bean in some other profound way as a food or flavoring source. Soybean curd, *dow foo*, is called "meat without bones" in China, since it is so nutritious and can be prepared in so many ways. Trish, a flight attendant on United Airlines, told me that she even made a bean-curd lasagne. Boy, I can hear you running to the kitchen for that one! It is best, in my opinion, to cook bean curd in the Chinese manner, and a few recipes follow.

The Chinese also use beans to make bean sprouts, soy sauce, soybean condiment, fermented bean cheese *(foo yee)*, bean-curd skin, and MSG, a natural derivative of the soybean. Beans are made into noodles, fermented for black-bean flavorings, and cooked into heavy sauces, both hot and sweet. In short, the Chinese serve beans in every way imaginable—except as beans.

You may also wish to consider:

Beans and Leeks Apicius *(page 452)*

SMOKED BEAN CURD

I offer this in an effort to show you how this food can be made to taste like many meat products, though it has no meat or animal-fat content whatsoever.

Cut a cake of firm bean curd, Chinese style, into ¾-inch slices. Drain them well on paper towels. Rub the rack of your smoker (I prefer a Cameron, page 19), with a bit of peanut oil and place the drained slices on the rack. Smoke them, according to instructions for your smoker, for about 15 minutes. Serve the slices with the following sauce for a terrific vegetarian dish.

Use any of the ingredients in any amount you wish. It is a matter of your personal taste. The amounts given are for my taste.

SAUCE

2 green onions, chopped

¼ teaspoon grated fresh ginger

⅛ teaspoon sugar

2 tablespoons light soy sauce

1 tablespoon rice wine vinegar

1 teaspoon sesame oil

Shot of Tabasco to taste

BEAN CURD WITH PORK

SERVES 4 AS
PART OF A CHINESE MEAL

Tai Tung restaurant, a Seattle institution, has been operating in Chinatown since the thirties. I have eaten there since I was about thirteen, and that is some thirty-seven years ago. Through the years the food has been inconsistent sometimes, but it is still a fine eating house. When one of the old crew is on duty in the kitchen, this dish is prepared in such a delicious manner that you think you could live on bean curd flavored with soybean condiment. Beans with beans, that's what this one is!

1 *pound bean curd, cut into ½-inch cubes and drained*

2 *tablespoons peanut oil*

3 *cloves garlic*

1 *slice fresh ginger root, size of a 25-cent piece, cut julienne*

½ *pound pork, sliced into thin julienne strips*

1 *tablespoon soybean condiment (mein see)*

3 *green onions, cut Chinese style (page 142)*

2 *tablespoons dry sherry or Chinese rice wine*

1 *tablespoon light soy sauce*

½ *teaspoon sugar*

⅛ *teaspoon salt*

Freshly ground white pepper to taste

Pinch of MSG (optional)

¼ *cup Chinese Chicken Soup Stock (page 113)*

1 *tablespoon each cornstarch and water, mixed together*

Cut the bean curd and allow it to drain for one half hour.

Heat a wok and add the oil. Chow the garlic and ginger for a moment and then add the pork. Cook for a couple of minutes over high heat and remove the meat to the serving bowl, leaving the oil in the wok. Add the soybean condiment and green onions to the hot wok and chow for a moment. Add the bean curd along with all remaining ingredients, except the cornstarch mixed with water, and the meat. Chow the bean curd until all is very hot and then add the pork and, finally, stir in the cornstarch mixture.

This dish is great over rice. It is versatile in that you can brighten the flavor simply by increasing the amount of garlic or soybean condiment.

LONG GREEN BEANS WITH BEEF

SERVES 4 AS PART OF A CHINESE MEAL

If you have never seen the long variety of Chinese string beans you are in for a surprise. They are over a foot long and can be found in large Chinatowns. The flavor is close to the bean we know but the texture is completely different as this long bean holds its crunchiness when cooked.

You must find some of these legumes . . . though the substitution of our green bean still makes for a delicious dish.

1 pound Chinese long green beans, cut into 1-inch pieces (You can substitute fresh green beans)

½ pound beef flank steak, sliced thin

MARINADE

½ tablespoon light soy sauce

½ tablespoon dry sherry or Chinese rice wine

¼ teaspoon grated fresh ginger

2 teaspoons cornstarch

3 teaspoons peanut oil for chowing

1 quart peanut oil for deep-frying

2 cloves garlic, chopped fine

½ tablespoon fermented black beans (dow see), rinsed, or soybean condiment (mein see)

¼ cup Basic Brown Soup Stock (page 132)

Pinch of sugar

1 teaspoon sesame oil

Cut and rinse beans and pat dry with kitchen towel.

Marinate the beef and chow on one side, using 1 tablespoon of the peanut oil. Chowing on one side on high heat prevents the overcooking of the beef. Remove from the pan and set aside.

Deep-fry beans quickly at 360°. These should cook for only a minute or so. Be careful of the spitting fat if the beans have not been dried properly. Drain well.

Place 2 tablespoons peanut oil in *hot* wok and add garlic and black beans. Chow for just a moment and add the green beans, beef, and remaining ingredients, stirring to form a light sauce.

GREECE

LIMA BEANS WITH GREEK TOMATO SAUCE

SERVES 4 AS A SIDE DISH

Yes, your child will eat lima beans if you cook them this way. This recipe is common in the tavernas in Greece and it is really very delicious. The tomato and onion seem to remove the bitterness from the bean, that bitterness that children so "bitterly" dislike.

½ *pound dried lima beans,*
soaked overnight

4 *tablespoons olive oil*

3 *cloves garlic, sliced thin*

1 *yellow onion, peeled and*
sliced thin

1 *tomato, large and ripe,*
cut in ¼-inch dice

3 *tablespoons tomato paste*

1 *cup Greek Tomato Sauce*
(page 204)

½ *cup dry red wine*

Salt and freshly ground
black pepper to taste

½ *cup chopped parsley*

¼ *teaspoon each cinnamon*
and allspice (optional)

Soak the beans overnight and drain.

Heat a 4-quart stove-top casserole and add the oil. Sauté the garlic and onion just until clear. Add tomato, tomato paste, and tomato sauce and sauté 5 minutes.

Add all remaining ingredients, including the beans, cover, and simmer until the beans are tender but not soggy, about 30 to 40 minutes.

NOTE: The addition of the cinnamon and allspice is up to you.

BLACK-EYED PEA SALAD SIGALAS

SERVES 6 AS
A SALAD OR SIDE COURSE

The taverna called Sigalas, in Monastiraki Square, Athens, has all of the dishes out on display for you to see. It is typical of a good taverna in that they want you to check out everything before you order. Craig, my cooking assistant, and I, found this dish on their buffet and we were somewhat surprised. Beans are American, and certainly black-eyed peas are from this country. In Greece they are very popular.

2 cups dried black-eyed peas
4 green onions, chopped
1 cup olive oil
Juice of 1½ lemons

½ cup chopped parsley
Salt and freshly ground
black pepper to taste

Place peas in saucepan and cover with ample water. Bring to a boil, cover, and turn off the heat. Let sit for 1 hour.

Drain the peas, add fresh water and simmer 10 minutes, or until tender. Do not overcook. Drain and allow to cool.

Blend remaining ingredients together to form a dressing and toss with the beans.

WHITE BEANS, GREEK STYLE

SERVES 6 AS A SALAD OR SIDE DISH

This dish is not to be confused with a hot bean dish for your dinner. In Greece dried-bean dishes are often served cold, as in the case above. This is close to the dish above but the flavor of the beans is a bit lighter. It is a very good salad course.

2 cups small white beans
½ cup peeled and chopped shallots
½ white onion, peeled and sliced thin
½ cup lovage, coarsely chopped, or substitute celery leaves

1 cup olive oil
Juice of 1 lemon
Salt and freshly ground
black pepper to taste

Place the beans in a saucepan and cover with ample water. Bring to a boil, cover, and turn off the heat. Allow to sit for 1 hour. Drain and add fresh water. Simmer for about 35 to 45 minutes, or until the beans are just barely tender. Drain and cool.

Mix remaining ingredients together to form a dressing and toss with the beans.

PASTA AND BEAN SOUP
(Pasta e Fagioli)

SERVES 8–10 AS
A VERY HEARTY SOUP

Everyone has heard the name of this soup, I am sure, but few of us have eaten a good version of it. This is a very decent recipe based on the dish that has been common in Italy for the last few hundred years. It is hearty, to say the least.

2 *cups small white beans*

1 *pound pork neck bones*

1 *or 2 drops liquid smoke or use smoked pork neck bones. Great for the soup, but hard to find. Smoked pork hocks are easier to find. Use about 1¾ pounds.*

1 *bay leaf*

2 *cloves garlic, peeled and chopped*

½ *medium yellow onion, peeled and diced*

1 *carrot, unpeeled and diced medium fine*

¼ *cup chopped lovage or celery leaves*

½ *cup Italian Tomato Sauce (page 208)*

6 *cups water*

1 *cup Basic Chicken Stock (page 129)*

Salt and freshly ground black pepper to taste

1 *cup small shaped pasta such as stars or shells*

Place the beans in a 4-quart pot and add ample water for cooking. Bring to a boil, cover, turn off the heat and let sit for 1 hour. Drain the beans and discard the cooking water. Add all ingredients to the pot, except the salt and pepper and pasta. Cover and simmer lightly for 1½ hours or until the beans are very tender.

Remove the pork bones and the bay leaf. Take the meat off the bones and set aside. Remove ⅔ of the contents of the pot and purée in a food processor or food blender. Return to the pot, along with the meat, and restore to a simmer. Add salt and pepper to taste. Add the pasta and cook until the pasta is just tender, about 15 minutes.

FRESH FAVA BEANS, ROMAN STYLE

This is the strangest practice, but a practice loved by the Romans. When the fresh fava beans arrive in springtime, people come to the market and purchase them, shell them, and eat them raw, some of them eating these right in the middle of the market. They dip them in a bit of salt and pepper mixed with olive oil. This delicacy is eaten with a fine Pecorino cheese along with a good red wine.

Yes, I tried it at Er Moccoletto restaurant, and I really cannot understand the excitement. You might want to try it sometime and see if your tongue is really Roman.

LIMA BEANS WITH LETTUCE AND ONION

SERVES 4 AS A VEGETABLE COURSE

You will find this dish in both Roman and Greek cuisines. It is usually made with fava beans in Rome, but frozen baby limas will work very well.

1 tablespoon olive oil

1 clove garlic, chopped fine or crushed

3 ribs of celery, sliced thin

1 medium yellow onion, peeled and sliced

1 10-ounce box frozen baby lima beans, defrosted

¼ cup Basic Chicken Stock (page 129) or canned broth

¼ cup dry white wine

½ head iceberg lettuce, torn into ½-inch pieces

Salt and pepper to taste

Heat a 3-quart stove-top lidded casserole and add the oil. Sauté the garlic, celery, and onion until the onion is clear. Add the beans, chicken broth, and wine, cover, and bring to a simmer. Cook the beans to taste and then add the lettuce. Cook covered for just a moment or two so that the lettuce collapses. Add salt and pepper to taste and serve.

BEANS, ARTICHOKES, AND PEAS
(Frittella)

W hen I saw this dish on the antipasti counter of La Carbonara restaurant in Rome, it was in the middle of the artichoke season, of course. This is as close as I can come to their version, which is just terrific, and I am pleased to tell you that it is served at room temperature. It can therefore be used as an antipasto, salad, or vegetable course. It sounds unusual but it is one of the best dishes that I found in Rome.

2 artichokes, cleaned and cored (page 400)

Juice of 1 lemon

4 tablespoons olive oil

¼ cup diced pancetta

¼ cup water

1½ cups peeled and thinly sliced yellow onion

4 tablespoons olive oil

1 10-ounce package frozen baby lima beans, defrosted, or use fresh fava or broad beans

1 10-ounce package frozen peas, defrosted

¼ cup Basic Chicken Stock (page 129)

3 cups sliced iceberg lettuce

¼ cup dry white wine

Salt and freshly ground black pepper to taste

Additional olive oil if desired

Clean the artichokes and chop them into bite-size pieces. Toss in the lemon juice. Heat a frying pan and add 4 tablespoons olive oil. Sauté the artichokes, along with the lemon juice, covered, until tender, about 15 minutes. Do not overbrown them. Set aside.

Heat a large covered frying pan and add the pancetta. Sauté for a moment and add ¼ cup water. Turn down the heat, cover the pan, and simmer for about 10 minutes. This will render the wonderful fat from the bacon. Turn up the heat to medium high and add the onions and 4 tablespoons olive oil. Sauté until the onions are transparent and then add beans and peas. Cook for a few minutes and add the chicken broth and lettuce, along with the cooked artichokes. When the lettuce is tender but not soggy, add the wine and salt and pepper to taste.

You may wish additional olive oil in this dish. In Rome it is served with a great deal of oil.

CHESTNUTS

There was a time not long ago when chestnut trees covered the United States. And we knew what to do with them. In 1904 a blight hit our trees and by 1940 few remained. We think of chestnuts now as a specialty food, but in the Old World they were a staple.

It is doubtful that we will ever get back to an appreciation of the chestnut since the trees offer the best nuts at age sixty, and the great trees live for hundreds of years. An 1850 volcanic eruption at the foot of Mount Etna, in Sicily, destroyed a tree that had been planted there by the Romans two thousand years before.

Affection for chestnuts as food is still common in all three of our ancient cuisines. They have never been considered food for the wealthy, except, perhaps, in China, since in early times they were so plentiful. The hunter-gatherer tribes could collect them easily since they simply fall from the tree when they are ripe. In ancient Rome the nut was crucial to the diet of the lower classes; it offered both starch and sweetness, and it was cheap. However, the Roman gourmet of the first century, Apicius, took great delight in chestnuts and suggested that they be cooked with wild greens in order to cut the sharpness of flavor found in the green vegetable. Further, the Roman legionnaires spread the chestnut throughout Europe. Wherever they went they planted the nut so that troops following behind them would have something to eat. Talk about long-range planning!

Originally the chestnuts were dried and ground to make a cheap flour substitute. Wheat flour was very expensive in the old days but chestnut flour could be had for little money. It could be made into breads, cakes, puddings, sauces, and polenta. Pasta is still made from the flour and there is good evidence that one of the ancestors of what we call the pizza was actually made from chestnut flour. In addition, the whole nut served as a vegetable, which explains why I have placed it in this section.

The Chinese have enjoyed the nut since the Han dynasty (210 B.C.) and I have included a dish or two showing its use in both the great kitchens and the peasant kitchens of China.

You can find chestnut flour in most Italian delicatessens. You will have a grand time experimenting with this sweet and flavorful substance, and you can help your children learn something more about the history of Rome. When Rome collapsed, nearly everyone was reduced to a diet of chestnuts.

You may also wish to consider:

Peking Dust *(page 495)*
Sweet Chestnut Purée *(page 500)*
Italian Chestnut Jam Cake *(page 501)*
Focaccia Romana *(page 482)*

CHINA

CHINESE BEEF AND CHESTNUT STEW

SERVES 6–8 AS
PART OF A CHINESE MEAL

Ken Hom taught me about this recipe. I hope you know who he is—he should be declared a national treasure on public television. He was born in Arizona of American Chinese parents and was raised in Chicago's Chinatown. He has a wonderful sense of who he is . . . and it is a bit complex, I can tell you. This fine chef uses chestnuts in the following Chinese stew. The nuts add a wonderful sweetness to the meat.

4 tablespoons peanut oil

3 pounds stewing beef, cut into ¾-inch cubes

SAUCE

1 tablespoon hoisin sauce (page 30)

4 tablespoons Chinese rice wine or dry sherry

4 tablespoons light soy sauce

1 tablespoon finely minced or crushed garlic

1 whole star anise

1 teaspoon roasted and crushed Szechwan peppercorns (page 40)

4 cups water

½ pound dried chestnuts, soaked overnight and drained

Heat a wok or large frying pan and add the oil. Brown the meat and place in a stove-top casserole. Mix all ingredients for the sauce and add to the pot, along with the browned meat. Add the drained chestnuts and cover. Simmer for about 1½ hours, or until all is very tender.

CHINESE CHICKEN WITH CHESTNUTS

SERVES 5–6 AS
PART OF A CHINESE MEAL

This is a simple recipe that will confuse your guests since they will think that you have been working for days on one dish. It is surprisingly rich because you are using both the richest part of the chicken—the thigh—and the sweet chestnuts. A little will go a long way.

10 chicken thighs

MARINADE

3 tablespoons light soy sauce

2 tablespoons Chinese rice wine or dry sherry

1 teaspoon grated ginger

3 green onions, chopped Chinese style (page 142)

Pinch of salt

Pinch of white pepper

4 tablespoons peanut oil for chowing

2 cups Chinese Chicken Soup Stock (page 113)

5 Chinese dried mushrooms, soaked for 1 hour and drained

$\frac{1}{2}$ pound dried chestnuts, soaked overnight and drained

GARNISH

$\frac{1}{2}$ tablespoon sesame oil

Chopped green onions

Prepare the marinade and soak the chicken in this for $\frac{1}{2}$ hour. Drain and reserve the marinade. Heat a wok and add the peanut oil. Brown the chicken in 2 batches. Remove to a sand-pot casserole (page 19) or covered stove-top casserole. Add to the pot the remaining marinade, chicken broth, mushrooms, and soaked dried chestnuts. Cover and bring to a simmer. Cook for about 40 minutes or until the chestnuts are tender. Top with the garnish before serving.

NOTE: You might wish to thicken this dish with a mixture of 2 tablespoons each cornstarch and water. Stir it into the dish when all is tender. Cook and stir until the sauce is thick and clear. Then top with the garnish and serve.

WATER CHESTNUTS AND GREEN BEANS

*SERVES 4–5 AS
PART OF A CHINESE MEAL*

While water chestnuts are not actually of the same family as the regular chestnut they do have a very important place in Chinese cuisine. This dish is quite simple and can be served with any number of main dishes that need not be Chinese.

1 *10-ounce package frozen green beans*

1 *tablespoon peanut oil*

1 *clove garlic, crushed*

½ *cup sliced water chestnuts*

¼ *cup Chinese Chicken Soup Stock (page 113) or Basic Chicken Stock (page 129)*

1 *teaspoon light soy sauce*

Pinch of ground white pepper

1 *teaspoon cornstarch mixed with 1 tablespoon water*

Defrost the green beans. Heat a wok and add the oil. Add the garlic and chow for just a moment. Add the beans and chow until they are hot and barely tender. Add the remaining ingredients, in the order given, and stir until a sauce forms. Serve immediately.

SHRIMP CHOWED WITH WATER-CHESTNUT FLOUR AND GIN

*SERVES 2–3 AS
PART OF A CHINESE MEAL*

Water-chestnut flour, which can be found in any Chinese market, has the wonderful ability to provide thick and rich coating on foods . . .

or a very crunchy one if you are deep-frying. This dish is a favorite at our house and certainly easy on the cook who is short of time after work.

½ pound raw shrimp in the shell (headless)

1 tablespoon water-chestnut flour

2 tablespoons peanut oil

⅛ teaspoon salt

2 cloves garlic, chopped fine or crushed

1 slice fresh ginger, the size of a 25-cent piece, cut julienne

3 tablespoons gin

Toss the shrimp in the water-chestnut flour and set aside.

Heat a wok and add the oil. When it smokes a bit add the salt, garlic, and ginger. Chow for just a few seconds and add the shrimp. Chow on high heat until they change color, about 2 minutes. Have a lid in your hand and pour in the gin. Cover immediately and cook for just a moment until the wonderful noise stops. Stir quickly over high heat. Garnish with the green onions and serve.

GREECE

ROASTED CHESTNUTS

I do not know why I was so surprised to find peddlers offering roasted chestnuts in the streets of Athens. I thought to myself, "Just like New York!" No, Greece had them first and shared them with the rest of us.

To roast fresh chestnuts, cut a small cross in the top of each. You can roast them in a hot oven but they taste best if roasted over a small charcoal fire in your barbecue. Roast them just until they are very hot and begin to brown a bit on the outside. Peel and eat an Old World treat. You can find a chestnut roasting pan to use in your fireplace. Now we are talking a very romantic evening!

CHESTNUTS SOAKED IN OUZO

Cut a cross in the chestnuts and soak them overnight in ouzo. Roast as on page 430 and serve. This is totally Greek!

ITALY

CHESTNUTS SOAKED IN WINE

Cut a cross in the top of each chestnut and soak them overnight in dry red wine. Roast as in the Greek Roasted Chestnuts recipe and serve. This is considered a great winter treat in Rome . . . and has been so considered for hundreds of years.

WILD GREENS AND CHESTNUTS

In the early days of Rome it was very common for the peasants to cook chestnuts with wild greens. The sweetness of the chestnuts cut the harshness of the vegetables. Try this with collard greens or mustard greens.

CHESTNUT PASTA

This sounds a bit strange, or at least "very nouvelle." It is neither. In the old days, when wheat flour was so expensive, pasta was commonly made from chestnut flour, since the chestnuts could be gathered free by just about anybody. The pasta has a bit of a sweet flavor and is very delicious. I am told by people who know that in Genoa, where pesto sauce developed and is still very prized, the best places serve their pesto sauce on chestnut pasta, not the plain wheat variety. I have tried it and it is wonderful.

1 *cup unbleached white
flour*
1 *cup semolina flour*
½ *cup chestnut flour*

Pinch of salt
3 *eggs*
1 *tablespoon olive oil*
1 *tablespoon water*

Combine all dry ingredients in a large bowl. Make a well in the flour and add the wet ingredients. Stir together and pinch into a dough. Knead until it all holds together and is smooth. Let rest, covered, ½ hour. Roll into sheets and let dry 20 minutes. Cut into noodles.

CHESTNUT POLENTA

This again sounds a bit strange to our ears. Corn was not commonly used in Italy until the 1600s, and prior to that time garbanzo flour or chestnut flour was used to make polenta. Many other grains were used as well, but this dish is particularly interesting because it is a bit sweet and when fried forms a wonderful crust.

1 *quart water*
1½ *teaspoons salt*

3½ *cups chestnut flour*
Olive oil for pan-frying

Bring the water to boil in a 2-quart saucepan and add the salt. Remove the pan from the heat and stir in the flour, using a wire whip. Work hard at this as you do not want lumps. Return to low heat and continue stirring and cooking until the mixture becomes very thick, about 10 to 15 minutes. Pour into an oiled loaf pan and chill overnight. Unmold and slice into ⅓-inch pieces. Pan-fry in olive oil over medium heat until golden brown and a bit crispy.

CHESTNUTS AND LENTILS APICIUS

SERVES 6 AS A VEGETABLE COURSE

I should like to chat with Apicius. He was so far ahead of his time, in terms of our standards, that I think he would have made a great dinner guest. Too bad he is not around for an informal chat. He died sometime during the first century A.D. but that does not stop me from fantasizing about a dinner party with Apicius, Mozart, Henry VIII, and Bach. I would do the cooking, of course.

This is a favorite dish of Apicius that is really quite contemporary.

2½ cups Basic Brown Soup Stock (page 132)

½ pound dried chestnuts, soaked overnight and drained

2 cups chopped and rinsed leeks

2 tablespoons chopped fresh coriander

½ teaspoon freshly ground black pepper

½ teaspoon coriander seed, crushed with a mortar and pestle

1 teaspoon dried mint

⅛ teaspoon crushed whole rosemary

1 tablespoon red wine vinegar

1 cup dried lentils

Salt to taste

2 tablespoons good olive oil

Place the stock and chestnuts in a 4-quart covered saucepan and simmer until tender, about 1 hour. Drain the liquid and measure it. Add enough water to make a total of 2½ cups liquid. Return to the pan and add all ingredients except the lentils, salt, and olive oil. Cover and bring to a boil. Add the lentils and simmer, covered, for about 20 minutes, or until the lentils are tender and the liquid is absorbed. Add the salt to taste and place the whole in a serving dish. Garnish with the olive oil and serve hot.

NOTE: The old recipe also calls for the addition of honey. I find the dish already very sweet. You can certainly do as you wish.

EGGPLANT

Ajunior high school viewer asked me why eggplant is so called. "Eggs are not purple!" he claimed. Well, he is right on that point, but he is talking about a vegetable that is very old and has appeared in many forms. It goes back about four thousand years, and in South and Southeast Asia, where it originated, it shows up globular and white (as well as purple and palest green and oblong and cigar-shaped too) and does live up to its name. It has been used as a popular food in the East for thousands of years. The West is another story.

The wonderful eggplant, which the Greeks and Romans now love dearly, did not reach Italy until the fourteenth century. It arrived with a rather bad reputation and was dubbed *mela insana*, which means "bad apple" (any strange or new vegetable seems to have been called an apple in those days), and the superstitious people of the Middle Ages claimed the vegetable was poison and would cause severe fevers! It took a while to catch on.

The Chinese, however, during the Sung dynasty (tenth to thirteenth centuries), made the plant very popular and it was considered proper for the rich households to nab the first eggplants of the season. The popularity of the vegetable has not decreased in China since that time.

Remember a few basic rules about cooking the eggplant. First, whether you are going to deep-fry it, grill it, bake it, sauté it, or pickle it, remember that the smaller the eggplant, the fewer the seeds and the less oil it will absorb. Eggplant is like a sponge when it comes to good olive oil and in the Middle East people joke about a man's wealth in terms of his ability to provide enough olive oil when his wife is cooking eggplant. I cook my eggplant with ample olive oil, and good oil at that.

The second rule is simple: Always slice and then salt the eggplant before cooking. Let it sit in a colander for an hour or so with ample salt, and then rinse it in fresh water and pat dry. This process will get rid of the bitter flavor that you remember from your childhood when your mother first decided to try eggplant on you. Prepared properly, it is one of the most delicious vegetables I know . . . in all three ancient cuisines.

You may also wish to consider:

Eggplant Stuffed with Shrimp *(page 98)*

EGGPLANT WITH PORK, CHINESE STYLE

SERVES 4–5 AS
PART OF A CHINESE MEAL

I wish Americans could appreciate the eggplant more. In China it has been revered for so long, and this particular recipe is so good, and so simple, and so delicious, and so . . . make it!

1 *pound long Chinese or Japanese eggplant*

1 *teaspoon salt*

MARINADE

½ *tablespoon light soy sauce*

½ *tablespoon Chinese rice wine or dry sherry*

¼ *teaspoon grated fresh ginger*

½ *pound lean pork, chopped into ¼-inch dice*

2 *tablespoons peanut oil for chowing*

2 *cloves garlic, chopped fine or crushed*

6 *green onions, cut Chinese style (page 142)*

Pinch of sugar

1 *teaspoon sesame oil*

Pinch of MSG (optional)

2 *green onions, chopped, for garnish*

Cut the eggplant into long sticks, about ½-inch square. Sprinkle them with the salt and place in a colander to drain for ½ hour. Rinse and pat dry.

Mix the marinade and soak the meat for 20 minutes. Drain and set aside.

Heat the wok and add 1 tablespoon of the oil. Chow the pork just until tender and remove from the wok to a serving plate. Add the remaining oil to the hot wok and add the garlic. Chow for just a moment and add the green onions and the eggplant sticks. Chow until the eggplant is tender. Return the meat to the wok and add the sugar, sesame oil, and the optional MSG. Chow until all is hot and place on the serving platter. Garnish with the green onions and serve.

Eggplant with Soybean Condiment and Hoisin Sauce

SERVES 3–4 AS
PART OF A CHINESE MEAL

This dish has a bit of a bright flavor due to the added sauces. It is quick and just filled with flavor.

½ *pound lean pork, cut julienne*

1 *teaspoon cornstarch*

1 *teaspoon light soy sauce*

1 *teaspoon dry sherry or Chinese rice wine*

1 *pound eggplant, cut into ½-inch cubes*

1 *teaspoon salt*

2 *tablespoons peanut oil for chowing*

2 *cloves garlic, chopped fine or crushed*

1 *slice fresh ginger, the size of a 25-cent piece, cut into slivers*

4 *green onions, cut Chinese style (page 142)*

1 *teaspoon sesame oil*

¼ *teaspoon hot pepper sauce (such as Tabasco), or more to taste*

1 *teaspoon soybean condiment (mein see)*

1 *tablespoon hoisin sauce*

Pinch of sugar

1 *tablespoon chopped Chinese parsley for garnish*

Mix the pork with the cornstarch, soy, and wine and set aside.

Mix the cut-up eggplant with the salt and set in a colander to drain for 15 minutes. Rinse and pat dry.

Heat a wok and add 1 tablespoon of the peanut oil. Chow the pork just until tender and remove from the wok. Set aside.

Heat the wok again and add the remaining oil and the garlic and ginger. Chow for a moment and add the green onions and drained eggplant. Chow over high heat until the eggplant is tender but not soggy. Add the remaining ingredients, except the parsley, return the pork to the wok and chow until all is hot and done to your liking. Place in a serving bowl and add the garnish.

EGGPLANT AND PORK MANDAR-INN

SERVES 3–4 AS
PART OF A CHINESE MEAL

When I first tasted this dish at the Mardar-Inn restaurant, located in Chicago's Chinatown, I was ready to grovel in order to get the recipe. I went in several times and tasted it over and over again. Though the owner, and the one who directs the cooks, is a charming woman, I did not have the nerve to ask her for the recipe. You just don't do that with people who make their living feeding the rest of us. I finally got up my nerve. I brought Craig, my cooking assistant, along for moral support. I was ready for anything. Then . . . I did it. "Sharon, will you give me the recipe for this wonderful dish?" She replied, "Sure, but I have to explain my secrets." Only a truly kind person would "explain her secrets." Such is the nature of this restaurateur. Sharon Jay offered the following recipe, and since it is very detailed, you may think it is complicated. It is not. Chinese cooking seldom is. Just read the thing through once and you will realize that it is very simple and just heaven!

This dish will be simple for you if you have everything ready, including the mixed sauce, before you turn on the wok!

MARINADE
½ tablespoon cornstarch
1 egg white
½ tablespoon peanut oil
Pinch of salt

½ pound pork, cut julienne
4 cups of peanut oil for deep-frying

1 pound eggplant, cut into ½-inch-square sticks, 2½ inches long (I prefer the long, thin Oriental eggplant for this dish)
1 teaspoon grated fresh ginger
3 cloves garlic, chopped fine or crushed
1 tablespoon minced celery

1 tablespoon garlic and red chili paste

MIXED SAUCE

1 tablespoon dark soy sauce

1 tablespoon light soy sauce

1 tablespoon oyster sauce

1 tablespoon dry sherry

1 teaspoon white pepper powder

½ tablespoon sugar

⅔ cup Chinese Chicken Soup Stock (page 113)

1 tablespoon cornstarch mixed with 1½ tablespoons water

GARNISH

1 Chinese red vinegar or cider vinegar

½ tablespoon sesame oil

2 green onions, chopped

Mix the marinade and soak the pork in this for 10 minutes.

Heat the oil in a wok to 375° and deep-fry the marinated pork for 1 minute. Remove from the wok and drain.

Deep-fry the eggplant pieces for 2 minutes, or until soft. Remove, drain, and set aside.

In another wok heat 2 tablespoons peanut oil and stir-fry the ginger, garlic, celery, and chili paste with garlic for about 1 minute. Return eggplant to the pan and add the cooked pork. Chow for about 1 minute. Add mixed sauce and soup stock and bring to a boil.

Thicken sauce with cornstarch and water mixture. Cook until the sauce clears and becomes a glaze, about 1 minute.

Sprinkle eggplant with the vinegar, sesame oil, and chopped green onions.

GREECE

EGGPLANT STUFFED GREEK STYLE

SERVE 6-8

This makes a nice individual eggplant dish; each serving looks like a little pie. Since there is no white sauce on the top, as in a moussaka, the dish is also a bit lower in calories.

2 medium eggplants, about
1 pound each, sliced ½
inch thick

½ tablespoon salt for the
eggplant

¾ cup olive oil

1 pound lean beef or lamb,
or a mixture of both,
ground

Salt and freshly ground
black pepper to taste

1 yellow onion, peeled and
chopped

2 cloves garlic, chopped fine
or crushed

1 teaspoon dried oregano,
crushed by hand

1½ cups Greek Tomato Sauce
(page 204)

1 cup grated kefalotyri
cheese (page 36)

Slice the eggplants and sprinkle with the salt. Arrange in a colander and
allow the vegetables to drain for ½ hour. Rinse off and pat dry.

Heat a large frying pan and add 2 tablespoons of the oil. Sauté the
meat, along with the salt and pepper, onion, garlic, and oregano. Cook
until the meat is browned and the onions clear. Add ½ cup of the tomato
sauce and simmer for 15 minutes longer. Set aside.

Pan-fry the eggplant slices in a bit of the olive oil, reserving ½ cup oil
for the final step. Brown on both sides. Place some of the meat mixture
between two slices of eggplant and arrange on an oiled baking sheet.
Drizzle the top of each serving with the remaining olive oil and the
remaining tomato sauce. Top with the cheese and bake at 350° until all
is hot and very tender.

MOUSSAKA

SERVES 10–12
AS A MAIN COURSE

This is a classic dish of Greece. The origins are probably Turkish, though
the white sauce used on top is certainly Greek. In any case, it is a very
old and beloved eggplant dish to be found in every taverna in Athens.

2 medium eggplants, about
1 pound each, sliced
¼ inch thick

½ tablespoon salt

MEAT SAUCE

2 yellow onions, peeled and
chopped

2 tablespoons olive oil

2½ pounds lean ground beef
or lamb

1 teaspoon salt

3 cups Greek Tomato Sauce
(page 204)

Cinnamon to taste
(optional)

1 cup freshly grated
Parmesan or Romano
cheese

½ cup olive oil

TOPPING

⅓ cup butter

½ cup flour

1 quart milk

1 teaspoon salt

¼ teaspoon nutmeg

½ cup freshly grated
Parmesan or Romano
cheese

6 eggs, beaten

Extra cheese for garnish

Slice the eggplants and sprinkle with the salt. Place in a colander to drain for ½ hour.

Prepare the meat sauce by heating a large SilverStone frying pan or porcelain-lined stove-top casserole and add the onions and 2 table-spoons olive oil. Sauté until the onions are clear and then add the meat. Sauté until the meat begins to brown. Add the salt and Greek Tomato Sauce and simmer for 30 minutes, uncovered. Taste for optional cinnamon and stir in the cheese. Set aside.

Rinse the eggplant slices and pat dry with paper towels. Pour the ½ cup olive oil onto a large baking sheet and dip the slices in it, coating both sides. Arrange the slices on the sheet and bake at 425° for 30 minutes, turning once during this time. The slices should be tender.

Prepare the topping by melting the butter in a small frying pan and stirring in the flour, making a roux. Cook for a few moments. Heat the milk in a saucepan and stir in the butter-flour mixture, using a wire whip. Stir over medium heat until it thickens. Stir in the salt, nutmeg, and cheese. Stir 1 cup of the hot sauce into the beaten eggs, using the wire whip. Stir this mixture back into the saucepan and stir the whole over medium heat until it is thick and rich.

THE CONSTRUCTION

Arrange ½ of the eggplant in the bottom of a 9 × 13-inch baking pan and top with the meat mixture. Place the remaining eggplant slices on the meat and pour the topping over the whole. Sprinkle the cheese for garnish on top and bake at 350° for 1 hour.

Cut into squares at serving time.

EGGPLANT SHOES

MAKES 6 SERVINGS

This is a wonderfully rich dish, and the name is a riot! They do look like shoes, shoes filled with a flavor that your whole family will love, even those supposed to be eggplant haters. You will find this dish in the tavernas all over Greece. If you have the good fortune to get outside the city and into the villages the versions of this dish that you will find there will be even better.

- 3 medium eggplants, each about 1 pound
- 2 tablespoons salt
- 2 yellow onions, peeled and sliced
- 5 tablespoons olive oil
- 3 cloves garlic, crushed
- Freshly ground black pepper to taste
- 2 cups Greek Tomato Sauce (page 204)

Cut the eggplants in half the long way. Salt them and allow to drain in a colander for 1 hour. Rinse and pat dry.

Dig out the eggplant meat to form boats with a ⅜-inch layer of eggplant, reserving the removed eggplant. Chop the reserved eggplant and set aside to drain.

Sauté the onions in 3 tablespoons of the olive oil until browned or even caramelized. Remove from the pan and set aside.

Sauté, in the remaining oil, the garlic, chopped eggplant, and pepper to taste. Place this mixture in the boats. Top with 2 tablespoons of the tomato sauce and then top with the onions. Place the remaining tomato sauce in a baking dish large enough to take the "shoes." You may need to use two pans. Set the shoes on top of the sauce and bake at 350° for 1 hour or until the eggplant is very tender.

> **HINT: TASTE BEFORE SALTING,** always, and consider what other sources of salt you already have in the dish. Cheese, pancetta, olives, dried foods, anchovies—all are examples of foods that need to be seen as salts. Be careful!

EGGPLANT SLICES BAKED

SERVES 6 AS A
SALAD OR VEGETABLE COURSE

This is a very common way of serving eggplant in Greece. Since the dish can be served cold or warm, it is also very versatile. I enjoy the utter simplicity of this dish.

2 medium eggplants, each about 1 pound

1 tablespoon salt

¾ cup olive oil

Juice of 1 lemon

½ teaspoon dried oregano, crushed by hand

Freshly ground black pepper to taste

Salt if needed

With a fork, score the eggplant lengthwise. Cut into slices ¼ inch thick and sprinkle with the salt. Drain in a colander for 1 hour and then rinse with water and pat dry with paper towels.

Pan-brown the slices using ¼ cup of the olive oil. When lightly browned place on a baking sheet and bake at 375° until very tender. Remove and allow to cool a bit.

Mix the remaining ½ cup oil with the lemon juice, oregano, and pepper. Dress the slices with this sauce and test for needed salt.

VARIATION: This eggplant is also terrific with garlicky Skorthalia Sauce (page 206).

EGGPLANT SALAD
(Melitzanosalata)

SERVES 6–8 AS A
FIRST COURSE OR SALAD COURSE

This is a relish/salad/sauce/type thing . . . and I cannot do better at describing it than that. You must try this. It has a smoky flavor because the eggplant is charred over a burner. There is an obvious connection between this dish and a similar salad found in Turkey.

- 3 medium eggplants, about 1 pound each
- 5 cloves garlic, crushed
- ½ medium yellow onion, chopped fine
- ⅓ cup parsley
- 2 medium tomatoes, chopped
- 1 teaspoon marjoram
- 1 teaspoon oregano
- ¼ cup of olive oil
- Juice of 1 lemon
- Salt and freshly ground black pepper to taste

Grill the eggplants over an open gas flame or under the broiler until the skin is a bit blackened and charred. I use a long barbecue fork and do this over my gas burner. Or, you can simply set them on a hot *asador* grill (page 19). When evenly charred, place them on a baking sheet and bake at 350° for 45 minutes. Allow to cool and then peel, discarding the peel, and chop the eggplant. Place in a bowl with the remaining ingredients and toss. Chill before serving.

ITALY

BROILED EGGPLANT BOLOGNA

This is a simple dish—very common food, but delicious. My friend Mrs. Nasi, in Bologna, served this for lunch one afternoon. I need only describe the dish for you as you will certainly have no trouble in making it.

Slice the eggplant thin and sprinkle with a bit of salt. Do not peel. Drain the slices in a colander for $\frac{1}{2}$ hour. Rinse with water and pat dry with paper towels.

Pan-fry the slices slowly in a bit of olive oil until they are brown. Arrange them on a baking sheet and sprinkle bread crumbs, which have been mixed with olive oil and fresh garlic, on top. Place under a broiler until the crumbs are browned and all is hot. Serve immediately.

BROILED EGGPLANT WEDGES

In Rome the antipasti tables often offer this dish. It makes a wonderful first course or salad and can be made ahead, so it is helpful at dinner parties, besides.

Pick out small eggplants and cut them into wedges, about 8 pieces from each vegetable. Do not peel. Salt them and allow them to drain in a colander for $\frac{1}{2}$ hour. Rinse with water and pat dry with paper towels. Arrange the wedges on a baking sheet, skin side down. Brush each with ample olive oil and broil until each is brown and tender. Allow to cool and dress with your favorite Italian dressing. I simply use olive oil, lemon juice, salt and pepper, and oregano. Delicious served at room temperature.

EGGPLANT, ROMAN STYLE
(Melanzane alla Romana)

This is a common lunch dish in Rome and it is simply a quick and easy form of Eggplant Parmesan. It is nice for a party because you can make it ahead and pop it into an oven at the last minute.

The eggplants are sliced $\frac{1}{3}$ inch thick and salted. Allow to drain in a colander for $\frac{1}{2}$ hour. Rinse with water and pat dry with paper towels. Pan-brown the slices on both sides, in a little olive oil. Arrange on a baking sheet.

Brown a bit of hamburger, along with some chopped yellow onion, crushed garlic, and salt and pepper. Place a bit of the cooked meat on top of each eggplant slice. Top with a bit of Italian Tomato Sauce (page 208) along with a sprinkle of grated Parmesan or Romano cheese. Place a slice of mozzarella cheese on top of each and sprinkle with a bit of oregano. Bake in a 375° oven until all is hot and bubbly. You may wish to broil at the last minute, thus browning the cheese.

GRILLED EGGPLANT AND FONTINA

I saw this dish in a quick takeout joint in a very fashionable district of Rome. You can wander in that city for days and eat from wonderful shops. I hope you can find this dish. Or make it now.

Slice eggplants the long way, about ¼ inch thick. Salt each slice and allow to drain in a colander for ½ hour. Rinse with water and pat dry with paper towels. Grill the slices on the charcoal barbecue with a bit of olive oil on each. Be sure to keep the heat low so that you do not burn them. Allow to cool. Roll each up with a thin slice of fontina cheese and secure with a toothpick. Drizzle a dressing of olive oil, lemon juice, salt and pepper, and oregano over each. Serve at room temperature.

LEEKS

Leeks are a mild and delightful member of the onion and lily family. They have been with us since the Early Bronze Age (3000 B.C.) and they were cultivated and loved in the gardens of Ur in Babylonia around 2100 B.C. The Bible mentions the vegetable when it says that the Israelites, after fleeing Egypt, lamented the fact that they had to leave leeks behind. The leeks had been cultivated in ancient Egypt, where they were a part of the ration package distributed to the pyramid workers. Further, they are mentioned in a 1500 B.C. Chinese guide to good eating.

The Greeks and the Romans all enjoyed this lovely long-stemmed lily. The Emperor Nero made sure he had a bowl of leek soup every day in order to keep his voice clear and sonorous so that he might deliver even more stirring orations. And our favorite Roman gourmet, Apicius, offered several wonderful recipes for the enjoyment of the leek during the first century.

The leek has been popular since ancient days, and only now are we Americans beginning to appreciate this vegetable. The Chinese use of the leek in the following recipes remains my favorite.

HINT: ON CLEANING LEEKS. Leeks are often full of mud. To clean, cut off the roots and slice the leek in half lengthwise. Then, cut into pieces 1 inch long and remove those outer pieces that are too tough to eat. The white part will be fine, but as you go up the stalk into the greener part, the outer layers are tough. Remove them and use the inner pieces. Separate the layers and rinse well in a sink full of water. Drain well before cooking.

CHINA

CHINESE LAMB AND LEEKS

SERVES 4 AS
PART OF A CHINESE MEAL

This is a most wonderful dish, and even those in your house who claim that they dislike lamb will enjoy this. It is a common winter dish in China.

¾ pound lean boneless lamb, sliced and cut into strips	4 cups leeks, cleaned and cut (see **Hint** on page 442)

MARINADE	SAUCE
1 tablespoon light soy sauce	1 teaspoon light soy sauce
1 tablespoon Chinese rice wine or dry sherry	1 teaspoon Chinese rice wine or dry sherry
½ teaspoon grated fresh ginger	2 teaspoons rice vinegar
1 teaspoon cornstarch	½ teaspoon sugar
2 tablespoons peanut oil for pan-frying	¼ teaspoon ground white pepper
½ teaspoon salt	GARNISH
2 cloves garlic, chopped fine or crushed	1 teaspoon sesame oil
	Hot pepper oil or hot sauce to taste

Cut the meat and soak in the marinade for 15 minutes. Heat the wok and add 1 tablespoon of the oil. Drain the marinade from the meat and chow the meat on high heat until tender. Remove to the serving plate. Heat the wok again and add the remaining peanut oil, salt, and garlic. Chow for just a moment and add the leeks. Chow until they are tender, just a few minutes. Return the meat to the wok along with the sauce. Chow until all is hot and garnish with the sesame oil and hot pepper oil.

PORK WITH LEEKS AND BLACK BEANS

SERVES 4–5 AS PART OF A CHINESE MEAL

This is another winter dish in China. The flavor of the winter leeks mingled with the fermented black beans will warm anyone, and it gets cold in the northern regions.

¾ pound lean pork, cut
julienne

MARINADE

1 tablespoon light soy sauce

1 tablespoon Chinese rice
wine or dry sherry

½ teaspoon grated fresh
ginger

2 tablespoons peanut oil for
chowing

2 cloves garlic, chopped fine
or crushed

½ tablespoon fermented black
beans (dow see), rinsed

4 cups leeks, cleaned and cut
(page 448)

1 teaspoon sesame oil

⅛ teaspoon sugar

Pinch of MSG (optional)

Cut the meat and soak in the marinade for 15 minutes. Heat the wok and add 1 tablespoon of the oil, along with the garlic and the rinsed black beans. Chow for a moment and add the drained pork. Chow over high heat until the pork is tender and remove to a serving plate. Add the remaining peanut oil to the hot wok, along with the leeks. Chow until they are tender. Return the meat to the pan along with the remaining ingredients. Chow for a moment and serve.

CHICKEN WITH LEEK BELTS

SERVES 3–4
AS PART OF A CHINESE MEAL

This is fun to make and a good one for your children. Tying the belt is a bit complicated for a child but he or she can have a good time trying.

This is formal banquet food in China.

2 leeks, cut into ribbons ½
inch wide, the long way

8 chicken thighs, cut in half

MARINADE

1 tablespoon light soy sauce

1 tablespoon Chinese rice
wine or dry sherry

½ teaspoon grated fresh
ginger

2 tablespoons peanut oil for
chowing

2 cloves garlic, chopped fine
or crushed

⅛ teaspoon sugar

Rinse the leek ribbons and dip into boiling water for just a moment in order to soften them. Set aside.

Hack each thigh in two, across the bone. I use my cleaver for this. Marinate the chicken for 15 minutes. Heat a wok and add 1 tablespoon of the oil. Brown half the drained chicken pieces and remove from the wok. Add the remaining peanut oil and garlic. Brown the second half of the chicken pieces. Return the first chicken pieces to the wok, add the sugar, and chow for a moment. Remove from the wok and allow the pieces to cool enough to handle.

Tie a ribbon of leek around each piece of chicken, as if it is a little package. Place the pieces in a steaming dish and steam in a bamboo steamer (page 97) for about 20 minutes.

ITALY

LEEK CAKES

SERVES 6
AS A FIRST COURSE

I tasted these in Rome, and they were used as a first course. It is so simple and so very good . . . and obviously a peasant dish that the cook learned from his grandmother.

4 cups leeks, cleaned (page 448) and chopped in food processor or chopped medium fine by hand

BATTER

2 eggs, beaten

1½ cups milk

1 cup flour

½ teaspoon baking powder

Pinch of sugar

Salt and freshly ground black pepper to taste

Olive oil for pan-frying

Cut up the leeks and prepare the batter. Mix the leeks into the batter and fry like little pancakes in a bit of olive oil.

ARTICHOKES AND LEEKS

I was impressed with the touch of leeks in sautéed artichokes. The leeks are not heavy enough to burden the artichokes. Simply prepare a batch of Artichokes Sautéed in Wine (page 401) and add a cup of cleaned and cut leeks (page 448) when you sauté the dish. It is very delicious.

SAUTÉED LEEKS

SERVES 3–4 AS
A VEGETABLE COURSE

Americans do not often think of a plate of sautéed leeks as a vegetable course. In Italy they are enjoyed throughout the winter and they are easy to prepare.

- 8 cups leeks, cleaned and cut (page 448)
- 1 clove garlic, crushed or chopped fine
- 2 tablespoons olive oil

- ¼ cup dry white wine
- ¼ cup Basic Chicken Stock (page 129) or canned broth
- Salt and freshly ground black pepper to taste

Clean the leeks and drain well. Heat a large stove-top casserole and sauté the garlic in the olive oil. Add the leeks and sauté until they begin to collapse. Add the remaining ingredients and cook, uncovered, until the leeks are tender.

BEANS AND
LEEKS APICIUS

SERVES 4–6 AS
A VEGETABLE COURSE

During the first century leeks appeared on Roman tables quite often. They are one of those vegetables that will hold well into the winter and so they were prized, both by the aristocracy and the peasants. Apicius gave us this recipe, and although you may not be terribly fond of the heavy use of herbs in these old Roman dishes, they are interesting nevertheless.

4 tablespoons olive oil

6 cups leeks, cleaned and cut (page 448)

1 pound green beans, preferably fresh, cleaned and cut into 2-inch pieces

Pinch of crushed coriander seed

½ cup dry white wine

¼ teaspoon dried rosemary

1 cup Basic Chicken Stock (page 129) or canned broth

Salt and freshly ground black pepper to taste

Heat a large stove-top covered casserole and add the oil. Put the leeks, beans, coriander seed, and wine in the pot and cover. Simmer until not quite tender and then add the remaining ingredients. Cook, uncovered, until all is tender and the stock is rich.

FAVA BEANS WITH LEEKS

You may use the same recipe as on page 452, substituting fresh shelled fava beans or baby limas. Frozen baby limas beans work well in this dish.

BOILED LEEKS WITH CABBAGE APICIUS

SERVES 8 AS A FUN VEGETABLE COURSE

The only reason that you would go to all this work for a vegetable course would be a Roman party. Maybe that is reason enough, but when you prepare this, please remember that Apicius had slaves. This dish takes a bit of doing but it is fun to eat. Those old Romans must have had wild dinner parties!

16 medium leeks, cleaned
   (page 448) and cut in
   half and then into 4-
   inch-long pieces

½ teaspoon salt

8 large cabbage leaves

3 tablespoons olive oil

½ cup Basic Chicken
   Stock (page 129) or
   canned broth

¼ teaspoon dried rosemary

Salt and freshly ground
black pepper to taste

Trim the leeks and cut them as directed. Wash them well while trying to keep the pieces intact. Place in a saucepan and barely cover with water. Add the salt and cook until the leeks are barely tender. Drain and allow to cool.

Bring a pot of water to boil and blanch the cabbage leaves for just a moment so that they will be pliable. Cool them quickly in cold water. Drain and set aside.

Divide the leeks into 8 little batches and place each batch in the center of a cabbage leaf. Roll the leaf up, folding in the ends of the roll so that you have a neat bundle. Tie with string in 2 or 3 places.

Place the bundles in a stove-top casserole and add the remaining ingredients. Bring to a simmer, cover, and cook until tender. Serve hot.

LEEKS AND
JUNIPER BERRIES

SERVES 3–4 AS
A VEGETABLE COURSE

This is another one of the dishes that the servants might have brought you had you been invited to a dinner party at the home of Apicius. The herbs and spices can always change but juniper seems to go nicely with leeks. However, as was the Roman custom, some Liquamen, a salty sauce made of fermented anchovies, would probably be added. You can get a similar effect if you add a shot of *nuc moom*, available in Vietnamese stores. I cannot take the flavor myself, but then maybe you want to be authentic.

1 *tablespoon whole juniper*
  berries

3 *tablespoons olive oil*

3 *cups leeks, cleaned and cut*
  (page 448)

Salt and pepper to taste

½ *cup Basic Chicken Stock*
  (page 129)

Crush juniper berries with a mortar and pestle or coarsely grind in a small electric coffee mill. Sauté the juniper berries in oil for a moment. Add the leeks and sauté, uncovered, for 2 minutes. Add broth, cover, and simmer just until tender. Salt and pepper to taste.

MUSHROOMS

Who ate the first mushroom? We can only guess that it was a prehistoric character and he was hungry. There have always been a thousand varieties of this wonderful fungus about, and many are poisonous—deadly poisonous. How did the first person learn which mushrooms were edible and which were not? We can only guess that it was by trial and error. And the error! The Great Buddha died of mushroom poisoning about 500 B.C. and one of the caesars died in ancient Rome of the same malady.

Since ancient times all three of our cultures have enjoyed mushrooms, though in China they were considered food for the poor and in Rome they were food for the rich. We have no records of Chinese peasants dying of mushroom poisoning, but a wild record of royal deaths in Rome. Apicius, the cookbook author of first-century Rome, lists some fifteen recipes for his beloved mushrooms and some are still used today. For instance, I expect he should be given credit for pickled mushrooms.

I think the Chinese have been the most creative with their recipes for mushrooms . . . and we have to admit that Americans really did not begin to enjoy fresh mushrooms until very recently. In Greece and Rome the mushroom has always been considered necessary to a good table.

You can find many varieties of mushrooms on the market. Some are dried and some can be purchased fresh.

White meadow mushroom: The common mushroom found in the American supermarket.

Oyster mushroom: Wide and white, these are delicious fresh.

Chanterelle: A wild forest mushroom very popular in my Pacific Northwest.

Portobello: Large Italian mushroom. Delicious and found fresh in very fancy food shops.

Cremini: A smaller Italian brown mushroom. Very rich and wonderful flavor. Find fresh in fancy food shops.

Porcini: Dried Italian mushrooms. The genuine imported will cost you about $60 a pound . . . so look for the South American variety. They will cost about $15 a pound and they are almost as good.

Chinese black mushroom: Fresh in the markets as *shiitake* (Japanese name) or *tong ku.* They can be purchased dried in any Chinese market. I prefer the dried since they have a much richer flavor.

Straw mushrooms: Imported from China in a tin. Very delicate and delicious.

Black fungus: Two types are brought in from China—Jew's-ears, and the smaller tree ears. Both are just wonderful.

White fungus: These round wooly balls of fungus are dried and can be found in any Chinese market. White fungus soup is very famous in China.

A note about cleaning mushrooms. All you need do is wipe them with a damp cloth. Do not wash them or soak them or splash them about. Just rub clean and slice. Nothing to it!

See also Pizza with Two Mushrooms *(page 448)*

CHINESE

ABALONE AND MUSHROOMS

SERVES 6 AS
PART OF A CHINESE MEAL

When I was a boy I could afford this dish. Abalone was not expensive and I could go to Tai Tung Restaurant, in Seattle's Chinatown, and enjoy myself. Now the price has risen to something like fifteen dollars for a one-pound can . . . and that is a little much. However, if you are feeling grand and have a special event to celebrate, this is one of the finest mushroom dishes in the world. In Hong Kong you would pay a fortune for this dish.

1 *16-ounce can abalone, drained (reserve the juice) and sliced very thin*	1 *teaspoon sesame oil*
	$\frac{1}{8}$ *teaspoon sugar*
	Pinch of MSG (optional)
1 *tablespoon peanut oil*	$\frac{1}{2}$ *cup Chinese Chicken Soup Stock (page 113)*
1 *clove garlic, chopped fine or crushed*	1 *teaspoon cornstarch mixed with 1 tablespoon water*
16 *Chinese dried mushrooms, soaked for 2 hours, drained and sliced*	2 *or 3 cups of shredded iceberg lettuce for garnish*
2 *tablespoons oyster sauce*	

Very carefully slice the canned abalone and set aside in the juice.
    Heat a wok and add the oil and garlic. Chow for a moment and add the drained mushrooms. Chow on high heat for a minute or two and

add the remaining ingredients, except the abalone, cornstarch, and lettuce garnish. When all is very hot, add the cornstarch mixture and stir until a sauce is formed. Add the abalone, drained (the juice discarded), and cook for a moment. When all is hot pour over the bed of lettuce and serve immediately.

NOTE: Do not cook the abalone too long. Since it is canned it is already cooked and all you need do is to warm it. Further cooking will toughen this precious seafood.

MUSHROOM SHREDDED CHICKEN

SERVES 4–5 AS PART OF A CHINESE MEAL

Mary Young, my adopted Chinese aunt, taught me this dish. It is simple if you have some leftover cooked chicken, and the flavors of the mushrooms and chicken simply belong together.

2 tablespoons peanut oil

12 Chinese dried mushrooms, soaked for 2 hours, drained, and sliced julienne

2 cups Chinese Poached Chicken (page 230), shredded

¼ cup ham or barbecued pork, sliced julienne

SAUCE

½ cup Chinese Chicken Soup Stock (page 113) or Basic Chicken Stock (page 129)

⅛ teaspoon grated fresh ginger

1 tablespoon oyster sauce

Pinch of sugar

Pinch of MSG (optional)

½ teaspoon sesame oil

1 teaspoon cornstarch

GARNISH

3 green onions, chopped

1 tablespoon pine nuts, toasted (page 38)

Have everything mixed and ready to go before you start this dish. It will take only a few minutes to cook.

Heat the wok and add the oil. Chow the mushroom slices for a few moments and add the chicken and ham. As soon as these are hot, add the sauce ingredients, all mixed. Chow until all is hot and the sauce thickens a bit. Remove from the wok and top with the garnishes.

PORK AND EGG WITH TREE FUNGUS IN PANCAKES

SERVES 6 AS
PART OF A CHINESE MEAL

This is the ever-popular Mu-shu Pork that seems to be on so many menus these days. It is not difficult to make and the wonderful flavor of the tree fungus will set your dish apart from those in restaurants that do not wish to serve the real thing.

1 batch Peking Pancakes (page 474)

2 tablespoons peanut oil for chowing

3 eggs, beaten

½ pound lean pork, coarsely ground

2 egg whites

1 tablespoon cornstarch

Pinch of sugar

2 cloves garlic, chopped fine or crushed

1 ounce dried tree fungus (page 31), soaked for ½ hour and drained

SAUCE

Pinch of MSG (optional)

¼ teaspoon salt

1 tablespoon light soy sauce

½ tablespoon Chinese rice wine or dry sherry

½ tablespoon cornstarch mixed with 2 table-spoons water

White pepper, ground, to taste

GARNISHES

3 green onions, chopped

1 tablespoon sesame oil

Prepare the pancakes and set aside. They can be reheated in a bamboo steamer (page 97) just before serving.

Heat the wok and add 1 tablespoon of the oil. Chow the beaten eggs just as you would scrambled eggs, over medium heat. Do not allow them to cook dry, and chop them up a bit. Remove and set aside.

Mix the pork with the egg whites, cornstarch, and sugar. Wash the wok and heat again. Add ½ tablespoon of the peanut oil and chow the meat until it falls apart but is not dry. Remove from the wok and set aside.

Heat the wok a third time and add the remaining oil. Chow the garlic for a moment and add the drained tree fungus. Chow for a moment and return the pork to the wok. Add the mixed sauce and chow until the mixture thickens. Add the eggs to the dish, stir, and top with the garnishes. Serve in the pancakes rolled up like burritos.

WHITE FUNGUS SOUP

This is a very delicate matter, and one of the five most famous soups of China. It is simple to prepare if you have some Chinese Chicken Soup Stock on hand. The fungus can be found in any good Chinese market.

Soak a small amount of white fungus, remembering that it will swell up. Cut the fungus into soup-size bits and cook in Chinese Chicken Soup Stock (page 113). It will take a very short time for the fungus to become very tender. Garnish with a bit of sesame oil and a tiny bit of chopped green onions. This is to be a very delicate soup. Add salt sparingly.

CLEAR MUSHROOM SOUP

This soup is used as a first course in a Chinese banquet because it will excite the palate. It is used as a middle course because it will cleanse the palate and as a last course almost as a dessert. It is very refreshing and quite easy to prepare.

Place 8 or 10 dried Chinese mushrooms in a double boiler and add 1 quart of Chinese Chicken Soup Stock (page 113). Cook in the double boiler for about 2 hours, thus giving you an extract of mushroom. This clear soup is served in very small bowls or teacups at any point in the meal. Be careful with the salt, but you might need some.

GREECE

The Greeks did not seem to get into mushrooms the way the other two cultures did. Very few recipes from the old Greek world even *consider* mushrooms. I don't know why. Seems to me all that traveling around the Mediterranean would have caused everyone to eat mushrooms. The Romans loved them!

MUSHROOMS STUFFED WITH FETA CHEESE

MAKES 15 APPETIZERS

This first course is from the excellent cookbook prepared by the women of St. Demetrios Greek Orthodox Parish in Seattle. The feta cheese is great with mushrooms.

15 *large fresh white mushrooms*

¼ *cup melted butter*

Salt and freshly ground black pepper to taste

2 *tablespoons butter*

3 *tablespoons chopped green onions*

1 *tablespoon flour*

¼ *cup milk*

3 *tablespoons finely chopped parsley*

1 *clove garlic, crushed*

Salt and pepper to taste

3 *tablespoons crumbled feta cheese*

¼ *cup grated kasseri cheese*

2 *tablespoons butter*

Brush the mushrooms clean. Remove the stems and reserve them. Brush caps with melted butter; arrange hollow side up in a baking dish. Sprinkle with salt and pepper.

Mince reserved mushroom stems. Heat small frying pan and add the butter. Add stems and onions and sauté until the liquid has been absorbed.

To the frying pan add the flour and mix well. Add the milk, stirring until thickened a bit. Add the parsley, garlic, and salt and pepper to taste. Mix well. Add feta cheese to mixture and fill mushroom caps.

Top with kasseri and a few dots of butter. Bake at 375° 15 to 20 minutes, or until stuffing has browned lightly and cheese has melted.

ITALY

GRILLED MUSHROOMS, ROMAN STYLE

The mushrooms used for this dish might be a bit hard to find. In Italy they use great big brown mushrooms, and the flavor is just heavenly. When you go to Milan you must go to Peck's Market, not far from the Grand Galleria. They have wonderful mushrooms, porcini, arranged like fancy tiles, but they sell them like gold. If you cannot get the large brown ones, use large meadow mushrooms.

The stems of the mushrooms are removed and reserved for another purpose. The mushrooms are then basted with a mixture of olive oil, chopped garlic, and parsley. A bit of salt and pepper is added and then they are grilled on a hot steel grill or over charcoal. Be careful not to overcook these and don't bother to try this in a frying pan as they will get mushy.

Serve them as a first dish or a side vegetable dish.

PASTA WITH MUSHROOMS NATALIE

*SERVES 6 AS
A PASTA COURSE*

Natalie is the concierge at the Halloran House Hotel on Forty-eighth and Lexington, in Manhattan. It is not a great hotel but a very nice one. She, however, is a great concierge. She can find you anything in New York. Since Alitalia crews stay in the hotel all the time she must speak Italian, and she is Italian. She told me of this dish from her childhood. If you can read this recipe and not immediately run to the kitchen, you have much more willpower than I!

2 ounces dried Italian mushrooms (page 37), soaked in water for 2 hours, drained and chopped

1 medium yellow onion, peeled and chopped

3 tablespoons olive oil

2 cloves garlic, chopped fine or crushed

$\frac{1}{4}$ cup whipping cream

1 teaspoon tomato paste

Salt and freshly ground black pepper to taste

1 pound favorite dried pasta, cooked al dente

GARNISH

Parmesan or Romano cheese, grated

Prepare the mushrooms and onion and sauté in the olive oil, along with the garlic. When all is hot and flavorful, add the cream, tomato paste, and salt and pepper. Simmer for a few minutes and toss with the pasta. Garnish with the cheese.

MUSHROOMS IN WINE AND CORIANDER
APICIUS

Evidently mushrooms were boiled for Roman banquets during the first century. All we have is a description of the process and I have tried it. If you do not overcook these morsels and do not use much water at all, they are quite good. I think Apicius was talking about a kind of steaming process.

A very small amount of salted water is heated, and to this is added olive oil and a bit of white wine. When all is boiling, the mushroom caps are set in the pan and blanched for just a few moments. The garnish for this Roman dish is fresh coriander leaves, slightly chopped. It is quite good . . . but you are supposed to have your slaves serve it on silver trays. So much for that part of the recipe!

MUSHROOM OMELET
APICIUS

Old Apicius, whoever he was, was certainly a mushroom lover. In this description of a dish the mushrooms are covered with scrambled eggs. It is really very good, though a bit sweet with the honey. Here is the description.

Mushrooms are sautéed with a bit of olive oil, dry white wine, and salt. They are placed on a formal platter and covered with very moist scrambled eggs. The whole is then topped with a sauce made with black pepper, celery leaves, honey, chicken broth, and olive oil. Heat the sauce, of course, before pouring it on the eggs and mushrooms.

ADDITIONAL VEGETABLES

SPINACH WITH OLIVE OIL, GARLIC, AND LEMON JUICE, GREEK STYLE

Sauté fresh spinach with olive oil and garlic and add fresh lemon juice just before serving. It is that simple and it is that delicious.

LETTUCE WITH FOO YEE

SERVES 3–4 AS A VEGETABLE DISH AT A CHINESE MEAL

Try chowing iceberg lettuce. It is simple and wonderful in flavor.

Heat a wok and add a bit of peanut oil and 2 cloves of garlic, chopped fine. Then add 1 head of iceberg lettuce, torn up. Chow for a moment and add 1 tablespoon of *foo yee* (page 29) mixed with 1 tablespoon of dry sherry. Chow until the lettuce is tender but not soggy. It is rich and surprisingly satisfying.

DEEP-FRIED VEGETABLES PIPERNO
(Fritto Misto)

The Piperno restaurant in the Jewish Ghetto in Rome is a fine eating house, though the bill will astound you. They serve a plate of assorted deep-fried vegetables that is just wonderful. This is as close as I can come to figuring out what it is that they do.

ARTICHOKES, FRIED JEWISH STYLE (page 400)

MOZZARELLA

The cheese is dipped in beaten egg and then rolled in bread crumbs. When you deep-fry this, be sure the oil is at about 360°.

POTATO GNOCCHI

Use our recipe on page 395, but add a good deal of lemon peel and nutmeg. The gnocchi are then dipped in beaten egg and rolled in bread crumbs, then deep-fried.

RICE BALLS *(Arancini)*

Cooked rice is placed in a bowl with a bit of Italian Tomato Sauce (page 208), just enough to color the rice. Salt and pepper are added and the mixture is rolled into golf-ball-sized balls. These are rolled in beaten egg and then in bread crumbs. Deep-fried, they make the finishing touch on the platter.

> **HINT: KEEP YOUR DEEP-FRYING OIL FRESH AND CLEAN BY** straining it through cheesecloth often. Keep it refrigerated so that it cannot become rancid. And you can freshen the oil by deep-frying a piece of fresh ginger in it now and then. Always use peanut oil or an inexpensive grade of olive oil (page 220) for deep-frying. Neither of these oils contains any cholesterol since they are pure vegetable oils, not animal fats. Remember, fresh, clean oil is much less likely to be absorbed by the food you are cooking.

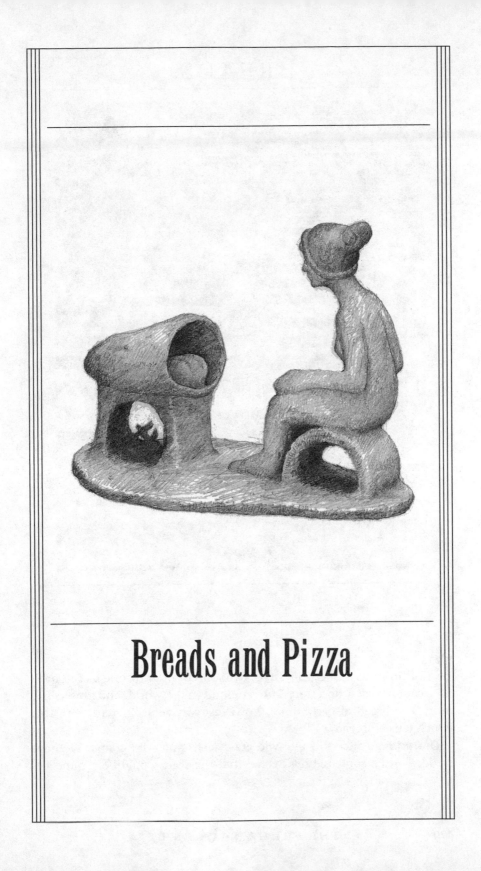

Breads and Pizza

BREADS

Bread from its earliest days has symbolized life. It is one of the most common and necessary forms of food in the world, and always has been. The bread of early times, however, was very different from that which we call bread.

Our primate ancestors ate wild grass seeds and wild grains. We have no idea when someone discovered that the seeds could be ground between two rocks and then dried on a hot rock by the fire . . . but that was the discovery of a crude form of bread. By 7000 B.C. we see bread ovens in the Middle East, though the rock-hard loaves, which contained no leavening, had to be soaked in water, soaked into a gruel, before they could be eaten. Yeast was to come much later.

Credit for the breads of Continental Europe must go in large part to Greece. By the seventh century B.C. the Greeks had added poppyseeds to some of their breads and by the fifth century B.C. an enormous variety of breads was available in Greece, both leavened and unleavened. Loaves, rolls, cakes made with whole wheat, rice, and barley were all baked, enriched, and enlivened with suet, lard, honey, cheese, milk, or oil, cooked in ovens, on griddles, roasted in coals, baked in ashes or on a spit.

By 170 B.C. Greek bakers appeared in Rome, typically as slaves. They taught their art of bread baking to the conquering Romans and bread became the staff of life all over the Mediterranean. One of the reasons for the fall of Rome seems to center around the fact that the Roman government, which controlled all the land, rented the agricultural properties to the rich, who decided to increase their fortunes by growing olives or grapes rather than the necessary grain for bread. The small farmers were forced off the land and grain had to be imported. The end of the Roman wheat supply coincided almost precisely with the fall of the Empire and its subsequent dismemberment by the barbarians. A government unable to feed its people is on very shaky ground. Thus did wheat and bread influence the history and destiny of the great Roman Empire.

The Chinese have enjoyed bread since early times as well. The northern regions of China began producing wheat as early as 1400 B.C., and it was baked along with other grains such as millet and, later, corn. Steaming is the most popular way of cooking bread in the north and the recipe for steamed bread that follows will please your family. It is very old, going back to about 220 B.C.

When you are in Rome you must go to the Forno Campo de' Fiori bakery. You will not believe the bread that is offered there. It is right next door to La Carbonara restaurant.

CHINESE FRIED BREAD STRIPS
(You Tiau)

This is a very delicious bread that is often served for breakfast along with Rice Congee *(Jook)* (page 378). It is not difficult to make but I find that frozen white bread dough works great for this dish and certainly saves a lot of time.

Defrost a loaf of frozen bread dough and let it rise as per the instructions. When risen cut the dough into strips, each about ½ inch in diameter. Cut the strips into pieces about 5 inches long. Stretch out the strips of frozen bread dough just a bit and put two strips together, one on top of the other. Press the two strips together with a chopstick, pushing down right in the middle of the dough, the long way, and pull or stretch it just a bit. Deep-fry in oil at 375° until golden brown, turning once or twice.

The bread is cut into 1-inch-long pieces and served in Rice Congee for breakfast or brunch.

The bread can be made a few hours ahead of time and quickly warmed up in the oven.

CHINESE STEAMED BREAD
(Bow)

Plain steamed bread is very popular in the northern regions of China. We Westerners seem to forget that northern China grows a great deal of wheat and these people live on wheat noodles and breads such as this one.

Use the bread dough recipe for the Steamed Meat-Stuffed Buns on page 109. Let the dough rise once and punch it down. Roll the dough out to about ⅓ inch thick and cut into strips 2 inches wide. Cut the strips into pieces each 5 inches long. Brush each with sesame oil and fold it over, making a little bun 2 inches wide and 2½ inches long. Top with toasted sesame seeds and put on small pieces of parchment paper. Place in bamboo steamers and allow to rise for a bit. Steam for 15 minutes over high heat.

These can be eaten along with any number of Chinese meat dishes and they are commonly eaten with vegetables as well.

SESAME DRAGON MOUTHS

MAKES 18 ROLLS

The name is for the kids, but the Chinese do have a habit of naming foods after wonderful concepts.

Prepare a batch of dough as in the Chinese Steamed Bread on page 472. Oil and fold the dough as instructed and place on an oiled baking sheet. Brush the top of each with a bit of milk and sprinkle with raw sesame seeds. Allow to rise until double in bulk and bake in a 400° oven for 20 minutes, or until golden. Cool on cake racks.

CORN CREPES, CHINESE STYLE
(Jian Bin)

MAKES 5 LARGE PANCAKES

This is a fine recipe from our *Sunset Magazine,* certainly one of the best regional magazines in the country.

When corn was taken to China it became a great hit. Sweet potatoes and peanuts were other gifts brought from the New World to the peoples of the Far East. These corn pancakes are thin and just perfect for eating with many Chinese meat dishes.

1⅞ cups water
1 cup yellow cornmeal
½ cup all-purpose white flour

½ teaspoon salt
Peanut oil for pan-frying

In a food blender combine the water, cornmeal, flour, and salt. Whirl until well blended. Preheat an electric griddle to 400° or place a heavy griddle on medium-high heat. When hot, brush the griddle with a bit of oil. For each pancake pour ½ cup batter all at once onto the hot griddle. Spread about with a ladle or spatula to form a thin, even round. Cook until the bottom is dry. With a wide spatula, turn the cake over and cook until the bottom feels dry to the touch and the sides are crisp, 3 to 4 minutes total time. Remove and repeat the process. You should have about 5 large thin pancakes.

Stack them to keep them warm or reheat before dinner in aluminum foil in a 350° oven for about 10 minutes.

PEKING PANCAKES

MAKES ABOUT 24 PANCAKES

These wonderfully thin wheat pancakes are most often served with Peking Duck. However, with any imagination you can think up all kinds of uses for them. Put meat and vegetable dishes in these pancakes and roll them up like burritos. The package is really very good.

Prepare one batch of Chinese Boiled Dumpling Dough (page 388) and let the dough rest the prescribed time.

Roll the dough into a snake about 1 inch in diameter and cut into pieces 1 inch long. Roll each into a ball and then press out flat to make a small pancake. Brush the top of one pancake with sesame oil and place another pancake on top of the first. Using a rolling pin, and additional flour if needed, roll out the two pancakes together until they are about 5 inches in diameter. Roll all and keep under plastic wrap.

To cook the pancakes, place them, one pair at a time, in a hot SilverStone-lined pan. Cook until tiny brown spots form on the bottom and then turn the pancake over, cooking the second side in the same way. When the pancakes are done they can be separated into individual Peking Pancakes. To reheat them simply warm them in a bamboo steamer (page 97).

NOTE: You can save a bit of work in this process if you use a tortilla press. Roll the cut dough into balls and flatten them with the press. Oil one, put another on top, and press the two. Then, using the rolling pin, finish the rolling-out process.

ONION CAKES

MAKES 6 ONION CAKES

This is a most unusual dish. I gave you a version of this dish in my first cookbook, but I used a cheater's method. I told you that when I urged you use tortillas for this dish. This is the legit method and it comes from a very fine cookbook by Pei Mei, the first in a three-volume set. If you are really serious about Chinese cooking you will look for these books (see Bibliography).

3 cups flour	3 tablespoons chopped green onions
1 cup boiling water	3 teaspoons salt
⅓ cup cold water	1 cup peanut oil for pan-frying
6 tablespoons lard	

Place the flour in a bowl and add the boiling water. Mix with chopsticks. Cover with plate and wait 3 minutes. Add cold water. Knead and let rest for 15 minutes.

Roll dough into a thick snake and cut into 6 pieces. Roll out each piece to 6 inches round. Place ½ tablespoon of lard on the pancake and smear around. Add salt and ½ tablespoon green onions. Roll up like jelly roll and into a snail shape. Press flat and then roll out to about ⅛-inch thickness. Fry in 2 tablespoons oil. Turn. Add more oil as you go along. These should be very flaky.

GREECE

OLD GREEK BREAD

MAKES 2 OR 3 LARGE LOAVES

I had the most wonderful experience on the Isle of Mykonos. It was February, off tourist season, and the little island was just going along for the sake of the regular inhabitants. A fellow took me to see a sight that tourists seldom see, the oldest bakery on the island. After a difficult search through the very narrow and wonderfully winding streets we stepped through a door and into a room so dark it took me several minutes to realize that the only light in the place was coming from the door of the wood-fired oven. The baker loads the oven twice a day and sells out twice a day. His ancestors built the ovens five hundred years ago, and there has not been a break in the family line.

Barley flour has been used by the Greeks since ancient times, and the windmills on Mykonos were originally used to power the grain-grinding mills. Grain would be shipped in from other ports in the Mediterranean and ground into flour on the windy Isle of Mykonos. This bread is as close as I can come to the wonderful bread of the Isle.

2½ cups tepid water (90°)

2 packages dry yeast (I prefer a quick-rising yeast)

2 cups barley flour

¼ cup rye flour

Unbleached white flour to make up total flour weight of 2 pounds 3 ounces

1 tablespoon honey

2 tablespoons olive oil

2 teaspoons salt, mixed with 2 teaspoons water

Cornmeal for the baking sheets

In a mixing bowl, dissolve the yeast in the tepid water.

Place a paper lunch sack on a scale and put in the barley and rye flour. Add enough additional unbleached flour to make up the 2 pounds 3 ounces.

Put the yeast water in an electric mixer bowl and add 4 cups of the flour mixture. (I simply use my KitchenAid for this whole process.) Add the honey and olive oil and mix to form a sponge, or very soft dough. Mix by hand or by machine until the dough begins to pull away from the side of the bowl, about 10 minutes. Mix in the salt mixed with water and finally the remaining flour. If you are using a hand mixer the last of the flour will have to be stirred in by hand. If you are using a powerful mixer use the dough hook.

Knead the dough until it is smooth and elastic. Place on a plastic counter and cover with a large bowl. Allow to rise until double in bulk, and then punch down and cover; allow to rise a second time.

Punch down and mold 2 or 3 loaves. Place on a baking sheet that has been sprinkled with a little cornmeal. Dust the loaves with a little flour and allow to rise again until double in size. Bake in a 450° oven for about 25 to 35 minutes, or until the bread is a rich dark brown and the loaf sounds hollow when you thump it on the bottom with your finger. Allow the loaves to cool on cake racks.

GREEK SESAME BREAD

MAKES 2 LOAVES

This is served all over Greece; the sesame seed has been popular there since ancient times. The Greeks were the ones who first started putting unusual seeds and flavorings into their baking. They taught the Romans to do the same.

1 *cup tepid water*

1 *cup tepid milk*

2 *envelopes fast-rising dry yeast*

2 *tablespoons sugar*

2 *tablespoons salad oil*

2 *pounds 3 ounces unbleached white flour*

1 *teaspoon salt dissolved in 1 tablespoon water*

TOPPING

$\frac{1}{4}$ *cup milk*

$\frac{1}{2}$ *cup raw sesame seeds*

Cornmeal for the baking sheets

Mix the warm water and milk in your electric mixer bowl. Dissolve the yeast. Add the sugar, oil, and 4 cups of the total flour. Whip for 10 minutes and add the salted water. If you have a very strong mixer, such as a KitchenAid, you can use the dough hook to blend in the remaining flour. If not, you must do it by hand. Knead the dough for several minutes so that it is smooth and elastic. Place the dough on a plastic counter, and cover with a large inverted metal bowl. Allow to rise double in bulk and punch down. Allow to rise a second time and punch down. Divide into 2 halves. Roll each into a ball and punch a hole in the center. Work with the dough until you have a round circle about 13 inches in diameter. Place each loaf on a greased baking sheet that has been dusted with cornmeal. Brush the tops of the loaves with a bit of milk and top with the sesame seeds.

Bake at 400° until golden and light, about 25 to 30 minutes.

SESAME CIRCLES

These are sold in the streets of Athens. Wagons and little carts park on the sidewalk around the great squares of the city and sell these tasty bread circles by the hundreds.

Make a batch of Greek Sesame Bread (page 477) and form only one loaf. With the other half of the dough make sesame circles in this way. Roll the dough out to about ¼ inch thick and cut it into strips ½ inch wide. Using a strip of dough 18 inches long make a circle. It will be about 4 inches in diameter. Place the strips on an oiled baking sheet and allow to rise. Brush with milk and top with sesame seeds. Bake at 425° until golden brown, about 15 minutes.

GREEK EASTER BREAD

MAKES 2 LOAVES

Easter is the most holy of the holidays in Greece, and certainly the most involved. The special meals go on for days and the Great Paschal Feast of Easter Day cannot be celebrated without this bread. It is great fun to make and it will wow the kids on Easter morning.

  1 cup warm milk
 *2 teaspoons Mahleb, ground (optional)
  2 packages fast-acting yeast
 1¼ cups tepid water
  2 tablespoons salad oil
  2 tablespoons sugar
  2 raw eggs

  2 pounds 3 ounces unbleached white flour
  1 teaspoon salt dissolved in 1 teaspoon water
  5 hard-boiled eggs, dyed a very bright red
  1 egg, beaten, for a glaze

Heat the milk, along with the Mahleb, and allow it to cool until tepid. In your electric mixing bowl, dissolve the yeast in the water. Add the warm milk, salad oil, sugar, and eggs. Measure out 4 cups of the total flour and add to the bowl. Mix for about 10 minutes. Stir in the salt and water. The rest of the flour must be added by hand unless you have a powerful mixer such as a KitchenAid. Use the dough hook and blend

*Available in Greek markets.

in the rest of the flour. Knead until smooth. Place the dough on a plastic counter and cover with a large inverted bowl. Allow to rise until double in bulk, punch down, and allow to rise again. (See, it *is* Easter Bread!)

Divide the dough into 2 pieces. Cover one half with the bowl and divide the other half into 3 equal parts. Roll each into a snake about 25 inches long. Lay the pieces side by side and pinch one end together. Braid the three pieces and form into a round loaf. Place the Easter eggs in the braid and allow the bread to rise until double in bulk. Brush with the beaten egg and bake at 375° for about 30 minutes, or until golden brown.

PITA BREAD WITH OLIVE OIL, GRILLED

The ancient Greek grill is a wonderful device. From it came our barbecue and a hundred gadgets in between. You can grill pita bread as they do in Greece and you can grill it on your gas or electric stove. Buy fresh pita bread at your market and brush a loaf on both sides with a small amount of olive oil. Place the loaf on a hot asador grill (page 19) and heat, turning once. You will be amazed at the difference in flavor.

PAXIMADI

This is not a recipe but a qualified commercial for the ingenious early Greeks. The Greeks invented toast! A baker in ancient times realized that bread sliced and cooked a second time, or toasted, would keep well on the road. He gave us a whole new possibility for travel, since his invention could feed us on long journeys. His name was Paxamos, and to this day you can find, in every bakery in Greece, sweet toasts called *paximadi*. You will also find signs outside coffee shops advertising the product. It is a funny sign, according to my sons, because it is translated into English and simply advertises "Toast." "Wow!" Jason laughed. "Let's get some!"

You probably have never thought about the fact that the invention of toast changed travel patterns in the ancient world. Neither had I!

ANCIENT ROMAN BREAD

MAKES
2 OR 3 LOAVES

We are quite sure that when the Romans invaded Greece they had their eating habits changed drastically. The Greeks were better bakers, for one thing, and the Greek slaves who were taken back to Rome taught the Romans to use several different flours in a single loaf instead of the one common flour that was used in Rome. I think this recipe is about as close as we can come to the flavors that were enjoyed during the early days.

- 2 *envelopes fast-rising dry yeast*
- 2½ *cups tepid water*
- 1 *cup whole-wheat flour*
- ½ *cup rye flour*

- *Unbleached white flour to make up 2 pounds 3 ounces of total flour weight*
- 1 *teaspoon salt dissolved in 1 tablespoon water*
- *Cornmeal for dusting the baking sheets*

Put the tepid water in your electric mixer bowl and dissolve the yeast.

Use a paper lunch sack for weighing out the flour. Put the whole-wheat and rye flour in the bag first, and then make up the weight with the white flour. Put 4 cups from the bag into the mixer and whip it for 10 minutes. Add the salted water. If you have a heavy mixing machine such as a KitchenAid, allow the dough hook to do the rest of the work. If not, you need to add the remaining flour by hand. Knead until the dough is smooth and elastic.

Put the dough on a plastic counter and cover with an inverted steel bowl. Allow it to rise once, punch it down, and allow it to rise a second time. Punch down and form into 2 or 3 loaves. I never use bread pans for this, as they will ruin the crust. Place the loaves on baking sheets that have been dusted with cornmeal and allow the loaves to rise until double in bulk.

Bake in a 450° oven about 25 minutes, or until the crust is golden and the loaf light to the touch. It should make a hollow sound when you thump your finger on the bottom of the loaf.

ROMAN BREAD

MAKES 2 OR 3 LOAVES

The bakeries in Rome produce a bread that has a crust so dark it looks almost burned. It has wonderful flavor and I think this method will produce something close to the crusty Roman version.

Prepare a batch of Ancient Roman Bread (page 480), but use only unbleached white flour. The total weight should be *only* white flour. Prepare the loaves and allow them to rise on pans dusted with cornmeal.

Preheat the oven to 450° 1 hour prior to baking. Place a sheet of baking tiles (page 22) on the middle rack of the oven. These will even out the heat. Place a 9 × 13-inch cake pan filled with water on the bottom rack of the oven. Add more water as needed. Bake the risen loaves in the oven at 450° for 20 minutes. Then turn the heat to 500° and bake another 10 minutes or until the crust is very dark.

BREADSTICKS, ITALIAN SESAME

These are simple to make and far superior to the fat, thick, pasty, flavorless things that we call breadsticks in this country. The Roman variety is very thin, closer to the size of a pencil. They are found on every restaurant table and they have a nutty, toasted flavor that goes beautifully with a glass of wine.

To make them, prepare a batch of dough using only unbleached white flour, as in the recipe above. Allow the dough to rise twice and then punch down. Roll it out into rectangles about ¼ inch thick. Cut into ¼-inch-wide strips and then cut these to the desired length for your breadsticks. Twist each strand of dough as you place it on a baking sheet dusted with cornmeal. Simply hold the strand of dough between two hands and turn the ends in opposite directions. Set on the baking sheet. Allow to rise for a short time and bake at 425° for 15 minutes or until golden brown.

VARIATION: If you wish to brush some of these with a bit of milk and then top them with raw sesame seeds, you will have a serious treat for the kids.

> **HINT: FOR MAKING BREADSTICKS** you might try using a noodle cutter. There is one on the market that has five large stainless blades, each $\frac{1}{4}$ inch apart. It is used for chopping noodles, but it also works great for cutting breadsticks. See page 20.

CRUSTULUM

I could not resist telling you about this delight. It is garlic toast, but made as in the days of the Roman Empire. I am quite sure that they learned the trick from the Greeks (see Paximadi, page 479). In our time the Italians call this *bruschetta,* but in the early days it was called *crustulum,* and from it we have our word "crust."

To make Crustulum simply toast good Roman bread on both sides over charcoal. None of this electric pop-toaster jazz! Rub the toast with an entire clove of garlic, and rub until the clove disappears. Drizzle extra virgin olive oil on the toast and enjoy. This is great with any Italian meal, and with a salad and a good wine it makes a meal in itself.

FOCACCIA ROMANA

Marion, who helps me in my studio kitchen in Chicago, does not eat a lot when she is working. None of us have time! But when I made this dish she ate as if I would never make it again for her. This recipe is for her.

Craig, my cooking assistant, and I tasted this version at the Forno Campo de' Fiori, the bakery in the great market center in Rome. People line up to buy this fabulous bread, and they bake throughout the day. They gave us the recipe . . . though it was just a description. We have worked out the following simple formula, and I think it is superb. It is a very old form of bread in Rome, going back hundreds of years. It is great for sandwiches and eating with dinner, and it forms the background of what was later to be called "Pizza."

2 packages fast-rising dry yeast

2 cups tepid water (90°)

2 tablespoons sugar

4 tablespoons olive oil

½ cup salad oil

1 teaspoon table salt

5½ cups unbleached white flour

3 cloves garlic, crushed

¼ cup olive oil for topping

1 tablespoon whole rosemary

1 tablespoon kosher salt for topping

Dissolve the yeast in the tepid water. Add the sugar, olive oil, salad oil, and regular salt. Mix in 3 cups of the flour and whip until the dough begins to leave the sides of the mixing bowl, about 10 minutes. I use my KitchenAid mixer for this whole process.

Mix in remaining flour by hand or with a dough hook and knead the dough until it is smooth. Allow the dough to rise twice, right in the bowl, and punch down after each rising.

Oil 2 baking sheets, each 13 inches by 18 inches, and divide the dough between the 2 pans. Using your fingers, press the dough out to the edges of each pan. Allow to rise for about 30 minutes and brush with the crushed garlic mixed with the oil for topping. Sprinkle the rosemary and kosher salt on top.

Bake at 375° for about 30 minutes.

VARIATION: Top with green onions instead of rosemary. Delicious.

OLIVE BREAD

This is a popular Roman treat that an olive lover cannot resist. Prepare a batch of Roman Bread (page 481) and knead in some stuffed green olives. Bake per instructions and get ready to surprise your guests when you slice the beautiful loaf.

OLIVE ROLLS

This is the same as above but you simply prepare rolls instead of loaves. Bake at 425° for about 20 minutes, or until golden brown.

PIZZA

We cannot date the first pizza, but we do know that flat, round loaves of bread go back to prehistoric times. It was peasant food from the beginning, and it has been raised to glory with a few wonderful toppings. Pizza is now the second most popular fast food in America.

The Greeks are credited with originating the concept of pizza in a refined form. They developed the "edible plate," for that is what pizza is, by topping the bread with an assortment of "relishes," here meaning anything that was put on the bread. A rim was put on the loaf so that it could hold the garnishes, and the pizza was born. It was actually a trencher! The Greeks took this with them into southern Italy and it became very popular there.

In the northern portion of Italy the Etruscans ate a *puls* or thick gruel made of grains. They customarily baked this on stones beneath the ashes of the household fires, seasoning these cakes with oil and herbs. The Romans adopted this ash cake and called it *focaccia* (from the Latin *panis focacius*, "bread from the floor of the fireplace"). *Focaccia* survives today and is certainly one the ancestors of what we call pizza.

It is easy to see how the Greek idea of flat bread with relishes combined with the Etruscan bread on ashes to produce pizza. The word "pizza" is derived from the Latin word *picea*, meaning the black ashes on the floor of the fireplace. This is still the way pizza should be made today. Two wandering peoples, the Greeks and the Etruscans, thus armed the Italian immigrant with a great treasure when he came to America. Our contribution to the cause was tomato sauce, of course. Since the tomato is a product of the New World, we can claim credit for the introduction of the sauce, which was first brought to Italy during the 1500s. Naples remains the center of great tomato-topped pies. Thus pizza has come full circle.

I understand that some character is planning on opening a pizza parlor in Beijing. Won't the Chinese be in for a surprise!

ANCESTORS OF WHEAT-FLOUR PIZZA

GARBANZO PIZZA, OLD ROMAN STYLE
(Cecina)

SERVES 6 AS A VERY INTERESTING HISTORICAL LESSON AND SNACK

Garbanzo beans, or chick-peas, are a very old food product. Apicius lists them in his first-century cookbook and we know they were used for common food long before wheat became popular. When wheat did become available in the Mediterranean it was very expensive, so people continued to eat the less-expensive garbanzo bean and the chestnut. Polenta and a kind of pizza were made from these products a thousand years ago. It had no yeast, nor tomatoes, of course.

This recipe is from Bugialli's wonderful book, *Classic Techniques of Italian Cooking* (see Bibliography). I am not sure that you are going to love this dish, but I do want you to know something about the history of pizza.

1½ cups dried garbanzo
beans, soaked in water
overnight

1 teaspoon salt

4 tablespoons olive oil

1 tablespoon fresh rosemary
leaves

Salt and freshly ground
black pepper to taste

Rinse the soaked beans and place them in a saucepan. Cover with fresh water, along with the salt. Bring to a simmer and cook, covered, for 1½ hours. You will need to add more water during the process. Cook until they are soft. Drain, reserving the liquid, and place the beans in a food processor. Grind them up using the pulse button—you do not want a fine mush. Add a bit of the reserved cooking liquid, about 1 cup, so that you have a nice thick paste. Stir in 2 tablespoons of the olive oil and add more salt to taste, if necessary. Use another tablespoon of the oil to grease a 14-inch pizza pan and spread the batter out in the pan. Top with the last portion of the oil, the rosemary leaves, and the black pepper to taste. Bake at 375° for 35 minutes. Slice up the pie and serve it while it is hot.

CHESTNUT FOCACCIA

This is also an interesting bit of history. When chestnuts were near free, the locals in the Old World used them to make flour. The flour was not suitable for what we call bread but it did make a flavorful baked pulse, or a flat polenta. That is the background of this very early pizza. The chestnut flour also made a good pasta (page 432).

1¼ cups chestnut flour

1¼ cups water

Olive oil for greasing the
baking pan

2 tablespoons pine nuts

¼ teaspoon whole rosemary

1 tablespoon olive oil

Beat water and flour to a batter consistency. Oil a 12-inch-round pizza tray and pour batter on tray. Spread out evenly and top with the pine nuts and herbs, and sprinkle the olive oil over the top. Bake at 380° for 25 minutes or until golden on top.

NOTE: In the oldest versions of this dish, golden raisins were also used, thus marking it as a favorite of the Roman palate. However, I think the raisins make it much too sweet.

Pizza Dough

The best pizza dough that I have ever come across is the bread dough for Focaccia Romana (page 482). Make a batch and then choose your topping. A single batch of dough will make 2 pizzas, each 13 inches by 18 inches. Follow the instructions for pressing out the dough but do not use the toppings for Focaccia. Use other creative toppings instead.

PIZZA TOPPINGS

Most of these call for an Italian Tomato Sauce topping (page 208). Just brush a bit on the dough and then go ahead and create any of the following pizzas. In Rome the items are generally not mixed but only a single item used on a pizza. However, don't let that stop your creativity.

Once the topping is on and you are ready to bake, drizzle some good olive oil over the whole thing. Then, into the oven!

Zucchini, sliced thin, and arranged like tiles over a bit of Italian Tomato Sauce and grated cheese.

Tomatoes, sliced thin, and arranged like tiles on top of sauce and cheese. Add lots of black pepper.

Onions, sliced thin and arranged like tiles on sauce with grated cheese.

Potato, sliced thin and arranged like tiles on sauce with grated cheese.

Eggs, hard-boiled and sliced, artichokes, sliced, and tuna. These items are placed on top of a tomato-sauce pizza while it is still hot. They are not baked.

Pancetta, sliced thin on top of tomato sauce and grated cheese.

Green olives, stuffed, sliced thin, arranged on a tomato-sauce pizza with grated cheese.

Mushrooms, sliced thin and arranged like tiles on a tomato-sauce pizza with grated cheese.

Two Mushrooms. Dried mushrooms (page 37) are soaked, drained, chopped, and spread on the tomato sauce. Fresh mushrooms are then sliced and arranged on top.

Anchovies, arranged in a neat pattern on a tomato pizza. No cheese on this one.

Old Roman. Olive oil, garlic, pine nuts, fresh rosemary, kosher salt. No cheese or tomato on this.

RUSTIC PIZZA

SERVES 4–6
AS A MAIN DISH

This is the original deep-dish pizza, I suppose, and it comes from southern Italy. It is not difficult to prepare and the presentation is just smashing. If you can eat more than 2 wedges of this I will give up on you!

CRUST

Use Focaccia dough pressed into a 10-inch-round cake pan.

FILLING

- ½ cup chopped ham
- ½ cup freshly grated Parmesan cheese
- ½ cup cream cheese
- 2 hard-boiled eggs, chopped
- 2 cups Basic White Sauce (page 205), enriched with 2 egg yolks
- Salt and pepper to taste
- 2 stiffly beaten egg whites

Mix all of the above except the egg whites. Taste for salt and pepper and then gently fold in the beaten egg whites. Pour this mixture into the crust and bake in a 375° oven for 30 minutes. Then turn down the oven to 350° and bake 10 more minutes or until the pie sets and is golden on top.

Desserts

Our Western desire for a sweet at the close of the meal was certainly not celebrated in our three ancient cuisines. There were exceptions, of course, particularly for special occasions and festivals, but the Greeks and the Romans most often ended their meals with a bit of fresh fruit. The Chinese have a bit of fruit, an orange perhaps, at the end of the meal, but even that practice is uncommon. Sweets were reserved for festivals and this practice continues in China even today.

The Greeks and the Romans make wonderful pastries, but even these are offered at some other time of the day, rarely after a meal. I offer these recipes with the understanding that I never serve desserts to my family, although I love each of the following recipes. My idea of a fine dessert is a good cup of Italian coffee, or perhaps a glass of fine wine. Just remember that we Americans eat much too much sugar, and we need to cut down. Diabetes was practically unknown in China until very recently. The Chinese have never been that concerned about consuming sugar, but now, with the invasion of Western tastes, soda pop and all of the evils that go with it are common in China. Diabetes in Beijing cannot be far behind.

CHINA

EIGHT-TREASURE RICE PUDDING

SERVES 8–10
AS CHINESE DESSERT

Boy, does this one take some doing. Rice is served here as a dessert, and I can just hear you commenting on the fact that the Chinese eat rice three meals a day and in all forms. Don't forget that rice pudding is very popular in America, too.

You will have fun making an attractive arrangement of the fruits. This dessert is served only on special occasions, and after making one I am sure you will know why.

2 cups sticky sweet rice (page 34)

1 tablespoon peanut oil for greasing the bowl

THE EIGHT TREASURES

1 tablespoon white raisins, soaked in water for 1 hour

1 tablespoon black raisins, soaked in water for 1 hour

6 Chinese dried red dates, soaked in water for 1 hour

3 dates, sliced into quarters the long way

6 candied red cherries, sliced in half

½ tablespoon diced candied lemon peel

1 tablespoon green candied peel or green pineapple, cut into diamond shapes or wedges

½ tablespoon pine nuts

1¾ cups water

2 tablespoons lard

3 tablespoons sugar

4 ounces sweet red bean paste (page 34)

THE SYRUP

1 cup water

3 tablespoons sugar

1 tablespoon cornstarch mixed with 1 table-spoon water

Rinse the rice several times in cold running water and then cover with water and allow to soak for 3 hours.

While the rice is soaking, select a 7-inch-diameter bowl, 3 inches deep. Oil the bowl with the peanut oil and arrange the soaked and drained fruits and nuts in an interesting pattern in the bottom of the bowl. You can make quite a production of this if you wish to take the time. Place things in circles, lines, wheel-spoke patterns. . . .

After the rice has soaked, drain and add 1¾ cups fresh water. Bring to a boil with the lid off and boil for 3 minutes. Turn the heat to low, cover the pot, and cook for an additional 7 minutes. Remove from the heat and stir in the lard and 3 tablespoons sugar. Very carefully place half of this mixture in the bowl, being careful not to mess up your colorful fruit arrangement. Place the sweet bean paste in a ball in the center of the bowl and top with the rest of the rice. Pat it down so that it will all stick together when it cooks.

Place the bowl in a bamboo steamer (page 97) and cook for 1 hour 15 minutes. Remove the dish from the steamer and place a plate upside down on top of the rice bowl and invert. Tap very gently so that the rice and fruit come out in one piece.

Prepare the syrup by bringing the water and sugar to a boil. Stir in the cornstarch and water and stir until thick. Pour over the pudding and serve.

FRIED CUSTARD

SERVES 4–5
AS A DESSERT

The cook who thought this one up has got to be credited with being very, very clever. The dish goes back many generations in China and it is popular at formal banquets in Hong Kong, since Westerners are so used to having a sweet dessert. It is not complex to prepare and it is a great deal of fun to serve.

3 eggs yolks, beaten

1 cup cold water

½ teaspoon almond extract

½ cup flour

6 tablespoons cornstarch

4 tablespoons sugar

4 cups peanut oil for deep-frying

3 tablespoons sesame seeds, toasted and ground (page 33)

In a 1-quart saucepan place the yolks, water, almond extract, flour, and 3 tablespoons of cornstarch. Add 1 tablespoon of the sugar. Mix thoroughly and cook over medium heat, stirring constantly, until the mixture thickens into a heavy custard. Remove to a flat dish that has been greased with a bit of vegetable oil and spread the custard out to a ½-inch thickness. Place in the refrigerator to cool. When cooled and firm, cut the custard into diamond shapes about 1½ inches long. Dust with the remaining 3 tablespoons of cornstarch. Deep-fry the coated diamonds in 360° oil until golden brown. Do this in 2 batches. Mix the remaining 3 tablespoons of sugar with the ground sesame seeds and sprinkle over the fried custard. Serve hot.

CANDIED BANANA FRITTERS

SERVES 6–8 FOR DESSERT

When the Chinese finally decide to serve a sweet dessert it is spectacular. Be careful with this classic as the sugar syrup is very hot and will burn.

BATTER

1 egg, beaten

3 tablespoons flour

3 tablespoons cornstarch

1 tablespoon water

3 medium bananas (not too ripe)

Oil for deep-frying

SYRUP

1 tablespoon peanut oil

½ cup sugar

In a small bowl mix the beaten egg, flour, cornstarch, and water to form a smooth batter. Slice the bananas into ½-inch-thick pieces and coat with the batter. Deep-fry at 360° for 20 seconds, in 2 batches, and remove and drain. Allow the oil to return to temperature and fry the slices, all at once, a second time just until golden brown.

While the slices are frying, heat the oil and sugar in a small saucepan. Cook on medium heat until the sugar dissolves and turns a very light golden color. Coat the bananas in the syrup and then plunge into a serving bowl of cold water and ice cubes. Serve at once so that the bananas are still hot and the syrup crystallized. Remove from the water with chopsticks for each serving.

CHERRIES IN ALMOND

SERVES 6 AS
PART OF A CHINESE MEAL

This dish is actually from Taiwan. It was given me by the same woman who gave me the Slow Simmered Pork Roast, Ann Gelow. We shared meals in my days as university chaplain in Tacoma, and my students had little money in the sixties. This was her clever Chinese solution to an inexpensive dessert. It cleans the tongue of the richness of the meal since it contains no sugar.

1 *16-ounce can unsweetened pie cherries (not pie-filling mix)*

1 *teaspoon almond extract*

Heat the cherries in their juice and stir in the almond extract. Serve just a few cherries, along with some juice, in tiny bowls to each guest.

CHINESE SESAME COOKIES
(Heung Yun Beng)

MAKES 100 COOKIES

These are very rich because of the heavy use of lard. They are a favorite with Chinese children, but they are generally reserved for special occasions and holidays. After you eat one, you will know why. They are delicious.

$\frac{3}{4}$ *cup brown sugar*

$1\frac{1}{2}$ *cups granulated sugar*

$1\frac{1}{2}$ *tablespoons powdered milk*

1 *tablespoon ice water*

1 *pound lard*

2 *eggs*

3 *teaspoons baking soda*

5 *teaspoons cream of tartar*

$5\frac{1}{2}$ *cups flour*

2 *cups raw white sesame seeds*

In an electric mixer mix all but the flour and sesame together. Then add the flour and do not overmix. Mix just until it holds together. Roll dough into walnut-sized balls and then roll in the sesame seeds. Place on a cookie sheet about 2 inches apart. Bake at 350° for 15 minutes until cookies have irregular cracks on the surface.

SWEET ALMOND CREAM SOUP

This is most unusual and very simple. You can buy the Sweet Almond Soup already prepared in a tin. Add one can of milk to each can of soup and heat. Serve small amounts to each person at the end of the meal.

PEKING DUST

SERVES 8–10 AS A DESSERT

This wonderful dish includes whipping cream, so I doubt that this version was served in early times in Peking. Cream was simply not used as we use it. As a matter of fact, the Chinese have never really gotten into dairy products. The cream is obviously a much more recent addition.

This is best made with fresh chestnuts, either roasted or boiled, peeled of course. If you wish to use fresh, use about 2½ pounds in order to prepare this elaborate dish.

THE CHESTNUTS

1 *pound dried chestnuts, soaked overnight and drained*

1 *cup water*

1 *cup regular sugar*

1 *teaspoon salt*

½ *cup powdered or confectioner's sugar*

1 *teaspoon vanilla*

WHIPPED CREAM

2 *cups whipping cream*

3 *tablespoons powdered or confectioner's sugar*

1 *teaspoon vanilla*

GARNISH

3 *tablespoons dark brown sugar*

Glacéed or candied fruit (optional)

Place the drained chestnuts in a saucepan and add 1 cup of water, along with the 1 cup sugar. Bring to a boil, cover, and simmer until the nuts are barely tender, about 1 hour. Drain, reserving the syrup. Place the nuts in a food processor and process, in 2 batches, just until grainy. Remove to a bowl and stir in the remaining ingredients for the chestnuts. Set aside.

Whip the cream and add the sugar and vanilla. Gently fold *half* of the whipped cream into the chestnut mixture and mound this on a serving plate. Make it look like a mountain. Cover the mountain with the remaining whipped cream and garnish with the brown sugar and optional dried fruits.

GREECE

HALVAH CAKE

SERVES 12–15 PEOPLE

This cake is unusual in that it has no flour in it at all. The farina soaks up the syrup that is poured on after baking and the result is very close to the sweet moist cakes that you find in the street cafés in Athens. This is truly a wonderful dessert.

BATTER

1 cup sugar

2 sticks (½ pound) butter

2 cups semolina flour or regular cream of wheat cereal

½ cup almonds, peeled, coarsely chopped in food processor

6 eggs, beaten

1 teaspoon baking powder

1 teaspoon cinnamon

½ cup whole pine nuts

SYRUP

2 cups sugar

3 cups water

1 whole clove

2 ounces brandy

Juice of 2 lemons

Using an electric mixer, cream the butter and sugar. Add the remaining ingredients, except the pine nuts, and blend to form a smooth batter. Spread the batter evenly in a greased 9 × 13-inch cake pan. Sprinkle the pine nuts on the top of the batter. Bake in a preheated 350° oven for 30 to 35 minutes.

In a small pan heat all of the ingredients for the syrup. Boil the syrup until it begins to thicken a bit, about 6 minutes. Remove from the heat and cool until just very warm to touch. Hold a saucer over the cake and drizzle the warm syrup onto the saucer and thus onto the cake. This will prevent your marring the surface of the cake.

Cover the cake pan with plastic wrap and allow the cake to sit for 2 hours so that the syrup will be absorbed.

BAKLAVA

It seems silly for me to give you a recipe for baklava when I know that you are not going to make the phyllo dough from scratch. It takes years to learn to do this, and I have tried several times. Mrs. Stergachis, my Greek friend in Tacoma, makes all of her phyllo by hand, and she supplies me with baklava for my restaurants. I could not believe the work involved, and she is still making the pastries for our Greek Orthodox Church.

Buy 2 pounds of phyllo dough from your Greek market or delicatessen. A recipe for baklava will be on the side of the box and you can bake the dish yourself. Pulling your own phyllo? Forget it.

STRAWBERRY YOGURT WITH HONEY

This is a classic dessert in Athens. There are shops just off Omonia Square that specialize in this very thing. It is great to sit in the Greek sun and enjoy a cool dish of yogurt made very sweet with fine Greek honey.

In the States one can simply purchase strawberry yogurt in the supermarket. Place a bit in a small bowl and drizzle a bit of good honey over the top.

Greek Heaven!

HALVAH

Sesame halvah can be purchased in fancy food stores and in Middle Eastern markets and delicatessens. It is a wonderful candy that is simply eaten at the close of the meal, as a dessert. It goes great with strong coffee. You will see it in several flavors, including vanilla and chocolate marbled.

COFFEE FRAPPÉ

The street cafés around the great Omonia Square in Athens serve a coffee drink that is very refreshing, and a great summer dessert. They call it a frappé, and it is served in tall glasses. You can make one with little effort.

Make some strong espresso coffee and chill it. Put 1 cup of whole milk, plus 2 tablespoons whipping cream, in a food blender and whip it a bit. Add coffee to taste, along with a bit of sugar, and whip again. Serve in a tall chilled glass.

ITALY

RICOTTA PIE, ROMAN STYLE
(Crostata di Ricotta alla Romana)

SERVES 8–10

I met the most wonderful woman in Rome. Her name is Jo Bettoja and she is married to a very famous Italian hotel owner. She has lived in Rome for more than twenty years but she was born in Georgia! She teaches Roman women how to cook American, Southern style, and she is good. She offered me this dish as being typical of old Roman eating. The dried fruits and pine nuts certainly bear out her case. This kind of baking is very old indeed. Mrs. Bettoja also teaches Americans how to cook Italian and she does know her history.

THE PASTRY

2½ cups all-purpose flour

½ cup plus 1 table-
spoon sugar

3 egg yolks, beaten

Grated zest (outer peel)
of ½ lemon

10 tablespoons unsalted
butter, at cool room
temperature

THE FILLING

1 pound ricotta cheese

1 cup sugar

2 eggs

2 ounces white raisins,
soaked in rum to cover
for 2 hours, and drained

2 ounces citron or green
candied lemon peel, cut
in a small dice

⅓ cup pine nuts, toasted in
a 375° oven until just
barely browned

Butter and dust with flour a 10-inch cheesecake pan with removable sides.

Place the flour for the crust in a large mixing bowl and make a well in the center. Add the sugar, egg yolks, lemon zest, and butter, cut into small pieces. Mix by pinching and rubbing the ingredients together until the consistency of coarse meal. Add a tablespoon of water, or perhaps 2, in order to form a dough. Knead just a couple of times.

NOTE: If using a food processor for this step, use well-chilled butter and just throw all of the ingredients into the machine. Process and add the water if you need it.

Cut the pastry into two pieces, one a little larger for the bottom crust. Roll out to about ⅛-inch thickness. (I find that a marble sheet and marble rolling pin work well for this.) Detach the pastry from the surface with a spatula or long knife and drape over the rolling pin. Unroll over the cake pan, leaving some overhang.

Cream the ricotta with the sugar, add all the other ingredients for the filling, and mix well. Pour this into the prepared cake pan. Roll out the remaining pastry and cut into ¾-inch-wide strips. Lay the strips across the pie in a lattice. Pinch or crimp the edges of the strips to the crust to seal.

Bake in a preheated 375° oven for 45 minutes or until lightly browned. Cool on a rack for 15 minutes before turning out. Serve warm or at room temperature.

SWEET CHESTNUT PURÉE

MAKES 2 CUPS
FOR USE IN DESSERTS

You can buy this product already made from fresh chestnuts . . . and it costs a fortune. This version will do you nicely for desserts and cake sauces and it will cost much less.

1 *pound dried chestnuts,*
  soaked overnight

1 *cup sugar*

⅛ *teaspoon lemon extract*

1 *teaspoon salt*

½ *cup brandy*

Drain the soaked chestnuts and rinse. Place in a 2-quart pot and cover with water. Bring to a boil, covered, and simmer for 1 hour or until tender. Drain, reserving the water.

Grind the chestnuts in a medium-size food processor until smooth. This will have to be done in 2 batches. Use some of the reserved liquid to get a smooth and very thick paste. Remove to a saucepan and add the remaining ingredients, along with enough of the reserved water to make a purée of desired consistency. Heat gently for about 5 minutes to dissolve the sugar.

WINE AND COOKIES

This old Roman custom is a delight. No preparation, no pain, and all of your guests will be delighted.

At the end of a heavy Roman meal, serve glasses of Vin Santo, available at Italian specialty shops, or you can use a good dry Marsala. A plate of *ghiottini*, almond cookies, are passed with the glasses. The fun comes when you instruct everyone to dip their cookies in the wonderful dessert wine. The flavor is ancient and contemporary, all at once.

ITALIAN CHESTNUT JAM CAKE

SERVES 8–10

This is a very dramatic presentation, though I have taken some gross liberties with this recipe. The older versions are just too complex to bother with and this one is both simple and delicious.

1 *pound cake, sliced horizontally into 3 equal layers*

SYRUP
Rind of one lemon, grated
1 *teaspoon vanilla*
½ *cup brandy*
½ *cup sugar*
2 *cups Sweet Chestnut Purée (page 500)*

BUTTERCREAM FROSTING
2 *sticks soft butter*
2½ *cups powdered or confectioner's sugar*
1 *teaspoon vanilla*
1 *egg white*

GARNISH:
1 *cup sliced almonds, toasted*
2 *milk-chocolate bars*

Mix the ingredients for the syrup together and heat for a moment on the stove or in the microwave. Dribble this mixture on all 3 slices of cake. Spread the chestnut purée on 2 of the slices and place on top of each other, the bare slice going on top.

Mix all of the ingredients for the icing with an electric mixer. Whip until light and smooth. Ice the cake and top with the toasted almonds. Melt the chocolate bars in a glass measuring cup in the microwave. Then stir in enough very hot water to make a very thick syrup. Dribble this over the top of the cake and allow to cool.

Epilogue
The Earth Is Too Small
for Private Dinner Parties

I am always concerned when I see a person in the supermarket with a basket filled with private food. You know what I mean by private food, of course. Little packages of instant and prepared foods that indicate that this person intends to eat alone again tonight. We see a lot of this among the older members of our culture, and we always mumble something about being pleased with their sense of independence. It may not be independence. It may be simple loneliness.

The three ancient cultures that we have looked at in this volume did not, and do not, understand private eating. For one thing it was economically impossible to eat by yourself in the early days. The fuel for the kitchen was too expensive, and the idea of living by yourself was unheard of. In America we claim that we value privacy and independence, and have therefore put a whole life-style on the market based on the ability to get along without anyone else. That is what private foods mean. We have sought a time of independence for everyone in our culture . . . and I am convinced that the result has not been pride in privacy, but rather an insight into the fact that privatude, in the end, offers only one thing—and that is loneliness.

Great food is not to be eaten by oneself. Eating privately is simply learning to sustain yourself, but dining is always done with other people. Please reconsider the plight of the people you know who live by themselves. Invite them in for a Roman dinner party, or for a Chinese or Greek dinner party. You and your children will be richer for it and your children will understand that the table is the proper place for sharing. And your guest? He or she, at the end of the evening, will give you a hug and say, "When can I come back?" That is what the ancient table was for . . . and what the table should be for in our time.

I bid you Peace.

Bibliography

*Indicates books of which I am particularly fond. You should look at them.

Allen, Jana, and Margaret Gin. *Innards and Other Variety Meats* (San Francisco: 101 Productions, 1974).

Bianchini, Francesco, and Francesco Corbetta. *The Complete Book of Fruits and Vegetables* (New York: Crown Publishers, Inc., 1973).

Boni, Ada. *Italian Regional Cooking* (New York: Bonanza Books, 1969).

Boni, Ada. *The Talisman Italian Cookbook* (New York: Crown Publishers, 1950).

Brennen, Jennifer. *The Cuisines of Asia: Nine Great Oriental Cuisines by Technique* (New York: Martin's/Marek, 1984).

Buehr, Wendy, editor in charge. *The Horizon Cookbook and Illustrated History of Eating and Drinking Through the Ages* (New York: American Heritage Publishing Company, 1968).

Bugialli, Giuliano. *Classic Techniques of Italian Cooking* (New York: Simon and Schuster, 1982).

Bugialli, Giuliano. *Foods of Italy* (New York: Stewart, Tabori, and Chang, 1984).

Burum, Linda. *Asian Pasta* (New York: Aris Books, 1985).

*Chang, K. C., ed. *Food in Chinese Culture* (New Haven: Yale University Press, 1977).

Chantiles, Vilma Liacouras. *The Food of Greece* (New York: Dodd, Mead, and Co., 1975).

Chinese American Women's Club of Santa Clara County. *Chinese Cooking Our Way* (Campbell, Calif.: Phoenix Press, 1971).

Chinese Parents Service Organization. *Flavors of China* (Seattle: Trinity Printing, 1975).
  Address: Trinity Printing, P.O. Box 68922, Seattle, Washington 98188.

Coyle, L. Patrick. *World Encyclopedia of Food.* (New York: Facts on File, 1982).

Cronin, Israel. *The International Squid Book* (New York: Aris Books, 1981).

Davidson, Alan. *Mediterranean Seafood* (New York: Penguin, 1981).

Defenbacher, D. S. (based on exhibition prepared by the Walker Art Center, Minneapolis). *Knife, Fork and Spoon* (Colwell Press, 1951).

di Schino, June. *L'Eterno Banchetto* (Rome: Commune di Roma, Assessorato alla Cultura, 1987).

Dosi, A., and F. Schnell. *Le Abitudini Alimentari dei Romani* (Rome: Edizioni Quasar, 1986).

Dosi, A., and F. Schnell. *Pasti e Vasellame da Tavola* (Rome: Edizioni Quasar, 1986).

Dosi, A., and F. Schnell. *I Romani in Cucina* (Rome: Edizioni Quasar, 1986).

*Edwards, John. *The Roman Cookery of Apicius* (Point Roberts, Wash.: Hartley and Marks, 1984).

Elegant, Robert, and the editors of Time-Life Books. *Hong Kong* (Alexandria, Va.: Time-Life Books, 1977).

Ellwanger, George. *The Pleasures of the Table* (New York: Doubleday Page, 1902).

Field, Carol. *The Italian Baker* (New York: Harper and Row, 1985).

Grist, D. H. *Rice* (London: Longman, Green, and Co., 1955).

Gunther, John. *Twelve Cities* (New York: Harper & Row, 1976).

Hale, William Harlan, editor in charge. *The Horizon Book of Ancient Greece* (New York: American Heritage Publishing Co., 1965).

Hazan, Marcella. *The Classic Italian Cookbook* (New York: Alfred A. Knopf, 1980).

Hazan, Marcella. *Marcella's Italian Kitchen* (New York: Alfred A. Knopf, 1986).

*Hom, Ken, *Asian Vegetarian Feast* (New York: William Morrow, 1988).

Kubly, Herbert. *Italy* (New York: Time-Life Books, 1965).

Lassen, Erik. *Knives, Forks, and Spoons* (Copenhagen: Host and Son, 1960).

Liebman, Malvina W., *From Caravan to Casserole: Herbs and Spices in Legend, History and Recipes* (Miami: Seemann 1977).

*Lin, Florence. *Florence Lin's Complete Book of Chinese Noodles, Dumplings and Bread,* (New York: William Morrow, 1986).

Lin, Hsiang Ju, and Tsui Feng Lin. *Chinese Gastronomy* (New York: Hastings House, 1969).

McNeil, William H. *History of Western Civilization* (Chicago: University of Chicago Press, 1986).

McNeil, William H. *The Rise of the West* (Chicago: University of Chicago Press, 1963).

*Mark, Willy. *Chinese Cookery Masterclass* (London; Macdonald & Co., 1984).

*Middione, Carlo. *The Food of Southern Italy* (New York: William Morrow, 1987).

Mock, Lonnie. *Favorite Dim Sum* (Walnut Creek, Calif.: Alpha Gamma Arts, 1979).

Montagne, Prosper. *The New Larousse Gastronomique* (New York: Crown Publishers, 1960).

*Norman, Barbara. *Tales of the Table* (Englewood Cliffs, N.J.:. Prentice-Hall, 1972).

Passmore, Jacki, and Daniel P. Reid. *The Complete Chinese Cookbook* (Los Angeles: Exeter Books, 1982).

*Pei Mei. *Pei Mei's Chinese Cook Book,* Volumes I, II, and III (Taipei, Taiwan, R.O.C.: Industrial Company, Ltd., P.O. Box 53-319).

Perl, Lila. *Rice, Spice and Bitter Oranges.* (Cleveland: World Publishing Co., 1967).

Revel, Jean-Francois. *Culture and Cuisine,* (Jersey City, N.J.: Da Capo Press, 1982).

Richards, Ersie, and Maria-Daphne Mavrelli. *The Tastes of Greece* (Athens: United Travel Press, Ltd., 1985).

Root, Waverly. *Food* (New York: Simon & Schuster, Inc., 1980).

*Root, Waverly. *The Food of Italy* (New York: Vintage Books, 1977).

Rudofsky, Bernard. *Now I Lay Me Down to Eat* (New York: Anchor Books, 1980).

*St. Demetrios Cookbook Committee. *Greek Cooking in an American Kitchen* (Seattle: 1982).
   Address: St. Demetrios Cookbook, 2100 Boyer Avenue East, Seattle, Washington 98122; cost is $20,00.

Seranne, Ann, and John Tebbel. *The Epicure's Companion* (New York: David McKay Co., Inc., 1962).

Sheraton, Mimi. *Time,* November 19, 1984, p. 143.

Simon, Andre L., and Robin Howe. *Dictionary of Gastronomy* (New York: McGraw-Hill, 1970).

Slomon, Evelyn. *The Pizza Book* (New York: Times Books, 1984).

Spoerri, Daniel. *Mythology and Meatballs* (New York: Aris, 1982).

Editors of Sunset Books and Sunset Magazine. *Sunset Chinese Cookbook* (Menlo Park, Calif.: Lane Publishing Company, 1979).

*Tannahill, Reay. *Food in History* (New York: Stein and Day, 1973).

Trager, James. *Foodbook* (New York: Grossman Publishers, 1970).

*Tselementes, Nicholas. *Greek Cookery* (New York: D.C. Divry, Inc., 1967).

Von Welanetz, Paul and Diana. *The Von Welanetz Guide to Ethnic Ingredients* (Los Angeles: J. P. Tarcher, Inc., 1982).

*Yianilos, Theresa Karas. *The Complete Greek Cookbook: The Best From Three Thousand Years of Greek Cooking* (New York: Funk and Wagnalls, 1970).

Encyclopedia Americana (Danbury, Conn.: Grolier, Inc., 1987).

Index

A

abalone:
  dried, with mushrooms, 336–337
  and mushrooms, 458–459
  soup, 115–116
almond(s):
  cherries in, 493–494
  cream soup, sweet, 495
  halvah cake, 496–497
  sesame chicken wings, 241
appetizers and first courses, 80–92
  antipasti bar, 90
  artichokes, chilled, Roman style, 401–402
  artichokes, stuffed Roman style, 403
  artichokes steamed with pesto, 402
  baby snails in Greek tomato sauce, 183
  baby snails in Italian tomato sauce, 184
  cheese pies, 88–89
  Chinese brine pickles, 83
  Chinese cold plate, 82
  cold chow fun and pork roll, 351
  glass noodles with peanut sauce, 356–557

gnocchi with cheese, 395
green tubes with meat sauce, 372
headcheese, 92
headcheese salad, 332
leek cakes, 451
looed beef, 312
looed beef tongue, 321–322
mortadella, 92
mushrooms stuffed with feta cheese, 462–463
pappardelle with pesto, 370
pasta all'amatriciana, 362
pasta carbonara, Roman style, 366–367
pasta carbonara with mustard, 367
pasta ears with cauliflower, 365–366
pasta ties with cabbage, 369
pasta with garlic and eggs, 364
pasta with mizithra, 357–58
penne carbonara, 367–368
peperonata, 91–92
pork tripe in hot sauce, 323
risotto with champagne, 384–385
risotto with mushrooms, 383
risotto with mushrooms and herbs, 384

risotto with seafood, 385–386
roasted quail appetizers Homer, 269
salted cod in tomato sauce, 343
shrimp Ananius, 181–182
smelt antipasti, 90–91
spinach pies, 89
stuffed grape leaves with egg-lemon
    sauce, 380–381
tahini bean dip, 88
taramasalata, 87
tzatziki, 86–87
walnuts fried with sugar, 85
see also salads; soups
appliances and machines, 17
artichokes, 398–405
    beans, and peas, 423–424
    chilled, Roman style, 401–402
    cleaning, Roman style, 400
    in Greek tomato sauce, 405
    with ham on toast, 403–404
    Jewish style, 400–401
    leeks and, 452
    with potatoes, Greek style, 404–405
    sautéed in wine, 401
    steamed with pesto, 402
    stuffed Roman style, 403
asparagus, 406–413
    with beef and black beans, 408–409
    blanching, Apicius, 411–412
    with cheese and eggs, Italian style,
        413
    cleaning, 407
    cold, Chinese style, 407–408
    cold, Greek style, 409
    custard Apicius, 412
    with oil and tomato, Greek style,
        409–410
    pickled, Greek style, 410–411
    scallop, and mushroom soup, 121

B

banana fritters, candied, 493
barley pudding with lamb, 283
bean(s), 414–424
    artichokes, and peas, 423–424
    black-eyed pea salad Sigalas, 419–
        420
    chestnuts and lentils Apicius, 433
    dip, tahini, 88

fava, with leeks, 453
fresh fava, Roman style, 422
green, water chestnuts and, 429
and leeks Apicius, 452–453
lima, with Greek tomato sauce,
    418–419
lima, with lettuce and onion, 422–
    423
long green, with beef, 417–418
and pasta soup, 412–422
white, Greek style, 420
bean(s), black:
    asparagus with beef and, 408–409
    chicken chowed with, 235–236
    with chicken salad, 139
    garlic ribs with green pepper and,
        106
    meatballs with green pepper and,
        311
    pork with leeks and, 449–450
    sauce, crab in, 178–179
    sauce, hot, smoked side of pork
        with, 291
    spareribs with, 297–298
    spareribs with, in sand pot, 298
    spareribs with pepper sauce and, 105
    steamed fish with, 160
bean curd:
    fish with olives and, 161
    with pork, 416–417
    side of pork with cod and, in sand
        pot, 296–297
    skin, stuffed, pan-fried, 102
    smoked, 416
    soup, 114
    steamed fish with soybean condi-
        ment and, 158
    stuffed, 103
bean sprout and Szechwan pepper
    salad, 139
beef, 305–319
    asparagus with black beans and,
        408–409
    avoiding high cost of flank steak,
        308
    and chestnut stew, Chinese, 427
    chow fun, 351–352
    filled ravioli, Roman-Jewish style,
        394
    fried meatballs, 314

beef (*continued*)
    ginger, 309–310
    hamburgers, Greek style, 315
    long green beans with, 417–418
    looed, 312
    looed, in sand pot, 312–313
    meatballs, 107–108
    meatballs in tomato sauce, 314
    Mongolian, 306–307
    oyster, 309
    pepper onion, 308
    poached meatballs in egg and lemon
        sauce, 313–314
    pot roast shredded, 318
    Roman Jewish style, 315–316
    slices with rosemary, 316
    on a stick, Roman style, 319
    stock, basic brown, 132
    tongue, looed, 321–322
    tongue in sweet and sour sauce,
        Roman style, 333
    tripe, Roman style, 329–330
black-eyed pea salad Sigalas, 419–420
breads, 470–483
    ancient Roman, 480–481
    breadsticks, Italian sesame, 481–482
    Chinese steamed, 472–473
    corn crepes, Chinese style, 473–474
    crustulum, 482
    focaccia Romana, 482–483
    Greek Easter, 478–479
    Greek sesame, 477
    noodle cutter for making bread-
        sticks, 482
    old Greek, 475–477
    olive, 483
    olive rolls, 483
    onion cakes, 475
    Peking pancakes, 474–475
    pita, with olive oil, grilled, 479
    Roman, 481
    sesame circles, 478
    sesame dragon mouths, 473
    strips, Chinese fried, 472
    see also pizza

C

cabbage:
    boiled leeks with, Apicius, 453–454

Greek village salad with, 144–145
    pasta ties with, 369
cakes:
    halvah, 496–497
    Italian chestnut jam, 501
cannelloni, 362–363
cauliflower, pasta ears with, 365–366
celery:
    fish fillets stir-fried with, 157–158
    fish with, in a hot plate, 156
    and mushroom salad Savini, 149–
        150
    pork with, Greek style, 302–303
    velveted scallops in, 176
cheese:
    asparagus with eggs and, Italian
        style, 413
    feta, mushrooms stuffed with, 462–
        463
    feta, shrimp in Greek tomato sauce
        with, 182–183
    fontina, grilled eggplant and, 446
    gnocchi with, 395
    lamb with pasta and, 279–280
    mizithra, pasta with, 357–358
    pappardelle with telephone wires,
        371–372
    pies, 88–89
    ricotta frittata, 227
    ricotta pie, Roman style, 498–499
    shaving, 151
    and spinach ravioli, 394
cherries in almond, 493–494
chestnut(s), 425–433
    and beef stew, Chinese, 427
    Chinese chicken with, 428
    focaccia, 486–487
    jam cake, Italian, 501
    and lentils Apicius, 433
    pasta, 432
    Peking dust, 495–496
    polenta, 432–433
    puree, sweet, 500
    roasted, 430
    soaked in ouzo, 431
    soaked in wine, 431
    wild greens and, 431
chestnut(s), water:
    flour, shrimp chowed with gin and,
        429–430

green beans and, 429
chicken, 229–247
  baked with honey and soy sauce, 232
  balls, fried garlic, 237
  beggar's, 233–234
  with black bean salad, 139
  Chinese, with chestnuts, 428
  and Chinese chive shu-mei, 106–107
  Chinese poached, 230–231
  Chinese sesame, 242–243
  chowed with black beans, 235–236
  devil's, 245–246
  fricassee of, Roman style, 244–245
  with leek belts, 450–451
  looed, 240–241
  mushroom shredded, 459
  and pork in lettuce, 238–239
  quick Chinese roast, 242
  roasted, Greek style, 243
  roast "lung kong," 240
  roast salt, 231–232
  roll, Greek style, 244
  roll, Roman style, 247
  salad, Ming's, 140–142
  shredded, sesame, 84
  shu-mei, 106
  soup stock, Chinese, 113–114
  and spinach ravioli, 392–393
  steamed with Chinese sausage, 238
  stock, basic, 129
  with sweet bell peppers, 246
  and sweet corn soup, velvet, 122
  with two onions in sand pot, 234–235
  wings, sesame almond, 241
  wings in five spice, 236–237
China, 52–61
Chinese herbs and spices, 39–40
Chinese ingredients, 28–35
chive(s):
  Chinese, and chicken shu-mei, 106–107
  and dried scallop soup, 337
  garlic, pork and, 292–293
  garlic, scallops with, 175
chowing, hints for, 293, 307
chow mein, Cantonese style, 347–348
chow mein noodles, to freeze, 348

cod, salted:
  in cream sauce, 342–343
  Greek style, 341
  in tomato sauce, 343
cod, side of pork with bean curd and, in sand pot, 296–297
coffee frappé, 498
condiments, 28–38, 212–215
  oenogarum, 215
  pinzimonio, 214
  roasted salt and pepper, 266
  Szechwan pepper and salt dip, 202
  see also sauces
cookies:
  Chinese sesame, 494
  wine and, 500
cooking methods and terms, 23–27
corn:
  baby, and quail eggs, 225
  crepes, Chinese style, 473–474
  sweet, and chicken soup, velvet, 122
crab (meat):
  in black bean sauce, 178–179
  fried milk with, 180–181
  garlic-steamed, 179
  with soybean condiment, 179–180
crepes, corn, Chinese style, 473–474
crustulum, 482
custard, fried, 492

D

desserts, 489–501
  baklava, 497
  candied banana fritters, 493
  cherries in almond, 493–494
  Chinese sesame cookies, 494
  coffee frappé, 498
  eight-treasure rice pudding, 490–492
  fried custard, 492
  halvah, 497–498
  halvah cake, 496–497
  Italian chestnut jam cake, 501
  Peking dust, 495–496
  ricotta pie, Roman style, 498–499
  strawberry yogurt with honey, 497
  sweet almond cream soup, 495
  sweet chestnut puree, 500
  wine and cookies, 500

dim sum, 93–110
    barbecued pork strips, 288–289
    beef meatballs, 107–108
    chicken and Chinese chive shu-mei, 106–107
    chicken shu-mei, 106
    cold chow fun and pork roll, 351
    deep-fried shu-mei, 100
    eggplant stuffed with shrimp, 98–99
    fried wontons, 108
    fun gor, 101–102
    garlic ribs with green pepper and black beans, 106
    ha gow, 95–97
    hot and spicy squid, 109
    meat-stuffed chow fun rolls, 353
    pork and taro meatballs, 100
    pork shu-mei, 99–100
    pork tripe in hot sauce, 323
    quail egg shu-mei, 100
    shrimp ball with pine nuts, 98
    shrimp boats, 97
    shrimp-stuffed mushrooms, 98
    shrimp toast, 97
    spareribs with black beans and pepper sauce, 105
    spicy pork tripe, 104
    steamed meat-stuffed buns, 109–110
    steamed pot stickers, 101
    stuffed bean curd, 103
    stuffed bean curd skin, pan-fried, 102
    wrappers, tortilla press for making, 97
dips, 201–202
    tahini bean, 88
    taramasalata, 87
    tzatziki, 86–87
dried foods, 334–343
    abalone, with mushrooms, 336–337
    duck, and pork, steamed, 257
    duck, Chinese sausage, and roast pork, sand pot, 340
    jellyfish, and duck salad, 138
    jellyfish, salad, 137–138
    oysters, and pork in lettuce, 338
    scallop, and chive soup, 337
    squid, steamed pork with mushroom and, 339

dried salt cod:
    in cream sauce, 342–343
    Greek style, 341
    in tomato sauce, 343
duck, 251–263
    Chinese roast, 252–253
    dried, Chinese sausage, and roast pork sand pot, 340
    feet, looed, 260–261
    Greek, with olives, 261–262
    grilled Greek style, 262
    and jellyfish salad, 138
    like a mandolin, 255
    Peking, 254–255
    salad, Chinese, 259
    soup, Chinese style, 259–260
    steamed dried, and pork, 257
    stewed, with mushrooms, 256
    tea-smoked, 258
    with turnips Apicius, 263
dumplings, 387–396
    beef-filled ravioli, Roman-Jewish style, 394
    cheese and spinach ravioli, 394
    chicken and spinach ravioli, 392–393
    Chinese boiled, 388–389
    coteghino–filled ravioli, 394
    to freeze gnocchi, 396
    to freeze ravioli, 393
    gnocchi fried, 396
    gnocchi with cheese, 395
    gnocchi with sauce Bolognese, 396
    lettuce circles for steaming, 107
    pot stickers, 390
    rolled, 390–391
    wonton, 391–392

E

egg(s), 222–227
    asparagus custard Apicius, 412
    asparagus with cheese and, Italian style, 413
    avgolemono soup, 126–127
    mushroom omelet Apicius, 465
    pasta with garlic and, 364
    and peas soup, 115
    and pork with tree fungus in pancakes, 460–461

quail, baby corn and, 225
quail, shu-mei, 100
ricotta frittata, 227
Roman "rag" soup, 133
salted, 224–225
salted, steamed pork with, 226
tea, 223–224
egg-lemon sauce, 205
  poached meatballs in, 313–314
  stuffed grape leaves with, 380–381
  tripe soup with, 325–326
eggplant, 434–446
  broiled, Bologna, 444–445
  grilled, fontina and, 446
  moussaka, 440–442
  with pork, Chinese style, 436
  and pork Mandar-Inn, 438–439
  Roman style, 445–446
  salad, 444
  shoes, 442
  slices baked, 443
  with soybean condiment and hoisin
    sauce, 437
  stuffed Greek style, 439–440
  stuffed with shrimp, 98–99
  wedges, broiled, 445

F

fava beans:
  fresh, Roman style, 422
  with leeks, 453
fennel:
  in innards, 327
  salad, Roman style, 150
feta cheese:
  mushrooms stuffed with, 462–463
  pies, 88–89
  shrimp in Greek tomato sauce with,
    182–183
first courses, see appetizers and first
    courses
fish, 154–167
  baked, Archestratus, 164
  braised, Oi Mann, 159–160
  with celery in a hot plate, 156
  chowder, Greek, 163
  cutting, 271
  fillets stir-fried with celery, 157–158
  fillets with sesame, 161–162
  grilled Greek style, 164–165

and lettuce soup, 119
with olives and bean curd, 161
pan-fried, with oil and lemon juice,
    167
removing smell of, from deep-frying
    oil, 160
salad, Chinese, 142–143
salted cod, Greek style, 341
salted cod in cream sauce, 342–343
salted cod in tomato sauce, 343
sardine and macaroni salad, 145
side of pork with cod and bean curd
    in sand pot, 296–297
small, deep-fried in olive oil, 162–
    163
smelt antipasti, 90–91
soup, Italian, 131
  soup avgolemono, 127–128
  steamed, with black beans, 160
  steamed, with soybean condiment
    and bean curd, 158
  stew for Christmas Eve, 166–167
  stock, 126
focaccia:
  chestnut, 486–487
  Romana, 482–483
food definitions, 28–38
fungus:
  tree, pork and egg with, in pan-
    cakes, 460–461
  white soup, 461

G

game birds, see poultry
garbanzo beans:
  pizza, old Roman style, 485–486
  polenta, 370–371
  tahini bean dip, 88
garlic:
  chicken balls, fried, 237
  crustulum, 482
  finely chopped, 178
  game hens with rosemary and, 271
  pasta with eggs and, 364
  ribs with green pepper and black
    beans, 106
  sauce, 206
  spinach with olive oil, lemon and,
    Greek style, 467
  steamed lobster or crab, 179

ginger:
  beef, 309–310
  to clean deep-frying oil, 160, 468
gnocchi:
  with cheese, 395
  to freeze, 396
  fried, 396
  with sauce Bolognese, 396
goose, 248–250
  Chiu Chow style, 250
  looed, 249
grape leaves, stuffed, with egg-lemon
    sauce, 380–381
Greece, 62–69
Greek herbs and spices, 41–42
Greek ingredients, 35–36
greens, wild, and chestnuts, 431

H

halvah, 497–498
  cake, 496–497
ham:
  adding to soups, 123
  artichokes with, on toast, 403–404
hamburgers, Greek style, 315
headcheese:
  appetizer, 92
  salad, 332
herbs, 39–43
honey:
  chicken baked with soy sauce and,
    232
  strawberry yogurt with, 497

I

ingredients, 28–38
innards, 320–333
  anise or fennel in, 327
  fried, Roman style Edmondo, 331–
    332
  grilled liver, Greek style, 325
  headcheese appetizer, 92
  headcheese salad, 332
  lamb innard soup for Easter, 327–
    328
  looed beef tongue, 321–322
  looed beef tripe, 322
  oxtails, Roman style, 330–331

pork tripe in hot sauce, 323
  spicy pork tripe, 104
  stewed oxtail, Chinese style, 324
  tongue in sweet and sour sauce,
    Roman style, 333
  tripe, Roman style, 329–330
  tripe soup with egg-lemon sauce,
    325–326
Italian herbs and spices, 42–43
Italian ingredients, 36–38

J

jellyfish salad, 137–138
  duck and, 138

K

kitchen equipment, 15–22
knives, 15–16

L

lamb, 274–285
  barley pudding with, 283
  with cheese and pasta, 279–280
  cubes, grilled, Greek style, 285
  fried innards, Roman style Ed-
    mondo, 331–332
  hot pot, Mongolian style, 276–277
  innard soup for Easter, 327–328
  and leeks, Chinese, 448–449
  Mongolian, 277–278
  with orzo pasta, Greek style, 280–
    281
  and pasta salad, Greek, 146
  rib chops, broiled Greek style, 282
  rib chops, broiled Roman style, 285
  roast, Greek style, 281
  roast, Italian style, 285
  souvlaki, 282
  stock, basic, 128
  stuffed grape leaves with egg-lemon
    sauce, 380–381
  stuffed tomatoes Hydra, 381–382
  and tomato sauce, Greek style, 278–
    279
leek(s), 447–452
  artichokes and, 452

and beans Apicius, 452–453
belts, chicken with, 450–451
boiled, with cabbage Apicius, 453–454
cakes, 451
Chinese lamb and, 448–449
cleaning, 448
fava beans with, 453
and juniper berries, 454–455
pork with black beans and, 449–450
sautéed, 452
lemon:
avgolemono soup, 126–127
juice, pan-fried fish with oil and, 167
juice, spinach with olive oil, garlic and, Greek style, 467
squid with oil and, 193
lemon-egg sauce, 205
poached meatballs in, 313–314
stuffed grape leaves with, 380–381
tripe soup with, 325–326
lentils and chestnuts Apicius, 433
lettuce:
adding to soups, 121
chicken and pork in, 238–239
circles, for steaming small dumplings, 107
cups, to prepare, 339
dried oysters and pork in, 338
and fish soup, 119
with foo yee, 467
lima beans with onion and, 422–423
liver, grilled, Greek style, 325
lobster, garlic-steamed, 179
luncheon main courses:
artichokes with ham on toast, 403–404
cheese pies, 88–89
Chinese sausage on steamed rice, 379
eggplant, Roman style, 445–446
Greek lamb and pasta salad, 146
Ming's chicken salad, 140–142
noodles in oyster sauce, 354

M

macaroni and sardine salad, 145
machines and appliances, 17

main courses:
baked fish Archestratus, 164
barley pudding with lamb, 283
beef, Roman Jewish style, 315–316
beef on a stick, Roman style, 319
chicken roll, Greek style, 244
chicken roll, Roman style, 247
chicken with sweet bell peppers, 246
devil's chicken, 245–246
duck grilled Greek style, 262
duck with turnips Apicius, 263
fish grilled Greek style, 164–165
fish stew for Christmas Eve, 166–167
fricassee of chicken, Roman style, 244–245
fried meatballs, 314
game hens with rosemary and garlic, 271
goose, Chiu Chow style, 250
Greek duck with olives, 261–262
grilled lamb cubes, Greek style, 285
grilled liver, 325
grilled squab, Greek style, 269–270
ground meat on skewers, 284
hamburgers, Greek style, 315
lamb and tomato sauce, Greek style, 278–279
lamb hot pot, Mongolian style, 276–277
lamb rib chops, broiled Greek style, 282
lamb rib chops, broiled Roman style, 285
lamb with cheese and pasta, 279–280
lamb with orzo pasta, Greek style, 280–281
meatballs, Roman style, 317–318
meatballs, in tomato sauce, 314
moussaka, 440–442
octopus in wine and tomato sauce, 197
octopus spaghetti Zorba, 196
oxtails, Roman style, 330–331
pan-fried fish with oil and lemon juice, 167
pasta with zucchini, 361
poached meatballs in egg and lemon sauce, 313–314

main courses (*continued*)
  pork souvlaki, 303
  pork with celery, Greek style, 302–303
  pot roast shredded, 318
  quail in tomato sauce, Greek style, 268
  quail or squab in creamed Italian sauce, 272
  quick Chinese roast chicken, 242
  roasted chicken, Greek style, 243
  roast lamb, Greek style, 281
  roast lamb, Italian style, 285
  roast "lung kong" chicken, 240
  roast pork, Roman style, 303–304
  roast quail Edmondo, 270
  rustic pizza, 488
  shrimp Ananius, 181–182
  shrimp in Greek tomato sauce with feta, 182–183
  souvlaki, 282
  spareribs with black beans in sand pot, 298
  squid pilaf, 192–193
  stewed oxtail, Chinese style, 324
  stuffed squid, Greek style, 194
  tripe, Roman style, 329–330
  see also luncheon main courses
meat(s), 273–333
  boiled, green sauce for, 209–210
  browning, 317
  cannelloni, 362–363
  Chinese sausage, chicken steamed with, 238
  Chinese sausage, dried duck, and roast pork sand pot, 340
  Chinese sausage on steamed rice, 379
  coteghino-filled ravioli, 394
  eggplant stuffed Greek style, 439–440
  fried innards, Roman style Edmondo, 331–332
  grilled liver, 325
  ground, on skewers, 284
  headcheese salad, 332
  innards, 320–333
  meatballs, Roman style, 317–318
  meatballs with black beans and green pepper, 311

moussaka, 440–442
oxtails, Roman style, 330–331
sauce, green tubes with, 372
smoked meatballs, 310–311
souvlaki, 282
stewed oxtail, Chinese style, 324
sticky sweet rice with, 377–378
stuffed buns, steamed, 109–110
stuffed chow fun rolls, 353
tongue in sweet and sour sauce, Roman style, 333
tripe, Roman style, 329–330
tripe soup with egg-lemon sauce, 325–326
tuna sauce for, 210
wonton dumplings, 391–392
see also beef; lamb; pork
meatballs:
  beef, 107–108
  bird's nest, 299–300
  with black beans and green pepper, 311
  fried, 314
  to keep from sticking to hands, 108
  pearl, 300–301
  poached, in egg and lemon sauce, 313–314
  pork and taro, 100
  Roman style, 317–318
  smoked, 310–311
  in tomato sauce, 314
mortadella, 92
moussaka, 440–442
mushroom(s), 456–465
  abalone and, 458–459
  and celery salad Savini, 149–150
  dried abalone with, 336–337
  grilled, Roman style, 463
  omelet Apicius, 465
  pasta with, Natalie, 464
  pork and egg with tree fungus in pancakes, 460–461
  risotto with, 383
  risotto with herbs and, 384
  scallop, and asparagus soup, 121
  shredded chicken, 459
  shrimp-stuffed, 98
  soup, clear, 461–462
  steamed pork with dried squid and, 339

stewed duck with, 256
stuffed with feta cheese, 462–463
white fungus soup, 461
in wine and coriander Apicius, 465
mustard, hot Chinese, to make, 289

N

noodles, 344–357
beef chow fun, 351–352
bird's nest meatballs, 299–300
Chinese New Year, 355–356
Chinese New Year, with olives, 356
chowed, with pork and sesame
    sauce, 349
chow fun, 349–350
chow mein, Cantonese style, 347–
    348
cold chow fun and pork roll, 351
glass, with peanut sauce, 356–357
meat-stuffed chow fun rolls, 353
in oyster sauce, 354
see also pasta

O

octopus, 195–198
baby, salad, 198
salad, Greek style, 197–198
spaghetti Zorba, 196
in wine and tomato sauce, 197
oil, deep-frying, to keep clean, 160,
    468
olive(s), 219–221
bread, 482
Chinese, steamed pork with, 301
Chinese New Year noddles with, 356
fish with bean curd and, 161
Greek duck with, 261–262
green, soup, 134
and pepper salad, 152
rolls, 483
olive oil, 219–221
buying, 221
omelet, mushroom, Apicius, 465
onion(s):
cakes, 475
chicken with two, in sand pot, 234–
    235
green, sauce, 202
green, to sliver, 142

lima beans with lettuce and, 422–
    423
pepper beef, 308
ouzo:
chestnuts soaked in, 431
hamburgers, Greek style, 315
oxtail(s):
Roman style, 330–331
stewed, Chinese style, 324
oysters:
dried, and pork in lettuce, 338
and side of pork in sand pot, 295–
    296

P

pancakes:
corn crepes, Chinese style, 473–474
Peking, 474–475
pork and egg with tree fungus in,
    460–461
pans, 16–17
pappardelle:
with pesto, 370
with telephone wires, 371–372
parchment paper, substitute for, 101
pasta, 344–346, 357–372
all'amatriciana, 362
and bean soup, 421–422
cannelloni, 362–363
carbonara, Roman style, 366–367
carbonara with mustard, 367
chestnut, 432
cooking ahead of time, 368
cooking "al dente," 370
ears with cauliflower, 365–366
fresh, 368–369
with garlic and eggs, 364
green tubes with meat sauce, 372
and lamb salad, Greek, 146
lamb with cheese and, 279–280
with mizithra, 357–358
with mushrooms Natalie, 464
octopus spaghetti Zorba, 196
orzo, lamb with, Greek style, 280–
    281
pappardelle with pesto, 370
pappardelle with telephone wires,
    371–372
pastitsio, 358–360

pasta (continued)
   pastitsio baked with phyllo, 360
   penne carbonara, 367–368
   sardine and macaroni salad, 145
   with sweet red peppers and ancho-
      vies, 364–365
   ties with cabbage, 369
   with zucchini, 361
   see also dumplings; noodles
peanut sauce, glass noodles with, 356–
    357
peas:
   beans, and artichokes, 423–424
   and egg soup, 115
penne:
   carbonara, 367–368
   green tubes with meat sauce, 372
peperonata, 91–92
pepper, black:
   onion beef, 308
   roasted salt and, 266
   and salt dip, Szechwan, 202
   Szechwan, and bean sprout salad,
     139
pepper, hot:
   sauce, for seafood, 202
   sauce, spareribs with black beans
     and, 105
   and shrimp on an iron plate, 174–
     175
pepper(s), sweet bell:
   chicken with, 246
   green, garlic ribs with black beans
     and, 106
   green, meatballs with black beans
     and, 311
   and olive salad, 152
   and pork on iron plate, 294–295
   red, pasta with anchovies and, 364–
     365
   roasted, salad, Roman style, 151
   roasting, 151
pesto:
   artichokes steamed with, 402
   pappardelle with, 370
   sauce, 211
phyllo:
   cheese pies, 88–89
   pastitsio baked with, 360

spinach pies, 89
pickled asparagus, Greek style, 410–
    411
pickles, Chinese brine, 83
pie(s):
   cheese, 88–89
   ricotta, Roman style, 498–499
   spinach, 89
pine nuts, shrimp ball with, 98
pita bread with olive oil, grilled, 479
pizza, 484–488
   chestnut focaccia, 486–487
   dough, 487
   garbanzo, old Roman style, 485–486
   rustic, 488
   toppings, 487–488
polenta:
   chestnut, 432–433
   garbanzo, 370–371
pork, 286–304
   balls, deep-fried, 299
   barbecued spareribs, 289
   bean curd with, 416–417
   bird's nest meatballs, 299–300
   with celery, Greek style, 302–303
   and chicken in lettuce, 238–239
   Chinese boiled dumplings, 388–389
   chowed noodles with sesame sauce
     and, 349
   and chow fun roll, cold, 351
   crispy roast, 290
   dried oysters and, in lettuce, 338
   and eggplant Mandar-Inn, 438–439
   eggplant with, Chinese style, 436
   and egg with tree fungus in pan-
     cakes, 460–461
   fun gor, 101–102
   and garlic chives, 292–293
   garlic ribs with green pepper and
     black beans, 106
   with leeks and black beans, 449–
     450
   pearl meatballs, 300–301
   and peppers on iron plate, 294–295
   roast, Chinese sausage, and dried
     duck sand pot, 340
   roast, Roman style, 303–304
   roast, slow-simmered, 292
   rolled dumplings, 390–391

shu-mei, 99–100
side of, and oysters in sand pot, 295–296
side of, with cod and bean curd in sand pot, 296–297
smoked side of, 281
smoked side of, with hot black bean sauce, 291
souvlaki, 303
spareribs with black beans, 297–298
spareribs with black beans and pepper sauce, 105
spareribs with black beans in sand pot, 298
spareribs with lotus root, 301–302
steamed, with Chinese olives, 301
steamed, with mushroom and dried squid, 339
steamed, with salted eggs, 226
steamed dried duck and, 257
steamed meat-stuffed buns, 109–110
strips, barbecued, 288–289
stuffed bean curd, 103
and taro meatballs, 100
pork tripe:
in hot sauce, 323
looed, 322
spicy, 104
potato(es):
with artichokes, Greek style, 404–405
Russian salad, Greek style, 147
salad, Greek style, 148
pots, 16–17
poultry, 228–272
basic chicken stock, 129
beggar's chicken, 233–234
browned quail, Chinese style, 267
browned squab with roasted salt and pepper, 265–266
chicken, 229–247
chicken and Chinese chive shu-mei, 106–107
chicken and pork in lettuce, 238–239
chicken and spinach ravioli, 392–393
chicken baked with honey and soy sauce, 232

chicken chowed with black beans, 235–236
chicken roll, Greek style, 244
chicken roll, Roman style, 247
chicken shu-mei, 106
chicken steamed with Chinese sausage, 238
chicken wings in five spice, 236–237
chicken with black bean salad, 139
chicken with leek belts, 450–451
chicken with sweet bell peppers, 246
chicken with two onions in sand pot, 234–235
Chinese chicken soup stock, 113–114
Chinese chicken with chestnuts, 428
Chinese duck salad, 259
Chinese poached chicken, 230–231
Chinese roast duck, 252–253
Chinese sausage, dried duck, and roast pork sand pot, 340
Chinese sesame chicken, 242–243
cutting, 271
devil's chicken, 245–246
duck, 251–263
duck and jellyfish salad, 138
duck grilled Greek style, 262
duck like a mandolin, 255
duck soup, Chinese style, 259–260
duck with turnips Apicius, 263
fricassee of chicken, Roman style, 244–245
fried garlic chicken balls, 237
fried quail, Chinese style, 266
fried squab, Chinese style, 267
game hens with rosemary and garlic, 271
goose, 248–250
goose, Chiu Chow style, 250
Greek duck with olives, 261–262
grilled squab, Greek style, 269–270
looed chicken, 240–241
looed duck feet, 260–261
looed goose, 249
Ming's chicken salad, 140–142
mushroom shredded chicken, 459
Peking duck, 254–255
quail in tomato sauce, Greek style, 268

poultry (*continued*)

quail or squab in cream Italian sauce, 272

quick Chinese roast chicken, 242

roasted chicken, Greek style, 243

roasted quail appetizers Homer, 269

roast "lung kong" chicken, 240

roast quail Edmondo, 270

roast salt chicken, 231–232

sesame almond chicken wings, 241

shredded chicken sesame, 84

small birds, 264–272

steamed dried duck and pork, 257

stewed duck with mushrooms, 256

tea-smoked duck, 258

tea-smoked game hen, 267–268

velvet chicken and sweet corn soup, 122

prawns:

with chili sauce, 171

velvet, 170

Q

quail:

browned, Chinese style, 267

in creamed Italian sauce, 272

fried, Chinese style, 266

roast, Edmondo, 270

roasted, appetizers Homer, 269

in tomato sauce, Greek style, 268

quail egg(s):

baby corn and, 225

shu-mei, 100

R

ravioli:

beef-filled, Roman-Jewish style, 394

cheese and spinach, 394

chicken and spinach, 392–393

coteghino–filled, 394

to freeze, 393

rib(s):

barbecued spareribs, 289

chops, lamb, broiled Greek style, 282

chops, lamb, broiled Roman style, 285

garlic, with green pepper and black beans, 106

spareribs with black beans, 297–298

spareribs with black beans in sand pot, 298

spareribs with lotus root, 301–302

rice, 373–386

congee, 378–379

to cook, 375

fried, 375–376

fried risotto cakes, 386

pudding, eight-treasure, 490–492

risotto with champagne, 384–385

risotto with mushrooms, 383

risotto with mushrooms and herbs, 384

risotto with seafood, 385–386

squid pilaf, 192–193

steamed, Chinese sausage on, 379

sticky sweet, with meats, 377–378

stuffed grape leaves with egg-lemon sauce, 380–381

stuffed tomatoes Hydra, 381–382

ricotta cheese:

frittata, 227

pie, Roman style, 498–499

and spinach ravioli, 394

risotto:

cakes, fried, 386

with champagne, 384–385

with mushrooms, 383

with mushrooms and herbs, 384

with seafood, 385–386

rolls:

olive, 483

sesame dragon mouths, 473

Roman herbs and spices, 42–43

Roman ingredients, 36–38

Rome, 70–78

S

salad dressings:

Greek, 144

sesame oil, 140

salads, 135–152

baby octopus, 198

beans, artichokes, and peas, 423–424

bean sprout and Szechwan pepper, 139

black-eyed pea, Sigalas, 419–420

broiled eggplant wedges, 445

celery and mushroom, Savini, 149–150

chicken with black bean, 139

Chinese duck, 259

Chinese fish, 142–143

duck and jellyfish, 138

eggplant, 444

eggplant slices baked, 443

fennel, Roman style, 150

Greek lamb and pasta, 146

Greek village, with cabbage, 144–145

headcheese, 332

Italian flag, 150

jellyfish, 137–138

Ming's chicken, 140–142

Mykonos, 149

octopus, Greek style, 197–198

olive and pepper, 152

potato, Greek style, 148

roasted pepper, Roman style, 151

Russian, Greek style, 147

sardine and macaroni, 145

seafood, Da Franco, 191

seafood, Roman style, 185

shredded chicken sesame, 84

squid, 190–191

vegetable, Greek style, 148

white beans, Greek style, 420

salt:

chicken, roast, 231–232

in foods, 442

and pepper dip, Szechwan, 202

roasted pepper and, 266

salted cod:

in cream sauce, 342–343

Greek style, 341

in tomato sauce, 343

sand pot:

chicken with two onions in, 234–235

Chinese sausage, dried duck, and roast pork, 340

looed beef in, 312–313

side of pork and oysters in, 295–296

side of pork with cod and bean curd in, 296–297

spareribs with black beans in, 298

sardine and macaroni salad, 134

sauces, 200–211

basic brown, 207

basic white, 205–206

Bolognese, 209

chowing, 202–203

dip, 201–202

egg-lemon, 205

garlic, 206

Greek tomato, 204

green, for boiled meats, 209–210

green onion, 202

Italian tomato, 208

looing, 203

pesto, 211

tuna, for meats, 210

sausage, Chinese:

chicken steamed with, 238

dried duck, and roast pork sand pot, 340

on steamed rice, 379

scallop(s):

asparagus, and mushroom soup, 121

dried, and chive soup, 337

with garlic chives, 175

in Szechwan spicy sauce, 177

velveted, in celery, 176

seafood, 153–198

assorted fried, 165–166

baby octopus salad, 198

deep-fried squid, Italian style, 192

deep-fried squid with spiced salt, 190

duck and jellyfish salad, 138

hot and spicy salad, 109

jellyfish salad, 137–138

octopus, 195–198

octopus in wine and tomato sauce, 197

octopus salad, Greek style, 197–198

octopus spaghetti Zorba, 196

pepper sauce for, 202

risotto with, 385–386

salad, Roman style, 185

salad Da Franco, 191

shark fin soup, 124

squid, 186–194

squid balls, 187–188

squid in Italian tomato sauce, 192

squid pilaf, 192–193

squid salad, 190–191

seafood (*continued*)
  squid with lemon and oil, 193
  steamed pork with mushroom and dried squid, 339
  stuffed squid, Greek style, 194
  two squid, chowed, 189–190
  see also fish; shellfish
seaweed soup, 118
sesame, 216–218
  almond chicken wings, 241
  bread, Greek, 477
  breadsticks, Italian, 481–482
  chicken, Chinese, 242–243
  circles, 478
  cookies, Chinese, 494
  dragon mouths, 473
  fish fillets with, 161–162
  halvah, 497–498
  sauce, chowed noodles with pork and, 349
  shredded chicken, 84
  tahini, homemade, 217–218
  tahini bean dip, 88
sesame oil salad dressing, 140
shark fin soup, 124
shellfish, 168–185
  abalone and mushrooms, 458–459
  abalone soup, 115–116
  baby snails in Greek tomato sauce, 183
  baby snails in Italian tomato sauce, 184
  crab in black bean sauce, 178–179
  crab with soybean condiment, 179–180
  dried abalone with mushrooms, 336–337
  dried oysters and pork in lettuce, 338
  dried scallop and chive soup, 337
  eggplant stuffed with shrimp, 98–99
  fried milk with crabmeat, 180–181
  fried shrimp Piraeus, 184
  garlic-steamed crab, 179
  ha gow, 95–97
  prawns with chili sauce, 171
  scallop, asparagus, and mushroom soup, 121

scallops in Szechwan spicy sauce, 177
scallops with garlic chives, 175
shrimp Ananius, 181–182
shrimp and oyster sauce, 173
shrimp and peppers on an iron plate, 174–175
shrimp ball with pine nuts, 98
shrimp boats, 97
shrimp-stuffed mushrooms, 98
shrimp toast, 97
side of pork and oysters in sand pot, 295–296
steamed shrimp with special sauce, 172
velveted scallops in celery, 176
velvet prawns, 170
shrimp:
  Ananius, 181–182
  ball with pine nuts, 98
  boats, 97
  chowed with water-chestnut flour and gin, 429–430
  eggplant stuffed with, 98–99
  fried, Piraeus, 184
  in Greek tomato sauce with feta, 182–183
  ha gow, 95–97
  and oyster sauce, 173
  and peppers on an iron plate, 174–175
  steamed, with special sauce, 172
  stuffed mushrooms, 98
  toast, 97
smelt antipasti, 90–91
snails, baby:
  in Greek tomato sauce, 183
  in Italian tomato sauce, 184
soups, 111–134
  abalone, 115–116
  avgolemono, 126–127
  bean curd, 114
  bird's nest, 125
  clear mushroom, 461–462
  double-boiled, 123
  dried scallop and chive, 337
  duck, Chinese style, 259–260
  fish, avgolemono, 127–128
  fish and lettuce, 119

Greek fish chowder, 163
green olive, 134
adding ham to, 123
hoko pot, 116–117
hot and sour, 120
Italian fish, 131
lamb innard, for Easter, 327–328
adding lettuce to, 121
pasta and bean, 421–422
peas and egg, 115
rice congee, 378–379
Roman "rag," 133
scallop, asparagus, and mushroom, 121
seaweed, 118
shark fin, 124
sweet almond cream, 495
tripe, with egg-lemon sauce, 325–326
velvet chicken and sweet corn, 122
white fungus, 461
zuppa imperiale, 130
soup stocks:
    basic brown, 132
    basic chicken, 129
    basic lamb, 128
    Chinese chicken, 113–114
    fish, 126
    to remove fat from, 114
souvlaki, 282
    pork, 303
spaghetti, octopus, Zorba, 196
spareribs:
    barbecued, 289
    with black beans, 297–298
    with black beans and pepper sauce, 105
    with black beans in sand pot, 298
    with lotus root, 301–302
spices, 39–43
spinach:
    and cheese ravioli, 394
    and chicken ravioli, 392–393
    with olive oil, garlic, and lemon juice, Greek style, 467
    pies, 89
    risotto with mushrooms and herbs, 384
    squid and, 193

squab:
    browned, with roasted salt and pepper, 265–266
    cleaning and cooking, 188
    in creamed Italian sauce, 272
    fried, Chinese style, 267
    grilled, Greek style, 269–270
squid, 186–194
    balls, 187–188
    deep-fried, Italian style, 192
    deep-fried, with spiced salt, 190
    dried, steamed pork with mushroom and, 339
    hot and spicy, 109
    in Italian tomato sauce, 192
    with lemon and oil, 193
    pilaf, 192–193
    salad, 190–191
    spinach and, 193
    stuffed, Greek style, 194
    two, chowed, 189–190
steaming food:
    bamboo steamer for, 97
    small dumplings, lettuce circles for, 107
stew:
    Chinese beef and chestnut, 427
    fish, for Christmas Eve, 166–167
stocks, soup:
    basic brown, 132
    basic chicken, 129
    basic lamb, 128
    Chinese chicken, 113–114
    fish, 126
    to remove fat from, 114
strawberry yogurt with honey, 497

T

tahini:
    bean dip, 88
    homemade, 217–218
tea:
    eggs, 223–224
    smoked duck, 258
    smoked game hen, 267–268
television shows and recipes, 44–57
tomato, asparagus with oil and, Greek style, 409–410

tomatoes, stuffed, Hydra, 381–382
tomato sauce, Greek, 204
    artichokes in, 405
    baby snails in, 183
    lima beans with, 418–419
    meatballs in, 314
    octopus in wine and, 197
    quail in, 268
    shrimp in, with feta, 182–183
tomato sauce, Italian, 208
    baby snails in, 184
    creamed, quail or squab in, 272
    salted cod in, 343
    squid in, 192
tomato sauce, lamb and, Greek style,
    278–279
tongue:
    beef, looed, 321–322
    in sweet and sour sauce, Roman
        style, 333
tripe:
    pork, in hot sauce, 323
    pork, looed, 322
    Roman style, 329–330
    soup with egg-lemon sauce, 325–
        326
    spicy pork, 104
tuna sauce for meats, 210
turnips, duck with, Apicius, 263

V

vegetable(s), 397–468
    artichokes, 398–405
    artichokes, chilled, Roman style,
        401–402
    artichokes, Jewish style, 400–401
    artichokes, stuffed Roman style, 403
    artichokes and leeks, 452
    artichokes in Greek tomato sauce,
        405
    artichokes sautéed in wine, 401
    artichokes steamed with pesto, 402
    artichokes with ham on toast, 403–
        404
    artichokes with potatoes, Greek
        style, 404–405
    asparagus, 406–413

asparagus custard Apicius, 412
asparagus with beef and black beans,
    408–409
asparagus with cheese and eggs,
    Italian style, 413
asparagus with oil and tomato,
    Greek style, 409–410
blanching asparagus Apicius, 411–
    412
boiled leeks with cabbage Apicius,
    453–454
broiled eggplant Bologna, 444–445
broiled eggplant wedges, 445
chestnuts and lentils Apicius, 433
cold asparagus, Chinese style, 407–
    408
cold asparagus, Greek style, 409
deep-fried, Piperno, 467–468
eggplant, 434–446
eggplant and pork Mandar-Inn,
    438–439
eggplant salad, 444
eggplant shoes, 442
eggplant slices baked, 443
eggplant stuffed Greek style, 439–
    440
eggplant with pork, Chinese style,
    436
eggplant with soybean condiment
    and hoisin sauce, 437
grilled mushrooms, Roman style,
    463
leek cakes, 451
leeks, 447–455
leeks and juniper berries, 454–455
lettuce with foo yee, 467
mushrooms, 456–465
mushrooms in wine and coriander
    Apicius, 465
mushrooms stuffed with feta cheese,
    462–463
pickled asparagus, Greek style, 410–
    411
salad, Greek style, 148
sautéed leeks, 452
spinach with olive oil, garlic, and
    lemon juice, Greek style, 467
wild greens and chestnuts, 431
see also bean(s)

W

walnuts fried with sugar, 85
water-chestnut flour, shrimp chowed
     with gin and, 429–430
water chestnuts and green beans, 429
wine:
    artichokes sautéed in, 401
    chestnuts soaked in, 431
    cookies and, 500
    mushrooms in coriander and, Api-
      cius, 465
    and tomato sauce, octopus in, 197

wonton dumplings, 391–392
wontons, fried, 108

Y

yogurt:
    strawberry, with honey, 497
    tzatziki, 86–87

Z

zucchini, pasta with, 361
zuppa imperiale, 130

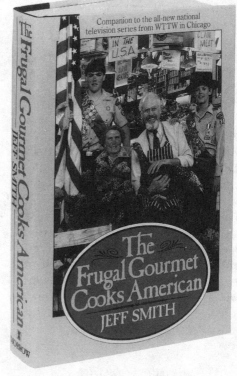